W9-BVL-710

Jewish Comedy

Jewish Comedy

A SERIOUS HISTORY

Jeremy Dauber

W. W. NORTON & COMPANY
Independent Publishers Since 1923
LONDON   NEW YORK

10   2017

For information about permission to reproduce selections from this book,
write to Permissions, W. W. Norton & Company, Inc.,
500 Fifth Avenue, New York, NY 10110

For information about special discounts for bulk purchases, please contact
W. W. Norton Special Sales at specialsales@wwnorton.com or 800-233-4830

Manufacturing by Quad Graphics Fairfield
Book design by Helene Berinsky
Production manager: Julia Druskin

Library of Congress Cataloging-in-Publication Data

Names: Dauber, Jeremy Asher, author.
Title: Jewish comedy : a serious history / Jeremy Dauber.
Description: First edition. | New York : W. W. Norton & Company, 2017. |
Includes bibliographical references and index.
Identifiers: LCCN 2017017864 | ISBN 9780393247879 (hardcover)
Subjects: LCSH: Jewish wit and humor—History and criticism. | Jews—Humor.
Classification: LCC PN6149.J4 D38 2017 | DDC 809.7/935203924—dc23
LC record available at https://lccn.loc.gov/2017017864

W. W. Norton & Company, Inc.
500 Fifth Avenue, New York, N.Y. 10110
www.wwnorton.com

W. W. Norton & Company Ltd.
15 Carlisle Street, London W1D 3BS

1 2 3 4 5 6 7 8 9 0

For Ezra
Whose laughter—like everything else about him—is a delight.

CONTENTS

INTRODUCTION

A Joke, Two Definitions, Seven Themes, Four Warnings, and Another Joke

Y‌OU CAN'T START A BOOK ON JEWISH HUMOR WITHOUT A JOKE. So here's one:

> "You want to hear a joke? I'll tell you a joke. What's green, is nailed to the wall, and whistles?"
> " . . . I give up."
> "A herring."
> "A herring's not green!"
> "*Nu,* you can paint it green."
> "But it's not nailed to the wall!"
> "You *could* nail it to the wall. If you wanted to."
> " . . . But a herring doesn't whistle!"
> "All right, fine, so it doesn't whistle."

Or: "I just threw in that part to confuse you."
Or: "All right, all right, so it's *not* a herring."
Or: "What am I, some kind of herring expert?" And on and on.

Is this joke, with its multiplicity of potential punch lines, a *Jewish* joke? And if so, why? Is it the syntax, with its faint Yiddish overtones? The slightly smart-ass sensibility? The comfort with its meta-jokiness, or, put another way, the subversive, near-parodic jab at the joke's very form? Is it the particular refusal to provide the closure of a punch line, which could be taken, by an overzealous interpreter, as a metaphor for a Jewish historical consciousness ever in wait for messianic redemption? Or is it just a joke about herring?

While you think about that, here's a story about *telling* Jewish jokes. It's an old story, a tale of the Preacher of Dubno, an eighteenth-century Hasidic rabbi famous for his apt and witty parables. Asked by an admirer how he always managed to find such an appropriate parable for each and every sermon, he answered, not uncharacteristically, with another parable. He told the story of a general visiting his troops who was struck by the results of their target practice: while most of the chalk circles drawn as makeshift targets on the wall revealed your regular variety of hit or miss results, one showed nothing but bullseyes—dead center, every shot. Gasping, the general demanded to see this marksman; he was even more surprised to discover the shooter was a Jew, a conscript forced to serve in the Tsar's army. He asked the Jew the secret of his success at arms. The Jew looked at the general as if he were cockeyed and responded: "Well, it's very easy. First you fire the gun, and then, once you see where the bullet hole is, you draw a circle around it." This had always been his technique, the Maggid concluded: find a good joke or story, *then* figure out the larger point to draw from it.

A joke, a story: a statement of the problem, an approach to solving it. The problem, of course, is how to define and describe Jewish humor as it's appeared in all its vast and variegated forms, from antiquity to yesterday. It's hardly a new enterprise: there have been previous efforts, especially over the last few decades, and especially in America, where for a while it seemed like Jewish humor *was* American humor, or at least a pretty central part of it. Steve Allen, who should know, referred to American comedy in 1981 as "a sort of Jewish cottage industry," putting Jewish participation in the field at approaching 80 percent. Some, though by no means all, of the approaches advanced in those efforts—arguments focusing on language, on sensibility, on history—are hinted at above.

But Jewish comedy tends to resist any single explanation. For every argument that's been advanced as to what it really is, a bit of thought immediately reveals all sorts of exceptions and counterexamples—so much so that other equally perspicacious critics have thrown up their hands and suggested any attempt to define a specifically Jewish humor is doomed to futility. What's more, the counterexamples themselves aren't just indicative: they're almost as vast and numerous as Jewish history itself, which covers a lot of ground, of both the actual and metaphorical variety. Writing a book that tries to touch on all of it, even representatively, as well as offer some explanatory power, is a pretty tall order.

Still, someone ought to do it.

The first time I walked into a Columbia University classroom to teach a course on Jewish comedy, *Seinfeld* had just gone off the air and Lena Dunham was entering high school. Judd Apatow was a respected television producer who no one outside the industry had ever heard of; and *The Producers* was still a movie, though there was talk of taking it to Broadway. I was a little nervous—a wet behind the ears twenty-seven-year-old assistant professor, lecturing to the largest class I'd ever had (apparently this was the kind of course that could attract a crowd), and I looked down at my notes to focus myself.

Jewish comedy is serious business, I'd typed across the top. And so it is.

Over the last fifteen years or so of teaching the subject, lots of things have changed—although, thanks to the magic of syndication, *Seinfeld* never really did go off the air—and my syllabus has changed with it; but the top line hasn't, along with the two central realizations that accompanied it.

First: The story of Jewish comedy was almost as massive in scope, as meaningful in substance, as Jewish history itself. In fact, I realized as I refined and developed the class, I was looking at a *tradition*. One with a history that could, and should, be *studied*. The story of Jewish comedy—what Jewish humor *did* and *meant* for the Jews at different times and places as well as how, and why, it was so entertaining—is, if you tell it the right way, the story of American popular culture; it's the story of Jewish civilization; it's a guide to an essential aspect of human behavior. The fact that it also happens to be immensely entertaining to read, talk, and teach about is something of a bonus.

But second: You can't include everything. Or even close. And so what you *did* include, I realized, had to work not just as a catalog of Jewish comedic production, but as an argument about what precisely Jewish comedy consists of. But even before you get to the cataloging and taxonomizing, there has to be some defining. Some inclusion and exclusion. Is the raw stuff of Jewish humor so capacious that it includes anything written by a Jew that might raise the faintest scintilla of a smile? Well, no. That would be, if not entirely ridiculous, at least ridiculously unhelpful. And literature is littered with brilliant comic thinkers who have warned against trying to define comedy too precisely: Samuel Johnson's "Comedy has been unpropitious to definers" is the most famous, though I kind of prefer Swift's rhyming couplet that "What Humour is, not all the tribe/ Of logic-mongers can describe." But this logic-monger would like to set two conditions nonetheless.

First: *Jewish humor has to be produced by Jews.* Maybe this is obvious, maybe it isn't, but it's part of our ground rules. How someone defines their Jewishness is a notoriously tricky subject—and, counter to some people's thinking, has been since the beginning of Jewish history—but anyone who defines themselves as Jewish in any way is potentially part of our subject; others, even if sometimes mistaken for Jews (Charlie Chaplin, looking at you), are out. This said, comedy—especially in performance media—is of course often collaborative, and oftentimes a great work of Jewish comedy is crafted in concert with non-Jews; this material is very much included.

The second, trickier condition: *Jewish humor must have some-*

thing to do with either contemporary Jewish living or historical Jewish existence. Jewish history is very long, and Jewish life extraordinarily diverse, both geographically and culturally. It would be surprising if all examples of Jewish comedy looked the same—and they certainly don't. But all those different times and places featured Jews commenting on what it meant to be a Jew in that culture. Usually, since most of Jewish history is diasporic history, as some kind of cultural outsider; but even if not, almost inevitably with that sidelong, half-immersed half-alienated glance so crucial to comedy. And frequently, they used those comic instincts to participate in long-running discussions that crossed centuries and continents about the meaning of Jewish history, theology, and destiny. Some of the examples we'll treat in this book are explicit about those discussions; some assign them to the spheres of subtext or allegory; some are snapshots of a lived present whose movement into the past render them part of the discussion despite their apparent intent. But they're all grist for the mill: as opposed to, say, a killer knock-knock joke written by a Silverstein or a Schwartz. (Unless, I suppose, there's some fairly potent allegorical or metaphorical component within.)

That's it. Certain subthemes will emerge again and again across the varying strands, of course—a particular playfulness with language, especially befitting the changing linguistic (and frequently multilingual) circumstances in which Jews lived; a contemplation of power and the lack of it; the relation of those two themes to questions of masculinity, along with the presence and absence of female voices. But those are more provocative preoccupations rather than essential parts of the definition. That still leaves a tremendous amount to wrangle, though, and the solution I've come up with, the one that serves as the organizing structural principle of this book, follows the Maggid's approach: Take a look at the long history of Jewish literature and culture, suss out the funny stuff that meets our definition, and then draw a defining circle around it—or, as I'm going to suggest, draw seven of them. Because, as it turns out, when you canvass the material—the entire breadth of the history of Jewish comedy, from the Bible to @crazyjewishmom's Instagram account and look for commonalities, seven major conceptual rubrics—seven strands—suggest themselves.

Immediately, I hear the cry: "Why not eight? Why not six? Your seventh is really a modified version of number four!" Look, this isn't a precise science; the writers and performers who produce this stuff aren't theoretical constructs, they're working artists trying to get a laugh and use multiple techniques at once; and comedy tends to blur boundaries anyway. So these are guidelines, ideal types.

And here they are, without further ado:

1. *Jewish comedy is a response to persecution and anti-Semitism.*
2. *Jewish comedy is a satirical gaze at Jewish social and communal norms.*
3. *Jewish comedy is bookish, witty, intellectual allusive play.*
4. *Jewish comedy is vulgar, raunchy, and body-obsessed.*
5. *Jewish comedy is mordant, ironic, and metaphysically oriented.*
6. *Jewish comedy is focused on the folksy, everyday, quotidian Jew.*
7. *Jewish comedy is about the blurred and ambiguous nature of Jewishness itself.*

So one strand of Jewish humor, for example, is its bookish, intellectual, witty side, appropriate for the self-proclaimed People of the Book, and bookish intellectual wits from Talmudic rabbis to Woody Allen can help trace our way through that aspect of the story. But Jewish humor can be vulgar as well—as raunchy and body-obsessed as any other group's comedy—and figures as varied as medieval scatologists and Mel Brooks can help show the way *there*.

Tracing the history of these seven strands—one per chapter—allows us to cover a lot of the history of Jewish comedy in an intellectually responsible way that also doesn't require the reader to wait hundreds of pages to get to the Marx Brothers. What it *does* mean is that I'll be returning to different periods of Jewish history and their culture—biblical antiquity, or the medieval period, or the age of Enlightenment, or postwar America, among others—several times over various chapters. I hope that's a feature, not a bug; with each successive essay, I hope you'll be introduced to yet another facet of Jewish history and culture, along with its comedy, and see each time period in a different light. Over the last half century, scholarship in Jewish studies has unlocked a dazzling variety of perspectives on how to think about the Jews: and comedy shows off those perspectives as well as anything else. Telling the story of each particular strand of Jewish humor through history not only makes an argument about what Jewish comedy is and how it works in different forms and venues, but also offers suggestions about how we understand Jewish history itself.

Drawing a circle, or seven circles, around the bullet hole, as the Maggid's marksman did, has its dangers along with its rewards. It creates an artificial sense of order where ragged chaos has bloomed; it runs the risk of being exposed as fallacious, as unfair or against the rules. On the other hand, doing it managed to impress both a Hasidic rebbe and a Russian general, bringing them together in shared admiration of an artist. So that's something.

WE HAVE A LOT of ground to cover, and we should be off. But four warnings before we do: ones important to any history of humor, and this one in particular.

1. *It's a history.* I'll be including things that, thanks to the vicissitudes of time, history, and critical fashion, may not necessarily be thought of as comedy anymore. Interpretive traditions become encrusted; literary traditions fall into inscrutability. Understanding the history of Jewish comedy, rather than simply celebrating it, or merely being entertained by it, means taking things as they *were*, not as they seem to us now. Put simply: Humor is cultural and context-dependent, and Jewish humor

is no exception to that rule. There will even be times—going back early enough—when it's my best guess that something had comic intent, but neither I, nor the extant scholarship, are absolutely certain. Research and instinct can get you far, but not everywhere.

2. *Humor isn't always funn*-ee. That "comic intent" in the last warning covers a lot of ground. One of the things constantly perplexing aestheticians and philosophers of comedy is the nature of its link with the physical phenomenon of laughter. Why, they wonder, do we smile or laugh at apparently unfunny things, like (for example) things that make us nervous? This isn't the book to answer that question (though we'll have occasion to encounter a number of theorists of comedy, particularly in the modern era, as our story becomes intertwined with the creation of a self-conscious category of "Jewish humor"). But it does bring up a related point: that we often don't laugh at things that are, unquestionably, comedy. I'm not saying this book uses "comedy" in the Elizabethan sense of the term, but we'll certainly be talking about areas of comic creation that go less for the laugh than the wry nod, the gentle smile, or even the horrified gasp. And that last leads to:

3. *Humor isn't always pretty, or polite.* Even a passing acquaintance with humor shows that we, as a species, like laughing at things society deems inappropriate for polite company or discussion. (In fact, some theories of comedy are pretty much dedicated to some form of that proposition.) This book has a lot of material in it some might find inappropriate; even deeply so. Some of that is the inevitable result of encountering works from periods with vastly different social norms than our own—humor we find almost unbearably racist, for example, was family fare far less than a century ago. And sometimes we'll find uncomfortable commonalities: fat jokes have been

in common currency from the beginning of recorded history, and they're doing pretty well right now, too. We're going to take certain kinds of moral considerations into account in our history—usually, the history of those kind of considerations themselves and the way artists dealt with, worked around, accommodated to, or shattered those taboos—but we won't shy away from including humor because it's misogynist, or homophobic, or obscene, or blasphemous, or xenophobic, or myriad other offensive characteristics that apply to different aspects of Jewish humor—as they do to any group's. You've been warned. Finally:

4. *Analyzing comedy runs the risk of killing it.* Probably the biggest danger of them all; as Lenny Bruce learned, it was far more dangerous to his career to be boring than to be dirty. What we enjoy about the great works of Jewish comedy—of all comedy—isn't *how* they work, it's *that* they work; and getting under the hood and seeing why a particular story or routine is, for example, a powerful expression of the anxieties and ambitions of postwar American suburban Jewry is certainly less entertaining than just listening to or reading it. But my job's to tell a story—seven stories in one, actually—and I can't do that without explaining. You want a joke book, buy a joke book.

That said, I don't want to end this introduction on that adversarial a note, so here's another joke. Befitting our warnings, it has no history (or, I'm sure it does, but I haven't yet been able to track down its provenance); you may not find it funny; it's not pretty or polite (the people I've told it to tend to split fifty-fifty between finding it terrible and hilarious); and I'm not going to explain it, at least for now. But it is, to me, one of the great Jewish jokes, maybe even the second-greatest ever (for the one that takes the top slot, you'll have to read on).

Two old men settle onto a park bench in Tel Aviv; after a moment, they recognize each other as long-lost friends. "Reuven!" says the first, "Reuven, how are you? It's been decades! Since we were young men from the same small town! How are you? How are your parents?"

"Oh," said the second man. "Oh, they died decades ago. We're old men now, Shimon."

"Yes, well, of course," Reuven replies. "To be expected, I suppose. My condolences. But your siblings—I loved spending time with them. How are they?"

"Oh," said Shimon. "Oh, you haven't heard. My brother died ten years ago. Cancer."

"I'm so sorry," Reuven said. "That's terrible news. But what about your sister? She was so lovely . . ."

"Oh," Shimon said. "Oh, we really haven't been in touch, have we? She died fifteen years ago. A stroke."

"Ahh . . ." Reuven replies, casting about. "Well, how is that beautiful wife of yours! I haven't seen her since she was a young mother . . ."

"Oh," Shimon said. "You didn't hear. She died five years ago. Bus bombing."

Reuven is now completely discombobulated. "Your kids!" he finally gets out. "How are your kids?"

"You'll laugh," Shimon said. "But they're dead too."

Jewish humor has always had bite to it. What it is, how it developed, how all its strands weaved together and in conversation with the Jewish story: that's our book.

Jewish Comedy

1

What's So Funny About Anti-Semitism?

For most of their history, Jews weren't particularly thought of as having much of a sense of humor.

In fact, a lot of outside observers considered them downright glum. The early-twentieth-century British philosopher Alfred North Whitehead, for example, remarked that Jews were "singularly humorless"; his slightly earlier contemporary, the historian and critic Thomas Carlyle, asserted that the Jews showed not the slightest trace of humor at any period of their history, and the novelist George Eliot suggested that "the Literature of the Hebrew gives an idea of a people who went about their business and their pleasure as gravely as a society of beavers." Let's put aside, for the moment, the problems of political correctness, and of assigning certain character traits to particular groups as a whole: people didn't have a problem doing it for most of human history, and a history of Jewish comedy is going to have to grapple with these conceptions, by Jews themselves as well as their neighbors. What's interesting is *why* people—and by "people," I largely mean Christians—had that opinion.

You could say it's all a matter of perspective. From the outsider's view, it's simple, in the way that all sorts of caricatured sketches are simple: there's something about Jews—about their essence, about their place in history—that prevents them from being happy. For Christians, through a lot of world history, that something was, of course, their bizarre unwillingness to accept Jesus Christ as their lord and savior. Whether that meant that they were metaphysically unhappy (that is, joy was literally unavailable to them without the genuine light of Christ in their hearts) or reflectively unhappy (looking around at Christianity's success in Europe and their comparatively beleaguered state, they realized they'd missed the boat: who wouldn't be sad under those circumstances?) is, for our purposes, a distinction without a difference. Later iterations of this approach, taking on racial or ethnic overtones, might posit some sort of quasi-genetic factor. The seminal nineteenth-century British anthropologist James Cowles Prichard, in his *Researches into the Physical History of Man*, spoke about the "choleric and melancholic temperaments" of English Jews, for example. But the general thrust was that unhappiness, and the corollary incapacity to engage in comic mirth and merriment, was a Jewish birthright.

Naturally, the Jews took the other side of that argument. We *could* be happy, they said, if it weren't for *all the anti-Semites out there making life so difficult for us.*

Now, dwelling on this approach overmuch leads to a condition famously diagnosed in the field as "the lachrymose approach to Jewish history": treating the Jewish story as one long trudge through a vale of tears, from the shaping event of biblical literature and the biblical period (the destruction of the Temple) to the shaping event of the twentieth century (the Holocaust), with stops for crusades, pogroms, and blood libels in between. Which has its problems, as a historical approach; but it does possess a certain explanatory appeal. Especially when it comes to Jewish humor.

At least this was what Hermann Adler, the chief rabbi of Britain in Whitehead's day, tried to gently point out to his British counterparts in an early and groundbreaking essay on our subject. After making some similarly sweeping generalizations about other peoples of antiquity—"The facetious element was not very strong in the

Egyptians: no laughter lurks in the wandering eyes and broad calm lips of their statues. Nor can the Assyrians have had any genius for comedy"—he suggested that the Jews, rather than being melancholy, in fact had a "faculty for saying witty and humorous things." And why? It was a "weapon with which a beneficent Maker has provided His feeble creatures, whereby they have been enabled to survive in the fierce struggle for existence," the "iron hand of bigotry . . . the soul-chilling venom of contempt." There's a direct line, suggests Adler, between bigotry and comedy.

That explanation has had many supporters in the century-plus since it was advanced. One of the most common moves of critics and students of Jewish comedy is to cast Jewish humor as a response to persecution—a kind of coping strategy, a display of resilience under historically tragic circumstances. Even with the best will in the world, though, this approach still defines the Jews as victims and sufferers, and tends to account for, feature, and even privilege a certain kind of Jewish humor that comes in two flavors: ironic and black. (Whitehead, for example, challenged on his assertion, acknowledged that yes, there were funny Jewish comedians, but "their laughter was generally ironic" because the Jews had always been "a people in a desperate position, feeling they were not getting their rights.")

I believe the comic impulse—for Jews and others—is like water, and it flows wherever and however people are willing to find it funny. But it flows through particular channels—in our case, the seven strands of Jewish comedy we've identified. Since this one probably constitutes the most common account for the particular nature of Jewish humor, it's the one we'll follow first, mindful of its partial nature.

WE DON'T have that many works of early Jewish literature (say, until the medieval period) that aren't, in one way or another, religious books. Which doesn't mean they don't have comic elements in them—boy, do they—but it does mean that they're generally created and disseminated by people with a theologically oriented worldview that they propound in the work. Works like the Bible and Talmud tend to frame the history of anti-Semitism and persecution through a lens that ties anti-Semitic depredation to a violation of God's covenant; Jew hatred has direct connection to sin.

What's funny about that? Not much—especially since it encourages to our mind a rather ugly blame-the-victim mentality. This perspective isn't played for laughs much in the Bible, especially in those books that are composed around and after the destruction of the First Temple, the defeats of the kingdoms of Israel and Judah, and the beginning of Jewish exile. One of those books—a book that stands at the beginning of a certain kind of Jewish history, a history of diaspora—is a work that, for centuries, was viewed by traditional Jews as *the* great source of Jewish comedy: the book of Esther. The book of Esther is so central, so fruitful, for our history that we'll return to it in every single chapter, the only work so honored: and in each case, telling another facet of its story exemplifies the questions behind that chapter's approach, its argument.

For those whose Bible-reading days are somewhat more distant, a very quick plot summary: The story of Esther takes place in a quasi-mythical version of the Persian Empire. The king, Ahasuerus, gets rid of his queen in a fit of anger after her refusal to attend him at a royal feast, and holds a sort of beauty pageant to find her successor. Esther is chosen, the cousin of Mordechai, a man who has recently foiled an assassination plot against the king. Esther and Mordechai are Jews, not members of the Persian majority, and, perhaps for that reason, Esther does not reveal her heritage to her royal consort. Mordechai refuses to bow down to the king's confidante, Haman; and Haman, not one to take his wildly disproportionate revenge retail when he can do it wholesale, vows to exterminate Mordechai's entire people—the Jews—and convinces Ahasuerus to give him the authority to do so.

Much of the rest of the book is dedicated to Haman's downfall. In a fit of insomnia, the king reads the royal chronicles, and determines Mordechai has never been rewarded for his role in foiling the assassination. He calls Haman, waiting suspiciously nearby, and asks him what should be done for a man the king wishes to honor. The vain and narcissistic Haman assumes the king is talking about *him*, and is humiliated when his suggested reward—being led through the streets on the king's horse while wearing the king's crown—is bestowed upon Mordechai. In the meantime, Esther has strategically arranged a private banquet for herself, Haman, and Ahasuerus. Haman, equally willing to believe he is the queen's favorite as well as the king's, is stunned when Esther reveals herself to be a Jew, begs for mercy for her people, and points the finger at Haman as her people's would-be génocidaire. The king, overcome, heads out for some air; Haman falls before Esther, begging for mercy; the king returns to find what he believes is Haman's attempt at a compromising situation, and that's it for Haman—hung on the same gallows he'd had built for Mordechai. After some final complications to which we'll return, feasting and happiness reign, along with Esther, and Mordechai is elevated to the king's second in command.

The diaspora-set book of Esther is the first work of Jewish literature to deal with something we'd recognizably call anti-Semitism: the persecution of Jews for motives, with tactics, and with rhetoric familiar through the long history of the Jewish diaspora. (Haman's arguments to Ahasuerus to grant him permission to exterminate the Jews—they're a people to themselves, they're hidden amongst the general populace, they're unfaithful to the regime, and so on—have had dark and dangerous echoes down the centuries.) As a result, it's the first work to feature the joyful celebration and comic pleasure that comes with an anti-Semite's downfall and the frustration of that form of persecutory intent. If there's any truth to the phrase "They tried to kill us, we survived, let's eat," it comes from the story of Esther and the festive holiday of Purim that resulted to commemorate the salvation she brought about.

But the book's investigation of anti-Semitic motives, for the first time in Jewish literature, raises uneasy questions that will pervade the history of this kind of Jewish comedy: *Why don't those people out there like us? What makes us so different from all of them, if we are, and why?* And, most uncomfortably: *Might they have a point?* The answers to those questions—by a wide variety of hands—are played for uncomfortable comic effect, and comically played for historical and national insight, over the next two millennia.

If anti-Semitism is portrayed in Esther as something that will be joyfully and relievedly vanquished, other books of the Bible have a different way of dealing with less easily disposed-of threats, like the imperial forces that destroyed temple and kingdom. They present the Jews' oppressors as simple pawns in a grand game between God and His chosen people—and stupid enough not to know it. (The prophet Isaiah, for example, is caustic on the subject of the boasting Assyrians in just this fashion: "Should the axe boast itself against him that heweth therewith? Should the saw magnify itself against him that moveth it?") Similar portraits appear in the book of Daniel, with its buffoonish Belshazzar and its childishly raging Nebuchadnezzar. And as Jewish literature developed, both these approaches—the triumphant and the uneasy—began to flow together.

Take some anecdotes from the essential text of Jewish elite culture, the Talmud, composed and edited in the centuries immediately following the closing of the biblical canon. The Talmud details numerous encounters between rabbis and some of the most imposing and terrifying authority figures of the Greek or Roman world, in which the former trip up the latter for basic errors in logic or theology. Two examples from the same page of Talmud, a page featuring a long series of purported conversations between non-Jewish leaders, particularly Roman emperors, and the rabbis, suggest the fraught and churning impulses represented in these almost certainly apocryphal encounters:

> Some say the Emperor said to [Rabban Gamaliel]: "I know the number of the stars in the heavens." Rabban Gamaliel replied:

"How many molars and [other] teeth do you have?" He put his hand to his mouth and began counting them. Rabban Gamaliel said, "You don't know what is in your mouth but you do know what is in heaven?"

Or:

The Emperor also said to Rabban Gamaliel: "I know what your God is doing, and where He is seated." Rabban Gamaliel became overcome and sighed. On being asked the reason, he answered: "I have a son in one of the cities of the sea, and I long for him. Please tell me of him." "Do I know where he is?" he replied. "You do not know what is on earth, and yet [claim to] know what is in heaven?!" he retorted."

The Talmud's message seems clear: despite their theological opposition to the Jewish God—and the temporal power to do something about it—if these gentile rulers aren't smart enough to understand these basic questions, then they're not really *threats*.

This smells like a pretty basic coping mechanism for a culture that's dealing for the first time with its loss of political independence and its central source of all its religious life. The genre of "stupid gentile" jokes, especially in contrast to the clever Jew—with the rabbis being the heroes of wit—really gets its start here, transcending the specifics of its origin to go on for centuries. But the impunity to call a Roman emperor an idiot to his face and get away with it exists most fully in literary form, on the Talmudic page, rather than in the life of late antiquity. And even on the page, the same page in fact, an ironic counterbalance emerges:

The Emperor proposed to Rabbi Tanhum, "Come, let us all be one people." "Very well," he answered, "but we who are circumcised cannot possibly be like you; you become circumcised and be like us." The Emperor replied: "You have spoken well. Nevertheless, anyone who gets the better of the king [in debate] must be thrown into the arena." So they threw him in, but he was not eaten. Thereupon a heretic remarked: "The reason they did not eat him is that they are not hungry." So they threw the heretic in, and he was eaten.

Yes, the emperor, with his oh-so-gentle suggestion of the eradication of Jewish difference, and the heretic, who wrongly ascribes supernatural salvation to natural causes, are brought a cropper. But the joke's on the Jewish reader as well, and it's a cautionary one. You can get off a good one at the emperor's expense, true, but he's the one who can throw you in the arena. And, looking about, miracles—outside the pages of the Talmud—tended to be in awfully short supply. Reading about them was one thing; but in real life, Jews needed to look to other approaches. In the comic literature of the medieval period, they found several.

IN THE LACHRYMOSE view of Jewish history, the medieval period is a pretty dim time for Jews, characterized by crusades and expulsions. Though all these things did occur in the medieval period, it's hardly an accurate reflection of medieval Jewish feelings about themselves (they didn't think of themselves as medieval, for one thing) or their neighbor, or of the nature of the violence perpetrated on them. That said, two types of humor popular at the time can certainly tell us something about the way they *did* think about dealing with anti-Semitism and persecution.

The first is that great repository of medieval wit and comedy, the animal fable. These tales had been around since antiquity: Most of us are familiar with the name of Aesop, the ancient Greek who may or may not have actually existed, but whose tales spread in revised form through the ancient world. They had their biblical parallels: one of the minor judges, Jotam, tells one, and the New Testament features a famous Jewish parable-spinner of its own. Animal fables grew even more popular in the medieval and early modern period; with their standard cast of animal characters who clearly stood for standard character types, they were pretty easy to understand, and they were easy to tell, which was important in an age of low literacy and high orality. They also gave advice about how to be in the world, how to use self-knowledge in order to navigate a hostile and dangerous universe. Like everyone in medieval society, fable animals had fixed positions in the social order, and any attempts to change their status—for the donkey to put on a lion skin and believe himself to be a lion, say—were met with comic disaster. The fable, in short, was a genre that counseled a certain degree of accommodation and even quietism: The joke was on those who might attempt to go against the divine decree and hasten the messianic end, and strong deference to the current political order was the clear message.

Though Jewish fables cast their protagonists in a number of different animal forms, fox fables were of particular popularity. In the diaspora, the fox—hunted by others, forced to scramble and live by its wits—became not only an unlikely hero, but a symbol of the Jewish presence. Such tales were told by Jews from the midrashic to the medieval to the modern period. Here's one that can stand in for many:

A sick lion who had not eaten for a long time acquired a bad breath. In the forest he met an ass. "Does my breath smell badly?" the lion asked him. "It does," replied the simple-minded ass. "How dare a common creature like you insult me, the king of beasts?" roared the lion, and forthwith he devoured the ass. A while later he met a bear. "Does my breath smell badly?" the lion asked him. "Oh, no!" exclaimed the bear. "Your breath is sweeter than honey." "Flatterer!" roared the lion. "How dare you deceive me?" And he devoured the bear, too. At last, he met a fox. "Smell me, my friend," asked the lion, "and tell me whether my breath is sweet." Now the sly fox saw the pitfall and was wary. "Pardon me, O king of the forest," said the fox most politely, "for I cannot smell at all! I have a bad cold."

The story's allegorical dimensions are pretty clear—it's a fairly transparent metaphor for the "damned if you do, damned if you don't" position we saw alluded to in the Talmud. Here, though, instead of a demonstration of power—either through insolent speech like Rabban Gamaliel's, or supernatural salvation like in the arena—what transpires is comedy that revolves around weakness, where resistance is couched in rhetorical deference, and in assertion of physical inferiority. Versions of this comedy of accommodation appear in the stories of Esther and Daniel, but the fable genre gave it greater prominence, tying it, arguably, to a kind of waiting game inflected by messianic expectation: Just hang on until the great ram's horn blows, and history ends. There's another animal joke, if not precisely a fable, to the same effect, in which a king directs the kingdom's chief rabbi to make his favored monkey talk or suffer the consequences. The rabbi agrees, but says it will take him five years. When his fellows ask him what he's doing, he replies: "In five years all sorts of things can happen. The king might die; I might die; the monkey might die; who knows? It might even learn to talk."

Compare this last joke to another genre popular in the medieval period: the riddle tale. Riddle tales, though slightly more realistic than their fabulous, allegorical counterparts, are still often historically anachronistic or mythically vague. But they're powerfully related nonetheless to some of the most important features of the medieval period. As anyone who has read (or seen) *The Hobbit* knows, riddles are inherently conflict-based: One party poses the question knowing the answer, the other has to assume all the risk of answering wrongly with a dubious promise of reward. (The basic reward for answering the Riddle of the Sphinx, for example, was not getting eaten.) This kind of situation echoed the Jewish situation in medieval Christendom quite nicely.

In the riddle tales, characters like the councilor Kunz (whose name comes from the German/Yiddish for "skill, cunning, trick") or other Jewish protagonists (or their stand-ins) are placed in seemingly impossible situations or presented with seemingly impossible challenges. (One such challenge, for example: The ruler insists the protagonist come to him neither clothed nor naked.) The character is able to solve the challenge through the exercise of wit, therefore escaping persecution or destruction. (In this case, the individual comes naked, but wrapped in a fishing net.) Many of these riddle tales, unlike the talking monkey joke, feature open-minded rulers willing to acknowledge the utility of such intelligent individuals: a faithful replica, or legitimate wish fulfillment, of the medieval European situation, where the Jews' position as *servi camerae regis* ("servants of the royal chamber") meant that they were largely protected by a strong monarch or leader, which kept other elements of the society in check. The utility the Jews provided, though generally of the fiscal variety in support of the royal tax revenue, could even, theoretically, have been the pleasure that came from the display of wit itself. Though Jewish jesters to Christian rulers per se were vanishingly rare, there seems to be some merit to the articulation of that noted medieval Jewish scholar, Mel Brooks, who famously put it in these terms: "If they're laughing, how can they bludgeon you to death?"

It's not coincidental, I think, that both these types of humor are adaptations of genres broadly popular throughout the medieval world. (With the exception of some details, many of the tales that appear in Jewish fable or riddle collections appeared elsewhere with little comment.) But that's not to say that Jewish comedy relating to anti-Semitism in the medieval period was limited to the humor of accommodation or resignation. There was another sort of humor about medieval Jewish-Christian relations, one which flourished out of sight of gentile eyes. In the safety of their own linguistic sphere, the Jews would, on numerous occasions, try to get back at those around them.

Perhaps the most infamous work of medieval Jewish comedy in

this respect is the *Toledot Yeshu*, a parodic work purporting to be the true history of Jesus. This "counterhistory," to use the scholarly term, portrayed the Christian god, his history and biography, in the worst possible terms, sparing no detail to reverse and degrade the circumstances of the Gospels. Take the virgin birth, for example: The *Toledot Yeshu* differed from the canonical account, suggesting, instead, that Mary was a menstruating prostitute impregnated by a Roman soldier—rendering Jesus a bastard—and proceeded to depict the Christian savior as a sexually depraved sorcerer defeated in mystical battle by being urinated on by a rival. Some scholars even believe the work might have been read communally on Christmas Eve. Call it a medieval war on Christmas.

This was the same kind of intellectual contempt Rabban Gamaliel had applied to the pagan emperors: You think you're so smart, but a moment's examination reveals your belief's shocking insufficiencies. You have the power to count the stars? Count your teeth without opening your mouth first; then I'll listen. Christian theology? Tell me why it makes more sense for me to believe that a pregnant woman was divinely inseminated, and to worship three gods in one, rather than a single, transcendent, omnipotent creator; then we'll talk. But since that kind of talk would get us expelled from our communities, if not worse, we'll make sure we do it in a language you can't understand.

Which was one of the reasons Jews were particularly anxious about Christians by choice, or, as they're better known, converts, who *did* know the language, and drew on (and often slanted) their knowledge to compose some of the most anti-Jewish manifestoes of the period. But Jews' attitude to these individuals—who were fairly rare in the medieval and early modern period—was generally scabrous, stemming from that same intellectual-theological superiority: Why would you possibly accept Christianity? It couldn't be out of *belief*. And, often behind the cloak of Hebrew, they let them know it. Around 1391, a Jewish doctor named Profiat (or Profayt)

Duran converted to Christianity in the Kingdom of Aragon and took the name Honoratus de Bonafide. While living an apparent life of Christian respectability, he wrote anti-Christian works in Hebrew. One of them, *Al tehi keavotekha* ("Do not be like your fathers"), composed three years after his conversion, is a satiric letter to David Bonet Bonjorn, another recent convert, who had apparently become a Christian out of genuine theological belief. The letter is framed as a congratulatory missive, but everything about it—including the complex byplay of biblical allusion that was a hallmark of witty Jewish writing at the time—shows it to be mocking the irrationality and absurdity of anyone purporting to possess a philosophical education who embraced Christian dogma. "Do not be like your fathers, who were brought by the principles of reason ineluctably to the natural, theological, logical and mathematical axioms," writes Duran, tongue lodged firmly in cheek, "this is their way in their folly, my brother." Or, more pungently, in the phrase credited to the sixteenth-century converso Juan Beltran from Brihuega: "I worship thee, Oh carpenter! I worship thee, Oh carpenter!"

This kind of comic Jewish triumphalism is reflected in one of the great narratives of the late medieval and early modern era: the Jewish pope, the child who's been converted to Christianity (generally forcibly) and by dint of his intellectual superiority makes his way through the ranks to the top spot. Later centuries will make the comic aspects of the tale more explicit—I'm thinking of the one where Mrs. Greenstein visits the Dalai Lama and speaks only four words: "Sheldon, enough is enough." But one can be forgiven for thinking the comic tone was there, at least mutedly, all along: *of course* if a Jew was a Catholic, he'd be the pope. All the others, after all, have *goyishe kep* (simply and manifestly inferior) gentile intellects.

But there was one occasion when Jews and Christians actually did engage in intellectual debate, comparing the relative merits of their theologies: the disputation. And one comic treatment of that very serious institution raises equally serious questions: what happens when that Jewish intellectual self-confidence, that sense of theological superiority, begins to waver?

First, the joke:

> Once there was a wicked bishop who wished to drive the Jews out of his local area. And so he decided to challenge a representative of the Jewish community to a debate, with the result that if the bishop won, he would be able to do with the Jewish community what he would. The Jewish community, naturally, was very frightened of the prospect, and no one wanted to be the one who would bear the burden of what might happen if they lost. And so they were about to forfeit, until one simple man, Yankel, stepped forward and agreed to take on the challenge. The problem was that neither Yankel nor the bishop spoke a common language, and so it was decided that the disputation would take place in pantomime.
>
> The bishop strode proudly to the center of the town square, and held up three fingers. Yankel, for his part, held up a single finger in return. Then the bishop, looking slightly flustered, pointed into the distance; Yankel responded with a finger stabbed sharply toward the earth. The bishop, now apparently entirely discombobulated, produced an apple from inside his cassock; Yankel took out a loaf of bread. And with that, the bishop stalked away, shouting, "Enough! The Jews have triumphed!"
>
> His fellow churchmen gathered about him, asking what happened. He said, "The brilliant Jew had a response for everything. First, I held up three fingers, to indicate the power and majesty of the Holy Trinity; in return, the Jew held up a single finger, to retort that majestic power is more fully embodied in a singular form, like the one God of the Hebrews, and what is more perfect in essence is finer. In return, I suggested to him that our Son of God would return

from afar, from where he is now, to show the Jews the error of their ways; the Jew replied, in turn, that faith must be judged not by some abstract happening in the distance or future but by what occurs in the present, at the moment, and where was our Messiah now? I had one more possibility: I produced Eve's apple, sign of the original sin that scourges us all; but when he produced wheat, the staff of life, showing Divine mercy, rather than prejudgment, I fell silent. I had nothing more to say." The churchmen shook their heads.

Back on the other side of the square, at the synagogue, there was great and festive rejoicing: and the rabbis said to Yankel, "Yankel! How did you do it? How did you best the brightest mind of the Church in theological disputation?" Yankel frowned. "Well, to be honest, I don't quite know," he said. "First he told me that he wanted three debates, and I suggested that one would be plenty. And then he thought we should do them over there, and I said that here would be fine with me; and then we had lunch."

The joke cuts two ways, testament, I think, to the doubled perspective of a lot of Jewish humor about anti-Semitism. On the one hand, it gets to the core sentiment that there's something both overly *mental* and overly *stupid* about anti-Semitism, something taking place largely in the heads of the anti-Semites themselves. Jew hatred is, almost by definition, a product external to actual Jews and their behavior itself; and so a lot of intellectual (or perhaps pseudo-intellectual) effort has gone into producing the structures necessary to explain precisely why to engage in it. These structures are easy to mock precisely in terms depicting their own collapse. In this instance, it's the bishop's overintellectualizing that brings himself down. That trait rests, ultimately, on his own deep-rooted sentiment that when it comes down to it he's the one with the weak, losing theological case—a position that certainly resonates with the Jewish joke-teller and audience.

On the other hand, it's not like the Jews come out particularly well in the joke, either. Their victory didn't emerge from an effective theological defense, or even a display of the kind of wit exemplified in the fox fables. Rather, they benefited from—literally speaking—dumb luck. On some level, this may reflect the corrosive nature of a type of comedy that assaults all its targets equally. But it also raises the uncomfortable question that the Talmudic texts by and large don't: maybe we *are* wrong, after all. Judging from the evidence around us, it's sure hard to prove that we're right.

This perspective is intriguingly echoed from the non-Jewish perspective in an anti-Christian satire by one of the greatest medieval humorists (one of the great humorists, full stop): Giovanni Boccaccio. In the *Decameron*, Boccaccio tells the story of Abraham, a Jew persuaded to convert to Christianity—but not by the blandishments of his Christian friend or by the virtues displayed by the Christian leadership in Rome. Abraham, as it turns out, finds that "nobody there who was connected with the Church seemed to me to display the slightest sign of holiness, piety, charity, moral rectitude, or any virtue," but converts for precisely that reason. If Christians are so successful despite their lack of virtue and poor conduct, they *must* be on the right track, he figures.

Boccaccio, a fourteenth-century Italian whose humanist, anticlerical tendencies pointed the way toward modernity, reminds us that as the world entered the modern period, Jews were hardly Christianity's only critics. European modernity as we know it was forged in the uneasy peace that came out of the mid-seventeenth century's wars of religion. A very rough definition of its most defining features—the development of a concept of religious tolerance based on a separation of church and state that derived from philosophically rationalist grounds—also led to significant potential changes in considering the "Jewish question" (another term that gained currency in the period). If the source of anti-Judaism was Jewish *difference*, if that's what made Jews so noxious and hateful (to the anti-Semites), that difference was based on a difference of theological opinion. And since there was no basis of judging the truth of any revealed religion as better than any others, if the main criterion of behavior was reason—a staple of Enlightenment thinking—then engaging in anti-Semitism simply wasn't reasonable. It should, therefore, vanish in a poof of logic, to be replaced by not only tolerance of the Jewish minority in these newly emerging nation-states, but even acceptance of them as equal partners, citizens (as the locution had it) of the Mosaic faith.

This didn't work in terms of abolishing European anti-Semitism, of course. Not in the slightest.

THE MOST obvious reason for the failure of Enlightenment rationalism to cure European anti-Semitism is a fact of human nature, one illustrated in literature and culture from *Romeo and Juliet* to *All in the Family* and *The Jeffersons*: prejudice dies hard. There's a vast difference between intellectual acceptance of a phenomenon and its emotional acceptance. Even people who genuinely believe in religious toleration don't necessarily want Jews as their neighbors or their in-laws.

Much of the Jewish humor that resulted from a cynical exploration of this phenomenon was written in the European languages Jews were embracing as part of the modern bargain. Some of it was by those who had, in the words of the brilliant nineteenth-century German lyric poet Heinrich Heine, taken baptism as the entrance ticket to European culture. That's Heine's phrase, and, befitting his caustic and unsparing comic sense, he, himself a convert, was also responsible for one of the best lines on the subject: "It is extremely difficult for a Jew to be converted, for how can one Jew believe in the divinity of another?"

Heine wasn't afraid to attack anti-Semitism using the old, familiar tropes of intellectual-theological contempt. In a long poem of his about a Jewish-Christian disputation, for example, he observes that the Trinity is

a mystery that only
Can be grasped if you dispense
With the reason's mental shackles
And the prison house of sense.

But he also twitted European anti-Semites for committing the worst of all possible crimes: failing to live up to their own standards of charm and class. Heine's biting image of the new anti-Semitism, "no longer with the gloomy, fanatical monkish mien, but with the flabby enlightened features of a shopkeeper afraid of being outdone in business dealings," encapsulates it nicely.

Most of Heine's anti-Semitic characters carry their hatred around with the same crudity and undignified nature as his other scatological and vulgar humor might suggest. (This was in marked contrast to his dignified and elegiac portraits of Jews, a kind of new solemnity and, indeed, class that one would find in contemporary and later philosemites like Gotthold Ephraim Lessing and George Eliot.) The new breed of European anti-Semite, in other words, would be guilty of socially cutting violence rather than any other kind, moving the comedy of persecution to the drawing room and to the realm of etiquette. Heine's comment that "when people talk about a wealthy man of my creed they call him an Israelite; but if he is poor they call him a Jew" is an indicative aperçu. True, the more biting versions of this suggest how at certain points this might, avoidably or otherwise, spiral into violence, but this was the regrettable outcome rather than the main point.

Heine's comic example took root in England, where Israel Zangwill, one of the most famous Jewish writers in the world before the World Wars, took on Jewish "bad habits" in his 1894 comic work *The King of the Schnorrers*. There, Zangwill embraces the stereotype English people had of Jews, but—crucially—in order to demonstrate the continuities between those stereotypes of scamming and financial chicanery to those practiced by the British upper crust. Zangwill's foreword to the book ends with a verse from an old English folk song beginning with the couplet "That all men are beggars, 'tis very plain to see/ Though some they are of lowly, and some of high degree." Zangwill demonstrated, along with Heine, the high crimes of hypocrisy and crudity associated with anti-Semitism that were—at least ostensibly—geared to create revulsion among the children of the Enlightenment.

Whether it was to alleviate the hypocrisy, or to assume the service that vice pays to virtue, the second phenomenon central in the persistence of anti-Semitism in the modern age resulted: the simple expedient of creating *different* reasons for rejecting the Jews. Zangwill also said that "if there were no Jews they would have to be invented for the use of politicians—they are indispensable, the antithesis of a panacea; guaranteed to *cause* all evils" and, as is well-known, anti-Semitism can flow tragically easily into new vessels, new conceptual schemas, as history offers them up and as earlier ones are blocked. This "flexibility" would make it possible for twentieth-century anti-Semites, for example, to simultaneously picture Jews as the secret capitalists who controlled the world's economies and the anarchist communists dedicated to overthrowing those economies. The shift that took place with the birth of racial anti-Semitism— roughly speaking, blaming the Jews less for what they believe than for who they are—simply accentuated the Jewish disillusionment with emancipation's prospects; and the belief spread among dismayed Jewish liberals that at least when it came to anti-Semitism, modernity was a mug's game, where the rules would be changed every chance their persecutors got. When Jews told a post–Great War joke about a meeting between the Polish politician and artist Ignacy Paderewski and Woodrow Wilson—where the Pole asserted that if all Poland's demands were not granted at the peace conference, his people will be so angry that many would go out and massacre the Jews, and if they were granted, his people would be so happy that many would get drunk and go out and massacre the Jews—they were relating the kind of story that spoke to the death of Jewish hope, even as a kind of liberal optimism reached its peak.

This stood alongside, and occasionally complemented, a third phenomenon of the modern period, one that led to a particularly discomfiting type of Jewish comedy of anti-Semitism: an internalization of some of the charges. That is to say, some Jews began to consider whether the anti-Semites actually had a point, and went on to attack Jewish behavior and blame *it* for anti-Semitism. It's obviously a different approach than the others, and rests on a notion of Jewish identity lying somewhere between the two definitions we've articulated before: something about the way Jews culturally and even nationally behave, it might go, has affected who they are. But—and this is the difference from racial anti-Semitism—if the former changes, perhaps root and branch, the latter could as well.

This kind of Jewish comedy is frequently called "self-hating": slightly inaccurately, because the Jewish haters were generally expressing their hatred of constituencies of Jews they weren't part of. Starting in the mid-eighteenth century in Western Europe, it was a phenomenon of Western European Jews aimed at the Eastern European immigrants in their midst. (There would be a similar phenomenon in America a century later: acculturated German Jewish emigrants of a previous generation denigrating the waves of immigrants who made their way through Ellis Island.) Occasionally it was produced for non-Jewish, or mixed, audiences: but it's the writers in Jewish languages that most profoundly influence the history of Jewish comedy at this point. The earliest members of the Haskalah, or Jewish Enlightenment, were, in their Western European phase, regular fellow travelers in this phenomenon.

The Haskalah plays an important role in our story, so it's worth taking a moment to explain what it is. To call it an ideology, or a movement, or a political program, or a literary style or sensibility, isn't quite right, although it was all—and none—of these. It consisted of, largely speaking, a set of men in European Jewish communities—first in Western Europe in the late eighteenth century, particularly Germany, and then, over the next few decades, admirers and disciples-by-reading in the Russian Empire, after they inherited their Jewish population via their conquest of Poland—who had really bought into the new ideals of philosophical rationalism and religious toleration.

They understood that this moment, exemplified by this argument, offered new prospects for Jewish political and social equality: but they also understood that these prospects wouldn't materialize without some change—and that the onus for that change was on the Jews. The proponents of the Haskalah, or *maskilim*, advocated reforms in Jewish social custom, in Jewish religious practice, in Jewish educational procedure, in Jewish literary style and content; and, in all those cases, "change" meant "attempting to more closely emulate the customs and culture of one's immediate neighbors"—pushing to speak their language, rather than (for example) Yiddish; prizing literary forms like the bourgeois satire or philosophical dialogue over the traditional Purim play; trying to force through state legislation to change aspects of Jewish dress, or school curriculum. As one can imagine, this hardly endeared the *maskilim* to many of their coreligionists: and they returned the favor, often depicting fellow Jews who had yet to get with the program, which was the overwhelming majority of them, quite negatively. But they were—particularly in Western Europe—aware that this might have deleterious consequences to Jews' image among their neighbors; so they ostensibly put their own best feet forward by explaining that all those stereotypes they had about Jews weren't *wrong*, precisely, just geographically inaccurate. They should be aiming their brickbats at these other, far less acculturated and (in their minds) acculturable Eastern European types.

In one play of the German Jewish Enlightenment, for example, 1797's *Silliness and Sanctimony*, the Eastern European Jewish character is presented as a hypocritical, oversexualized monster, a Tartuffe in traditional dress, the better to distinguish him in non-Jewish eyes from all the good German Jews who just wanted to dress and speak and read like everyone else. Here's how that character, Reb Yoysefkhe, is presented in his first appearance onstage: "He creeps and crawls, his head deeply bowed, his eyes fixed on the ground and his hands folded [ostensibly piously]." We're not particularly surprised when, at play's end, we find him in a house of ill-repute, attempting to pawn his ritual phylacteries in order to fund his continued activity.

That desire by the German Jews to fit in, and the comedy of self-hatred (or self-criticism, if you prefer) that it fueled, was conditioned on hope that if and when this social, cultural, and linguistic transformation *did* take place, the barriers would fall between Jews and their non-Jewish neighbors. Such a hope, if ultimately vain, was at least plausible in Western Europe; but the modernizing movement's Eastern European successor and counterpart, despite inheriting the idea of those imagined opportunities of assimilation and acculturation, had far harsher and more anti-Semitic legislation to remind the Jews of their place in society and the impossibility of those means realistically achieving such goals.

Whether it was the restriction of Jews to a specific swath of the Russian Empire—the "Pale of Settlement"—or, particularly after the Tsar's assassination in 1881, the growth of specific and quasi-organized anti-Jewish violence in the form of the newly dubbed "pogroms," Eastern European Jewish history suggested a very different approach for those who broke away from that centuries-long tradition of comparative quietism. Increasingly, the portraits of Jewish powerlessness in the face of anti-Semitism, when placed in a comic key, mocked those bienpensants for not understanding how anti-Semitism really worked. Take this joke, for example:

> Once a bear escaped from a circus. The chief of police ordered that the bear should be shot on sight. When one Jew heard that, he decided to get out of town. "Why are you running away?" asked his friend. "You're not a bear." The Jew replied, "Listen. Before you know it, they'll shoot a Jew—and then go prove he's not a bear!"

This progression from liberal optimism to cynical disillusionment is evident in some of the best Yiddish literature of the period. While there are lots of people who are willing to dub Yiddish language funny by its very essence, that's deeply inaccurate. As the lingua franca of Eastern European Jewry, Yiddish was the vehicle for the most somber eulogies as well as the earthiest jokes, lyrical poetry along with shaggy doggerel or comments about gastrointestinal distress. But there's no question that Yiddish *literature* had a sense of itself, from the beginnings of its modern iteration, as an underdog, a second choice for writers who'd rather be writing Hebrew or for an audience who didn't have the skills or inclination or background to learn Russian or Polish. And the reason many of the authors first indulged in Yiddish—reaching a mass audience for their progressive polemics—did, at first, suggest inserting a crowd-pleasing spoonful of comic *zuker* to let the medicine go down.

Which is not to say that the comedy wasn't serious, especially when it came to anti-Semitism. Consider the man dubbed "the grandfather of Yiddish literature," S. Y. Abramovitch (although everyone knew him by the name of his literary persona, Mendele the Book Peddler), and how his thinking progressed. Born in 1835 in modern-day Belarus, Abramovitch turned to literature after a dramatic period of begging as an orphan through the Jewish Pale of Settlement and finding solace in the house of an early Eastern European *maskil*; the conditions of Jewish life he witnessed on his travels, and the hope the Haskalah offered of alleviating them, marked him. In an 1878 novel of his, *The Travels of Benjamin III*, Benjamin and his traveling companion Senderel the Housewife are stymied in their grand journey not primarily by the Russian military into which they are impressed, but by the Jewish press-gangers who impress them. Jewish power is stunted not only by Jews' own lack of perspective about their own place in the political order—armchair Jewish generals sitting around the bathhouse debating points of military strategy of the Crimean War while resolutely refusing to take a clear-eyed look at their own situation—but, perhaps even more troublingly, by their seeming pride in their own impotence.

Benjamin and Senderel are released from the Tsarist army, for example, on the basis of Benjamin's testimony that "We hereby declare, the two of us, that we are, have been, and always will be ignorant of military matters; that we are, God be praised, married men with other things on our minds than your affairs, which are totally alien to us; and that we cannot possibly be of any use to you!" Judging from the plucked and scrawny image they present, there's no disagreeing with them: but the bemused Tsarist soldiers are, in the scheme of the novel, largely blameless. The best prescription for a better Jewish politics, the book seems to suggest, is a change in Jewish perspective: the kind the Jewish Enlightenment specialized in.

But the author was simultaneously cynical about the possibility of Enlightenment actually changing things, in no small part thanks to the failure of Russian liberal institutions to grapple appropriately with the Jewish question; a cynicism that grew as the years passed. In his novel *The Mare* (1873; substantially revised 1889), a student's entry into Russian society is stymied, as the entrance examinations to Russian university are stacked against Jews. He goes mad, hallucinating a talking horse who is a metamorphosed personification of the Jewish people, downtrodden and beaten in exile. Even the liberals of Russia—personified in turn as the Society for Prevention of Cruelty to Animals—don't care about the horse, and assume it's the horse's fault that it's been beaten. Their approach—"Let [the mare] become more presentable," they say. "When she has learned all the tricks required of a trained horse, she will be worthy of our commiseration, and our society will stand by her." That is a position that Abramovitch might once have sympathized with, but did no longer: not when, as on the next page, his student/stand-in, seeing a Russian peasant beating a horse, proudly identifies himself as a member of the society and is greeted with the response: "I'm gonna bash your head in, you nut! Go to hell with all your societies!" At some point, personal responsibility begins to look pale and, indeed, laughable in the face of other malicious causes.

Take another of the canonical turn of the century Yiddish writers, I. L. Peretz. In his late 1890s story "The Shabbes Goy," a resident of Chelm, the archetypal Jewish fools' town, is constantly explaining away a fellow townsman's beating at the hands of the local gentile bully with increasingly specious (and comic) rationalizations:

> "It's all very clear, Yankele! . . . Just like that, you say, 'murderer.' About one of God's creatures, *murderer*? There's no such thing. If there were murderers in the world, would God permit the world to exist? So what then? But since you are relating an incident that happened, after all, and I believe you, and I see with my own eyes the knocked-out teeth I must conclude, you understand, thus. . . ." He pauses to catch his breath and expounds: "The guilt, Yankele, in reality belongs to your teeth!"

As the beatings worsen, the Chelmites finally come to a conclusion: to banish Yankele, because of his tormentor's fixation on him, and to attempt to appease the eponymous goy through increased portions of challah and brandy. Peretz's sardonic conclusion lingers: "You're laughing? Still, there's a little of the rabbi of Chelm in each of us."

Peretz wasn't the only one diagnosing this dismaying foolishness, stemming from, in his diagnosis, a combination of a religious tradition counseling quietism and a liberal modern agenda that located Jewish troubles in their own behavior. An iconic joke of the period depicts two Jews before a Russian firing squad, both offered blindfolds. One accepts, the other scornfully refuses. His friend urges him: "Shh . . . don't make trouble." And a more elevated, if no less stinging, treatment came from the pen of the Hebrew (and Yiddish) poet H. N. Bialik, who crafted an epic jeremiad after the 1903 Kishinev pogrom filleting the Jewish men who watched their wives be violated in pogroms and then crept off to ask if the rabbinic law permits them to the men. His poem "The City of Slaughter" is either the fullest embodiment of national and divine wrath, the blackest of all cynical satire, or both.

If Bialik began to champion a kind of Jewish nationalism expressed by his support for Zionism, the fulfillment of the Jewish national dream, Peretz, writing just a few years earlier in the 1890s, advocated an approach to combating anti-Semitism far more popular at the time: replacing the current order with a revolutionary brotherhood of mankind that would look beyond petty divisions, including crusty and reactionary religious division. Of course, it wasn't so easy to sweep away ancient hatreds. And as the idealism behind the first Russian Revolution collapsed into spasms of reactionary anti-Semitic violence, and the October Revolution curdled into permanent assault against the same old marginalized group, the European Jewish comedy of anti-Semitism metastasized into a kind of permanent black humor, a grim state of resignation. One illustrative Soviet joke: "Haim is walking down the street when someone calls him a Jew bastard. He mutters, 'Ay, if only there were meat in the shops, it would be like czarist times.' "

IF JEWS of the premodern period felt anti-Judaism to be *wrong* but *logical* (taking into account the other's theological position); and modernizing Jews felt it to be *logical* (since it was, in their view, based on an organic outgrowth of specific, explicable, and correctable circumstances) and to some limited extent even *right* (even if it wasn't fair); modern Jews—and modern Jewish comedy—is predicated on a picture of anti-Semitism as both *wrong* and *illogical* (since any attempts at corrective behavior aren't accepted, and the bases for such hatred are rejected as increasingly specious). A joke that perfectly illustrates this sense of modern anti-Semitism's increasingly free-floating, illogical nature:

A Jew was stopped on the street by a bully and challenged to say whose fault it was that Europe was in such a mess. "The Jews," said the Jew, knowing his audience and being no fool, "and the bicycle riders." "The bicycle riders?" replied the bully, nonplussed. "Why the bicycle riders?" "Why the Jews?" the Jew replied.

That joke is usually told as a Holocaust joke, with the protagonist some sort of brownshirt. Here's another, even more specific one:

Two Jews are sitting on a park bench, reading newspapers. One looks over and notices, with some surprise, that the second Jew is reading *Der Sturmer*, the viciously anti-Semitic Nazi paper. "Why are you reading that?" he asks. The second Jew sighs and looks at his paper. "What does your paper say about the Jews?" he asks. "Well," says the first Jew, looking at his Zionist weekly. "It says that the Jews are being harassed; that they're being beaten, and their property is being taken away from them; that they're being gathered up and taken away in trains to who knows where." "Exactly," nodded the second Jew. "Now look at this paper. In this paper, we control the world's economy; we have our men inside all the world's governments; we're an unstoppable force. Now, tell me the truth: which Jews would you rather be?"

The joke bites, perhaps because it so neatly reverses the humor of the previous era. In the streets of Berlin during the period of the Enlightenment, a Jewish response to complaints and canards was to internalize and to accept (even if the parties accepting were so doing on behalf of another part of the Jewish people) in the hope that changing their behavior might change their destiny. Here, in the face of such persecution, there was no sense, no sense at all, that the Jews were culpable for the situation they had placed

themselves in. All they could do was laugh bleakly at the role
history had cast for them.

As the Nazi noose tightened, and the bleakness and despair deepened, the Jewish comic sensibilities remained of a piece: perhaps
because they'd been tempered by so many centuries of contemplation on the topic. Lion Feuchtwanger, a notable German-Jewish
writer who spoke out against Hitler early on, ironically reduced the
assaults against his home and property to other entries in a long
list of calculations in his comic essay "Balance Sheet of My Life":
"The writer L. F. committed 22,257 venial sins, resulting mostly
from indolence and a somewhat phlegmatic search for pleasure. . . .
He possessed, when the National Socialists came into power, 28
manuscripts, 10,248 books, 1 auto, 1 cat, 2 turtles, 9 flowerbeds, and
4,212 other objects which were either destroyed, killed, lost, or otherwise removed when the National Socialists ransacked the house."
The noted Warsaw Yiddish cabaret performer Shimon Dzigan, in a
1935 sketch "The Last Jew in Poland," pictured a Poland in which
the anti-Semites got their wish—to make Poland *Judenrein*. But
then the Poles realize the result: an economy in ruins, a nonexistent
culture, no one for the anti-Semitic fraternities to attack, and so
on. Luckily, they find one final Jew in Poland, just about to leave:
a governmental delegation begs him to stay. A call goes out across
the land to find someone who knows how to prepare gefilte fish and
cholent. They give him the highest medals in the land . . . which he
pins to his behind. The skit ends with them serenading him with a
well-known Polish song, "May You Live a Hundred Years." That
image of a Poland free of Jews, haunting a specter as it was in 1935,
achieved a bloody reality just a few years later that was almost
beyond imagining.

And yet, the Jewish comic impulse to comment, to investigate, to
contemplate, continued. Franz Werfel, the great Austrian-Jewish writer
of the period, returned to the ironies of Jewish modernity in his 1944
play *Jacobowsky and the Colonel*, in which the Jewish protagonist,

an ironic bearer of Jewish fortunes in Nazi-occupied Europe, says: "My great crime was German culture. I admire it fervently: Goethe, Mozart, Beethoven! And so I founded a school for modern architecture in Mannheim, and a chamber music society in Pforzheim, and a workers' library in Karlsruhe. The Nazis will never forgive that." Years later, the French novelist Romain Gary, in *The Dance of Genghis Cohn*, a blackly comic novel about a murdered Jewish comedian possessing the body of a former Nazi, put it even more succinctly: "Culture is when mothers who are holding their babies in their arms are excused from digging their own graves before being shot."

That observation is told to the comedian-ghost, the eponymous Cohn, right before he is shot to death (while digging his own grave, as it happens). And the spirit comments: "It was a good *khokhme* ["joke"], and we both had a good laugh. I'm telling you, there's no funnyman like the Jewish funnyman." Later in the novel, Cohn tells a joke—if that's the word—about a relative of his: "It was his wife whom the Cossacks raped in front of him. She had a child after that adventure and my uncle, who was very vindictive, revenged himself cruelly on the Russian goyim. *He treated the child as his own son, and brought him up as a Jew.*" Jewishness becomes tragedy, a cataclysmic punishment: and, given the circumstances, how easy is it to argue the alternative proposition?

All four of these comic artists survived the Holocaust. Feuchtwanger and Werfel managed to escape the Continent and settle in the United States; Dzigan and his partner would survive the war in Russia, even touring the Soviet Union as they did (though they would subsequently spend several years in prison); Gary fled to England and spent the war fighting with the Free French Forces. Millions of others, of course, would not have that good fortune.

And what of *their* laughter? Because, by all accounts, humor *did* flourish, in ghetto newspapers, like Warsaw's *Morgen Freiheit*'s "Political Joke" section, and in Theresienstadt's weekly satirical paper *Salom na patek* ("Hello Friday"); in revues in places like Westerbork; even in the camps, in jokes passed along inside the latrines and in songs sung in makeshift, temporary cabarets in Auschwitz. One song from Sachsenhausen, for example, takes on the beatings that were a horrific staple of camp life:

> The first kick and you will feel much better,
> They bash your face—do not raise a sweat,
> The third kick, really, is a laughing matter,
> After the fourth—your pants are rather wet!
> Four big bullies kick you in good rhythm,
> Spit six of your teeth out when they are quite done,
> The seventh heel is dancing on your tummy,
> It stamps on it, and it's all really fun!

A second, from the Lodz ghetto, is an extensive, loving, ode to a potato: "Oh, potato, oh dream of my life! For you do I yearn, for you do I strive. . . ." And a third, from Theresienstadt, titled, simply, "Invitation," ironically, and self-consciously troublingly, places the singer in the imaginative position of sharing the aim of the Nazis who deported them:

> Friends and loved ones, do you suffer
> From a life of want and fear?
> Are things at home becoming tougher?
> Pack your bags and join me here.
>
> [. . .] Do you dream of ease and pleasure,
> Tea and coffee, wine and beer,
> Concerts, theater, endless leisure?
> Pack your bags and join me here.
>
> Here's a wacky world of show biz,
> So stunning that I can't explain.

The only thing we'd like to know is
How we will get out of here.

Was it a coping mechanism? Viktor Frankl, the Auschwitz survivor and founder of logotherapy, wrote that there were "songs, poems, jokes, some with underlying satire regarding the camp. All were meant to help us forget, and they did help." And certainly some of the comic sentiments seem in no small part to be of the "what can't be cured must be endured" variety. Ruth Wisse, among others, has sensitively written about the Yiddish aphorism uttered in occupied Europe—"God grant that this war not last as long as we are able to endure it"—and one can never begrudge those in such unimaginably hellish circumstances whatever crumbs of solace and resilience humor was able to give them. Frankl, for example, helped a fellow laborer at Auschwitz by proposing they invent "one amusing story" each day about something that could happen after the Nazi defeat; a Yiddish couplet, *lomir zayn freylekh un zogn zikh vitsn, mir veln noch hitlern shive nokh zitzn*—"Let's be happy and tell jokes, we'll yet live to sit shiva for Hitler"—tells the tale. A children's play in the Warsaw ghetto reflected a long-standing Jewish strategy of theological endurance by presenting Hitler as Haman, leading him to the gallows to mirror Haman's end.

Another strategy of endurance was to provide, through the jokery, a kind of humor of psychic resistance. Take these three jokes:

A man is saved by a Jew from a streetcar accident; the man turns out to be Hitler; Hitler grants the Jew one wish; the wish: "Don't tell anybody!"

A Jewish fortune-teller tells Hitler that he will die on a Jewish holiday. "How can you be so certain?" the Fuhrer asks. "Oh, I'm certain," the fortune-teller replies. "Any day you die will be a Jewish holiday."

> A Nazi sees a Jew walking toward him. As the Jew passes by, the Nazi says, "Schwein." The Jew tips his hat and replies, "Cohen."

Which is not to say that such comedy couldn't be an actual form of resistance as well. Certainly the regime saw it that way. Hitler set up "joke courts" to punish and silence mocking opponents; between 1934 and 1945 the People's Court handed down 5,286 sentences of death, many of which went to political joke tellers. (One Nazi prosecutor was asked how he determined when a joke became criminal: He responded that the better the joke, the more dangerous the effect, and therefore, the greater the punishment.) And Dzigan was called into Polish police headquarters for questioning about his "Last Jew" skit.

But for many, perhaps even for most—whether under swastika or sickle—humor was far more jagged, a way of probing at the gaping wounds inflicted on them, rather than balm. Was it an ironic rejection of earlier theological promise? An inmate painted the words "Road to Heaven" on a sign indicating the way to Sobibor; Germans were referred to as "men of valor" in an ironic use of the biblical locution. Was it simply the most radical version of the mug's game of history? Or was it, as the Romanian filmmaker Radu Mihaileanu said about his 1998 film *Train of Life*, where a comic tale of a village's plan to survive the Holocaust by building a train to "deport" themselves and instead ride to Palestine is revealed in the film's final moments as a literal fool's tale, related from behind a camp's barbed wire fence, that the "language of comedy" is used "to strengthen the tragedy. Laughter, after all, is another form of crying."

Let a joke from Treblinka have the last word: "Cheer up—we'll meet again some day in a better world. In a shop window, as soap."

IN 1951, Irving Kristol wrote that "Jewish humor died with its humorists when the Nazis killed off the Jews of Eastern Europe . . .

Just as humor cannot mature in a life of utter religious faith, so it cannot survive a life of sheer nihilism." Looking back over a half century from Kristol's remark, you can take issue with both sides of his equation while being sympathetic to the impulse that generated it. A contemporary joke about a survivor still stings today, but, in the world of the early fifties, must have bitten deep:

> A Jew survived the gas chambers, having lost every one of his relatives. The resettlement officer asked him where he would like to go.
> "Australia," he replied.
> "But that's so far," said the officer.
> "From where?" asked the Jew.

As the postwar era continued, though, the world's largest remaining Jewish constituencies, concentrated on two spots on that globe—the United States and Israel—would each in their own way deal with almost the precisely opposite issue: a *decreasing* level of anti-Semitism and persecution.

This is hardly to say that the United States welcomed its Jews with open arms from the beginning. And there were similar dynamics of Jewish self-hatred, for example, between German and Eastern European Jewish immigrants, and, more broadly, between greenhorns and ex-greenhorns, ruing the fact that the people just off the boat were ruining it for the people who had gotten there ten years earlier. But in the twentieth-century United States, much of the energy of the comedy of Jewish self-hatred was exercised so strenuously precisely because the external pressures were, comparatively speaking, so low: there were no pogroms, no Hitler; the discrimination was of another kind entirely.

The great Yiddish writer Sholem Aleichem—the man who invented Tevye, who would gain universal immortality in his Broadway incarnation—wrote a brief piece in 1907, after he first visited America, called "Otherwise, There's Nothing New," featuring an exchange of letters between an American immigrant and his European relative. In it, the European correspondent demonstrates ironic resignation, borne of long traumatic experience, to his family's travails: no big deal, he reports, "all our family got through [the pogrom] safely, except for Lippi, who was killed with his two sons, Noah and Mordecai; first class artisans, all of them. Oh, yes, and except Hersh. Perel was found dead in the cellar, together with the baby at her breast. But as Getzi used to say, 'It might have been worse.'" This is juxtaposed to the worst thing imaginable in the American context: violence done, not to the Jewish body, but to the Yiddish language, with all these terrible English words worming their way in to the mother tongue thanks to the seductions of accultura- tion. American Jewish comedy of anti-Semitism was, by and large, built on a playing field of comparative gratitude for the possibility of Americanization; which meant that the careful observation of Jew-hatred—of which America certainly had its share—had to be exercised quite differently.

Or, to illustrate with a joke:

During the Great Depression, two Jewish bindlestiffs, hoboes, are walking along a country road; they haven't had a good meal in weeks. They pass by a church with a sign posted in front: CONVERT TO CHRISTIANITY. GET FIVE DOL- LARS. The first Jew looks at the second and says, "How about it?" The second one says, "Are you crazy? I'd never give up my faith, and certainly not for something like five dollars." The first replies, "Of course not! I'm not talking about *really* converting; just go in there, mumble some lines about Jesus, cross yourself, take the money, and get a big steak dinner and a hot bath thanks to the goyim." The second says, "Look, I'm not comfortable with that, but if you want to do it, go ahead. I'll wait outside." The first one says, "Fine; I'll be five minutes." The second one leans against the sign and waits. Five minutes pass. Then fifteen. Then an hour. Then two hours. The second Jew is getting more and more worried. Finally, after four hours, his companion emerges from the church. The second Jew is beside himself. "Are you all right?" he asks. "Did you get the money?" His friend shakes his head sorrowfully. "All you people think about is money."

This is the other side of the story of anti-Semitism in America: the Jewish side. The joke here is predicated not on a Jewish failure to be ineradicably different, but the remarkable success in overcoming that difference: the Jews are so successful that immediately they are able to participate in that prime action of the majority. And it's significant, in this telling, that that archetypal action is hating, or at least stereotyping, Jews. Compare this to an analogous joke from a different geographical context:

A Jew emigrates to Britain, leaving his family behind him. Twenty years later, coming to join him, they see him for the first time in two decades, waiting on the docks, unrecognizably dressed in Turnbull and Asser, the picture of a true English gentleman. On seeing them, he bursts into tears. "We're so glad to see you too, *tatele*, after all this time!" his tear-faced daughter responds. "Oh, no, my dear chaps, it's not that. I'm crying because we lost India."

If the response here is that assimilation—where assimilation is possible—is to be more British than the British, in the American joke, empire is replaced by that old-time religion once more, with its emphasis on Jewish distinctiveness and differentiation, despite the kind of toleration that could only have been dreamed of in Europe.

This process became even more pointed as acculturation became more of an option after the Second World War, and the sphere of social possibility became more permeable. Jewish comedy became a way of indicating that these processes had their flash points, and, with them, their limits. Perhaps the seminal cultural document of

American anti-Semitism is the 1947 filmed version of Laura Z. Hobson's novel *Gentleman's Agreement*. Gregory Peck's journalist pretends to be Jewish in order to get a firsthand view of anti-Jewish prejudice in the United States. *Gentleman's Agreement* depicts practically no sense of physical threat against Jews, an almost unimaginable characterization of anti-Semitism anywhere else in the world. But it amply displays the unspoken set of limitations and circumscriptions of Jews' entrance into gentile territory—hotels, country clubs, and the like. (An infamous mid-century postcard from Miami Beach's Gulf Hotel emblazoned with the slogan "Always a view, never a Jew," makes the point far more bluntly than usual.)

Ring Lardner, Jr., satirically noted that the moral of *Gentleman's Agreement* was "that you should never be mean to a Jew because he might turn out to be a Gentile." Unpacking the subterfuge and hypocrisy of discrimination was fertile ground for mid–twentieth-century American Jewish comedy. It mixed in another dose of Jewish unease about the prospects, and the meanings, of their attempts at acculturation, of joining a club that wasn't necessarily so crazy about having them. Or, to put it another way, it explains the contemporary rise and fall of the country club joke.

Take this one:

> All the Greensteins wanted to do was to join the local country club. But, of course, it's restricted: they don't admit Jews. So what do they do? They fly to Paris; they spend months working on their accents; they receive tutoring in the finest details of cookery, art appreciation, table manners; they get the requisite amount of plastic surgery; and then, finally, they change their names, move back, and apply to join the country club. They sail through all the opening events with ease; soon it's all over but the formality of the final interview. "What do you do, Mr. Grenville?" flatters the interviewer. "Oh, dabble, mostly," the former Mr. Greenstein replies, shooting his French cuffs. "A little investing, some watercolors, you

know how it is." "I do indeed," says the interviewer. "And Mrs. Grenville?" "*Madame, s'il vous plait.* I paint as well. And work on my sauces." "Well," the interviewer says. "I don't want to speak out of turn, but I'm certain the two of you will be a remarkable addition to our little family here. Just one final question. What religion are you?" Mrs. Grenville draws herself up haughtily: "I, my good man, am a goy."

The ineffable trace of Jewishness persists—here defined both in the use of Yiddish, in the word for "gentile," and their notion of embracing that gentile otherness precisely *as* something foreign. (And it comes out in times of duress: a similar joke has Mrs. Grenville shouting "Oy vey!" when a piping hot consommé is spilled on her dress at the welcome dinner, only to look around and intone, "Whatever *that* means.") When it comes right down to it, the jokes suggest, efforts to please the anti-Semites, or even oneself, by escaping one's Jewishness implode into futility, because the Jewishness will always be there, lurking. In Yiddish. Shades of the most basic thinking about comedy, ranging back to Plato: comedy comes, essentially, from a lack of self-knowledge.

In this kind of setting—the country club joke of the 1950s—you can see the explosion of Yiddish as a return of the repressed, since many of the protagonists of the joke would have either been Yiddish speakers as kids or grown up around Yiddish speakers (and comfortable with Yinglish). But the appearance of this kind of Jewish language or speech, or tone of voice, as proof that people are "really" Jewish is present even in people who don't know any Yiddish at all. These jokes offer a bracing countercharge to melting-pot narratives, one with uneasy commonalities to certain anti-Semitic charges: the Jew will *always* be a Jew and not a goy, no matter what efforts are made to close the gap.

So why not own it? The mid-twentieth-century comedienne Belle Barth tells a joke about a suspicious clerk of a restricted Miami Beach hotel administering an admissions test to a gentleman request-

ing a room he suspects of Jewish ancestry: "Who was our lord?"
"Jesus Christ." "Where was he born?" "In a stable in Bethlehem."
"And why was he born in a stable?" "Because a rat bastard like
you wouldn't rent him a room, that's why." More famously, the
breakthrough fifties stand-up comic Lenny Bruce, the man who may
have done more to create the comic trope of ineradicable difference
between Jews and gentiles than anyone else in American Jewish
culture, framed it unforgettably in his bit about Jewish and goyish,
where Jewish and hip are as synonymous as goyish and square: "Now
I neologize Jewish and goyish. Dig: I'm Jewish. Count Basie's Jewish.
Ray Charles is Jewish. Eddie Cantor's goyish. B'nai Brith is goyish;
Hadassah, Jewish. . . . All Drake's Cakes are goyish. Pumpernickel
is Jewish, and, as you know, white bread is very goyish. Instant
potatoes—goyish. Black cherry soda's very Jewish."

On the other hand, Bruce was able to have his pumpernickel and
eat it too. In an immediately infamous routine, he continued and
expanded his definitional activities:

> Now, a Jew, in the dictionary, is one who is descended from the
> ancient tribes of Judea, or one who is regarded as descended
> from that tribe. That's what it says in the dictionary; but you
> and I know what a Jew is—One Who Killed Our Lord . . .
> Alright. I'll clear the air once and for all, and confess. Yes,
> we did it. I did it, my family. I found a note in my basement.
> It said: "We killed him. Signed, Morty." And a lot of people
> say to me, "Why did you kill Christ?" "I dunno . . . it was
> one of those parties, got out of hand, you know." We killed
> him because he didn't want to become a doctor, that's why
> we killed him.

The shock value here is doubled. First, admitting—*for laughs!*—and
speaking out loud the most powerful anti-Semitic canard in Western
history, and daring—*daring!*—the Christian audience to do some-

thing about it. Only in America could worries about a resulting pogrom reflect more on the worrier than the joke-teller. And second, ringing the changes on a kind of ethos of self-hatred, here of the hip for the postwar, aspirational, bourgeois Jew in the grey flannel suit: if there's a reason to hate those Christ-killing Jews, it's because they, boringly, want everyone to be doctors and lawyers, like they now—thanks to American vistas of possibility—can be. (Bruce's flaying of the Scheckners, Jewish squares he meets on tour, is a case in point.) Whither American Jewish comedy of anti-Semitism then, when persecution becomes a dead letter and Jews can get into (almost) all the best clubs?

The interesting comparand here is Israel itself. Israel constitutes the second pole of Jewish historical success, where a Jewish state means a relief from state-sponsored anti-Semitism and the sentiment of minority culturehood. Well, that would be the theory, anyway. As Arthur Koestler put it, writing before the establishment of the state, "Palestine has the size of a county and the problems of a continent." In reality, Israel not only faces the constant threat of military aggression from enemies on all of its borders who specialize in genocidally eliminationist rhetoric that would have done Haman proud, but also a kind of increasing pariahhood among members and citizens of other liberal states. For some, this feels like a double standard that comes uncomfortably close to anti-Semitism itself, whether or not Israel has committed actions that were wrong or criticism-worthy. (As Israelis and others point out, this pretty much describes every state almost all of the time.)

This is not a recent Israeli sentiment. One of the blackest versions of this I've seen came from the pen of Ephraim Kishon, one of Israel's leading humorists in the decades immediately following the establishment of the state. Kishon generally engaged in gentle satire of Israeli life, in newspaper columns that show how classic Jewish tropes—verbal one-upsmanship, puffed-up fake knowledge, and the like—persist in the transference from the diaspora to the new society.

But in "How Israel Forfeited World Sympathy," written after the 1956 Suez Crisis, he ventured into much darker territory.

Satirically castigating Israel for its military triumphs, Kishon suggests that the key for the world to find genuine sympathy for Israel will be for the state to be destroyed. After the remnants of the Jewish state are gathered "on the shores of bombed-out Tel Aviv and Haifa," Kishon writes, "then, world conscience awakened." Kishon's detailed accounting of the copiousness and variety of the world's crocodile tears—although that's not quite accurate, since the bite of the satire is that the tears are genuine, now that Israel has been moved out of the pesky status of actually existing—is bone-chilling; you don't know whether to laugh or shiver. The piece ends: "Israel did not wait until May, 1957, but rashly smashed the Egyptian war machine in the Sinai Peninsula and thereby lost the opportunity to win the whole world's sympathy. And that is a great pity. God knows when we shall again have such a chance." Kishon died in 2005, having seen, alas, how many other chances would come to suggest themselves.

Notwithstanding Israel's frequent efforts to separate itself from diasporic cultural stances, this comic stance shows real continuities with the Jewish past, even if the self-consciousness of that continuity ebbs and flows. It may have been most pervasive during the first Gulf War, where international politics forced Israelis into a particularly inactive mode of response to Saddam Hussein's bombings, but it persists. There's the black humor that results from the recognition of free-floating hatred (high school students, army-bound, may part from each other with the phrase: "We'll meet on the memorial plaque"), matched, perhaps, by the rueful acknowledgment that the hatred seems to violate all dictates of common sense and moral proportionality. These sentiments are often linked—in Kishon's piece, implicitly, if patently—to the Holocaust; and it says something about the vicissitudes, and continuities, of history, that the following joke could have the resonance it does:

Sara in Jerusalem hears on the news about a bombing in a popular café near the home of relatives in Tel Aviv. She calls in a panic and reaches her cousin, who assures her that thankfully, the family is all safe. "And Anat?" Sara asks after the teenager whose hangout it had been. "Oh, Anat," says her mother, reassuringly. "Anat's fine. She's at Auschwitz!"

Such sensibility is shared, I think, by some of the increasingly beleaguered Jewish communities of Europe. There, the ever more straitened gap between liberal and Europeanist and universalist affiliations and a sense of growing inhospitality to the Jewish state—and an increasing comfort by some of those inhospitable elements to blur the lines between Israeli and Jew—leads to works like the British writer Howard Jacobson's biting comic novel *The Finkler Question*, which won the Man Booker Prize in 2010. In that novel, Jacobson, like Heine in reverse, excoriates the Jewish left and their Israel-shaming stances for playing into the hands of more traditional cases of anti-Semitism. Jacobson depicts a charged relationship between two old friends, Julian Treslove and Sam Finkler. The former becomes increasingly obsessed with matters Jewish after being mugged by someone who may or may not have hissed "You, Jew" at him; the latter joins a provocatively named group, "ASHamed Jews," which protests Israeli policies toward the Palestinians. The spiraling, traumatic conclusion, shrouded and shot through all about with fundamental concern about the possibilities and prospects for an Anglo-Jewish community, seems impossibly alien to an American context.

Which may explain why much of the twenty-first-century American humor of anti-Semitism has turned away from country club humor, from aggressions that for all intents and purposes no longer exist, and back toward the hoariest, most archetypal tropes of anti-Semitism, which can loom large in the American imagination—even if in the imagination is where they largely exist. And there's no better person to illustrate this than a man who depicts himself, in the climax of an episode of his television show, as literally being chased by a furious, cross-wielding Jesus.

LARRY DAVID—by which I mean the character that shares his creator's name and appears on a series of quasi-improvised half-hour blocks on HBO—has nothing to complain about. He, like his namesake, has made fortunes beyond his wildest dreams as the cocreator, along with Jerry Seinfeld, of one of the most successful television programs in the history of the medium. He is respected for his talent and envied for his success by peers and sycophants alike. David's golden California lifestyle is as far away from the eliminationist anti-Semitism suggested by his attacker than at any time in two thousand years of Jewish history. And yet he's constantly dissatisfied, constantly irked, and constantly picking fights and alienating friends, neighbors, potential business partners, random passersby, and, on more than one occasion, Ted Danson. What's up with that? Or more precisely, what's up with *him*?

The question is sharpened by David's enthusiastic willingness on *Curb Your Enthusiasm* to include far more explicit Jewish content and theme, and embrace a far more explicit Jewish identity for his character, than he ever did for his alter ego George Costanza and friends on *Seinfeld*. That decision is illustrated most profoundly by the way David often presented the primary structural domestic tension in the show, between himself and his wife Cheryl, as a set of differences between a Jew and a Christian that revolve around religious strife, rather than simply ethnic or cultural stereotypes, despite the fact that neither is particularly religiously observant.

And not just any old Jewish-gentile friction: David, who was expelled from Hebrew school for laughing at his rabbi, is replaying medieval Jewish-Christian relations for laughs—uncomfortable laughs as they may be—presenting himself as the Jew Christians, and indeed Christendom, love to hate. There's the episode where

Larry eats some of the cookies that were part of his wife's family's Christmas manger diorama (thus participating in one of the oldest of anti-Semitic stereotypes, the desecration of the Host). And then there's the one in which he prevents his potential future brother-in-law from getting baptized. And then the one in which he actually (if accidentally) urinates on a picture of Jesus, where the urine drops are then taken by credulous Christians for a miraculous display of Christ's tears. And, of course, the one where he's being chased down the hall by Jesus (a man named Jésus, actually, who believes, through a series of misunderstandings, that Larry has attempted to seduce his wife).

That last isn't the only mock-pogrom on offer in *Curb*: On one episode, set on Halloween, David's house actually ends up getting attacked by gentiles. The attack consists only of toilet paper and graffiti; the attackers are just disgruntled trick-or-treaters; and I wouldn't make much of the fact that Halloween is originally All Hallow's Eve, a Christian holiday. But I do think the *reasons* for the assault speak, in a nutshell, to Larry David's difference, and the way others respond to it. David refuses to offer candy to two teenagers who come to his house and who aren't wearing costumes. He's *got* plenty of candy, of course; it's the principle of the thing that matters. He awakens the next morning to find his house TP'd and the words BALD ASSHOLE spray-painted on his door; an argument with his gentile wife ensues; Larry defends his position; finally, in utter exasperation, Cheryl shouts, "No one understands your rules, Larry!"

These discussions about rules, one of *Curb*'s main continuities with *Seinfeld*—what are the boundary lines in nebulously defined situations? What constitutes the limits of social acceptability? When does *this* status change to *that* one?—were dubbed a "dark Talmud" by Larry Charles, the longtime *Seinfeld* and *Curb* writer, producer, and director. For Charles and David, adherence to those rules—in fact, an identity built around following those rules—creates a different approach to the world which is not only the basis for comedy, but hatred. David, when it comes right down to it, is certain that he's right: and there's a kind of antiheroic pride that he, along with *Seinfeld*'s Jerry, and George, and Elaine—not Kramer, usually; he's too popular and beloved, despite or perhaps because of his particular kind of weirdness—takes in avoiding the tyranny of the (polite, decent, and moral) majority. *Seinfeld* itself, as a show, seemed to take on this attitude toward the character of its lead protagonists, their difference from the rest of the world: an attitude evoked—and responded to—in the show's controversial, David-penned series finale.

In that hotly anticipated program, the foursome end up in jail because they refuse to help someone in trouble. In fact, not only do they not help, but they stand on the sideline and make jokes. Now, standing on the sidelines and making jokes—observing life and placing it through your own societally askew lens—is the province of comedians. But it is also, in its own ways, the province of minorities, and Christendom's great minority in particular—and I don't think it's totally coincidental that David makes much of the fact that the crew end up in jail for having violated a Good Samaritan law. They're not, in short, behaving like Christians; they violate the standards of regularly upheld social behavior, which makes them a threat that must be purged from the community. Jailed, in fact. In this sense, as David—and the *Seinfeld* characters—repudiate everything that the culture stands for, it's hardly a surprise that, in the finale, they become nothing less than enemies of the state. (The judge tells the "New York Four," as they're known, with all the Jewish subtextual coding that implies: "Your callous indifference and utter disregard for everything that is good and decent has rocked the very foundation upon which our society is built.") Such claims remind us uneasily of Haman's whispers to Ahasuerus—and, perhaps more uneasily, of the idea that there's some truth to those whispers. All great comedians, at heart, take themselves as a target first and most of all.

But let's not be too quick to call Larry David—or "Larry David," at any rate—a self-hating Jew. When challenged with just this epithet by a man who hears him whistling Wagner, identified by his antagonist as the Nazis' favorite composer, David's response is "I hate myself, but not because I'm Jewish." Which is, of course, a direct lift from Woody Allen, who had a thing or two to say about Wagner, Nazis, and anti-Semitism himself. Fans of Allen's film work can remember Alvy Singer's testimony in *Annie Hall* about New York, that, per Bruce, essentially and entirely Jewish city, and his jabs at neurotic obsessiveness with vestiges of anti-Semitism where none exists ("*Wagner*, Max. *Wagner*," those unmistakable adenoidal tones say, plaintively). But they also remember Granny Hall, who envisions the man who enthuses over "dynamite ham" in black hat, full beard, and sidelocks.

Both Allen and his contemporary Mel Brooks—who David also pays tribute to; the entire fourth season of *Curb* is dedicated to a brilliant meta-joke reproducing *The Producers*—have a less complicated take on anti-Semitism, perhaps befitting their pre-Boomer status and identification. (Brooks fought in the Second World War; Allen was slightly younger, but still identifies more strongly with the prewar generation; David, by contrast, had just turned twenty-one when *The Producers* came out.) Both older figures stress the importance of comic minimization in "triumphing" over anti-Semitic threats like Nazism—a triumphalism that, one could argue, could only be advanced in the flush of success of the allies (with Jews in their forces) over the anti-Semitic Axis. Brooks makes the point explicitly, in interview after interview about *The Producers*; Allen less so, and his treatment of the subject gathered nuance as his career continued. Even in that classic dinner scene from *Annie Hall*, it's a bit difficult to determine precisely who the joke's on. But in works like "The Schmeed Memoirs," purporting to be the tale of Hitler's barber, Allen cast the Nazis in no less bumbling, preening, and feckless a light as Franz Liebkind does in writing the script seized upon by Messrs. Bialystock and Bloom. ("The world needs to know that Hitler was a terrific dancer!")

As much as he repurposes Brooks and Allen on these matters, though, David goes further. There's the notorious Holocaust set piece on *Curb*, in which David invited two survivors to his house, think-

ing they'd have a lot in common because they both went through
the Holocaust (though agonizing about whether such thinking was
offensive). The twist: the "survivor" his friend brought to dinner
was actually a reality show contestant from the television program
Survivor who attempts to equate his trials with those of the former
prisoner of Auschwitz—there'd been mosquitoes, after all, and he
and the other contestants had been deprived of snacks. But it's *Curb*'s
fifth season that truly stretches the limits, despite its seemingly innoc-
uous and sitcommy premise.

After discovering his father (played by the old-time Jewish comedian Shelley Berman, another tip of the hat to his comic heritage)
may not be his biological ancestor, Larry hires a private detective
to check out his roots. Believing he's found proof positive of his
Gentility, he begins behaving, as Lenny Bruce would have put it,
goyishly. But if Bruce's response to non-Jewish discrimination is a
reverse discrimination that casts the goyim as squares, David goes
the other way, turning the joke on himself. For David, Jews are
pushy, cowardly, and selfish, cast, perhaps in his own Costanza-
ish image; whereas the gentile Larry is polite to flight attendants,
cheerfully offers to provide a leadership role in the case of airline
disaster, and, most prominently, offers to donate a kidney to Richard
Lewis—something the "Jewish" Larry was avoiding like the plague.

In short, David's fantasia is, in its own way, a classic fantasy
shared by genocidal anti-Semites: Wouldn't it be great if there weren't
any Jews? Jews, who have all of these negative characteristics, and
none of the positive ones? Even the season's deflationary finale—
Larry is told, on the way to the operating table, that it's all been a
mistake and that he's Jewish after all, but it's too late to do anything
about it—seems in its own way to be a cautionary tale, the same
from *Seinfeld*, the same from the medieval era: Don't try to change.
It always ends badly.

David isn't the only one who's employing these classic models
of the comedy of Jewish anti-Semitism in an age when we might
have thought, or hoped, that they'd lose their relevance. Take the

stand-up comic and film and television actress Sarah Silverman, for example, who handled the topic of interfaith relationships—which has increasingly lost its transgressive power in American society as social acceptance of Jews has become the norm—by describing her very public (former) relationship with the comedian Jimmy Kimmel in consciously medieval terms. She claims that she wears a St. Christopher's medal he gave her:

> It was cute the way he gave it to me, you know, he said, if it doesn't burn through my skin it will protect me, which is . . . [makes *aww, cute* face] who cares, different religions, you know, I mean, I guess the only time it's an issue I suppose would be like, if you're having a baby, you gotta figure out how you wanna raise your baby or whatever, you know, which wouldn't even still not be an issue for us because we'd be honest, you know, and just say, mommy is one of the chosen people and, uh, and daddy believes that Jesus is magic!

Starting with an image that would not have been out of place in Chaucer—of Jewish flesh repulsed by the Christian saint—she has her revenge in those same medieval terms, articulating that same Jewish contemptuousness of Christian theology, of Christian irrationalism compared to rational Jewish faith.

This is, it should be said, part of Silverman's generally transgressive approach, aided immeasurably by the faux-innocent, mock-inarticulate delivery I've tried to replicate above, which means you hardly see the shiv coming. Her brief but brilliant update on a previously mentioned Lenny Bruce bit, delivered less than a minute later, is particularly apropos: "Everybody blames the Jews for killing Christ, and then the Jews try to pass it off on the Romans. I'm one of the few people that believe it was the blacks." In some ways, this is a particularly twenty-first-century move: if we're going to be throwing around charges of anti-Semitism and ethnic hatred, it says, let's be good liberals and make sure we don't exclude ourselves, too. We're not just victims of discrimination; we're practitioners, too, and so the joke's on us. Sort of.

Compare this to the work of the British television and film star Sacha Baron Cohen, who takes *his* transgressive delight in displaying (or purporting to display) a hidden or not-so-hidden seam of anti-Semitism in famously tolerant America. He does this primarily by means of one of his characters, the Kazakhstani journalist Borat, who attempts, in interviews, to get his subjects to accede to his rabid anti-Semitism. (Borat's, of course, not Cohen's; Cohen, a veteran of Zionist youth programs who insisted that his wife, the comic actress Isla Fisher, convert to Judaism before he married her, has a much more positive approach to Jewish history and culture; and it's a doubly subversive and ironic note that Borat's "Kazakhstani" is actually Hebrew—a point largely lost on most of Cohen's viewing audience.) As it turns out, it's often the case that the greatest tolerance that is displayed by the subjects is toward Borat himself, as they look awkward and refuse to take the bait as Borat asks (for example) a martial arts instructor what he should do to defend himself against someone attacking him with the "Jew claw." On other occasions, though, such as when he leads an audience at a Country and Western bar in a rousing rendition of an (ostensible) Kazakhstani classic, "Throw the Jew Down the Well," their seemingly eager participation is slightly more unsettling. But frequently, as in the case of Cohen's other character Brüno, who uses a fashionista thumbs up/thumbs down model to vapidly ask his interviewees if a given clothing line is, say, "on the train to Auschwitz"—and have them cheerily play along—is basically a testament to the docility and occasional inanity of people caught in the media spotlight; whether it pulls the cover back on anti-Semitism, as some watching the show indicated, may be less plausible, especially given the deeply contrived, if hilarious, circumstances Cohen creates to let his art flourish.

Regardless, the comic performances of David, Silverman, and Cohen mark the position of confidence and strength Jews have in the American culture. And in that vein, there's one final point worth

noting about David's assault on the Christian majority: his aston-
ishing protestations of ignorance about that culture. In one episode,
in which he stops a Jew's conversion to Christianity by disrupting
the prospective convert's baptism, he claims he doesn't know what
a baptism is, or what it looks like. David's character's cluelessness is
a comic foil, of course, but suggests two opposed lessons.

On the one hand, David's ignorance is a kind of fuck you to
the ostensible majority power, an apotheosis of Lenny Bruce's
approach—I don't *need* to know. But it's also a telling accentuation
of his difference, reminding his viewers that David, that comedians,
that Jews, *are* different, so essentially so that they can know little
about the outside world. And the ignorance *does* tend to blow back in
Larry's face. Which begs the question: Is it the safety and security of
the American Jewish community that allows David, Silverman, and
Cohen the comfort to wallow in such neurotic (not to say self-hating)
comic behavior? Is it simply the comedian's temperament? Or is it
an ongoing feature of this strand of Jewish comedy through history,
even in more endangered precincts?

Here's one answer, probably not the only one: in 2006, when
a major Iranian newspaper hosted a competition to see who could
come up with the most anti-Israel and anti-Semitic cartoons, Amitai
Sandy, an Israeli illustrator, announced a second, similar competition, this one open to Jews only: "We'll show the world we can do
the best, sharpest, most offensive Jew hating cartoons ever published!
No Iranian will beat us on our home turf!"

Black times *do* call, it seems, for black comedy.

2

Not-So-Nice Jewish Doctors

ONE OF THE WORST OUTCOMES OF THE LACHRYMOSE THEORY of Jewish history—not of anti-Semitism itself, that is, but of presenting the story of Jewish history as essentially a response to anti-Semitism—is the portrait it presents of Jewish society as essentially reactive, contingent on external circumstances: all foreign policy, no domestic affairs. But it's easy to overcorrect and commit the opposite error: to consider Jewish history and culture not as largely unchanged by external forces (which isn't true), but as somehow *unchanging*, locked into sepia-toned, *Fiddler on the Roof*–inspired notions of an eternal shtetl which remained basically static until explosive outside events turned it upside down.

We can even pretty easily sketch out the contours of what that society might look like: songs and Sabbath candles, poor but happy, communally cohesive, and largely rural. And, though it's most frequently applied to the communities of Jewish-speaking Eastern Europe, there are analogues for other Jewish communities from the biblical, medieval, and early modern periods as well. This doesn't have a name as catchy in the scholarship as "the lachrymose theory of Jewish history," but we might call it the "life is with people" theory, after the best-selling book of the same name by Mark Zborowski and

Elizabeth Herzog. Published in 1952, it helped implant this approach into the minds of many American readers.

This misreading of Jewish history was perpetuated in no small part by Jewish writers who knew better. There's plenty of Yiddish fiction of the shtetl, for example, written by people who were there, that purposefully and inaccurately represents those market towns as harmonious Jewish presences in tune with the flows of the Jewish calendar and sometimes even the natural order. They often do it for pious reasons of elegy or nostalgia; but whatever the reason, the approach tends to downplay or overlook the internal political or social ferment that constantly took place within Jewish society, as it does in every society.

Sometimes that ferment was over perceived communal failure of their duties as observers of Jewish religious practice. Sometimes it stemmed from concern over alarming new social trends, or, conversely, the community's unwillingness to adapt to new social trends or circumstances. Sometimes it was a small group advocating the power of a new idea; sometimes it was about chastising the failure to live up to old ideals. But all of it is indicative of a community constantly thinking, talking, deliberating, evaluating. And since one of the most pungent means of advocacy or chastisement is through comedy, albeit often of the barbed and stinging variety, satire (comedy whose job it is to oppose and to conflict, afflict, reflect, and catalyze reform) offers a particularly rich strand of Jewish humor for us to explore—and a particularly good lens on the Jewish story more generally.

Unlike in the last chapter, our focus here is internal. This isn't to say some of the criticisms posed to the life and culture of the Jewish community weren't echoes of the outside world's; or that proposed solutions weren't borrowed from there. But in this chapter, the emphasis is less external—"What are the goyim doing? How should we react?"—but internal—"What are we doing wrong? How should we change it? What killer joke, or cutting scene, or biting turn of phrase, will change people's minds, and get them to adopt our undoubtedly correct point of view about the Jewish present and future?" Which leads to a related question, *the* question: Did it work? Does Jewish satire ever achieve the change it sets out to effect?

In judging its success, we'll also have to balance how it deals with two related risks. The first is its potential to fail on the comedy side. Remember the infamous characterization of satire by the noted (Jewish) theatrical wit George S. Kaufman: "Satire is what closes on Saturday night." To Kaufman, the question of satire's efficacy is not unrelated to its entertainment value: and that it runs the risk, all too often, of failing on both counts. But there's an even greater danger than that. Joseph Addison, the great eighteenth-century British journalist and comic force, wrote that "lampoons and satires, that are written with wit and spirit, are like poisoned darts, which not only inflict a wound, but make it incurable." Addison's remark, venomous on its own, suggests not only that targets of satire are wounded beyond repair, but that the process of satirizing—the taking up of comedic arms—destroys the possibility of repair more generally; it scorches the earth.

This is a far different, and bleaker approach, from the view of the satirist as society's doctor championed by thinkers as varied as Molière and Lenny Bruce, and encapsulated in Dryden's pungent definition: "The true end of satire is the amendment of vices by correction." *That* was the view, unsurprisingly, adopted by the majority of the Jewish satirists themselves: idealists and, often, prophets without honor. But whether the communal body actually takes their medicine—well, that's another question indeed.

THE BIBLICAL PROPHETS are known, in the critical literature and the wider world, for being champions of social justice; for speaking truth to power, whether held by priests or kings; and for the magnificently wide spectrum of their poetic vision, in desolation and in comfort. They're not generally, however, thought of as being particularly funny.

But satire was among their main weapons. The prophets scourged the world they saw around them: a world of lazy, hedonistic materialists, whom they portrayed as ridiculous and ultimately disastrous. "They lie on ivory beds, lolling on their couches," fumes the prophet Amos, "feasting on lambs from the flock and calves from the stalls. They hum snatches of song to the tune of the lute—they account themselves musicians like David. They drink [straight] from the wine bowls and anoint themselves with the choicest oils—but they are not concerned about the ruin of Joseph." But the satiric portraits the monotheistic prophets paint of society as a whole are sharpened to their keenest when they take on their opposite numbers: the idolaters.

The pagan religions of antiquity were rich, complex systems, focusing on spirit cultures and using material and physical representations—idols—as the focus of devotion and commitment, whether at home or at the temple. One of the proofs of the power of this approach is that it was subscribed to by the great majority of the denizens of the Near East: it was the monotheistic Jews that were the exception. Technically speaking, it seems that the earliest Hebrews practiced *monolatry*, rather than *monotheism*: it was all right to have other gods, but Jehovah was the main one. As it says in the Ten Commandments, you should have no other gods before me—but *having* other gods was okay. By the time you get to the prophets, though, monolatry has given way to monotheism—the prophet Hosea, for example, rewrites the Ten Commandments to assert that God says there are no other gods *besides*, not *before* him—which in its turn requires the humiliation and minimization of other approaches by its champions.

Satire, as the great critic Northrop Frye put it, is a kind of humor that's particularly founded on a sense of the grotesque or absurd, and the prophets pithily express that. The prophet Habakkuk writes: "What has the carved image availed, that he who fashioned it has carved it for an image and a false oracle—that he who fashioned his product has trusted in it, making dumb idols? Ah, you who say 'Wake up' to wood, 'Awaken' to inert stone! Can that give an oracle?

Why, it is encased in gold and silver, but there is no breath inside it."
Jeremiah goes into even more depth, turning the clarion call into a
story: "For the objects that the nations fear are delusions: for it is
the work of a craftsman's hands. He cuts down a tree in the forest
with an ax; he adorns it with silver and gold, he fastens it with nails
and hammer, so that it does not totter. They are like a scarecrow in
a cucumber patch, they cannot speak. They have to be carried, for
they cannot walk." Hosea may even turn the idea into a dirty joke:
when he suggests that the typical population of idolaters "consults
its stick; its rod directs it," he may just be implying that there's little
difference between following the wood of idols and the wood that's
been comically ascribed as driving male behavior throughout history.

And in at least one instance, this mockery expands into a comic
set piece: on Mount Carmel, where Elijah mocks the prophets of
Baal in a competition where they fail, despite great effort, to elicit a
response from their divinity. "Call with a loud voice, for he is a god,"
Elijah sneers. "Perhaps he is talking, or he is pursuing enemies, or
he is relieving himself, or perhaps he is sleeping and will awaken."
All this is part of a more general phenomenon where idolatry is
satirically reduced to the spectacle of a bunch of morons worshipping
sticks and stones—neatly tying in with the general portrait of the
society as unmistakably materialist: they can't get past their objects,
putting ultimate value in them.

This anti-idolatrous satire perfected by the prophets would
find its echoes centuries later in rabbinic literature. The Talmudic
authority Rabbi Nachman, for example, explicitly opines that "all
joking is prohibited except jokes about idol worship." And a potentially ideologically fraught biblical moment—the matriarch Rachel's
absconding with her father's household idols, suggesting she finds
value in them—is not only reinterpreted by the rabbis as a virtuous
act (the righteous Rachel was trying to save her father from his own
idolatrous sinfulness) but transformed into another opportunity to
satirize the idiots who *do* worship them. How powerful can these
guardian idols be, the rabbis say, *if someone can just steal them?*

There are other, similar expansions, but I'll cite only one other midrashic example in this vein, a famous one which expands the story of Abraham, who has, by now, been reinvented as the first monotheist. His youth—undiscussed in the biblical text—is invented in the form of a full-fledged satiric sketch. Abraham's father Terach, who is briefly characterized as an idolater, is now operating an idol store; and we are treated to the spectacle of Li'l Abraham not only logically arguing with the father's clientele and ruining the walk-in traffic ("A man came to him and wished to buy one. 'How old are you?' Abraham asked him. 'Fifty years,' was the reply. 'Woe to such a man!' he exclaimed. 'You are fifty years old and would worship a day-old object!'") but also, after Terach has stepped out, smashing all the idols, then—to counter his father's wrath at the destruction of his stock—claiming the idols did it themselves, arguing over which of them would get first crack at a customer's meal-offering. When Terach challenges this interpretation ("Why do you make sport of me? Have they then any knowledge?"), Abraham offers the triumphant rejoinder, "Should not your ears listen to what your mouth is saying?" If Terach doesn't even believe the idols can even do these limited actions, how can he believe they shape the world?

Aside from this rabbinic story casting the young Abraham as a proto-rabbinic smart-ass, it's also a strong indication that prophets—and satirists—are remarkably difficult to live with. They may be a necessary social scourge, but who wants them around the house? They're so *sensitive*, for one thing: always on you about your behavior, and so sure they're right. And what's more, in behavior not unknown among the community of satirists, the prophets are particularly humorless when it comes to themselves and their mission. Elisha, who brought down she-bears to consume forty-two schoolchildren who were taunting him, was a case in point. Not to mention the fact that the behavior they adopt to illustrate their points can be offputting, sometimes even—in its absurd or grotesque excess—persuading their audience of precisely the opposite point they're trying to articulate. Isaiah went naked for three years; Jeremiah walked around wearing a yoke of wood, then iron; Ezekiel shut himself up in his house, speechless, lying first on his left side, then his right, for 390 days, along with eating barley cakes (then seen as animal fodder) cooked over a fire fueled by human feces. You can kind of understand the ancient Israelites for not exactly looking to these figures as unimpeachable authorities—or, in terms more familiar to us, not getting the joke or mistaking the piece of performance art. "I have become a laughingstock all day long," moans Jeremiah. "Everyone mocks me . . . For the word of the Lord has become for me a reproach and derision all day long." Talk about laughing at, not with.

And having their Temple destroyed as a result; at least, that's how the later, theologically oriented readings have it. Since what becomes doubly clear is that (a) the prophets' intended audience, the vast majority of Israelite society, turned a deaf ear and (b) the choir they *were* preaching to became the custodians of Jewish history, literature, and culture. This twin notion—of satirists' questionable power to change the society around them and their remarkable power to influence later writers and historians—is something we'll see again and again in our story. This will not be the last time the prophets go unheeded in Jewish history.

If the biblical satirists of the period before the destruction of the First Temple are outsiders taking on the entrenched authorities, the satire of the diaspora takes a different approach, one where Jewish power is radically circumscribed and focused largely toward those aspects of culture that Jews themselves have the power to change. A lot of the book of Esther's satire consists of quick jabs at royal incompetence (as we mentioned, it features a king so uninterested in matters of governance, he reads royal documents to cure his insomnia), but the larger shape of the book's political satire is much more profound. Sometimes it takes on the black comedy of the law, Jewish life, and fate in the diaspora under the whim of a despot. (Even after Haman is defeated, it transpires that the genocidal decree sealed with the king's seal can't, as a political-bureaucratic matter, be overturned, even by the despot itself; only counterlegislated with *another* decree). Or it expresses a cynical resignation at the prospects of political change: after all the action dies down, the narrative takes special pains to end on an account of a tax hike. In other words, everything returns to its usual equilibrium: people are going to end up getting it in the neck, one way or another. Issues of monumental import get lost in the gears and ground down in utterly undramatic ways; and nothing much changes anyway. This is the stuff that satire feeds on, the continuing fuel for its engine of outrage, but at the same time expressing the cynical belief that the oil is sufficiently slippery that it's hard to get any traction to make any real changes. As Jews begin to develop their own diasporic social, cultural and political organizations, these—dare we say it—organizing principles of human social behavior become grist for the Jewish satiric mill.

IF THE BOOK of Esther's Mordechai (at least in the rabbinic imagination) incorporates both temporal power and theological expertise, by the end of antiquity those roles had been, culturally speaking, largely separated. A schism had developed between two main empowered classes that worked their uneasy way around another: the rabbinic authorities, who contained the intellectual and theological underpinnings of the society, and what we might call the commercial and the professional classes, the wealthy, who supported the scholars, and whose attitude toward them vacillated between respect and contempt. These are ideal types, of course—there were wealthy rabbis, and intelligent and cultured cosmopolitan businessmen—but the satirical sensibility tended to separate Jewish society into these broad brushstrokes, which would be the background of socially satiric material well into the modern era.

The Talmud is inordinately influential in establishing the contours of the division: and, given the authorship of the Talmud and almost all literature of the rabbinic period by, well, the rabbis, there's very little reformist-oriented satire of rabbinic culture writ large in those texts. To use a particularly Talmudic metaphor, it would be their own ox that's gored. That's not to say, as we'll see, that the rabbis don't have a sense of humor about themselves; it's just that generally speaking they take the *idea* of rabbinic mind and culture very seriously. There are, on occasion, the jabs at local rabbinic academic structures, or even particular types of rabbinic modes of interpretation, that are too abstruse to go into. But they're not that interested in satirizing the rabbinic project writ large.

And the other sphere? There is, on more than one occasion, the image of the rabbis speaking truth to the centers of temporal Jewish power—particularly the exilarchs, the member of the Davidic house who led the Jewish community-in-exile in Babylonia. But overall their presentation of the vastly larger segment of Jewish society that *weren't* rabbinic jurists is to minimize their import—and when they're mentioned, it's with a light brushing of satirical presentation, chided for not leading the life of the mind, or insufficiently recognizing the accomplishments of the rabbis, coupled with an acknowledgment that they're necessary—one supposes—for society to run.

Our considerations here are limited by the fact that we have few surviving texts from the rabbinic period from those other segments of society—that is, that aren't rabbinic texts. As we move to the medieval period and the early modern period, and with the concomitant preservation of more material, other details begin to emerge. Some—and there's some of this in the rabbinic material as well—follow in the prophetic mold, social satires intended as communal moral correctives; generally portraits of communal law-(or norm-) breaking types. Responsa, legal opinions by rabbinic jurists on matters of Jewish law from the period of late antiquity and beyond, contain the occasional pointed comment, focused as they are on prescribing appropriate communal behavior. Works of medieval pietists like the Hasidei Ashkenaz will often include an occasional prophetic-style castigation of the community that brings a smile or a wince to the reader.

Here's an analogous satire, by the fourteenth-century Provence physician-satirist Kalonymus ben Kalonymus, writing about pious hypocrisy:

> Though he seems pious, night and day
> And ne'er forgets his prayers to say,
> And still performs his meet devotion,
> With bended head and endless motion,
> Yet friend, as well as e'er you can,
> Avoid this crafty, godless man,
> Whose piety is dissimulation,
> To God a base abomination.
> Well may he sit with downcast look,
> With eyes glued to his Hebrew book,
> And shake his body to and fro
> His splendid holiness to show.
> But yet, in truth, his heart within
> Is hard as stone, and black with sin;
> And he is ever a sad disgrace
> To Jewish creed and Jewish race.

Rabbinic satirists also at times sharpen their focus to take on particular trends or movements they perceive to be antinomian, or rule-breaking, or philosophically and theologically corrosive. (Take, for example, the thirteenth-century scholar Meshullam da Piera, whose stance in the complex medieval philosophical debate known as the Maimonidean controversy—he was anti-Maimonides—was expressed in equally complicated satiric poetry.) Satires of false messiahs, the movements they spawn, and those who follow them, are a case in point; and rabbinic manifestoes against, for example, the seventeenth-century false prophet Sabbatai Zevi drip with contempt.

But not all medieval and early modern Jewish satire was related to theological doctrine or religious observance. Increasingly, the creation—and preservation—of quasi- or nonreligious documents remind us that there were all sorts of other political and cultural trends that fell under the satirist's scrutiny. Medieval European poetry and prose takes on the predilections and vogues of their cosmopolitan readers and writers, tweaking them for their slavish interest in the matters of the day. Yiddish-language broadsides from eighteenth-century Amsterdam discuss a communal division, each side taking on the other in satirical terms that wouldn't be unusual in twenty-first-century blogs about income inequality, gentrification, and NIMBYism.

Still, all this satire is largely contingent on a self-constructed notion of a coherent and essentially closed Jewish community. Whether that was by choice or by duress, it was the fact itself that shaped and conditioned the direction of the satire. The medieval composition of Jewry as its own largely self-regulated community, tied to set places within the larger structures of Christian Europe— with the authority and possibility of excommunication, *cherem*, arrogated to its leaders, an outcome which would have been close to literal and not merely spiritual anathema—allowed for power to be exercised and thus satirized.

Modernity and the prospect of Jewish emancipation changed all that. With the creation of what historians have called at least "semi-neutral" spaces, the gradual easing of residential restrictions, and the opening of national political space to minority participation, it was possible—at least in theory—for Jewish political and cultural engagement, and its satirical and critical version, to take place in a less delineated sphere. Accordingly, communal satire became less a matter of cleaving to internal norms than transposing external ones into an internal context.

This is not exactly the same as participating in the burgeoning general atmosphere of Enlightenment satire—since this period, the eighteenth century particularly, is perhaps the high point of satirical prose, featuring the efforts of Swift, Addison, Voltaire, and Diderot, among many others. On the rare occasions Jews *were* able to participate in that conversation, they did so *as* Jews, or as "the Jew," and so their satirical barbs were leavened with the uncomfortable and straitened double consciousness that necessitated. Easier—and, in many senses, more important—for those satirists to continue their efforts, for the time being, within their own community.

The Jewish Enlightenment, or Haskalah, responded to emancipation by critiquing the behavior of their own community, assuming that internal social and cultural transformation would lead to external acceptance. A great deal of that effort was done through satire, which was, for its wielders, also a way of demonstrating their comfort with the broader literary forms and techniques of the Enlightenment—another way of offering the proof of their qualifications for emancipation they felt would be necessary to acceptance. (Like in many reformist movements, however, there were plenty of humorless practitioners as well. In 1808, for example, the *maskil* Menachem Medel Lefin wrote that "the way of education is to open the heart to the intellect while the mouth does not open . . . if a joke stirs his intestines he should accustom himself to swallowing it back down.")

Much of the great first wave of Haskalah comedy—the first great wave of modern Jewish literature—is dedicated to this kind of satiric approach, predicated on liberal and optimistic beliefs, that their work would be efficacious, that it would transform society. While figures like Moses Mendelssohn were producing the canonical texts of the Jewish Enlightenment—treatises like 1783's *Jerusalem*, which suggested a place for a Jewish religion alongside other revealed religions—writers like Isaac Euchel, Aaron Halle-Wolfssohn, and Joseph Perl were writing satires on contemporary Jewish life, taking on religious hypocrites in the manner of Molière's *Tartuffe*, a major Haskalah influence. At the same time, they realized that an unchecked embrace of the Enlightenment might lead to unwanted consequences, such as the abandonment of Jewish identity altogether. The satirist is rarely posed with the question of possibility of too much success for their chosen agenda: but—with a very generous assist from an engine of modernization already well in action—it was something for Western European satirists to consider.

Both Halle-Wolfssohn's *Silliness and Sanctimony* (ca. 1797) and Euchel's *Reb Henokh, or, What Are You Going to Do About It* (ca. 1793), for example, are set among the rising Jewish businessmen and bourgeoisie of Berlin, then booming in the post–Thirty Years' War recovery and in its new role as the center of the Kingdom of Prussia. Wolfssohn takes aim not only at the Eastern European Jews who aren't acculturated, but the parvenus who are so spoiled, silly, or frivolous that they get themselves into trouble, the family daughter even being kidnapped for nefarious purposes by a gentile after (seemingly) leading him on. (Note the "silliness" in the title, which in the original also has the sense of foolishness.) Halle-Wolfssohn wrote in an introduction to his play that he was specifically interested in looking at different social groups within the Berlin Jewish community, each with their own fallacious behavior, and that "if from my words they recognize and understand [their errors] . . . and then turn away from their paths, I have achieved my purpose," a classic satirist's manifesto. *Henokh* broadens its satiric vision to travelers from foreign regions who make their way through the city, reminding the reader that Jewish satire could range further afield, but hits the same notes: the Scylla and Charybdis of pious hypocrisy and false Enlightenment, and the difficulty—and necessity—of navigating that narrow and treacherous route.

If the satire of Western European enlightenment was dedicated to portraying a Jewish society in the process of looking like everyone else, their Eastern European counterparts had neither the luxury nor the necessity of doing so. The satirists of the late eighteenth and early nineteenth century—the real forerunners of this aspect of modern Jewish humor—turned their attention to a cultural war raging through the Jewish communities of Poland and Russia, one which spoke volumes about tradition and change: the rise of the Hasidic movement.

Hasidim was a pietistic, mystically oriented movement that rapidly and shrewdly pulled the middle class over to its side by the end of the eighteenth and early nineteenth century. But that wasn't how the satirists of the Jewish Enlightenment saw it. They viewed the enterprise as particularly superstitious, pernicious, and retrograde, the prime stumbling block in the prevention of Eastern European Jews embracing their inner Berliner. They saw Hasidic rebbes as financially and sexually predatory; a common charge was that childless mothers who went to their rebbes for assistance received something a little more hands-on than prayer, for instance. And they considered the Hasidim, those leaders' followers, a flock of uneducated, gullible sheep. This might sound unfair, a tendency not uncommon in satire. It was certainly not unknown amongst the Eastern European *maskilim*, who had often come face to face with the social opprobrium and communal hostility aimed at them as godless sinners cloaking themselves in guise of altruistic virtue, and who may have let some of their resulting aggrievedness seep in. (Swift's contention in his "Verses on the Death of Dr. Swift" that "Yet malice never was his aim;/ He lashed the vice but spared the name," in other words, might have been less apposite for the Eastern European critics of Hasidism.) But the works themselves that they produced, the best ones anyway, rise above it.

The granddaddy of these works was written in the second decade of the nineteenth century by a Galician reformist named Joseph Perl. His *The Revealer of Secrets* (1819), sometimes considered the first Hebrew novel, purported to be an exchange of letters among Hasidim who were thrown into dismay by the circulation of a book revealing all their hypocrisies. (Satire is a great lover of puncturing hypocrisy: think of all those clips Jon Stewart played of Fox News anchors saying things 180 degrees from their comments just a few weeks before.) One letter tells of a non-Jewish prince who tells a Hasid he will not lease him a mill "because in that book it says you're allowed to cheat us." The letter continues:

"Perish the thought!" I cried. "It doesn't say that in the book!"
He looked in his book and says to me, "On page 14, paragraph 6, doesn't it say this explicitly?"

I took the holy book and looked at it and cried, "Perish the thought, sir! He wrote here that it's okay to cheat *idolaters*, that is, worshipers of stars and planets, but not *you*!"

When I said this, he went through the roof and he says, "I know you say this . . . [but if that's true] why did that Rabbi Nakhmen [a Hasidic contemporary] write . . . that it's a mitzvah for the Tzaddik to give a bribe to the idolator? Maybe he also meant "to give a bribe to idolators who lived eighteen hundred years ago?"

And to this the Hasid has no answer.

The book—in another characteristic typical of satire—attempted to incorporate the rhythms of Hasidic Hebrew; and was apparently successful enough in doing so that, at least apocryphally, a good number of Hasidim believed it to be true. (The hoax was later discovered, and it is also said that Hasidim would regularly dance on Joseph Perl's grave.)

In *The Revealer of Secrets*, the book-within-the-book is triumphant, persuading state authorities to take an anti-Hasidic position. But what's particularly telling for our history of the power and possibility of Jewish satire is the fact that that same book was actually based on a real book Perl had written himself and submitted to the authorities, with the hope that they'd shut down the Hasidic movement, in the interests of modernization. No such luck: Hasidism grew and grew without the interference of the Austro-Hungarian authorities, who appreciated the movement's helpfulness in the kingdom's tax collecting efforts. (Ahasuerus and the author of the book of Esther would have been proud.) Satire, it seems, works best, if at all, in the fictional world imagined by the satirist: there, the writer has the benefit of creating his audience along with his bon mots and brickbats.

Part of the reason for the anti-Hasidic satirists' failure was linguistic. Satire is predicated on reaching an audience, even if the audience will reject it. In order to do that you need to speak their language, literally before metaphorically. This wasn't always an obvious matter when it came to the Enlightenment, whose first wave of satirists largely felt more ideologically comfortable with Hebrew or German. But this wasn't much of a possibility when it came to Eastern Europe. Not if you were looking to achieve real social change. The Hasidim of Perl's opprobrium—the ones who were being viciously satirized, whose politics, culture, and organization were being neatly filleted—were becoming a mass movement on a scale the Haskalah could barely imagine, their tales of rabbis and unbelievers becoming believers capturing the imagination widely. And no small part of their success was their willingness to use Yiddish—in stories, teachings, even prayers—to get their message across. Perl's Hebrew novel, biting and accomplished as it was, couldn't possibly compete for reach and spread.

The Hasidim used satire, too, of course. Some of their "conversion" tales were satirical—the first collection of Hasidic tales, a collection featuring the movement's founder, Israel Ba'al Shem Tov, featured caustic portraits of individuals who didn't get with the reformist program that Hasidism, in its eyes and those of others, comprised. Generally, those portraits consist of comic humiliation: robbers who try to attack the Ba'al Shem Tov discover their axes come to life and lay about them; the Ba'al Shem Tov's brother-in-law—who thinks his sister has married a fool, because the Hasidic leader has not yet publicly revealed himself as such—is constantly shown up and embarrassed. There were also the jokes: "What's the difference between a *misnaged* [opponent of Hasidism] and a dog?" a Hasid asks his friend. "I don't know," the friend answers, "What *is* the difference?" "I don't know either," the Hasid says.

The Haskalah and its fellow travelers, seeing this, realized they would have to turn to Yiddish, despite ideological discomfort with the prospect. Jokes were an obvious mechanism, given that their generally oral nature meant they were easy to deliver in the Yiddish vernacular. Here are two that give the flavor of the anti-Hasidic charge, one more expansive than the other, both following the same form:

A rabbi is trying to get home for the Sabbath, but is running late, having lingered a little too long over his Friday lunch. He insists his coachman whip the horses faster and faster, but nonetheless, it's getting near sunset, the beginning of the Sabbath, and home is nowhere in sight. This doesn't bode well: as it's against Jewish law to ride on the Sabbath, the only other option is to hunker down in the cold, snowy woods on the side of the road. The rebbe takes counsel within himself a moment, prays, and—miracle of miracles!—a remarkable thing occurs. On one side of the road, it's the Sabbath; on the other side of the road, it's the Sabbath; but on the road itself, it's still Friday! And the rebbe rides home in style.

Or, if that's not clear, here's the second joke:

Two groups of disciples are gossiping, and begin to engage in a familiar custom: telling stories in praise of their rebbe. A member of the first group boasts, "Let me tell you how holy our rebbe is. One Friday afternoon, he goes over to his wife's cookstove, and asks her what's for dinner. She begins to curse and harangue, saying that there's nothing for dinner because her good-for-nothing husband is such a terrible provider. But is the rebbe perturbed? Not one bit. 'Just look in the pot,' he says, pointing to the pot sitting on the cookstove. 'For what?' she shrieks. 'It's empty.' 'Just look,' he says, and she does, and what do you think she discovers? Five fish!"

"That's nothing," says a member of the second group. "Wait until you hear *this*. So my rebbe was playing poker with a few of his disciples, and it's time to call. So one of them lays down his cards and he says, 'With all due respect, rebbe, I've got you beat.' And he shows his cards—it's a royal flush. And what do you think? Cool as a cucumber, the rebbe doesn't blink. He just turns over his hand. Five aces. *Five aces.*"

"That's impossible," says the first storyteller. "A deck of cards only has four aces in it, total."

"*Nu,*" said the second, totally unabashed, "you take away a fish, I'll take away an ace."

It's surprising how many things are going on in this joke. The portrait of the rebbe as a cool gambler—a dissembler with poker face, a cardsharp to boot—fits nicely with the financial chicanery and dishonesty their opponents claimed of them. But this behavior is, of course, shoehorned into the framework of a Hasidic miracle tale— much as in the first joke, where the rebbe's seeming easiness with blatantly violating the Sabbath to preserve his own material comfort is reworked into a standard Hasidic motif, the bending of the natural world to protect the holy. But the screw turns again: the disciples who are swapping the stories with each other are satirized, too. Not, as in the implied, credulous narrator of the first joke, because they're so gullible that they buy the rebbe's claims of miracle. But because they're *not*: they understand the whole thing's a marketplace, a competition for the top spot, and the details of miracle are just another commodity, to be swapped and peddled like that extra fish.

But jokes—pungent and powerful as they were—were brief encounters. The satirists would soon expand to greater lengths, and greater impact. A contemporary of Perl's, the early nineteenth-century writer Isaac Ber Levinson, perhaps seeing the writing of linguistic necessity on the wall, took to Yiddish to write a play, whose title, *Di Hefker-Velt* (The Topsy-Turvy World), suggests the essence of the satirical vision: that the clear-sighted author can diagnose to others the nature of a world gone mad. Levinson certainly isn't afraid to take on Hasidism, and Hasidic rebbes are targets within his play, but he saw it as part of a larger societal illness. *His* vision of the problems with traditional Jewish society has less to do with a particular social movement than the broadest definition of Jewish society itself: That the Jewish world continues, generation after generation, to perpetuate the same inequities and injustices. The powerful prey on the weak, the poor get it in the neck at the hands of the holy. A similar play of the period by an anonymous author by the title *The Deceived World* made the point even more explicit in a programmatic introduction:

> Our holy Talmud says that . . . it is proper to reveal the shame of false people, who disguise themselves and who say they are pious, but in truth they are great evildoers: they bow down to the ground and blaspheme to high heaven. . . . One must not be ashamed, but rather one must openly let the world know that they are swindlers and that their piety is pure deception. . . . it is a great mitzvah to tear the false masks off these people's faces and to show the swindle to the world. . . . It may happen that some individuals will get angry when they read [this play, dedicated to this aim]. To them I say: if the shoe fits, then wear it; if you don't eat garlic, then your breath won't stink. Do you understand what I mean?

Others followed in this dramatist's footsteps, and, as the nineteenth century continued, writers both sticking to Hebrew and embracing Yiddish birthed a series of biting social critiques. Bitterly satiric poems by Yehuda Leib Gordon told of cozened rabbis who rendered a poor woman's geese unkosher, sending her starving into the street, or ignorant ones who rendered a woman a "chained widow" for life because of the smallest of scriptorial irregularities; and the satirist M. D. Brandstadter told the story of credulous zealots who confronted a woman who had refused to shave her head after marriage, blaming her for a plague that had killed several children in the community. There, Brandstadter gives the (very slightly) modernized woman the last word: She tells them if they don't back away, she would grow her hair even longer, and then the plague would spread. They folded. One of the most important Hebrew satirists of the nineteenth century, Isaac Erter, would employ Samael, the archfiend, in the service of virtue. In an encounter at Tashlikh, the communal ceremony on Rosh Hashanah afternoon where one symbolically rids oneself of sin, the maleficent one ironically reveals the real deceivers and sinners: Hasidic hypocrites who look pious but are very much the opposite.

Erter, along with his contemporary satirist Isaac Mayer Dik, used another supernatural guide—the *gilgul*, or reincarnated spirit—for similar satiric purpose. In Dik's comic novella, the same soul passes through numerous cycles of being. Each of his incarnations allows the author to satirize some aspect of the contemporary Jewish community—allowing for a good deal of free-floating social satire that doesn't have to strictly hew to an anti-Hasidic program. Along with doctors (giving advice to potential MDs: "Put a skull on your desk and a stillborn embryo in a jar of alcohol on your windowsill. Any visitor will be thunderstruck by your vast wisdom"), he takes on both Hasidim ("When praying, I blared and bellowed like a wild bull so that no one understood a single word . . . and when my voice became hoarse and my tongue dried out, I wet my whistle with endless streams of liquor") and even members of the Haskalah. There, Dik once more reveals the corrosive effects of satire, where the protagonist's consciousness turns inward to effect himself as well: "And that was my total erudition—to do anything I felt like. I scoffed and laughed at all Jews . . . I despised my brethren, my people—I couldn't stand the very word *Jew*."

This last skeptical note in Dik's novella marks a turn in Jewish satirical sensibility. From the prophetic period on, through the Enlightenment, most of Jewish political satire was, at base, idealistic. Isaiah and Ezekiel scourged their fellow men for the sake of religious reform; the Enlightenment satirists did so to inculcate a new religion of secular civility and progress. But as time went on, it grew harder and harder for the individuals not to turn the satire on themselves and their cause, as events made those causes harder to bear. The late nineteenth-century Jewish satirists might not have agreed with Swift's comment in his preface to *Battle of the Books* that "Satire is a sort of glass, wherein beholders generally discover everybody's face but their own"; they saw it, at times, all too clearly.

THE NEXT few decades in the history of Yiddish satire are instructive in following that increase in ambivalence. Start, on one end of the spectrum, with Isaac Linetski (1839–1915), arguably the next great Eastern European satirist after Erter and Dik, whose anger at traditional Jewish society—particularly Hasidic society—knew no bounds. You can understand why: when he began to entertain Enlightenment ideas, his family forced him to divorce the wife of his youth and married him off to a woman who was deaf and mute so that he could not "infect" her with his blasphemous considerations. Linetski returned the favor as soon as he could. When an enterprising newspaper publisher created a Yiddish-language supplement to his Hebrew text, the author published a pseudo-autobiography whose assaults would set a new height, or depth, for Jewish satire.

Anger and the desire to inflict pain, say the critics, are essential components of satire; and *The Polish Lad* (first serialized in 1867) is quite angry. No portrait of the Hasidic rebbe was ever quite so corrosively funny; no evocation of the timid, superstitious, and stunted people who result from their leadership was ever so influential. Those who read *The Polish Lad* were convinced: Hasidism was the wrong way to go. The only question, of course, was whether the only people who were reading *The Voice of the Herald,* the more modern-oriented newspaper in which it appeared, weren't at least half-convinced already. One might make a similar point about Israel Aksenfeld's *The Headband* (1861), which touches on the same theme in a broader vein: that modernizing individuals are licensed to use certain aspects of the society (such as the eponymous headband, that represents both material greed and the arranged marriage) in order to trick it to change against its own desires. "When it comes to worldly things," says the novel's ostensible hero, "when people are only after money or silly ornaments or wasteful things, then they deserve to be punished, we ought to fool them."

Sholem Yankev Abramovitch/Mendele the Book Peddler, whom we met in Chapter One, begins his literary life as a classical liberal Haskalah satirist, calling out the traditional institutions of Jewish society as corrupt and with the explicit aim of changing them. His first novel, *The Little Man* (1864), often if inaccurately termed the first modern Yiddish novel, also appeared in *The Voice of the Herald* and is a textbook example: Mendele is called upon to read the will of a recently deceased local magnate, who, it is revealed, made his way to the top through the most deceitful ways, methods that cast shadows on every aspect of Eastern European Jewish society. One vivid example from the book, saturated in the little man's sharp ironic retrospection, should illustrate. Here's his tutor in the ways of dubious virtue, another local magnate named Issar Varger (or "Issar Throttler"):

> Maybe you want to say: "But it is a pity on the poor?" You silly fool, with your empty, meaningless word—*pity!* Pity was invented by the weak, the unlucky ones, by the sheep, who, knowing that they are weak and incapable of obtaining what they desire because they lack the teeth and claws to fight, have invented this word *pity* and use it as their weapon. . . . I have, blessed be His Name, a fair knowledge of the ways of the world, although I am no great scholar. It's not scholarship that is needed here, but good hard common sense.

The book ends with the magnate realizing the error of his ways and begging Mendele to help create a series of schools to provide the training and education he never had, education which would have set him on the right road. Gentile society is secondary; it rarely, if ever, appears in the book. (Reform of the educational system was a constant topic of agitation, both satirical and otherwise, among Haskalah writers: Linetski, the Hebrew writer Peretz Smolenskin, and many others took on the traditional cheder as part of their cherished, Enlightenment-inspired belief that proper education would make the proper man.) What mattered, Abramovitch argued, was fixing Jewish society, not addressing its relationship to the non-Jewish world; and he hoped to hold up a satirical mirror to society's currently crooked reflection to get it to straighten up and act right. But that was early in his career. By the time he wrote *The Mare*, he had retreated into a more cynical stance, wondering whether there even was a possibility of real social change. What good is satire, or the comedic ethos of self-improvement, if the world doesn't take any account of the satirists' literature, or even the results it brings?

That novel located much of its skepticism about social satire's efficacy in external, anti-Semitic cause; but the satiric work of the next great Yiddish writer turns inward. Sholem Aleichem, Yiddish literature's greatest writer and one of the foundational figures of modern Jewish comedy, was Mendele's self-proclaimed disciple. In an introduction to one of his novels, he referred to himself as the "grandson" to Mendele's "grandfather," even though the two were only twenty-something years apart. Sholem Aleichem was born in 1859, and over the course of a three-decade career, he would become famous, in the Jewish world, for taking what was going on in that world and reflecting it back to them. And at the turn of the twentieth century, with the tremendous outgrowth of political activism in the Jewish community, and the increasing emigration from shtetl to city and from Europe to America and to the *Yishuv* in Palestine, there was plenty to reflect. The respect—and love—his community felt for him was reflected in the tens of thousands of Jews, of all political, religious, linguistic, and geographic orientations, who turned out for his 1916 funeral in New York City: Jews who could agree on nothing else agreed on the centrality of the man who created Tevye and a host of other characters unforgettable to Yiddish speakers— the failed businessman Menakhem-Mendl, the perennially cheerful cantor's son Motl, and the denizens of the shtetl Kasrilevke, to name just a few.

Almost all of Sholem Aleichem's voluminous satirical reflections on Jewish historical, political, and cultural matters, though, have one thing in common: an extreme doubt about the Jewish community's ability to achieve anything permanent or lasting at all. ("I want your idea to be adopted no less than you do," he wrote to a literary friend of his asking him to contribute to a Zionist anthology. "But what shall I do when I know my people Israel so well that I can't believe they will take it to heart?") Part of this, he seems to suggest, comes from extrapolating the same tendency he finds in himself: a predilection to mock, to satirize, that was so powerful that it would inevitably turn on and sabotage anything even potentially meaningful and positively programmatic. "What shall I do," he once wrote, "when laughing is a kind of illness for me, God save us, from childhood on?" Satire, Sholem Aleichem believed, was less a positive, constructive mechanism—a healer of social illness—than an instrument to cynically reflect the malady. Throw up your hands and laugh; there's not much else to do.

His shtetl stories tell the tale. Sholem Aleichem's invented shtetl, Kasrilevke—which means something like "happy pauperville"—takes its joy from a somewhat expected and a somewhat unexpected source. The expected one is the joy that the shtetl Jews take in talking, and, in what for Sholem Aleichem and others is virtually synonymous with talking, arguing. A satirist's dream approach: in which to speak is to take a position. (Whether the Kasrilevkans or other Jews in this view are taking an *informed* position, or are simply reflexively argumentative, is another matter; in the words of another great Jewish comedian, whatever it is, I'm against it.) In stories like "Dreyfus in Kasrilevke," or in his Zionist stories like "Lunatics" or "The Red Little Jews," there's a fairly common structural path: an idea—perhaps one which might change the Jewish situation, or at least impact Jewish history—would come into the fairly closed-off world of the Jewish small community, at which point it would be the source for uninformed argument. I've never come across a Sholem Aleichem tale in which he retells the old joke about the Jew stranded on a desert island—he builds two synagogues, the second the one he *doesn't* go to—but he'd certainly have appreciated the joke if he heard it.

So far, this approach isn't that much different from scenes in earlier Yiddish satire. But Sholem Aleichem goes further: in stories like

"A Yom Kippur Scandal" and "On Account of a Hat," he makes it clear that there is a propensity, within this Jewish culture, to satirize and mock so much that it would actually destroy what it seeks to save. In the two stories, faced in each case with the destruction of a symbol of possible progress—a bright young man who, it transpires, has eaten on Yom Kippur, and a businessman who had the opportunity to arrive home for Passover in style, but failed for the stupidest of reasons—the correct response, the stories suggest, are to weep for what is lost and to try to learn from the lessons. But Sholem Aleichem, with his self-proclaimed compulsion to mock, creates a community that simply jeers at internal frailty. Here's a selection from the ending of each of the stories:

Poor Reb Yosifel! He turned away in shame. He could look no one in the face. On Yom Kippur, and in the synagogue. . . . As for the rest of us, hungry as we were, we could not stop talking about it all the way home. We rolled with laughter in the streets. ("A Yom Kippur Scandal")

It was all very simple [he said, trying to explain his lateness]: the reason he came home late, after the holidays, was that he had made a special trip to inspect a wooded estate. Woods? Estate? Not a chance—no one bought *that*! They pointed him out in the streets and held their sides, laughing. ("On Account of a Hat")

In the hands of any other writer but Sholem Aleichem, whose devotion and love for his people was universally known, it might have been viewed as self-hatred. Increasingly, this approach would accentuate the complications of Jewish action *as* Jewish action (although Sholem Aleichem was a committed Zionist), and many of the individuals who sought improvement of the Jewish condition through non- or a-Jewish approaches—emigration, communism, simply acculturation—might have drawn some resonance from Sholem Aleichem's self-consuming satire.

Failure of effect, accusations of self-hatred, self-doubt: these are bad enough for the satirist. But perhaps an even worse fate is when the forces of adulation and acceptance muffle the satirist's sting beyond recognition. It's a double tragedy, after all: first as someone who tries to change history finds their efforts manipulated and misused, intentionally or no, which offends them both as activist and as comic artist. Most of the recognizably satiric work of the third of the trio of classic Yiddish writers, I. L. Peretz (1852–1915), came early in his career, when he was actively involved in socialist causes (until a stint in a Tsarist jail dampened some of his more overt enthusiasm for the cause). But one of those early stories—a story that has become so famous in the Jewish tradition that it has largely been purged of its satirical bite in its countless retellings—is worth reclaiming.

"Bontshe the Silent," first published in 1894, is a tale set in the most classical of Jewish spheres, one even more iconic than the shtetl: the seat of judgment in Heaven, where all souls (so they say) are placed into a courtroom, to weigh their sins and their merits to determine whether they go to Heaven or Gehenna. The eponymous Bontshe takes his turn, and the facts of his life are rehearsed—essentially, an unending catalog of misuse and maltreatment, to which his response was, always, silence. Bontshe, who for most of the proceeding is unsure if the litigants are actually speaking about him, is told that had he spoken—had he cried out—the metaphorical walls of Jericho, of injustice, would have fallen, that the earth could have changed its ways. But as it is, it is time for his reward, and he can choose anything that he wants. "Really?" he asks. "Really! Really! Really!" the heavenly hosts chorus. Anything at all, they say. Well, Bontshe says, if that's so, then what he would like above all else is a hot roll every morning. With fresh butter.

This is sometimes where the story, when it's retold, ends, and it's of course not very funny. I was told it in my youth as a paean to the virtues of humility in a religious context. *See how modest Bontshe is*, the teller would end. *The opportunity to get anything, and this is all he asks for.* But that's not actually Peretz's point, as the tale makes clear at its end, since Bontshe's request, like a joke, elicits laughter from the court—bitter laughter, to be sure, but laughter nonetheless. This is the destruction of the personality that has been created by the world and the community: that faced with the opportunity for anything, he has been so limited, so trodden down, that *all* he can request is a roll and butter. What possibility of change then? What possibility for the benefits of satire—even the satire of "Bontshe the Silent" itself—if this is the audience the writer has to work with?

Perhaps this isn't being quite fair to Peretz's satirical sense, and to his sense of possibility. But there is no question that his move into other realms of Jewish literature left, at best, a bad taste in his mouth about social change. Take the lovely story "Neila in Gehenna," written toward the end of his life, about a man who through extraordinary circumstances manages to ensure that no one will be sentenced to Gehenna, sentencing himself there in the process. But, Peretz points out, this was only temporary. Hell fills up soon again, in the last sentences of the story; in fact, they need more room. The role of the extraordinary man—a cantor whose voice inspires repentance, standing in for the writer/satirist/social advocate—is largely stilled by the circumstances. Things continue as they did before, is the message of Peretz's that seeps through. On the path to an expanding hell.

During his lifetime Peretz saw, and participated in, a massive expansion of the Yiddish press, which featured more than its fair share of satirical publications—in the Russian empire between 1862 and 1916, around 25 percent of the total. These included occasional "holiday journals" that could circumvent some of the Tsarist restrictions on publishing; supplements to mainstream Yiddish newspapers like *The Broom* (with "a stated policy of sweeping the metaphorical dirt out of Jewish political and cultural affairs"); or journals like St. Petersburg's *The Sheygets* or Warsaw's *The Bee*, which took on topics related to contemporary political partisanship and communal fragmentation. The manifesto of a slightly later one, *Der Bluffer*, even satirizes the satirizers. It proclaimed, tongue firmly in cheek, that it was "the only bluffer in the world who calls himself by his true name and does not demand that you call him, instead, 'righteous,' 'seeker of justice'. . . . we shall not deal with any socially [beneficial] activity. . . . Our task shall be dispersal of the heavy atmosphere created by the nudniks of the Jewish community."

But Peretz died early in the Great War, just beginning to see how the guns worked to still satiric possibility from an internal Jewish perspective. For, say, British satirists, the war provided a remarkable if brutal occasion for juxtaposing the ideals for which they claimed to fight and the horrific circumstances of war. But the Jews were largely victims of geography as they lay between the Russian and German homelands (and were believed to be agents for each side by the other), and they lacked the possibility of an empowered satirical voice. The exceptions—works like Sholem Aleichem's apocalyptic "Tales of a Thousand and One Nights," which chronicled a shipboard refugee's harrowing and tragicomic circumstances under his town's various occupiers—were more ironic than satiric: drowning in their own lack of agency, the impossibility of meaningful action. And not because of Jewish inattention, or self-destructive attitude, but because of the soldiers.

FOR SOME JEWS, the notion of changing and remaking society took (you should excuse the expression) a great leap forward in the years immediately *after* the First World War, as revolutionary change in Russia provided a sense of great things aborning. Of course, it wasn't so easy to suggest any problems with those changes—not internally, at least. Most of the satire coming out of the newly established Soviet Union was about people who wouldn't get with the program, since any other kind was strictly prohibited.

Yiddish literature did pretty well under the Soviets, at least at the beginning, since it was considered a language of the people (useful for catering to the Bolsheviks' proletarian concepts) and was consciously juxtaposed, and opposed, to the clericalism of Hebrew. Moyshe Kulbak's *Zelmenyaner*, published serially between 1929 and 1935, takes on the question of revolutionary change, satirizing earthy members of a Jewish family in Minsk who just wouldn't get with the modernizing program by their very nature, which is redolent of, according to the novel, "a faint odor of musty hay mixed with something else." Even as electrification comes to their courtyard, the older generation is just stuck in a rut, wondering what this has to do with them. But *Zelmenyaner* was published in two parts—one before, one after the First All-Union Congress of Soviet Writers presided over the straitjacketing of artistic expression in the name of socialist realism; and Kulbak's satire turns to asking how intelligently the revolution is taking account of human nature and its general unchangeability itself. Or, as the joke puts it:

> A left-wing intellectual, in the years before the revolution, is speaking to a group of unconvinced community members. Enthusing about the transformative nature of the revolution, he boasts, "Comrades, when the revolution comes, you will have strawberries and cream every morning!" One of the young men in the back, a scrawny type, pipes up. "But, ah, comrade," he says. "I don't *like* strawberries and cream." The young intellectual fixes him with a stare. "Don't worry, comrade," he says. "When the revolution comes, you will."

This combination of intellectual magical thinking and the (not very hidden) implication of coercive pressure to change one's nature was there from the very beginning of the Soviet era. Take, for example, the great Russian Jewish writer Isaac Babel (1894–1940), whose *Red Cavalry* stories suggest that revolutionaries, Jews, and Jewish revolutionaries, with their totalizing perspectives, can't see the problems with their own approaches. In one of the vignettes that compose the work,

Cavalry's protagonist, the Babel stand-in Lyutov—himself a Jew who in no small part yearns to be easily and uncomplicatedly one of the newly Soviet troops he rides with—encounters a store owner, Gedali, who asks him: "So let's say we say 'yes' to the Revolution. But does that mean we're supposed to say 'no' to the Sabbath?" Lyutov answers:

> "The sun cannot enter eyes that are squeezed shut," I say to the old man, "but we shall rip open those closed eyes!"
>
> "The Pole has closed my eyes," the old man whispers almost inaudibly. "The Pole, that evil dog! He grabs the Jew and rips out his beard, *oy*, the hound! But now they are beating him, the evil dog! This is marvelous, this is the Revolution! But then the same man who beat the Pole says to me, "Gedali, we are requisitioning your gramophone!" "But gentlemen," I tell the Revolution, "I love music!" And what does the Revolution answer me? "You don't know what you love, Gedali! I am going to shoot you, and then you'll know" . . . "The International, *Pan* Comrade, you have no idea how to swallow it!"
>
> "With gunpowder," I tell the old man, "and seasoned with the best blood."
>
> And then from the blue darkness young Sabbath climbed onto her throne.
>
> "Gedali," I say to him, "today is Friday, and night has already fallen. Where can I find some Jewish biscuits, a Jewish glass of tea, and a piece of that retired God in the glass of tea?"

The conversation reveals multitudes. Though one of Babel's great gifts is to layer satire with a deep dose of irony, we can still recognize that same intellectual from the joke about strawberries and cream—here both through the ideas of Gedali, for whom he plays the latest iteration in a long role of illogical oppressors (in the form of the Revolution) and through his own satirized doubleness (wanting to oppose Gedali and what he stood for while simultaneously being pulled toward Jewish biscuits and tea). No one escapes Babel's critical gaze.

Still, outright satire of the Soviet Union from someone who lived there was a dangerous thing, and even Babel—the prized writer of the Soviet Union—could last only so long. Babel was disappeared, to be executed in 1940, and became an unperson in the USSR for over a decade. (He survived Kulbak, who had far less celebrity, by three years.) To take on the Soviet Union—and the left more generally—you had to turn to the emigres, not just from Russia proper, but from Europe more broadly.

The work of one émigré in particular remains the apotheosis of a certain kind of political satire, both its promise and its pitfall. Born in 1892, Ernst Lubitsch left Germany for Hollywood after the Great War; he'd trained with the great Austrian-Jewish director Max Reinhardt and himself directed and starred in a series of short comic films as "Meyer," a "roly-poly comic Jew." In America, he was, at least by some accounts, a strong contender to direct *The Jazz Singer*, that crucial moment in the history of Jewish American film and American film more generally, but—thankfully for our story—decided to focus on comedy instead, developing the "Lubitsch touch" for which he became immortal. His 1939 film *Ninotchka*, in which Communism is presented through the person of Greta Garbo, is more a fizzy confection than a poisoned dart: the real problem with the Soviet Union, personified through Garbo, is that, essentially, it doesn't crack a smile. They all just need to lighten up, with all that talk about farm production and historical materialism.

Ninotchka was co-written by fellow Jewish émigré Billy Wilder, whose path to America was the result of far more duress. As he put it: "It wasn't my idea to leave; it was Hitler's." Though Wilder's own masterful satires would have little Jewish presence to them (the occasional Yiddish in *The Apartment*'s script notwithstanding), his story of suffering under fascism's shadow, along with those of millions of others far more unfortunate, shaped Lubitsch's next political satire.

If *Ninotchka* showed that in 1939 the Soviet Union was still capable of being taken unseriously, in 1942, it was impossible for anyone in America not to take the Nazis very seriously indeed. And the movie Lubitsch directed that year, *To Be or Not to Be* is all about the possible power of comedy, and, specifically, satire.

The movie begins, in fact, with the staging of a satire about Nazism in Warsaw, complete with a Hitler impersonator who will prove central to the film's caper of a climax. As it transpires, this group of actors, through a series of improbable events, are revealed to be essential to the war effort, by preventing the names of Polish resistance members from falling into enemy hands. The convoluted plot is not our business here, though; what is is how that famed "Lubitsch touch" takes a dark turn through that plot's twists and corners. When the actor Josef Tura (played by Benny Kubelsky, better known as Jack Benny) meets the man they call "Concentration Camp Ehrhardt," his efforts at small talk fall away in the face of the monstrousness concealed behind the buffoonish face before him. Tura is coming face to face with the limits of comic performance, there, in occupied Warsaw; and simultaneously realizing how the mockery and imitation they perfected in their previous career can assist—but takes a clear second place to—a kind of purposive action in which comedy falls away. One of Tura's acting troupe—the clearly Jewish actor Greenberg, played by the recognizably Jewish actor Felix Bressart—constantly repeats the phrase "it will get a tremendous laugh" throughout the film. But his valiant contribution to the great escape that marks the film's end is not about getting a laugh at all. When he steps out before a group of Nazi soldiers and delivers Shylock's "Hath not a Jew" speech from *The Merchant of Venice* in order to distract them, his performance is deadly serious. Satire, it seems, fails in 1942, or at least reveals its own insufficiency. Tragedy has taken its place.

LUBITSCH'S FILMS were hardly the first example of American Jewish satire. Like so much of American Jewish culture, it had taken its primary form several decades before at the hands of other European Jewish immigrants, largely Eastern European. Satire frequently takes on institutions and institutional behaviors, and the dislocation and transformation of that massive immigrant community, over two million strong, as it encountered America between roughly 1880 and 1920, created a new set of targets for humorists.

Take, for example, the series of sketches by the American Yiddish comic writer known to his audience as Tashrak (the name's a joke: *tashrak* is a mildly esoteric form of acronymic wordplay favored among kabbalists). Tashrak, who was popular in the 1890s and the first two decades of the twentieth century, was perhaps best known for his stories featuring an immigrant named Chayim, whose travails tended to show off the more ridiculous features of the American immigrant community. Whether it was discussing politics (as the only citizen, every member of his family chimed in for him to vote for another party; the story ends with his realization that someone has forged his vote) or real estate (where he meets a bunch of immigrants who are halfway to making their fortunes—sellers they've got, but no one can find a buyer), American adjustment wasn't easy. New American Jewish institutions, like the *landsmanshaftn* or cooperatives based on Eastern European cities of origin, were perfect examples of the continuities of Jewish, and human, nature. The Yiddish writer Zalmon Libin composed a feuilleton in which he is, in a scene that would have faced plagiarism charges from *Monty Python's Life of Brian* had it not been written decades earlier, confronted angrily by the "United Brotherhood of Taracan" because he has written for the "fake" "Independent Taracan" society.

Tashrak and Libin's stories satirized immigrant action as part of a living, often sympathetic effort to assist in Americanization; but a darker strand of American Yiddish satire took a more cynical position. There's a Yiddish saying to the effect that America is a place where a shoemaker becomes a "Mr." and a "Mr." becomes a shoemaker (it rhymes in the Yiddish), and if the first part of the clause suggests how economic and social transformation may lead to hypocritical, parvenu, and materialistic behavior—hardly anything new there—the second reminds everyone, including the teller, that it's not so easy to get America right. Satire of both the greenhorns who just can't get their heads around their new home and of the *alrightniks* who have become caricatures of the American way flourished in the American Yiddish and early American Jewish press, and burgeoned with a self-righteous confidence at odds with its fate at the hands of American acculturation. Some of the pieces appeared in Yiddish satirical journals like *The Yiddish Puck* and *The Big Stick*, featuring a wide variety of cartoon art (some of it swiped from contemporary humor magazines like *Judge* and *Puck* and given new Yiddish captions). Other works appeared in the newspapers, and two short stories by Sholem Aleichem, "Mr. Green Has a Job" and "A Story of a Greenhorn," take on that omnipresent figure in American Jewish society at the turn of the twentieth century, the greenhorn, in very different ways.

The first story is about a new immigrant who thinks he's got the system figured out: he signs up to blow the shofar for Rosh Hashana services at a variety of different synagogues, simultaneously. It's a hilarious misapplication of the American mass production system then revolutionizing the needle trades which consumed most of the Jewish immigrant labor. Sholem Aleichem wasn't the only one to mock the mangling of the American capitalist impulse. The great American Yiddish humorist Moyshe Nadir (a pen name for Isaac Reiss, with the rough meaning of a gentler version of "up yours") chronicled the tale of a man hired by an enterprising Jew to work at a picturesque locale that, to become a real tourist magnet, lacks only one thing: an echo effect. The creative solution: hire someone to serve as said echo. The problem is that the employee gets carried away, and so when someone shouts "How are you?" the echo replies, "Not bad, and how's by you?" Jewish propensities from way back—Sholem Aleichem and many others had rung the comic changes on Jewish logorrhea—trump American possibilities for transformation.

Was some of this rooted in anger that the Promised Land had failed to live up to its promises? *America goniff*, went a Yiddish phrase that could be translated something like "America—it'll screw you"; "A curse on Columbus!" went another one. That second tale of Sholem Aleichem's is about a wised-up former greenhorn and his anger at a young couple whose sense of possibility hasn't yet been tarnished. He destroys their livelihood, and then their marriage, under cover of helping them out: the comedy is of the sort sometimes characterized, in Yiddish, as "laughing with lizards," to laugh rather than to cry, or scream. This could be played in a gentler key. The Yiddish writer Avrom Reyzen, for example, wrote a bittersweet satire about an immigrant who is constantly trying to find America but his finances prevent him from really discovering it: His ambitions shrink from California, to Chicago, to Detroit, to Boston, to Philadelphia, to Paterson, to Brownsville. But the punch line still stings: "Hard, it's hard, brother, to reach America, once you fall into New York."

But if some of those early satirists were unsure about the possibilities of America's promise, the history of the twentieth century showed that the difficulty of reaching America grew smaller and smaller. In the process, though, as the American Jewish community became less and less an immigrant community, American Jewish satire became less concerned with matters directly related to European Jewish history—and, perhaps, Jewish history itself. With increasing acculturation, the culture they satirized was either this new thing known as "American Jewish culture," the new creation birthed at the interaction between the phrase's two adjectives, or American culture writ large.

Taking the latter first, which illustrates, more than anything else, how "Jews in comedy" increasingly diverges from "Jewish comedy in America." Topical satire was put on a new footing in the United States by Mort Sahl, who first appeared at San Francisco's hungry i in 1953, a decade after *To Be or Not To Be* had left theaters. The press at the time weren't always sure what to make of Sahl. While noting some continuities with previous American satirists, most notably the vaudevillian cowboy-humorist Will Rogers, they largely saw the man who walked onto a bare stage with a rolled-up newspaper and told biting jokes about the golf-loving President Eisenhower ("If you are in the Administration, you have a lot of problems of policy, like whether or not to use an overlapping grip") and Joseph McCarthy ("I got a McCarthy jacket; it's like a Nehru jacket, but the flap buttons across the mouth") as a "strange sort of comic . . . whose routines are anything but routine" and a significant break from the "old stand-up joke book comedians." Sahl, for his part, had this to say about his most illustrious American predecessor: "There's quite a bit of difference between Rogers and me. Rogers . . . impersonated a yokel who was critical of the federal government. I . . . impersonate an intellectual who is critical of yokels who are running the American government."

Certainly Sahl was a shock to the system. As the new cellar and coffeehouse satiric movement expanded from San Francisco to Chicago (Mister Kelly's, the Gate of Horn), New York (the Bitter End, the Village Gate, Café Wha?), and beyond, almost every major American comic who took aim at the way things were for the next two decades would claim him as a major, disruptive influence. He was shocking enough to lead Lenny Bruce to experiment with working clean, which is shocking indeed. Some of that was a matter of form—Sahl, unlike most of that previous generation, wrote his own material. Some was his improvisatory skill. But a lot of it was the fact that, as an anonymous 1959 article in *Time* put it, his humor—along with that of a number of like-minded compatriots who had come to prominence during the fifties—was "a symptom of the twentieth century's own sickness . . . partly social criticism liberally laced with cyanide, partly a Charles Addams kind of jolly ghoulishness, and partly a personal and highly disturbing hostility towards all the world." Sahl was dubbed "the original sicknick," but Shelley Berman, Lenny Bruce, Tom Lehrer, Don Adams, Jonathan Winters, and Mike Nichols and Elaine May all appeared in the piece, cast in his image. A new generation, a new approach.

Is it coincidental that almost every one of those comedians is Jewish? (Winters is the lone exception.) And how does that reflect, if it does, on the Jewishness of their satire? Sahl—like most, though not all of the comedians here—rarely mentioned religion on stage; his press never mentioned his Jewish heritage; and his autobiographical reflections, short of a brief mention of hanging around Berkeley in his formative years with "a cadre of left-wing Jewish kids with fervor," don't discuss his Jewish background. Does that intellectual and political fervor—shades of the famous alcoves in the dining halls of City College for a slightly earlier generation—equal Jewish? Is this part of our story?

That *Time* magazine piece suggested that the new generation's comic achievement—even if its author was ambivalent, perhaps downright negative, about the quality of that achievement—was that no subject was taboo, even if the comedians lumped in this group differed in method and degree of approach. This focus on real issues was a bold step in the world of comedy, and, you could argue, it moved a kind of Jewish comic sensibility—one where every aspect of behavior was scrutinized under the microscope—onto the stand-up stage. Or, as Sahl put it: "I don't have any kinship with a Jewish background . . . If the role of the Jew is to rock the boat and to be inquisitive—intellectually curious, that is—fine. Classic role." Or, you might argue, that these comics' (or their parents') immigrant Jewish backgrounds, with their exposure to the Yiddish-inflected culture of the left or an abstract affiliation with a Jewish sensibility of American promise, might create a particularly sharpened sense of outrage when that promise came up short.

But this is getting us onto some awfully dicey ground. Even if you posit the sensibility as Jewish, in its expansiveness of approach and its willingness to confront the jugular—and it's pretty iffy to limit this to Jews—these comedians' topics weren't. (Unless you consider the studied attempt at broad resonance and American universalism a definition of an American Jewish impulse, and that's kind of circular reasoning.) A notable exception that may prove the rule came from down south. Harry Golden, a remarkably popular and influential satirist, took on matters of national import with a satiric flair, particularly when related to civil rights. His "vertical negro plan," for example, offered a solution to the integration question by noting that southern whites seemed only to be perturbed by African-American presence when they were sitting, at lunch counters, or on buses. So he came up with the obvious solution: just eliminate seats for everybody. Golden, however, was not merely thought of as a Jewish comic for a general audience, but, as the publisher and writer of the *Carolina Israelite*, a representative of Jewishness and the American Jewish people. He was sometimes referred to as "the Jewish Will Rogers," for example, something that never would have occurred to any of the critics speaking about Mort Sahl, and was often asked to do national media representing a Jewish viewpoint on this or that matter. His satire, in short, even when it addressed the same topics as Sahl, was explicitly seen as flowing from a Jewish moral, cultural, and political stance. Unlike Sahl et al.

But it was a lot like Lenny Bruce, the major mainstream satirist of the fifties who bridges the gap between American and Jewish in his work. If Sahl's satire was oracular, delivered from the perspective of Everycomedian, Bruce's was avowedly particularistic, alienated, apart from the mainstream. Bruce was happy to own up to the satirist's sobriquet: "I am a satirist basically," he said; "I am irreverent politically, religiously, or any things I think need discussing and satirizing." Responding to that same charge of sicknickness, he used that same classic trope of the satirist: "I'm not a comedian. And I'm not sick. The world is sick and I'm the doctor." What set Bruce apart from the pack, in many ways and certainly for our purposes, is not what he says. Bruce's routines don't hold up well on recording. He would regularly play to the band. His almost pathological hatred of phoniness (even as he made a career of phony-style impersonations) can weary.

But it's the rhythms and flows of the way that he says it. It's the voice, the language, and particularly the Jewish voice: his embrace of his inauthentically authentic self, or vice versa, which leads to an approach markedly different from the one set out by Sahl. Perhaps the most indicative comment he ever made came late in his career, in a show after he was arrested for obscenity in San Francisco. "I wasn't very funny tonight," he said. "Sometimes I'm not. I'm not a comedian. I'm Lenny Bruce."

Though Bruce (born Leonard Alfred Schneider in 1925) was notoriously unreliable when it came to narrating his own life, both in his routines and his autobiography, he was open, in public no less than private, about his ethnicity, and how it played a role in crafting his stage language. Bruce, in his autobiography, talks about putting "the jargon of the hipster, the argot of the underworld, and Yiddish" together in conversation, and given the evidence, this is one of the few things there we *can* trust. Thanks to other comics and entertainers he spent time with in the late forties and early fifties, most importantly Joe Ancis, he learned and mastered what's been called "the art of the *shpritz*," giving himself a patina of Yiddish authenticity, a *heymishness*, as part of a rapid-fire patter of words, ideas, jokes, general *geshrying*: culminating in his ventriloquizing a Jewish judge in his indecency trials who has been entrapped by a young hooker. ("Give it to me, you litvak Lolita!" is the immortal phrase in question.)

Rodney Dangerfield said, speaking of Bruce: "All you guys who try to get away from being Jewish by changing your last name always give the secret away by forgetting to change your first name. What kind of goy name is Lenny?" What Dangerfield didn't see—or maybe he did; he changed his name from Jack Roy *Cohen*, after all—is that Bruce's point was to be a living contradiction, a bit of a satire on himself. He wanted to be a hipster, but he also wanted to be someone who made fun of people who wanted to be hipsters; he spoke the lingo of jazzmen (both he and Sahl released comedy albums on jazz labels) and excelled, in language, with the art of the *shpritz*. But onstage he was always aware of the audience watching him put on an act, even as he was improvising and thus *not* doing something posed, rehearsed. Bruce's Jewishness was a performance, something reclaimed: which made it part of his art, and his art thus part of our story.

Other great American Jewish satirists of the period fall somewhere on the spectrum of identification between Sahl and Bruce. The cartoonist Jules Feiffer (b. 1929), who came to prominence with his late fifties *Village Voice* strips entitled *Sick Sick Sick* (published in book form in 1958), was able to take some of the new basic staples of postwar American culture—the slick newscaster, the gray-flannel-suited businessman, the leotard-wearing bohemian—and turn them into an indictment of logical inconsistencies that masked truly monstrous, moral possibilities. Feiffer's political satire, which lasted for years, wasn't vulgar, though he was lumped in with the sick comics, for obvious title-based reasons. It was daring in every sense of the term, perhaps especially for the way that it took a more conventional form, the newspaper strip, and turned it into a forum for a sustained comic vision. (With a soundtrack, presumably, by Tom Lehrer, who was doing the same thing with the tradition of the American popular song.) But although many of the cultural luminaries and bohemians who flittered around the *Village Voice*, where Feiffer's "Explainers" appeared, were culturally Jewish, and shared Feiffer's preoccupations with intellectualism, psychoanalysis, and paralyzing and neurotic self-doubt, they were rarely explicitly so in their work.

Sometimes the Jewishness seemed pervasive, but disguised. Joseph Heller's *Catch-22*, published in 1961, predates anything but the most minimal American incursion into Indochina, but it would become a bleakly comic touchstone for the war to come. Critics and biographers have asserted that Yossarian, the novel's Armenian protagonist, was Jewish in earlier drafts; Heller suggested otherwise, though he acknowledged Jewish characters existed in his notes for the novel. But his characters' struggles with and against the military machine, taken in tandem with Stanley Kubrick's 1964 film *Dr. Strangelove, or: How I Learned to Stop Worrying and Love the Bomb*, reminds us not only of that Jewish neurotic tendency, but also the political satire of bureaucracy and groupthink run wild that grinds the little guy under the gears.

Kubrick's work was among the most prominent examples of the replacement term for "sick comedy" that was increasingly circulating: black humor, referring to the dark comedy that satirically focused on the anxious undersides of an ostensibly confident and booming postwar American culture. (*Catch-22*, taking on the haloed American military that won World War II, was a seminal predecessor.) The flagship text of the movement was *Black Humor*, a 1965 mass market paperback edited by Bruce Jay Friedman, featuring figures like Thomas Pynchon, Edward Albee, John Barth, and Terry Southern. Friedman would later distance himself from the term "black humor," preferring "tense comedy"—which gives a better sense of the psychoanalytic anxiousness behind the work, but never quite caught on—but at the time found it *le mot juste* for

> a nervousness, a tempo, a near-hysterical new beat in the air, a punishing isolation and loneliness of a strange, frenzied new kind . . . a new, Jack Rubyesque chord of absurdity [that] has been struck in the land . . . one that can only be dealt with by a new, one-foot-in-the-asylum style of fiction . . . the satirist has had his ground usurped by the newspaper reporter. The journalist who, in the year 1964, must cover the ecumenical debate on whether Jews, on the one hand, are still to be known as Christ-killers, or on the other hand are to be let off the hook, is certainly today's satirist. The novelist-satirist, with no real territory of his own to roam, has had to discover new land, invent a new currency, a new set of filters, has had to sail into darker waters somewhere out beyond satire and I think this is what is meant by black humor.

Friedman's presentation of the material as transcending satire, rather than reshaping it, may strike the reader as less compelling than his presentation of the movement (like Sahl) as a broadly American one, rather than his particular ethnic group. His own anthological selections for the volume, for example, featured largely non-Jews, the exceptions being Nathanael West, Heller, and Friedman himself. Is black humor Jewish satire, then? No, or at least, not necessarily; but Friedman's own "tense comedy"—particularly his 1962 novel *Stern*—not only shaped the American black comic consciousness, but along with Bruce's Yiddish hijinks set the postwar American Jewish satire into motion.

Stern (*pace* the Yiddish satirists above) was not, culturally speaking, about how to deal with the specter of cultural and economic failure but how to deal with the anomie and dysfunction of incomplete success, with a move to the suburbs complete with blighted foliage and a neighbor who pushes his wife down, seeing up her dress in the process, and tells his son "No playing here for kikes." All of what follows—the petty slights and cruelties that nature and society play upon Stern, and, perhaps even more to the point, the way Stern sorrowfully internalizes them—are delivered in such a flat, affectless tone, drenched in ironic force, that the reader doesn't know whether to laugh at the powerless figure the protagonist has cut for himself, or to ache along with him.

A number of these sad sacks, or satiric schlemiels, appear in American Jewish works of the period. Beside Friedman's 1963 short story "When You're Excused, You're Excused" (where a man's pas-de-deux with his wife about liberation from the humdrum regularity of postwar life is expressed in his desire to avoid Yom Kippur services and go to the gym), there are the various characters who strut, then fret, their way through the pages of Philip Roth's 1959 National Book Award–winning collection *Goodbye, Columbus*. Epstein, of the eponymous short story, whose attempts to reclaim some of his suburb-neutered masculinity lead to a social disease and familial neutering; and Mr. Patimkin in the title novella, the bathroom fixture king brought low by social expectations for, and of, his daughter. Or some of Bellow's early shvitzers; Leventhal, the protagonist of his 1947 novel *The Victim*, who manages to find the one gentile who claims to be a victim of anti-Semitism; or Tommy Wilhelm's flailing in *Seize the Day*.

But *Stern*, in its own way, encapsulates it all, despite selling only about six thousand copies. (At least, as Robert Gottlieb told the author, they were the "right copies.") Friedman's work—along with that of Roth, Bellow, and others—would help usher in a new direction for satire.

THESE MID-CENTURY writers' focus on the norms, ideals, aspirations, and failures of the American Jewish community complemented the Bruce stand-up approach—to ground the satirical in the personal, and the personal in the communal—and that approach in turn led to a kind of seventies comedy, perfect for the Me Generation, that had a specific and explicit autobiographical focus, in contradistinction to the more institution-oriented, political satire of the fifties and sixties.

Harry Golden, again, had been an underrated transitional figure, maybe even leading the way. In books like *Only in America* (1958) or *For 2¢ Plain* (1959), he delivered epigrams characterizing American Jewish progress as "from sha sha to cha cha" (later "from shul to pool") and wrote tours de force on topics like the American Jewish fundraiser, complete with cameo by the comic George Jessel, known to American Jews as much for his tireless devotion to Jewish causes as for his monologues. But he also treated his audience to scenes from his American Jewish autobiography that mixed large dollops of fondness and nostalgia in with the satire: his portraits of a mother buying a child a suit on the Lower East Side, or instructions on how to buy two cents plain seltzer, burst with a kind of gentle affection that would have come hard to Lenny Bruce, with all his Yiddish, or the Philip Roth of the 1971 anti-Nixon satire, *Our Gang*, with its gleeful puerility. Instead, it was Golden's path that would serve as the future of mainstream American Jewish satire, and it was a path that came easily to Robert Klein.

Klein, whose dad was a friend of the comedian Myron Cohen's, did summers in the Borscht Belt growing up, occasionally delivering punch lines in Yiddish. He used his experiences on the streets of the Bronx and the improv halls of Chicago's Second City to create a loose, energetic style that earned him regular appearances on Carson and the first of HBO's highly influential *On Location* specials. Klein wasn't actually apolitical; but he worked in a kind of political-is-personal vein epitomized by the title of his first album, 1973's *Child of the 50s*. Jay Leno, speaking about Klein, suggested that he "didn't have a hook—the black guy or the Jewish guy. He was just a funny guy"—but Klein, who admired Lenny Bruce greatly, was a Jewish comic for a new era, whose Jewishness inflected his comedy necessarily, rather than ideologically or linguistically: if you were going to draw on your own life for your comedy, and your own life had a Jewish tinge, then you were going to have to incorporate Jewishness into your own routines, no more—but also no less—than other aspects of your identity. That same untroubled, even fond satiric approach appeared in the work of his contemporary David Brenner, whose autobiography, *Soft Pretzels with Mustard* (1983), is in its own way as Jewish a coming-of-age narrative as Henry Roth's *Call It Sleep*, if one with less literary merit.

Several decades later, this autobiographical anthropological approach shows up clearly in some of the most influential works of American Jewish satire in the twenty-first century. Perhaps most prominently in the Coen brothers' *A Serious Man* (2009), which—among the many other things it does—holds a certain kind of Conservative Judaism up to scrutiny in a way that takes on American Jewish consumerism, acculturation, ignorance, and questionable quest for spirituality. David Wain and Michael Showalter's *Wet Hot American Summer* (2001), and subsequently its Netflix 2015 miniseries sequel, has become a touchstone of contemporary American Jewish comic nostalgia. It takes an American Jewish adolescent rite of passage that in itself contains more Jewish identity and sensibility than content and invests it with meaning by calling attention to its pervasive, if superficial, Jewishness. There's an extended riff on the

Jewish last names of campers; Wain's portrayal of an Israeli counselor, Yaron; and a "shofar dick sword fight" that chains adolescent male behavior with Jewish ritual in a manner that would have made Lenny Bruce proud.

But before we leave the 1970s behind entirely, we might revisit the blurring that lies at the heart of the personal-as-political approach through the work of one of the great American satirists, who created a set of indelible characters who demonstrated an American society in social upheaval by Americanizing the Jewish milieu of his upbringing. Norman Lear—arguably the most important figure in the history of the sitcom—would, in shows like *All in the Family* and *Maude*, take on the issues of the day and place them in the mouths of extraordinary ordinary Americans. Though Lear's characters weren't explicitly Jewish (and *All in the Family* and *Sanford and Son* were based on British shows), Lear insisted that many of the interactions and situations in his sitcoms were influenced by ones he had heard and experienced in his own home. If Jews were becoming American, then Americans—and for some, there were no more archetypal Americans than Archie and Edith Bunker, love them or hate them—were also, in their own disguised way, Jewish.

Lear wasn't the only one working in satiric masquerade. As the seventies gave way to the eighties and nineties, director Paul Mazursky would do the same thing in a smaller vein on a bigger screen, with his 1986 film *Down and Out in Beverly Hills* (Richard Dreyfuss and Bette Midler, playing characters named the Whitemans, is as close to explicitly putting a gentile mask on Jewish social satire as you can get) and the more explicitly Jewish 1991 film *Scenes From a Mall* (Woody Allen and Bette Midler taking the leads, and the mall taking the role of Nick Nolte).

But, overall, the American Jewish satirist was, largely speaking, an American satirist who happened to be Jewish. There were Abbie Hoffman and Paul Krassner on the radical left; and Art Buchwald, the noted columnist, in the center; but Hoffman was more of a performance artist, Krassner would deny his Jewishness, and Buchwald was interested in reaching a mainstream audience with a mainstream approach. And America's most unquestionably influential venue for political satire of the last four decades—*Saturday Night Live*, the show originally described by its Canadian-Jewish founder as "Monty Python Meets Sixty Minutes"—isn't particularly Jewish, as that one-line statement of its influences showed. (Most of SNL's political sketches were overseen, and often written, by the non-Jewish Jim Downey; perhaps the most direct influence Michaels ever had on Jewish satire—and almost certainly on US elected politics—was hiring future Jewish senator Al Franken to his writing staff.) And in America, at least, the role of political satire has become less and less intertwined with Jewish life and fate, as that life and fate becomes more and more American.

This had consequences for the personal-as-autobiographical satire, too, of course: as the American Jewish experience became more acculturated, less pronounced, the Jewish part of the comedian's biography frequently became less resonant, offered less grist for the comedic mill. There were significant exceptions, of course: but they tended, more and more, to cluster in the area known as "American Jewish literature," which, in the last quarter of the twentieth century, flourished primarily as a kind of niche, narrowcast literature, which, though in English, was written largely by and for members of the American Jewish community with high levels of affiliation. The satire, then, subjects that community to withering scrutiny by writers who, almost by definition, are intimately involved with its doings and whose satires are well-known within the Jewish community and little-known out of it.

There's Tova Reich's take on the American obsession with Holocaust remembrance (2007's *My Holocaust*); Tova Mirvis's gimlet skewering of the close and occasionally suffocating circles of American Jewish sisterhood, in all senses of that word (2000's *The Ladies' Auxiliary*); and Shalom Auslander's arguments with the religious world he left behind (2005's *Beware of God*), among many others. These satires are steeped in a level of literary sophistication, textual familiarity, and anthropological intimacy that would have shocked a previous generation, which would have assumed American acculturation would have rendered the next generation incapable of the privileged position of the satirist's knowledge. But they attract a limited audience: whether they're preaching to, or castigating, the choir, the pews are increasingly empty. One exception that may prove the rule: Gary Shteyngart, whose rollicking satiric novels—particularly for our purposes his 2002 debut, *The Russian Debutante's Handbook*—have achieved wider crossover success, but lack most of the identifying features above; focusing, as it does, on a post-Soviet Russian-Jewish immigrant milieu in which the constitutive features of Jewish identity are somewhat different.

THE SITUATION is very different in Israel, where by definition the satire of the politics and culture of the world's only Jewish state is significantly more suffused with Jewish identity and determination. To speak broadly, one major approach within Israeli satire is to focus on continuities with a previous Jewish politics. Take, for example, the famous joke about when President Eisenhower met with the first Israeli prime minister, David Ben-Gurion. Eisenhower confessed it was extremely difficult to be the president of 170 million people, to which Ben-Gurion responded, "It's harder to be the prime minster of two million prime ministers." Jews, the joke suggests, all talk and kibitz in the same way they did in Mendele's bathhouse or in Sholem Aleichem's Kasrilevke; even in the Jewish state, Jewish politics is largely shtetl politics. This perhaps helped explain the focus on the comic sensibilities of Israel's third prime minister, Levi Eshkol, who was famous for his sense of humor, and particularly his Yiddish-inflected speech and sensibility. (American Jewish humor about Israel strikes an analogous tack, reframing Israel as an outpost of American Jewish sensibility. Two illustrative jokes: one where, during the Six-Day War, Syrians broke into the Bank of Tel Aviv, escaping with over a million dollars in pledges. And then there was the one Milton Berle told about

Israel's unknown soldier, whose tomb reads HYMAN GOLDFARB, FURRIER: "As a soldier, he was unknown; but as a furrier he was famous!")

But there are two counterpoints to this approach. The first is that that wasn't—according to Zionist thinking—the way that it was supposed to be. The new Jewish state, in the transformative dreams of its founders, was supposed to lead to a new Jewish culture, associated, logically, with a new Jewish humor (as a certain conception of "Jewish humor" itself was seen as an example of problematic, accommodationist or quietist, diaspora culture); and the attempts to fulfill those revolutionary dreams were themselves viewed satirically. Take, for example, the *chizbat* jokes of the Palmach, the predecessor of the IDF. The jokes themselves—essentially, tall tales, shaggy dog stories, or joke riffs concerning things Palmach members did—were often adaptations of general joke forms to the new landscape; but occasionally they were about the "humorlessness" of the soldiers, the constant attentiveness to the serious matters at hand that was the hallmark of the new, empowered Jew. In the Palmach's case, of course, these were military matters, and so there was often a focus on the rifle. Here's one famous example:

> They came to one of the instructors, I don't remember the name, and said, "Listen. It's not possible that you teach only rifle, rifle, rifle. You need a little history, a little culture, a little sociology. You can't do only rifle. Greenhorns come to you and you start with the rifle. Start with something from the Bible. Get to the rifle afterwards." He said "O.K." When the greenhorns came he said, "In the beginning God created the heavens and the earth. After that he created the rifle. Now this is the rifle."

Talk about a rupture from the past.

Except, of course, that Israeli history *wasn't* discontinuous from the past—and they knew that. Some of the most biting satirical moments of Israeli comedy focus on a propensity to over-remember, to see Jewish history as overlaying too much on contemporary Israeli life. A skit from the 1990s Israeli satirical troupe *Hahamishia Hakamerit* ("The Chamber Quintet") called "Ghetto," for example, depicts a young man getting directions to a Tel Aviv party: "Take Warsaw Ghetto Street, then a U-turn onto Concentration Camp Avenue, then park in Dachau Square." "Is it nearby?" "Dachau? Dachau is right here, just around the corner."

And what's more, this sort of talk of continuity obscured a second counterpoint: the fact that Israel's Jewish population (to say nothing of its non-Jewish population) is increasingly diverse, its culture more multivariegated, and is increasingly dissociated in one way or other from the history of Israel's founding Ashkenazic elite. Some of the most important Israeli humor comes precisely from those marginalized communities, starting with the "*bourekas* films" of the sixties and seventies which, though generally directed by Askhenazim, trafficked, with popular comic success, in stereotypes of Yemenite, Moroccan, and other Sefardi and Mizrahi Jews.

Although the portraits were stereotypical, they at least rendered these minorities visible, taking on questions of their place within Israeli culture. Those movies often featured Romeo-and-Juliet romance plots, but with a happy marriage at the end often accompanied by the repeated slogan "we're all Jews." They accentuated a wish for unity, a sentiment shared by the trio known as *Hagashash Hahiver* ("The Pale Trackers"), Sephardic Israelis whose speeches of truth to Ashkenazic power were less about class conflict than a hoped-for integration. Even the popular series of jokes in the late 1990s about Israeli foreign minister and deputy prime minister David Levi, an immigrant from Morocco, show off his Mizrahi identity as evidence of sameness to, not difference from, his fellow Israelis.

More recent iterations of the *bourekas* movies, though, have focused more on fissures rather than joins, satirizing the dream of unity rather than the specter of difference. And a newer immigrant community, the emigrants from the former Soviet Union (who've created their own brand of "pierogi films"), also tend to cast a more skeptical eye at Israeli society and its promise, not always achieved, of integration. Authors like Igor Guberman and Dina Rubina satirize their community, Israeli practice, and their position in it by juggling multiple languages and often using the humor honed by their community under Soviet oppression to frame the challenges of their new society. ("Soviet Jews!" went one joke in *Beseder* [All Right], a humor supplement aimed at Russian emigrants from the early 1990s. "Immigrate to Israel! Only here your long-cherished dream of becoming Russians can come true!")

What does it say, in the end, if you can make the same jokes about the Israelis as the Soviets, that the names change, but not the jokes? Maybe something about the continuity of satiric consciousness; maybe something about the continuity of Jewish experience. And maybe, just maybe, something about the incompleteness of the satiric effect: that not only is the satirist generally never satisfied, but that such a goal is as impossible as is the ultimate correction of human nature.

ONE FINAL EXAMPLE, returning to the American context, to speak for all of them.

From 1999 to 2015, Jon Stewart's *The Daily Show* was one of the most lauded, most noticed, most respected shows on television. As Stewart would yell "Welcome to the Daily Show!" over the roaring cheers of the studio audience, as the camera dollied in on him, leaning forward, messing with those iconic blue sheets of paper, his voice almost seemed to carry the strain of bearing the outrage of his constituency, over and over again: a bemused, weary, outrage, seasoned with just enough resignation and irony to remind you that he did the best fake news on television, just enough fire to let you know that he honestly cared—deeply—that what he had to report actually matters, and that he hoped to change some minds along the way.

On *The Daily Show*, Jon Stewart frequently injected a Yiddish word, or acquired a Jewish vocal inflection or inserted a reference to his Jewishness. Probably the defining moment of Jewishness on *The Daily Show*, though, took place, as it were, *off* the show's set—at the Emmy Awards, in 2003, where Stewart brought his writers onstage to accept the second of their nine Emmys in the category for best writing for a comedy or variety show. As the line of white men stretched out behind him, Stewart made fun of their demographic unanimity. "I've always felt that diversity is the most important part of a writing staff," he said, to the broad laughter of the audience. "I don't know if you can tell, but Steve has a beard, and J. R. isn't Jewish."

A great line; and its implications matter. Was there something Jewish about *The Daily Show*'s satire during Stewart's run? And if so, precisely what might it have been? Certainly the vast majority of Stewart's viewers didn't focus on his evident and unselfconscious Jewish identity; at most, it was a shtick, it helped to sell the general-interest material. But the long tradition of Jewish—and American Jewish—satire leaves open the question of precisely what kind of Jewishness Jon Stewart's Jewish satire demonstrated.

One that it certainly seemed to, alas, was its questionable success. As comedy, absolutely; as insightful and clarifying comedy, of course. But was he able to, in the partial title of his popular one-time rally on the Washington Mall, restore sanity? Or even (though you got the sense that he clearly felt it was a symptom rather than the disease) muzzle the outrages and idiocies of cable news?

Jeremiah couldn't do it; so the best we can do, probably, is thank Stewart for trying.

3

The Wit of the Jews

For all the talk of the Jews as intellectual, bookish, clever, or people of the book, there's little talk of this in the Book of Books itself. For most of biblical literature, books come in for fairly little respect. Moses breaks the tablets. A king, notably, throws a scroll of prophecy into the fire. Moses' law is lost for a while, and has to be discovered in the course of some temple renovations. (And you get the sense that no one's missed it very much; plus, the discovery was probably a "discovery"—the latest monarchists finding something to legitimate the current rulers.) Before the destruction of the Temple, the kind of intellectualism that comes from mastery of reading (and writing) texts mattered a lot less than war-leadership or direct access to the Lord.

Maybe this isn't surprising, given the largely oral nature of biblical society; especially when we consider that some analogous skills—like the verbal sophistication and manipulation of knowledge and reference known as wit—find champions likely and unlikely throughout the Bible. Take, for example, one of the first extended displays of biblical wit: the riddle game in Judges 14. Riddle games are perfect mechanisms to show off the clever display of creative intelligence and the facile and flexible use of language. But the riddler here is hardly known for his wit—it's Samson, the strongman par excellence—and he tells his riddle not to participate in the gracious and harmonious sense of a shared community of text and language, but to express his annoyance with his wife's family (non-Jewish, though of course that has a different valence in the biblical period).

We know that because Samson's riddle, "Out of the strong came forth sweet," is unsolvable unless you happened to be present when Samson, as the Bible has earlier related, accomplished his remarkable feat of slaying a lion with the jawbone of an ass. The lion in question then became a hive for bees that produced honey. You can say that this riddle's failure to obey the conventions of its genre serves as a nice metaphor for the lack of effective communication between Jews and other peoples, or between Samson and his wives. But it's certainly not wit, perhaps even anti-wit: it may not even, strictly speaking, be a riddle, as biblical commentators intent on justifying Samson's behavior nervously noted. And the story's outcome, in which Samson's wife provides her family the answer, and his response is to kill them all, is hardly a shining example of wit itself.

Even the paradigmatic example of intelligence and wit in the Bible—King Solomon—is more complicated than it first appears. In the most famous biblical story of Solomon's wit, two mothers, each with newborn sons, one living, one dead, come to the king for justice. Each claims the surviving child to be their own. Solomon's ruling: cut the living baby in half, and present half to each mother. Equity is served. At which point one mother acquiesces to the idea—fair is fair, after all—and the second protests, offering the child to the first rather than seeing it harmed. Solomon, in what seems presented as a show of intelligence, then presents the child to the mother willing to give it up rather than see it harmed, as she has been proven to display the requisite qualities of maternity.

First of all, this famed display of intelligence doesn't seem *so* intelligent: for one thing, it obviously depends on a level of idiocy so staggering on one party's part that it beggars belief. One possibility might be to suggest this is actually a comic parody of Solomon's wisdom: certainly the idea has tickled modern comic fancies, and at least two separate treatments have played up the idea that Solomon isn't all he's cracked up to be. Joseph Heller, in his rollicking and underappreciated 1984 comic novel *God Knows*, an ostensible autobiography of King David, presents Solomon as such an idiot that he actually *wanted* to cut the baby in half. And in a 1996 episode of *Seinfeld*, Kramer and Newman come up with the idea of how to divide a bicycle in exactly the same way—and neither Kramer nor Newman has ever been upheld as a paragon of intelligence.

But Solomon's suggestion could be construed in another way, a way that demonstrates wit's other face, its cruel, mocking side. Wit can unite, true, but it can also divide: it can create a shared community in on the joke, or demonstrate the vast schism between the wit-maker and the butt of his or her comedy. Riddles, to take our earlier example, can do either; and in this story Solomon does both, serially. One can imagine Solomon's first response, in other words, as a kind of wittiness: "You want to know how to divide one child—it's easy enough; all you need is a sword." Such wit would carry a particular bite in an autocratic monarchic society where such an idea—to split the baby in half—could indeed be the capricious and cruel response of an unjust king faced with what he feels to be wearying stupidity. (Think of this question being presented to the psychopathic boy-king Joffrey Baratheon on *Game of Thrones*, for example, and shudder at the image HBO might provide you.) If that's so, his second response, then, is a kind of anti-wit, an empathetic engagement with the lives of the mothers that a reliance on wit, the abstract intellectual play of language and ideas, can blind one to. It's a caution about the price of wit, the need for emotion and sincerity. In other words, wit becomes wisdom, cruelty empathy.

The specter of wit's failure—or, more precisely put, its insufficiency—is brought up clearly in the book of Esther, that grand unifying comic text of ours. Though Esther has her plans and stratagems, preparing banquets and luring Haman into a false sense of security, her final appeal to Ahasuerus is to the heart as much as the intellect: and the real planner in the book is not Esther, but Haman, with his schemes. It's *his* use of language, *his* rhetorical flourishes, that seduce Ahasuerus into approving genocide. And we see how well *that* worked out: the plots and strategems of the overly clever are destined to come to naught in a world ruled by chance, comic coincidence, personal whim and empathetic attachment, or the secret workings of the rule of the Lord. Too much wit, the book evocatively suggests, blinds one to the importance of faith.

If the third strand of Jewish comedy we choose to follow is about the power and currency of wit, its practitioners have constantly—even as they make those bookish, allusive, intellectual efforts—been alive to its insufficiencies.

THE RABBIS of the Talmud, of course, would prefer you privilege faith over wit; although they're naturally conflicted about it.

On the one hand, their post-biblical transformation of Samson, based on that riddle game, into a wordplayer and champion of wit is understandable. People like to retell stories in their own image, and the image of the archetypal Jew was undergoing a radical reshaping with the destruction of the Temple and the shifting center of Jewish life to Babylonia, the shifting focus to text rather than rite, to scholarship and legal interpretation rather than cultic service or prophetic pronunciation or military service. (They even reshape the riddle. "Who is wise?" Ben Zoma remarks in the Ethics of the Fathers. "He who learns from every man," he concludes, uncomically.) The Jewish champion should be one of intelligence, of learning, of erudition, of verbal verve—and Samson's got just enough of that in the biblical version of his story to allow the rabbis to create more.

But they also have to address the danger that you can be too smart for your own good. Like Samson's strength, wit and wisdom, when unharnessed to the will of the Lord, ends up not being real at all. And here's the thing: when you have the best minds of Jewish life sitting around the Babylonian and Jerusalemite academies for the better part of a few centuries, all of them trying to make extremely fine distinctions on legal questions which become so rarefied that their practical ramifications often cease to exist, a certain kind of immediately recognizable intellectual Jewish smart-assery results. A kind which leads to the central question that undergirds any discussion of rabbinic humor, which is: *Did these guys* (and they were all guys, of course, with one or two exceptions who are subject to a lot of bizarre treatment) *think that the whole thing was ridiculous?*

On a superficial level, the answer was, of course, no. The Talmudic enterprise is based on the theological understanding that halakha—Jewish religious law—is the essential explication of the oral complement to the written Torah received by Moses at Sinai from God Himself, and that since that last is somewhat vague about many of the details of making the laws work in everyday life (What exactly does it mean to rest on the Sabbath, anyway? Precisely?), the rabbis are doing God's work, literally. On the other hand, digging into the details at such depth and at such levels, entertaining hypothetical cases that might never occur, and the like means that occasionally there are some reasons to wonder whether intellectual play and byplay is actually taking precedence over juridical contemplation.

Take, for example, the case of the pigeon. There's a discussion, in the Talmud, of establishing the ownership of a particular pigeon that's found some distance from a coop: how far away does it have to be before we assume that it's actually a wild pigeon, and finders keepers, rather than having to return it to its (presumed) owner? A reasonable enough question. Here's the discussion:

> A baby pigeon that is found within fifty cubits of a coop belongs to the coop's owner. If it is found outside the fifty cubits, then it belongs to the finder. Rabbi Yirmiyah asked: If one foot of the pigeon is within the fifty cubits and one foot is outside, to whom does it belong? . . . It was for this that they expelled Rabbi Yirmiyah from the academy.

It's obviously possible that this kind of thing was designed, as one critic puts it, as a "pedagogic device" to elucidate or get at legal principles, like the extraordinarily unlikely case of a knife flying through the air that somehow manages to properly slaughter an animal according to all the ritual punctilia en route or driving a wagon using a goat and a fish to determine if it violates principles of interspecies mixing. . . . but then it's not a firing offense. At least not compared to the response given by Rebbi when asked by Plimo: "If one has two heads, on which one should he place his phylacteries? Rebbi responded: 'Either go into exile or accept excommunication.'" The Talmudic editors—and the rabbis—are well aware of the dangers of witty mockery; it could bring the whole thing down around their ears, like the temple of Dagon in the Samson story. On the other hand, the unnamed editor of the Talmud seems to have the last word on the subject: "Meanwhile, a man came to the academy saying that he just begotten a two-headed son and wanted to know how much must be given to the priest for the redemption of the first-born." Wit is one thing, but the world can also be stranger than wit itself.

Which is a way of explaining the difference between three different types of rabbinic wit, epitomized by three different figures: Rabban Gamaliel, Hillel, and Rabbi Akiva. We've encountered Rabban Gamaliel in an earlier chapter, where he takes on—and puts down—the gentile authority figures or heretics who come to him with questions. The reason for returning to him here is that those challenges are framed as battles of wits, centered around both facility with language and knowledge of textual tradition. Here's a similar example, employing a different rabbi:

> A certain heretic whose name was Sason once said to Rabbi Abahu, "You are destined to draw water for me in the world to come, for it is written, 'Therefore be-sason [in joy] shall we draw water,' (Isa. 12:3)." "If," the other retorted, "it had been written le-sason, it would be as you say, but as it is written

be-sason, the meaning must be that a water-skin will be made of your skin, and water will be drawn with it."

In other tales, even an emperor cites biblical texts of his own, becoming a (defective) Talmudist—playing according to the rabbis' rules.

But this is often *not* the way of the Talmud. Some of the greatest moments of the rabbis are the defeat of pseudo-wit—as we saw in Solomon's case—with a kind of wisdom that short-circuits cynicism or mockery in the name of emotion, a kind of wit that arises from a display of what we might almost call anti-virtuosity in the subject. Perhaps the most famous example of wit's failure is the case of Hillel, who is besieged by men trying to get him to lose his temper by thinking of (quasi-)clever insults or by challenges, such as to teach him the Torah while he stands on one foot. (The insults are delivered in the form of just-so stories, where the questions are, apparently, targeted at Hillel's own ethnic and personal characteristics.)

While his more mercurial colleague Shammai drives the individuals away, Hillel stands his ground (on two feet, presumably), and treats these mocking occasions not as the opportunity to unleash more satire or wit, nor to retreat into ironic quotation marks, nor—unlike Samson or Shammai—to resort to violence. Instead, he answers the questions calmly (including, in one response, the famous Golden Rule of loving thy neighbor as thyself), and it's only at the end of one story—where he suggests to the man it would be better to lose twice the amount of his bet than for Hillel to lose his temper—that we see the wry sensibility behind the apparently placid surface. In this sense, he may resemble Solomon, where ultimately the display of wit is aimed not at his interlocutor but himself, his God, and, perhaps, his readers (depending on how you view the editor's role).

"Love thy neighbor as thyself" is not Hillel's own formulation but a quotation from the Bible. The Talmud, and rabbinic literature more generally (particularly the collections of rabbinic explications of legal and narrative material known as the midrash) is where another kind of display of wit—allusion—really comes into its own. (In fact, Hillel himself is technically alluding, not quoting: he actually slightly alters the biblical formulation to "What is hateful to you, do not do to your neighbor," in what may be a slight verbal jab at his current treatment.) Such witty displays by definition require an earlier literary tradition, and, although there is intra-biblical allusion, it tends not—very generally speaking—to be the kind of full-throated basis for a story or joke as it is in the post-biblical literature.

The wit of allusion may take the form of a basic recognition of another word or phrase that sheds a double light on the current interaction. Looked at this way, the pun or spoonerism is a kind of allusion, and so are many classic punch lines ("I don't know, but his face sure rings a bell," for example). Or it may be a kind of playfulness that comes with understanding the contextual literary universe a text evokes by introducing an entirely other book or canon as a frame of additional reference. Allusion can lead to two different kinds of relationship to the earlier material, both of which rely on taking it intensely seriously—because, after all, you have to know it inside and out in order to chop it up and use it as the basis of your wordplay, or, in another context, your legal analysis.

Take the story of Rabbi Akiva and the foxes, which involves laughter as a means of maintaining faith. It's not funny, exactly, but it is witty; and it shows how such sentiments can flourish even in the most dire of locales—in this case, in the ruins of the destroyed Temple. Rabbi Akiva and some of his rabbinic colleagues are walking the ruins, the story goes, and see a fox running out from where the Holy of Holies once stood. The rabbis begin to weep; Akiva, incongruously, smiles. The rabbis ask Akiva why he's smiling; he asks them the same question about their weeping. The rabbis recite a verse of Jerusalem's glory, and juxtapose it with its desolation. Akiva, for his part, replies that this is precisely why he laughs: such a manifestation proves the predictive power of the biblical text, and so other verses—and he recites three to their one—must share that same power, including ones about the ultimate redemption and the Temple's reconstruction in messianic times.

In other hands and other sensibilities, Akiva's one-upsmanship would have been a witty retort demonstrating ridicule of the less textually supple and knowledgeable. Here, however, Akiva's laughter isn't the comedy of superiority; it is the warm happy glow of faith fulfilled. (The rabbis' reply: "Akiva, you have comforted us; Akiva, you have comforted us.") How hollow the comfort that wit supplies may prove to be is a question played out over the centuries of diaspora to come: a question played out in Akiva's own connection to laughter. On the one hand, Akiva's laughter recurs frequently through the Talmud as a means of expressing his own comfort with tricky metaphysical questions—he laughs, for example, at the suffering of Rabbi Eliezer, but only because he now understands the latter's place in the world to come is secured. And yet the same Rabbi Akiva states explicitly that laughter and frivolity lead to licentiousness.

Akiva's seemingly conflicting statements are a good representation of a generally bifurcated rabbinic attitude toward laughter. On the one hand, rabbis could say that "since the day of the destruction of the Temple there is no laughter for the Holy One, Blessed Be He," and that a student of Torah should only allow a minimum of laughter. One rabbi, Rav Ashi, accordingly broke a glass at a wedding when the merriment got too much, one of the antecedents for today's common custom at Jewish weddings to break a glass under the chuppah. In fact, one particularly pietistic community of Jewish antiquity that predated the Talmud, the Essenes, had a rule that "Whoever has guffawed foolishly shall do penance for thirty days."

Were they worried that excessive frivolity would lead to an abridgement of the Torah study that was their highest value? Perhaps; one midrash reads:

> Just as if a full container of oil were in your hand and a drop
> of water fell into it an equal amount of oil would spill over,
> so too for every word of Torah that enters one's heart a word

of *letsanut* (humor) leaves it; and for every word of *letsanut* that enters one's heart a word of Torah leaves it.

The rabbis may also have associated this kind of frivolity with the pagan activity of stadiums, theaters, and circuses, and their anticomic efforts should then be seen as part of a wide range of anti-idolatrous sentiment and activity.

On the other hand, they certainly understood that humor could serve a beneficial pedagogic purpose, not just a baneful one: the Talmud notes that the sage Rabbah, before starting his lecture, would open with a joke, and Rabbi Simon noted that "If your inclination comes to incite you to merriment, make it merry with Torah." And even more powerfully, they could recount that the prophet Elijah—a man who occasionally knew how to deliver a satiric zinger, as we saw in the previous chapter—praised two simple men because by their jests they made sad people merry and stopped them feuding. The question of the moral status of laughter continues in rabbinic circles to this day.

Some of the ambivalence, though, must have stemmed from the observation that this kind of allusion—where intellectual and linguistic play run the risk of becoming superior to everything—can serve as the basis for profanation and parody. Since you're not subordinate to the demands of the text, they bend to you, grist for your own playful literary mill. Or, as a joke from the yeshiva milieu, the successor to the rabbinical academies in later centuries, would have it: Kopl told his friend he should be the happiest man in the world. "Why's that?" his friend replied. "I have an answer, a wonderful answer, a perfect answer!" "Mazel tov! Then what's the problem?" "I have the answer, but I don't have the question."

AFTER THE CLOSE of the Talmudic canon, the next great period of Jewish wit and intellectualism reached its cultural and literary height in the Iberian peninsula in what some have referred to as "the Golden Age of Spain" (very rough estimate: from the early tenth century, on and off, through the expulsion of Jews from the Iberian peninsula in the late fifteenth century, but primarily between the late tenth and early twelfth century). Much has been written about Sephardic Jews' status under the Muslim caliphate, whether it was an idealized age of *convivencia* or an enshrined sense of servitude and inferiority. Either way the period gave rise to a wide range of remarkable Jewish cultural production, particularly Hebrew-language poetry often constructed on contemporary Arabic models.

To talk about Spanish-Jewish poetry and focus on the funny parts is a little like writing a biography of Shakespeare and only mentioning the sonnets. But there are two points that have real import for our discussion of wit. The first is that much of this humor, like so much of the art and effect of poetry, is based on the careful manipulation of language. That manipulation takes place in two main ways. The first is the employment of phrases from the biblical canon, which were often used in subversive ways to provide a frisson of witty blasphemy for writers like Solomon ibn Gabirol or Judah Halevi and their largely elite, cosmopolitan audience. (Almost no one else would be able to make their way through the recondite Hebrew to get the meaning of the line, much less the joke.) Here's a simple one, scanted by translation, from the twelfth- to thirteenth-century poet Judah Al-Harizi:

> You ruthless flea, who desecrates my couch
> And draws my blood to sate your appetite,
> You know not rest, on Sabbath day or feast—
> Your feast it is when you can pinch and bite.

> My friends expound the law: to kill a flea
> Upon the Sabbath day a sin they call;
> But I prefer the other law which says,
> Be sure a murderer's malice to forestall.

The poem pretends to take a Jewish legal approach in order to privilege the sensation of joyous pleasure, or at least the cessation of displeasure, over traditional observance. The idea is to frame it in witty language that transcends theological fidelity. The fact that the fleabite would be often used in poetry as a symbol of sexual desire, by poets like John Donne among others, heightens the frisson of forbiddenness.

A second thing Spanish-Jewish poetry does, though, is take into account the surrounding language—Arabic—in order to create witty bilingual interactions between the two languages. For example: long riddles in verse were in vogue in Spain and Italy from the Middle Ages to the seventeenth century whose comprehension frequently depended on understanding Hebrew and the local language and how they might work independently and complementarily. This kind of "macaronic" material—where words from one language are introduced and incorporated into text in another—is more common in more multilingual societies than in America. In some ways, it's the flip side of a different kind of humor of wit, one that becomes increasingly prominent in Jewish comedy as we have staged or performed material preserved. The malapropism, for example, in which the character doesn't know they're mangling the language, but the audience, ironically, is well aware of the differences. As Jews in the diaspora are often between and among languages—the language of the society they live in, the sacred Jewish language of Hebrew, and vernaculars like Yiddish, Ladino, Judeo-Arabic, and others that are themselves fusions of various languages—the ability to navigate between them provides its own source of playfulness and comic joy.

This dynamic played out in the courtyards and around the fountains of medieval Spain, where its gracious and elegant poetry hid puns and dirty double entendres. But you can find it throughout the breadth of the medieval Jewish diaspora. A medieval wedding song, to take one example, blasphemously weaves together French and Hebrew in a performance filled with double entendres, most powerfully telling the bridegroom that he will rule on Mount Seir, which sounds, in Hebrew, like "the hairy mountain" (you can guess). It's worth noting that the recondite Hebrew lines, as opposed to the French, are the raunchiest ones, pitching the sexual comedy more to the men in the audiences. This kind of division of the sexes wasn't uncommon in medieval times. The Dante-modeled comedy of the early fourteenth-century *Notebooks* of Immanuel of Rome reminded its cosmopolitan audiences of the fun that could be had in juxtaposing Hebraism and Hellenism. This would be an even more seductive and pronounced challenge as the Jewish community follows Dante's heirs into the modern world. Witness the fact that a century later, Joseph Karo, the author of the greatest Jewish law code, prohibited people from reading the *Notebooks*.

IF THE ELITES of the medieval period linked wit, text, and wisdom, they also understood the fine and often blurred lines between wisdom and folly. This wasn't only a Jewish concern, of course. Christians, taking Paul's dictum that "If anyone among you think that he is wise, let him become a fool that he may be wise," were enamored of this dynamic, too. People have been finding foolishness an appealing subject for philosophical, theological, and aesthetic consideration—and comic entertainment—for as long as there have been fools around. In First Samuel, the not-yet-king David plays the fool in order to escape captivity, wrapping wisdom in foolishness to establish superiority over the non-Jew who can't tell the difference. The author of the book of Proverbs, so obsessed with wisdom, is particularly astringent on the relationship between its literary representation and folly: "Like a thorn that goes into the hand of the drunkard, so is a parable in the mouth of fools," he says.

But it's the medieval period that really takes it to a new level, and where the theological understanding develops (in the Christian context, certainly) that knowledge can itself be a tainted goal, since—after all—the search for it led to the Fall. Folly and its offshoots branch in many directions—some of which, like the vulgarity and parody associated with it, we'll discuss in the next chapter—but chief among them is foolishness illustrated through the use of the tools of wit, the application of logic (or choplogic) unmoored by wisdom or common sense to reach ridiculous conclusions. Which leads us to a magnificent innovation of the early modern period: the Jewish fools' town, best known as Chelm.

Fools' towns weren't invented in the medieval and early modern period, though the image was particularly popular then, and Chelm isn't an invention at all. It's an actual place, not far from Warsaw, in the same region that the majority of Isaac Bashevis Singer's stories are set. (Singer would go on to feature Chelm in a series of stories.) But despite its actual existence, it's really a metaphor above all else. In a classic Chelm story, the identifying feature is not simply the display of stupidity: it's the application of intellect of a kind of Talmudic mien to a problem, without a trace of the self-awareness possessed by those rabbis who kicked people out of the yeshiva, that generally results in making the situation worse than before. One example: the time when the Chelmites, enamored with the beautiful, unbroken snowfall that covered their town's streets, wanted to ensure that the civic employee whose job it was to wake everyone up for morning prayers wouldn't disturb it. And so they hired four people to carry him around on a table—that way his feet wouldn't touch the ground.

As a crucial corollary, the Chelmites don't *realize* they're worse off; they take the satisfaction that comes from the solving of the intellectual problem as the important thing, despite the worsening of their "real-life" situation. (In another story, for example, the poor townspeople of Chelm enable their impoverished citizens to eat rich cream by the simple expedient of renaming sour milk by that sobriquet.) Wit has its pleasures in the absence of other goods, but, in a culture that prizes wit so, it may end up inuring its practitioners to that absence. In so doing, it encourages (in its most exaggerated form) quietist indifference to its own suffering or problematic situation. The most extreme form of this may be Nathan Englander's story "The Tumblers," a tale of twentieth-century Chelmites who encounter the Nazi menace. Their not-so-comic incomprehension of the perils they face, of their magnitude, may suggest that foolishness, in this allegorical context, is a national and historical issue of great seriousness indeed.

The tension between the prizing of witty play and the concern that a surfeit of it may lead to no good was a hallmark of the beginnings of modern Jewish literature. Following the Jewish Enlightenment's general adherence to the cultural—and comic—standards of the Western European world around them, the would-be sophisticates and boulevardiers of the Haskalah attempted to master the art of wit. They saw their efforts in doing so as a continuation of the flexibility with language demonstrated by the Sephardic medievals, whose culture they admired deeply, and hoped their demonstration of same would lead to a social outcome like the one they pictured the Golden Age of Spain to have been: cosmopolitan, convivial coexistence. This linkage of wit, and humor, with full participation in the modern emancipated state loomed so important for many Jewish modernizers—and, in fact, some of the anti-Semites who opposed Jewish emancipation—that it led to the identification of the possession of a sense of humor with a truly civilized nature. And it led, in some precincts, to an identification of "Jewish humor" with the modern period itself.

That's a lot of pressure, and, as Oscar Wilde has taught us, nothing strains wit so much as the effort to be witty. A good bit of Haskalah comedy suffers from this malady; all too often the authors, self-congratulatory about their latest biting aperçu, seem to have failed to realize that they were more tendentious than funny. That said, what more often held them back in their entrée to the salons was more anti-Semitism than wit's failure—and, as the Haskalah made its way into Eastern Europe, it was wit itself which once more came into question. The challenge to it was posed by one of the Haskalah's opponents—a Hasidic rebbe who understood, perhaps better than anyone, the moral dangers of wit.

It would be easy to tell this story and suggest that polemical comedy was solely the province of the forces of modernity, bearing right on their side against the benighted figures of traditionalism, stuck in the Dark Ages. But this would hardly be fair to the dynamism, intelligence, change, and sense of humor of traditional Jewish culture, who saw, in these newfangled Haskalah idealists, fools ready to throw out the baby of centuries of Jewish tradition for a bathwater of uncertain temperature. The Enlighteners reserved much of their ire for Hasidim, as we suggested in the previous chapter; and the Hasidic master Nachman of Bratslav fought back, in a little story that took on the entire issue of Jewish modernity and neatly wrapped it up in a few short pages.

Nachman is not normally thought of as a comic writer, to put it mildly. Despite having died in 1810 at thirty-eight and having left no dynastic successors, he has an ever-increasing number of followers, many of whom poster the walls of the cities of Israel with slogans dedicated to him and who flock to his grave in Uman. He is best known for his mystical-ecstatic thought and a series of pseudo-fairytales which seem to be deeply disguised allegories of kabbalistic struggle and redemption. But those tales also have a great and wide sense of the human comedy about them, with a keen attunement to the reversals of understanding central to comedy.

This is particularly true of "The Tale of the Wise Man and the Simple Man," a not-at-all-simple fable in which the eponymous wise man, a clear stand-in for the members of the Haskalah Nachman would have encountered in his travels, is so clever that he outsmarts himself. Relying only on the hallmarks of the Enlightenment—empiricism, the data of his senses, and the logical reasoning he holds dear—he ends up reaching conclusions that are both treasonous (he denies his king because he has never actually seen him) and foolish (he steps into a deep muddy mire and won't get out because he insists it isn't there). Nachman takes the prerogative of the satirist—and the mystic—of turning things upside down, suggesting that it is the simple man who possesses wisdom and the wise man who is foolish.

Nachman's adoption of the forms of the folktale, in a story delivered in *proste mame-loshn* (simple Yiddish), also embraces the wisdom of a long-lived genre of Jewish wit: the folk saying, in its epigrammatic or psycho-ostensive varieties. Folk sayings, blessings, curses, hopes, and fears were often prime examples of a witty sensibility that one can find as early as the Talmud. ("If your friend calls you a donkey, put a saddle on your back," goes one such saying. "A pot in charge of two cooks is neither hot nor cold," goes another.) Jews all over the world have such pithy expressions—take, for example, the Judeo-Spanish *refrán*, which boasts sayings like "Because of just one little knife, we are Jews"; "Two Jews, three congregations"; and "A rabbi without a beard is worth more than a beard without a rabbi"—but for Ashkenazic Jews, at least, they may have reached their height in Eastern European culture, where the Yiddish curse can, at its best, be the baroque essence of witty play.

They can be creatively allusive. There's "May Titus' worm crawl into your skull," for example, referring to a midrashic legend depicting the punishment of the general, later emperor, who sacked Jerusalem, and his fateful punishment; or, alternatively, the more straightforward "may your bones be broken as often as the Ten Commandments." Or simply baroquely imaginative: "May you own one hundred houses with one hundred rooms in each house and twenty beds in each room, and may fever toss you from bed to bed." Or: "May you be blessed like a Sabbath candle—to burn at the top and melt at the bottom." Or: "May all your teeth fall out, except one to give you a toothache." Or the deceptively simple and pungent "May this happen to anti-Semites." There was a saying in the nineteenth century: "Spare me from gentile hands and Jewish tongues," and you can see why. The form has taken modern, Yiddish-inflected English iterations as well; from Ernst Lubitsch's version, "You should have a lot of money, but you should be the only one in your family with it" to the more recent politically charged internet sensation, "Yiddish Curses for Republican Jews." (One example: "May your child give his bar mitzvah speech on the genius of Ayn Rand.") But all of this can be seen, in its own way, as a rebuke to the elites who believe themselves to have a monopoly on wit.

AS THE PROMISES of the Enlightenment came to nothing, and as the forces of conservative reaction roared their way across Russia, the wittiness of the *maskilim* turned in upon itself, questioning the entire value of the intellectual project. Take, for example, this anticlerical joke whose bite goes beyond the rabbinical portrait:

> A rabbi who is trying to adjudicate between congregants. The first gives his side of the story; the rabbi, listening and cogitating, says, "You're right." The second, protesting, tells *his* side, and the rabbi says, "You know what? *You're* right." The rabbi's wife, hearing this exchange, bursts in and says, "They can't both be right!" To which the rabbi responds: "You know what? You're right, too!"

The intellectual ability to see both sides of a question can allow for the ability to cope with a wide variety of situations. But it's not particularly suited for the exercise and implementation of strong positions. (William Hazlitt termed wit "the eloquence of indifference" in his *Lectures on the English Comic Writers*.) Which has led some critics, such as Ruth Wisse, to suggest that Jewish comedy, certainly the Jewish comedy that exemplifies and elevates these sort of approaches, has ultimately been bad for the Jews, has replaced action with paralyzing wit. Or, to put it another way, in a joke Wisse tells in her own work on Jewish comedy:

> Two Jews traveling by wagon along a narrow road see boulders blocking their path. They stop to consider what to do, and as they sit there, a wagon approaches carrying two peasants. The Gentiles get out, roll up their sleeves, and shove the

rocks away. "There's goyish thinking for you," says one Jew
to the other. "Always with force."

Certainly there were writers for whom that position resonated. The
twentieth-century writers S. Y. Agnon and Eliezer Shteynbarg—to
take examples in Hebrew and in Yiddish—approached wit, during
the period between world wars, not as a cultural saving grace,
or even as an escape mechanism, but as an ironic way of ruefully
reflecting on their current circumstances. Shteynbarg's fables provide
wittily modernist versions of a very old genre, drawing on every
register of the Yiddish language to suggest the tensions of art and
life; Agnon's novels, demonstrating the clever, bookish allusions of
a world of Eastern European culture, are written after the desola-
tions of the Great War, and are consciously created and presented
as tombstones to a certain kind of intellectual life.

But that's not the whole picture: one could find channels for
witty vitality in the first half of the twentieth century, too. One
prime center of that energy was in Odessa, and particularly in Isaac
Babel's *Odessa Tales* of Jewish gangsterism, in stories like "Liubka
the Cossack" and "The King," in which Jewish gangsters take bribes
inside Torah scrolls and ambush opposite numbers from inside mock
Jewish funeral processions and shoot in the air because if you don't,
you might kill someone. But even that has an air of what has been
left behind: the wit of the streets is not the same as the wit of the
boulevards, and certainly not of the rows of yeshiva benches.

A joke along those lines:

A newly Enlightened young man, formerly of the yeshiva
world, goes to Krakow to visit the famous Krakow Heretic. He
presents the latter with a particularly pungent contradiction in
a late medieval rabbinic work; the Heretic mumbles that he's
unfamiliar with that particular work. Mildly discomfited, the
young man presents another proof, this one from a famous
Biblical commentator. The Heretic doesn't seem to follow.

This goes on, until the young man exclaims: "I thought you were a heretic. It turns out you're just an ignoramus!"

In the modern world, the heroes of wit, who had so often, for some at least, been masters of a particular kind of Jewish knowledge, had to grapple with the fact that that knowledge was being devalued as the coin of the realm. Transgressiveness didn't resonate if you no longer shared the same norms to transgress.

Decades later, a similarly barbed, ironic, rueful, and witty comment of Agnon's was recalled by Saul Bellow, who visited his fellow Nobelist in Jerusalem in the fifties, before either of them had won the prize. According to Bellow, Agnon gleefully reports that Heinrich Heine's work has been translated into Hebrew—now, Agnon says, "it's safe." An ironist like Agnon is well aware of the discrepancy between Heine's circulation in Hebrew and in German—as aware as he is of the notions of Jewish faith and perception that suggest that Hebrew is indeed, as the language of the Chooser who selected the Chosen People, the only eternal option. And of the recent historical circumstances that have rendered the ultimate rejoinder to the power of wit as an acculturating mechanism. . . . and yet, on the other hand, here are Bellow and Agnon in the Jerusalem of a Jewish state. The wheel turns round and round.

Bellow's literary reputation—in English—is in no small part based on his mastery of one of the strains of wit we've been discussing. Although the challenges of Jewish wit based on traditions of allusion-based wordplay might seem practically insurmountable in a language that bears little to no trace of them, Bellow's Judaization of the Anglo-American liberal and philosophical tradition is, along with Cynthia Ozick's "New Yavneh"–based Jewish English, probably the closest American Jewish literature has gotten to a comedy of high wit. Theirs is literature that demonstrates the intellectual quicksilver of the deeply educated, as they blend Joyce and James and Bertrand Russell and the Talmud and Maimonides. And they do this, crucially, to portray individuals who are all too often—to put it mildly—losers.

In that, they're different from the criers and kibitzers of such writers as Stanley Elkin, Bruce Jay Friedman, and Bernard Malamud: they have pretensions. The comic failure that the protagonists of works like *Herzog, Mr. Sammler's Planet*, and *The Puttermesser Papers* stumble into is a world that in their eyes should, at least, still operate on the animating belief in intelligence and culture, along with their belief that a philosophical solution that provides order, coherence, synthesis of the world is possible. (Bellow was frustrated with people who didn't read *Herzog* as a comic novel; "I was making fun of pedantry!" he said.)

The closest to high wit, perhaps, but only if you define "high wit" to exclude one of the high-water marks of American Jewish wit: the far more demotic—to use a word Bellow and his University of Chicago colleagues might have liked—world of the golden age of the American musical theater, of George Kaufman, Moss Hart, Stephen Sondheim. In all these cases, we can see the image of the outsider with a nose pressed against the glass looking to come in, and using cleverness and facility with language—as well as a knowledge of the language's repositories, its nooks and crannies and odd slang and slant rhymes, that outdoes many of the majority culture's representatives—that leads to the outsider becoming the culture's central ventriloquist. This was a feature of America, in which the old European idea of wit as a cultural doorkeeper was always complicated by the radical impulse to welcome the newcomer with a fast sense of humor ready at the draw. American salons—or, at least, their temples of mass culture—were willing to go where their European counterparts refused.

American temples of high culture were slightly slower to open their gates. The newspapers and magazines were more clubbable and gentile in the twenties, thirties, and forties, though there were exceptions. The one that proved the rule, S. J. Perelman, essentially wrote the book on wit. Perelman's work isn't deeply Jewish, the occasional Yiddishism notwithstanding. Though those occasions are delicious, like in the opening of his parody of Clifford Odets, "Waiting for

Santy," which takes off on Odets' leftism, relocating its Jewish roots to the North Pole. ("A parasite, a leech, a bloodsucker—altogether a five-star no-goodnick! Starvation wages we get so he can ride around in a red team with reindeers!" complains Riskin the gnome.) Perelman described his style as "mélange . . . a mixture of all the sludge I read as a child, all the clichés, liberal doses of Yiddish, criminal slang, and some of what I was taught in a Providence, Rhode Island school by impatient teachers." His approach—to mess with logic, to attack language by pulling it apart and putting it back together in deliciously absurd ways—has real continuities with the smart alecks and pastiche poets of Jewish yesteryear.

But his comments about mélange and clichés also serve as a harbinger for the fate of wit in American mass entertainment. By the middle of the twentieth century, as the glittering days of the Algonquin Round Table were fading, the concept was beginning to be surrounded by quotation marks. Jewish acts were probably as responsible for this as any. Not so much the Borscht Belters, whose rapid-fire patter and machine-gun punnery were avatars of an earlier kind of banter, albeit rendered in a yiddishe key; but rather the likes of Shelley Berman, Nichols and May, and Woody Allen.

Mike Nichols and Elaine May—the former a Russian immigrant, the latter a child of the Yiddish theater who played a character named "Baby Noodnik" on the Yiddish radio—were an inseparable twosome from their days at the University of Chicago. Incalculably influential in their brief performing career in the late fifties and early sixties, Nichols and May brought the improvisational scene-based sensibility of the Compass Players to the nightclub and stand-up milieu; they helped introduce a variety of "real people" to the stage; and, most important for our purposes, they articulated a different kind of wit in their routines, a simulacrum of wit, that rewrote the book on allusion. The medievals wrote poetry that demanded a deep knowledge and understanding of allusion's context in order to get the joke. Nichols and May, in their portrayals of show-biz phonies and blathering upper-middle-class professionals, name-dropped and buzzworded phrases and concepts that you only needed to know just enough to be in on it. The audience and author were united in the joke precisely *that* you didn't know any more than the basic things that everyone kind of knew. Everyone was faking.

Nichols did a sketch with the Compass Players called "How to Appear Cultured." With May, he did a ten-second version of Dostoevsky (in which May laughed wildly for ten seconds, Nichols said "Unhappy woman!," then: blackout). May had often not read or seen the things she was parodying; and Nichols, in 1961, put it most neatly when he said: "I object to the whole thing about 'intellectual' comedians. . . . These days you can be an intellectual in twenty seconds just by saying certain names: Nathanael West, Djuna Barnes, Dostoevsky, Kafka. Intellectual used to mean a process of thinking, or a body of knowledge. For some nutty reason, it doesn't anymore." In the same period, Shelley Berman, a fellow Compass Player who had worked intensely with them and the first comic to win a Grammy Award, did a routine with a booking agent on the phone which included Picasso, Hemingway, Albert Schweitzer, and the pope.

And then there was Woody Allen, the ne plus ultra of the phenomenon. Legend has it Woody Allen's first joke was that he was "at two with nature." That may not be technically accurate, but it tends to sum up something essential about the man: the idea that he'd rather be caught dead than caught outside, his intellectualism, the frantic name-checking of Kierkegaard and Dostoevsky. Whether it's in his frequent pieces for *The New Yorker*, his stand-up routines, or the dozens of films he's written and directed, the man born Allan Stewart Konigsberg in 1935 has been obsessed with matters of the mind over half a century. Accordingly, he's been portrayed as the apotheosis of a certain kind of Jew, and in turn, a certain kind of Jewish comedy.

As a stand-up comedian, Allen was never far, at heart, from the joke-writing sensibility he originated with. His most successful routines, by and large, involved painting word pictures for his stage (and record) audiences that would have often been impossible to render visually, although he would try with some success in his early films. (He called them "verbal cartoons.") But it was intellectualism—in no small part the middlebrow pseudo-intellectualism practiced and punctured so finely by Nichols and May, who at first had far more cultural credibility than Allen did—that played a small but increasing role in his work, particularly in the pieces he wrote for *The New Yorker*. Then, as now, *The New Yorker* was considered a bastion of cosmopolitan sophistication—Allen had idolized Perelman as a young writer—and so to write pieces tweaking the cultural concerns of its readers (literary biographies, Scandinavian plays, existentialist philosophy) was a natural, and became essential to Allen's reputation as an intellectual comic.

Allen's own intellectualism—his voracious reading, his engagement with philosophical and metaphysical questions—is undeniable, despite his protestations to the contrary. "I submit to you that I've been called an intellectual more times than I can count," he said in an interview. "I'm not an intellectual. It shines great on show business that I would be called an intellectual. After all, I *quote* intellectuals." And indeed, Allen's own intellectualism is often confused, or conflated, with his comedy's, which more precisely relies on the simulacrum of intellectualism.

"If the Impressionists Had Been Dentists," "The Kugelmass Episode," and "The Whore of Mensa" all rely, for their comic effect, on having some knowledge of the materials in question (Impressionism, *Madame Bovary*, and the contemporary New York cultural scene writ large, respectively). And at times, Allen, who took two and a half years of Hebrew in school, employs the same approach with Jewish-themed materials. "The Scrolls" and "Hasidic Tales, with a Guide to Their Interpretation by the Noted Scholar" picked up on the discovery of the Dead Sea Scrolls and the enthusiasm around the English-language version of Martin Buber's translation of and commentary on Hasidic tales. But in all these cases, Jewish and non-Jewish alike, nothing more is demanded than basic cocktail-party knowledge. Remarkable Judeo-Allenisms like "Whosoever loveth wisdom is righteous but he that keepeth company with fowl is weird" or "Why pork was proscribed by Hebraic law is still unclear, and some scholars believe that the Torah merely suggested not eating pork at certain restaurants" hardly require extensive familiarity with Jewish law and lore. Deploying such familiarity might actually dampen the comic effect.

Allen's O. Henry Prize–winning story, "The Kugelmass Episode"—in which Flaubert's Emma Bovary comes to New York–ish, Jewish life under the neurotic, sweaty hands of her Jewish Henry Higgins, the eponymous Kugelmass, with hilarious results—can be described as the encounter of Jews and Western literature played for comedy. One of the story's best jokes—that Kugelmass's antics change the actual text of Flaubert's novel—is a tribute to characters', and readers', vague handle on a book they claim to cherish. " 'I cannot get my mind around this,' a Stanford professor said. 'First a strange character named Kugelmass, and now she's gone from the book. Well, I guess the mark of a classic is that you can reread it a thousand times and always find something new.' " And in "The Whore of Mensa," that lovely noir parody in which the protagonist is hired to investigate a ring of intellectual prostitutes (when you can't talk to your wife about your need to discuss Melville, they're who you call), *everyone* is faking: the prostitutes are just going through the verbal motions, and even the Hunter College Bookstore is a front.

This may have started aspirationally for Allen. "Teachers were amazed in school because my references were sophisticated references," he's said. "I wasn't literate, but my references were witty. What I made jokes about at the youngest ages, before I really knew what I was talking about, were Freud and martinis, things like that, because I was emulating the witty patois of films that I saw, who I wanted to be, what I identified with." But, in his more mature work, this pseudo-intellectual comedy of surface wit, expanded to a sensitive look at the strained and effortful anxiety behind a witty façade. Recall those subtitles in 1977's *Annie Hall*, the same year "The Kugelmass Episode" was published, when Allen and Diane Keaton are trying to make intellectual conversation: "He probably thinks I'm a yo-yo," Keaton worries. "I don't know what I'm saying—she senses I'm shallow," frets Allen.

Joan Didion, writing about the iconic list of reasons to live that Allen's character gives at the end of 1979's *Manhattan*, writes: "This list . . . is the ultimate consumer report, and the extent to which it has been quoted approvingly suggests a new class in America, a subworld of people rigid in apprehension that they will die wearing the wrong sneaker, naming the wrong symphony, preferring Madame Bovary." This *New Yorker* (and New Yorker, with all that implies) audience—its circumscribed horizons best comically sketched in the famous Saul Steinberg cover of *The New Yorker*, "The View of the World From Ninth Avenue," published a year before *Annie Hall* premiered—was no less enamored of the currency of wit than the Jews of the Haskalah, or the rabbis of Babylonia.

And the anxieties, discontents, and concerns are no less present: Woody Allen, who is almost never anything less than dedicated to intellectualism in his movies, even the early comedies, is equally dedicated to the proposition that, to quote *This Is Spinal Tap* (sadly, not a part of our story), there is a fine line between stupid and clever. Intellectual characters in his comedies—Fielding Mellish in *Bananas*, Alvy Singer in *Annie Hall*, Boris Grushenko in *Love and Death*—are typically laid low through a kind of short-circuiting of their own intelligent intentions. Sometimes, Allen contends, intellect is nothing in the end compared to other human forces (most notably lust in the early movies; by the later films, such as *Mighty Aphrodite* or *Shadows and Fog*, that has given way to something like chance, necessity, or the simple fact of human frailty). And sometimes, he even entertains realization that intelligence itself is at fault for alienating the individual from his own best interest. Creepy as it is, this may be what Allen is suggesting in *Manhattan*: that Mariel Hemingway's Tracy might be the best thing for him. A difficult and questionable proposal, from Jewish comedy's most famous representative of wit. And one which reflects long-running concerns.

WHO ARE the heirs to Allen, Bellow, Ozick, and Nichols and May, in our postmodern cultural moment? If the barriers between high and low culture were blurring in Allen's *New Yorker* pieces, or under assault by the demands of humanity in Bellow's novels, today's magpie and pastiche culture threatens to obliterate those barriers entirely.

Threatens, but hasn't yet succeeded. Take, for example, a new talent for a new medium unimagined in Bellow's day (and one that hasn't managed to crack Allen's filmic consciousness). Twitter has served as an incubator for innumerable new comedians, and one of the best is Megan Amram, who tickles the intellectual funny bone by proudly flaunting her non-intellectuality. In her 2014 book *Science—For Her!*, she cultivates a persona that reflects the product of fevered misogynist thinking about women's perceived inability to excel in science. But her strong work on Twitter frequently refers to Jewish themes, particularly Holocaust-related ones. Despite her studied attempts to create a witless persona, or personae, she's a master of the medium, which suits the epigrammatic display of intellectual byplay known as wit. "No one knows if you're cool when you're a Jew because backwards yarmulkes look the same as normal ones," she notes. Or, on the first day of Passover: "DAMN today's the ONE day I forgot to smear my door post with lamb's blood." Or, not quite Jewish but apropos to the themes of this chapter, "I'm gonna go binge watch some words (read)."

On the other hand, it doesn't have to be short to be witty. Joshua Cohen's monumental novels, which cannot be accused of being epigrammatic, shine with his deep erudition. If Bellow's comedy comes from witnessing the failure of Western liberal enlightenment thinking at the hands of the barbarism of the Nazis and the follies of the sixties radicals (not that I'm comparing the two), Cohen's 2010 novel *Witz* suggests that language—witty, almost Joycean language—could be the only thing left as all the Jews on earth but one disappear. Mordantly, the world within *Witz* (and, perhaps, not just there?) seems to admire everything about Jews—their culture, their sensibility—except, of course, for the Jews themselves. And his most recent novel, *The Book of Numbers*, is a master class in that other field of wit, allusion, as its title suggests, rewriting Israelite desert wandering for the Internet age. Cohen's writing bristles with intelligence, playful, referential, and reverential.

Other contemporary works of modern American Jewish wit are analogously educated but more inner-directed—in good contemporary liberal fashion, they mock themselves for their education, partially ashamed (or "ashamed") of their pretensions, their wit, even as they express them. Take, for example, the spinning structure of Jonathan Safran Foer's 2002 novel *Everything Is Illuminated*, where the joke is clearly on the eponymous traveler, who's so highly educated he can't possibly succeed in the world around him (and whose flailings are imparted to us via the broken language of his tour guide Alex, whose comic creation is a linguistic tour de force). And in a different medium, there's the HBO series *Girls'* main character Hannah Horvath, as created and portrayed by Lena Dunham. You may empathize with the character or not; you may or may not view her, in her famous words, as "the voice of my generation. Or at least, a voice of *a* generation." But Horvath's constant self-sabotage and short-circuiting of her own artistic and intellectual possibility—out of liberal discomfort with her own privilege; out of a studied mismatch between cosseted education and the practical challenges of adult life; out of the difficulties of articulating a woman's voice in a society in which women's roles are in complex transition—provides one of the most indelible portraits of recent comic culture.

Many of today's Jewish comedians of wit, in short, are hyper-articulate, deeply educated, but often convinced of their own ignorance—or of the failures of the benefits of their own wisdom. In that, they're not much different from all of their predecessors. And knowing that is wisdom of its own, of a sort.

4

A View from the Bottom

Okay, ENOUGH SMART STUFF. LET'S TALK ABOUT FARTING.

Jews have been called the people of the book often enough, but there's recently been a movement among scholars to reclaim their history as people with bodies—and who find pleasure, comic and otherwise, in those bodies. Thus, the farting.

Flatulence, one might prefer; but not Mel Brooks, whose penchant for the vulgar punch line is as widely known as his fondness for expressing his Judaic affiliation. The classic scene appears in Brooks's 1974 parody Western *Blazing Saddles*, the movie that connected him with a mass audience and made him a household name during a decade in which the conception of American mass entertainment—comedy included—was being reshaped. (Soon after its release, it was second only to *M*A*S*H* as the highest-grossing screen comedy of all time.) A bunch of grizzled cowboys are sitting around the fire zestily consuming that frontier staple, beans. What follows is only what, presumably, comes naturally—at least to a particular cast of mind, and for someone attuned to what one Hollywood treatment after another had left out. Gas is expelled copiously as the grizzled cowboys, one after another, shift and stand to let one fly. That's it. That's the scene.

There was, it's fair to say, no farting on John Ford's range. But, in some ways, that made it not feel like home, not *heymish* at all. "In every cowboy picture," Brooks expostulated, "the cowboys sit around the campfire and eat 140,000 beans, and you never hear a burp, let alone a bloozer. For 75 years these big, hairy brutes have been smashing their fists into each other's faces and blasting each other full of holes with six-guns, but in all that time, not one has had the courage to fart. . . . What could be lower low comedy than a bunch of cowboys breaking wind around the campfire? But it worked. People were ready for it. It was a broad, brave truth that had always been on the back of everyone's tongue when they were watching straight Westerns."

Vulgarity and parody go hand in hand for Brooks. Parody— whether it be vulgar, obscene, or blasphemous—is always about bringing a dose of Brooks's "broad, brave truth" to something whose own traditions have become a little too stuffed-shirt, a little too accreted, too iconic. Brooks, describing his reworking of the script *Tex X*, famously commented that "we're trying to use every Western cliché in the book—in the hope that we'll kill them off in the process." This might seem like cultural vandalism, but it's exactly the opposite. To take Roger Ebert's immortal phrasing, borrowed from Brooks himself, it rises below vulgarity.

To be a parodist requires love, knowledge, and intelligent, even intellectual familiarity with a culture one feels oneself to be outside of. To parody a Western, or a silent movie, or a spy series, or a horror film, or a historical epic, or a sci-fi space saga, or a Hitchcock suspense flick, or . . . well, you get the picture, you have to have deep love for the material, in order to pay the close attention that allows you to hit the jugular while you're taking it down. And to be a clever vulgarist—rather than merely being vulgar—involves an intimate understanding of the pressure points of human society, of understanding that the human body's ridiculous nature is only ridiculous under the right times, conditions, and places—in the same way that the hallowed precincts of culture are ripe for being deflated by the right people.

The noted mid-twentieth-century psychoanalyst and scholar of Jewish wit Theodor Reik wrote in his treatise on the subject that "Jewish jokes almost never make fun, for instance, of physical handicaps or frailties, almost never mock at body deformities and ugliness." This may have been polemic, or lack of exposure to the broader canon of Jewish comedy, or just plain wishful thinking; but it's certainly not true. And it's not just Mel Brooks. Jewish humor *has* been body-obsessed, raunchy, vulgar, obscene, and blasphemous, from the very beginning. And it has always been precariously balanced between the poles of love and distance: of an intimate relation to the materials being parodied, of propping them up and taking them down.

SCHOLARS portraying Jews as "the people of the body" find their earliest evidence in the Bible. There are books in the Bible that are strange, and parodic, and vulgar, and, to use a favorite jargon term of the academics, "embodied." The first laughter in Jewish history—Sarah's laughter when she hears of God's promise of an heir to Abraham—trades on classic comic anxieties about male potency. Is a hundred-year-old man really going to be able to do what he needs to in order to provide her with an heir? Dick jokes are as old as comedy itself; just think of Aristophanes and all those on-stage phalluses. The body—and this body part in particular—has always been about power, having it and not having it. So it's not surprising that the greatest biblical jokes of this sort appear in and around the book of Judges, the closest thing Scripture has to action heroes.

One such judge is Ehud, whose opponent is Eglon, the king of Moab. Eglon himself is cut down to size by the author of the book in a simple, straightforward way: by making fun of his body and its functions. Quite simply, he's fat. Very fat. (His name, in Hebrew, derives from the word for "calf," and he's a fatted calf ready for the slaughter, there's little question.) When Ehud kills him, he does so in a particularly ignominious way, adding a scatological fillip to the comic mixture: he offers to tell Eglon a secret while the king sits in his bathroom. The king, not being the smartest tool in the shed, dismisses all his guards, whereupon Ehud stabs him in his fat so deeply that, in a detail relished by the usually fairly-laconic Bible, the offending dagger disappears entirely, not to be seen. The resulting smell from the viscera and suchlike is treated by the guards outside as Eglon's normal bathroom production, allowing Ehud to make a getaway. The sniggering intimation is that they're used to these sort of smells coming out all the time.

This kind of physical humor repeats itself in the book of Judges in the very next chapter. Sisera, the Caananite general opposing the Israelites, also meets his end ignominiously (from the biblical perspective): after being fed milk by Yael, he gets a phallic tent peg in the head, and expires both infantilized and feminized. Other enemies of the Jewish people meet similar fates elsewhere in the Bible. In the book of Numbers, the prophet Balaam is rendered professionally inadequate. Not only is he forced by God to bless Israel when he has been hired to curse them, in a scene that recalls to the modern reader Jim Carrey's truth-telling lawyer in the 1997 film *Liar Liar*, although with more moving poetry; he's mocked by his own donkey, who castigates his master for the kind of blindness even an ass can see through, crushing him into a wall to boot. (Rabbinic legend, interested in midrashically embroidering the humiliation, renders the talking ass as a romantic partner, reproaching its bestiality-inclined master.) The Babylonian king Nebuchadnezzar is stricken with insanity, forced to fend in the fields and eat grass like an animal; the great and mighty King Belshazzar, upon seeing the Writing on the Wall, pisses himself like a frightened child. Or, to put it in the slightly more refined language of the Bible, "the knots of his loins were released, and his knees knocked one against the other."

Much of this certainly seems vulgar, but not necessarily very funny, at least not by modern standards, and the connection to *parody* isn't necessarily so clear. To which one might say two words: Thomas Hobbes. Perhaps not surprisingly for a political philosopher whose whole worldview was structured around might—who's got it, who hasn't, who's giving it up to whom—Hobbes's theory of comedy was based on power. Hobbes suggests that comedy is based on what the critics have come to call *superiority theory*: you laugh at something because you find yourself superior to it. Or, as Hobbes put it in his typically elegant prose: "The passion of laughter is nothing else but sudden glory arising from a sudden conception of some eminency in ourselves by comparison with the infirmity of others, or with our own formerly." Usually this kind of superiority comes into play in one or two ways: physical or intellectual. We laugh, as Plato suggested in his *Philebus*, at people who are less knowledgeable than we are, or than they should be, and at those who are physically inferior. It's hard to argue with Hobbes that people *haven't*, over history and to this day, found the stupid, the slow, the defective, a source of merriment and mirth. If you don't like what that says about the human condition, you're probably better off not talking to the guy who famously defines that condition as nasty, brutish, and short.

Hobbes, who knew his Plato well, was also a subtle and careful reader of the Bible—*Leviathan*, for example, is studded with biblical references—and it's not surprising that his vision of comedy is influenced by some of the scenes depicted there. But as a champion of mainstream might, he focuses only on one side of the equation—the comic power of the strong. We've seen this scornful laughter, so common in the Bible, in other chapters; what's interesting here is the way this "ethnic humor" is manifested through vulgar, scatologically oriented, or low comic depictions of those mocked.

None of these manifestations display much of a parodic sensibility, but that's probably because they're also—in a condition rare in Jewish history—manifestations of a sense of Hobbesian superiority. They represent a comedy coming from the confidence that the Jews *are* the majority culture, the ones on top. The counterexamples from the Bible—the ones that *don't* seem to be about this kind of superiority and in fact, throw this very vision of superiority into question—appear, by and large and most prominently, after the challenge to Jewish superiority that was the destruction of the Temple. And these questionings—as questionings of received narratives so very often are—take that parodic form.

A powerful example, is the post-exilic (that is, post-destruction of the First Temple in 586 BCE) book of Jonah. It was probably first disseminated in late fifth century BCE; roughly the time of Aristophanes. It's an eccentric example, because the book of Jonah is generally not considered a work of comedy—in fact, since Talmudic times, it has been read on the holiest day of the Jewish year, in the afternoon service for Yom Kippur, with the result that it's usually thought of as a testament to the power of repentance. But any close look at the book suggests that it really doesn't fit into a straightforward model of repentance—or, for that matter, of anything.

Jonah, it seems clear, is a prophet of the Lord. Or, at least, the Lord contacts him to prophesy—not to Jews, but to the people of Nineveh, who have sinned mightily. Jonah runs away from the job, a not unknown strategy among prophets of the Lord (see: Moses, Jeremiah), but it's the only case of such a flight whose protagonist ends up being swallowed by a great fish (whether it's a whale or not isn't clear in the Hebrew original), prays from inside it, and is vomited out.

Jonah is also the only prophet whose prophecy is successful. In fact, he's *deeply* successful: if you go by word to action ratio, there's never been a more successful speaker in Jewish history. In the Hebrew, Jonah only gets the chance to say five words—*od shivim yom venineveh nehpakhet*, or "Nineveh will be overturned in seventy days"—when the entire city-state goes into a regular orgy of weeping and wailing, putting sackcloth and ashes even on their animals. This strikes me—and many scholars before me—as something of an overreaction. (It should not go unnoticed—as it certainly didn't to its contemporary readers—that this remarkable prophetic success may be in no small part thanks to the fact that the word of the Lord was, in this case, not rendered unto Jews.) Jonah's response to his remarkable success is surprisingly grumpy (at least, until you recall his generally dour mien throughout the book), and, in an ending to the book that has puzzled readers for centuries, he gets into a big argument about a gourd with God.

Most of the book's puzzles, though, can be solved by changing our frame of reference and thinking of the book as a parody of prophetic mission, rather than an account of the mission itself. This was an approach to the text, incidentally, adopted by the pamphleteer and Revolutionary War figure Thomas Paine, among others: "A fit story for ridicule," he wrote in his *Age of Reason*, "if it was written to be believed; or of laughter, if it was intended to try what credulity could swallow; for if it could swallow Jonah and the whale, it could swallow any thing." Jonah, unlike other prophets, doesn't verbally protest; his mission consists of him sleeping through the epic storm in the hold, during what should be a time of trial—and, for that matter, God's greatness is accepted by the other sailors, not him; and Jonah's prayer is a parody of the psalmic cry to God *de profundis*, from out of the depths, by literally being from out of the depths, the comic "realization" of an already clichéd poetic image.

Parodies are usually told by individuals on the margins, who don't have quite the same access to cultural power. The name Jonah ben Amittai appears earlier in the Bible: He was a man executed by Jereboam II, one of the evil northern kings. That's all we know about him. Whoever wrote the book of Jonah seems to have taken a minor, marginal prophetic figure and crafted a parodic narrative around him. One that not only tweaks his name, which can be translated as "Dove, son of Truthfulness"—unlike his Noahide predecessor, this dove sinks, not floats, and he hardly seems to have truth's best interests at his heart—but shows off the failures of Jewish prophecy by portraying a remarkable, incredible success. The comedy there is almost precisely that of, say, telling the story of someone who tried to make a failure by doing everything wrong and then went right.

If that line sounds familiar, it should: it's Max Bialystock's plaint, as he hears the raves coming in for *Springtime for Hitler*. Jonah isn't *The Producers*, not quite. But there are threads.

BY THE second century BCE, the book of Jonah had become sacred scripture, its parodic and vulgar elements sanded down by the sages along with any anxieties about prophetic power and relevance they might have raised. While the book of Esther achieved a similar status, canonically and liturgically speaking, *its* parodic and vulgar aspects went unchecked. To the contrary; they were actively encouraged, befitting its central location as part of the carnivalesque Purim holiday.

Comedy and carnival go hand in hand, even etymologically. The Greek origins of the word "comedy" probably come from the words for "processional celebration" or "revelry" (which itself meant "village festival," which probably shaped Aristotle's definition of comedy as revolving around improvisations in the form of "phallic songs," whatever that may mean.) Certainly the Jews' celebrations in Shushan/Susa at the end of the book of Esther are celebratory. And while almost all Jewish holidays have some form of festive component, Purim was different from the very start, in that it seemed to allow for a kind of bodily celebration, a safety valve to let off some steam. We'll get to the phallic songs momentarily; let's first focus on the drunkenness and murder slapstick.

Wine and festive celebration are directly associated in Jewish culture; and, in the famous dictum of the Talmud, one is required to get so drunk on Judaism's most festive holiday that one is incapable of distinguishing between the genocidal anti-Semite Haman and the Jewish hero Mordechai. The rabbis' eagerness to fulfill that commandment, relates the Talmud, leads to what I think may be one of the earliest rabbinic jokes:

> Two rabbis, Rava and R. Zeira, get together for the Purim feast, and Rava, in his cups, takes out a sword and beheads his colleague. When he sobers up and sees what he's done, he's of course horrified and brings him back to life. Rava invites his friend to a Purim feast the next year; R. Zeira declines, saying: "Miracles don't happen every year."

A typical Jewish comic balance, putting wild revelry against ironized caution: safety valves are all very well and good, but enough's enough.

Rabbis' bodies get a lot of ink in the Talmud, whether it be one rabbi's gross obesity, another's remarkable penis size, and so forth. Precisely why these elements survived the editor's quill is a matter of much speculation, but one reason must be that parody and vulgarity is in some part a cultural safety valve. If the rabbis' intellectualism—the power and the authority that comes with their mastery of various kinds of wit—is the font and foundation of their cultural power, they're well aware of the possibility that it makes them seem like, well, understuffed shirts, and they need a little obesity and vulgarity to even up the scales for their less elite audiences. This allows their culture—and their cultural text, the Talmud—to truly contain everything: parodic and vulgar elements are part of the same structure, as the safety valve is part of the machine. (Which also allows for the possibility, of course, that the rabbinical elites and editors of the Talmud were also human beings who were fond of penis jokes.)

Anyone who's watched *South Park* or *Family Guy* is well aware of the cartoonish nature—and comic appeal—of scatology. Treating the body as a kind of bag of disgusting stuff is the exact opposite, the parody one might say, of the same philosophical and theological principles that render the human as the image of the divine. It really shows off the difference between the original and the reproduction. The book of Jonah is a case in point, with all that vomit. This prophetic parody may have created a parody of its own: the Apocryphal book of Tobit, probably written in the second or third century BCE. Tobit features an arrogant and unpopular protagonist who is blinded because a bird shits in his eyes and is cured because a magical charm made of fish gall smeared on him by his son smells so bad even the demons afflicting him can't tolerate it. I'm not making this up.

Tobit is a book set in the diaspora, and its lessons—essentially, that Jews should keep their faith and marry one another only, though the extremely quarrelsome and grumpy relations in Tobit's family suggest the author may be presenting this ironically—are diasporic lessons. Which brings us back to the book of Esther, not so much in the original text, but in the way that the book was expanded and used through the ages, starting with the rabbinic period. For most of traditional Jewish culture the prime instances of parody, vulgarity, and scatology—those potentially subversive elements—were given their safety valve within the culture, carefully attended to within a very specific and bounded context: the Purim holiday. The fact that Purim takes place between winter and spring—that time where death gives way to rebirth, where the calendars both pagan and Christian are filled with carnival festivals, shouldn't go unnoticed. As we've seen over and over again, Jewish comedy often invests its particular content in neighboring cultural forms.

One particularly interesting example is the midrashic piling on, literally, of Haman's humiliations. Drawing on a textual crux that describes Haman, after leading a triumphant Mordechai through the streets, returning to his wife and family *avel vechafui rosh* ("mourning, and with his head covered") the rabbinic authorities use this as an opportunity to create a mocking, scatological scenario that expands on the words in a way that allows for some sniggering at Haman's expense. The midrash relates that Haman's daughter, who is certain, given Haman's own previous confidence about his place in the king's favor, that the figure leading the king's horse through the streets will be Mordechai, is prepared for the parade: She stands at a rooftop with a pile of excrement, ready to douse the Jew. She dumps the bucket, but, given the switch in persons, the human waste falls on her father instead. When he looks up, dripping, and she realizes what she has done, she is so distraught and mortified that she plunges from the roof to her death. And so Haman returns home, in mourning for the death of his daughter and with his head covered—dripping and reeking with ordure.

Those who wonder about the cavalier disposal of Haman's daughter for the comic effect of the narrative (and, indeed, to solve a textual puzzle) miss the point: Haman's daughter is not so much "real" as a set piece designed for both the joy of explaining the text elegantly and for getting to envision a Haman, the traditional archenemy of the Jewish people, *covered in shit.*

One might think that this kind of vulgar comic perspective on the Purim story would begin and end with Haman (or, perhaps, Haman's family). But the real comic engine of the piece ends up being Mordechai. In a move that will have remarkable consequences, the Talmudic and midrashic Haman is portrayed as an *agelast*—that is, the man who doesn't laugh, who has no sense of humor, the "killjoy," as the critic Harry Levin called the type. We could also see him, if we want to get into classical comedic terminology, as an *alazon*, "the pompous fool, the pretender who affects to be more than he actually is": for Jewish comedy, Haman becomes a never-ending catalyst. Agelasts make their debut in Roman comedy—they were a staple of Plautus's plays—and the move from "stupid, fat gentile" to "unfunny gentile" as an ultimate mark of disfavor will resound down the centuries of Jewish history, and Jewish comedy. But to understand the history of its inverse—that it's the Jew who gets all the punch lines—we have to talk about Jews and theater, since for most of Western civilization, the theater is comedy's birthplace.

Perhaps surprisingly, Jews started out with a good deal of antipathy to the theater. Or maybe not so surprising, given the theater's origins in pagan religious custom. Rabbis prohibited attendance at theaters and circuses, suggesting that those who did attend were unworthy of rendering testimony. And in a setting in which all actors were male, the portrayal of female roles violated the biblical interdiction of cross-dressing.

There was one period of the Jewish calendar, though, that was an exception to the general rule, a rule which softened into something more like a cultural more in the medieval and early modern period, as theater became increasingly detached from its religious origins. That period, of course, was around the holiday of Purim. Then, amateur groups would put on performances in styles not too dissimilar from those adopted by their Christian neighbors: biblical plays of drama and spectacle, such as Jonah and the whale and the selling of

Joseph, were particularly popular. The most popular of all was the dramatization of the Esther story. It was generally performed, before the birth of the professional Jewish theater in the late nineteenth century, by traveling students seeking to make money for their family and their journey home for the Passover holiday.

These amateur theatricals, like their fictional companions in Shakespeare's *A Midsummer Night's Dream* (staged around the time these Purim plays were at their height), were often rude in both senses of the word. Staged in the long end of someone's living room or the hall of an inn, they weren't heavy on scenery or props. They relied instead, it seems, on physical business, dance, and performance heavily indebted to the Italian commedia dell'arte. They could also be shockingly crude. Take these selections from one of the few *purim-shpils* of the period that have survived. Here's Mordechai talking up Esther to the king (well, sort of):

> King, my dear, I heard it announced,
> That there was a search on for a young delight for you,
> I mean, a whore, or should I say a virgin. . . .
>
> First of all: She is shaped like a frog.
> A nose like a hare's.
> A brow like a bear's hind parts.
> Ears like a donkey's, front and back.
> A pair of tits—whoever wants to can use 'em.

And, to get a sense of the original Yiddish, an unforgettable couplet from the period. Mordechai says to Ahasuerus: *Halt mir der shtekn/ In arsh zolst mikh lekn*: "Hold my stick, and lick my ass."

Perhaps cutting down biblical figures to size is old news. We've seen Abraham the little rascal, after all, and Jonah the parodic prophet. But the Purim plays really press those sexual/scatological limits, and their parody even ventures into the sphere of the theological—or, to put it another way, the seemingly blasphemous. Take Mordechai's parody of the *Vidui*, the sacred Jewish confessional (the capitalized words are in Hebrew, almost all, except a few of the latter names, taken from the original text):

FOR
I go gladly with young girls into the stable.
THE SIN
Much more gladly to bed.
THAT WE HAVE COMMITTED
Even with a widow.
BEFORE YOU
Quite quickly I do it.
ABRAHAM SINNED
Has a large shop,
Makes all the young girls lame.
ISAAC SINNED
His thing is quite sharp,
Makes all the girls witty.
GEDALIAH sinned
He has a large awl,
Makes all the girls brides.
GUMPL SINNED
He has a big hobble,
Makes all the girls a big rumble.
MOSES SINNED
He has a big one,
Pokes all the girls with it.
MEYER SINNED
He has a big pair of jewels,
Like the door of a barn.

Where to begin? There's the intrusion of crass sexual innuendo into the Purim story—and by the ostensibly virtuous Mordechai, no less. If that's not bad enough, it seems he holds nothing sacred, not even the patriarchs (who are largely commended for their penis size rather than their ethical behavior or religious fidelity; here are those Aristotelian phallic songs we were talking about). And, perhaps most blasphemously of all, the Mordechai character—who served as the narrator, the audience's stand-in, and was the most prone of all the perfomers to "break the fourth wall" and offer asides to the audience—offers the latter comments in a parody of the prayer recited on Yom Kippur explicitly to express a catalog of one's sinful behavior. Suffice it to say Mordechai doesn't seem too apologetic.

There's another thing to note, less vulgar, perhaps, but equally parodic, and certainly not as obvious in translation. Mordechai's speech is bilingual, mixing the *Vidui*'s Hebrew with his Yiddish comments, which also allows it to parody the then common style of biblical and Hebrew interpretation. And the rhymed linguistic playfulness—less pungent, maybe, but no less important to the comedy—working off the juxtapositions between the high, sacred Hebrew, and the regularly spoken Yiddish reminds us that the word "vulgar" is, of course, etymologically related to the common speech. Jewish comedic artists used this linguistic byplay to achieve the heights of learned wit; and they could use it in brilliantly low keys, too.

The fact that a parody of learning, or at least of liturgy, sneaks into the Purim play is a reminder that Purim parody—and Jewish parody more generally—is located all over the intellectual spectrum. Witty parodies of rabbinic interpretation and Christian writings are located in the Talmud, for example. Many of these are too technical for readers unacquainted with Talmudic logic, but an analogous example can be found in a remarkable text dating from eighth- to tenth-century Iraq, *The Alphabet of Ben Sira*. This book, which, like the Purim stories, mixes its share of scatology along with its wit, focuses loosely around a wunderkind named after the Ben Sira who wrote the Apocryphal book of Ecclesiasticus: his birth, the result of accidental incest (involving the prophet Jeremiah's semen floating in bathhouse water his daughter bathed in, after he was forced to publicly masturbate), his miseducation, his smart-ass answers to Nebuchadnezzar (along with curing his daughter of excessive flatulence), and so on.

Consider Ben Sira's claim on his paternity. Born with teeth and the power of speech, he opens his mouth and says:

> "The son of Sira am I, the son of Sira!" His mother said to him, "My child, who is this Sira—is he a gentile or a Jew?" Ben Sira responded, "Mother, Sira is Jeremiah, and he is my father. And why is he called Sira? Because he is the *sar*, the ruling officer, over the officers [of the gentile nations], and he is destined to make all of them and their kings drink the cup of punishment. . . . Just add up the numerical equivalents of the letters in the name Jeremiah, which come to 271, and those in the name Sira, which also add up to 271 [thus proving that Jeremiah is the same as Sira]!" His mother said to him, "But if this is true, you should have said, 'I'm the son of Jeremiah.'" Ben Sira replied, "I *wanted* to say that, but it was too shameful to suggest that Jeremiah had sex with his daughter!"

In order to understand the comedy here, you have to know how *gematria*, a kind of numerological interpretive move common to rabbinic midrash works, as well as possess some basic etymological chops (for the *sar/sira* pun). In order to really *get* it, you have to know the specific biblical and midrashic Jeremiah-related texts that the book is hilariously parodying. Different people, depending on their levels of knowledge, education, and textual familiarity and sophistication, appreciated the parody in different ways: which is true of almost all parodies, and certainly the other types of Purim parodies that flourished through the medieval and early modern period.

For example, medieval Purim festivities were well known, following the Christian traditions of carnival and king-for-a-day, for their "Purim rabbis." The Purim rabbi might simply be the local fool, participating in the overthrow of social hierarchy common to the carnival, but individuals so dubbed could also deliver *purim torah*—which could be extremely detailed and recondite parodies of rabbinic sermons which would be hilarious, but to an extremely limited audience. (This wasn't just a Jewish thing: the Goliards, clerical students at the new universities of the early medieval period, did this sort of thing regularly, though scholars have yet to find a connection between the Goliards and the Jewish learned parodists.)

Though the sermons, orally delivered as they were, largely didn't survive, similar written parodies of rabbinic material from the same period may give us a sense of them. Take the Talmudic parody *Tractate Purim*, for example, probably written in the early sixteenth century, although the tradition goes back centuries earlier, to include works written by figures we've seen before—Kalonymos b. Kalonymos and Immanuel of Rome. (The earliest parody we know of, a circa twelfth-century *Hymn of the Night of Purim*, which parodies one for the night of Passover, plays on the idea of the latter being a night of divine protection, a *leil shimurim*, and transforms it—*à la* the garb of the medieval wine song—into a night for drunkards, a *leil shikorim*.) A sample:

> Said R. Keg: said R. Jug: Scripture says, "Remove the evil from your midst" (Deut. 21:21). And evil is none other than water, for it is written "but the water is bad and the land causes bereavement" (2 Kgs 2:19). This supports the view of R. Old Wine, for R. Old Wine said the generation of the flood was only punished because they drank water on Purim, as it says of them, "every plan devised by his mind was nothing but evil all the time" (Gen 6:5). It was also thus taught, whoever drinks water on Purim has no portion in the World to Come, as it says, "the people quarreled with Moses: 'Give us water to drink,' they said (Exodus 17:2)." The meaning is that had they asked for wine, they would have a portion in the world

to come, as it says, "and Noah began to plant a vineyard" (Gen 9:20).

Trust me, if you were deeply enmeshed in a rabbinic background and had studied the Talmud for years, you would find this a dead-on, hilarious parody of rabbinic literature. Parodies of this sort—and, as one of the earliest scholars of the topic noted, "It is no exaggeration to say that Jewish parody contains the entire Jewish literature in miniature; it would indeed be easy to make a collection of parodies representing the Bible, Talmud, Midrash, Liturgy, Zohar, Codes, Responsa, and Homilies"—continued through the middle ages and into modernity, particularly in the rabbinical seminary culture of the yeshiva. An illustrative anecdote, about *purim torah* in the famed nineteenth- and twentieth-century yeshiva located in Volozhin (currently in Belarus):

> During R. Itzeleh's tenure as head of the yeshiva [Isaac Volozhin, head of the yeshiva 1821–1849] . . . R. Mordechai Gimpel Yaffeh, one of the best of the students, was chosen as Purim rabbi. When it came time for him to deliver his lecture, the students gathered around him. R. Itzeleh, too, listened. The Purim Rav delivered a sharp and well-reasoned discourse to answer an apparent contradiction between a dictum of the Jerusalem Talmud and a legal ruling cited by Maimonides. The students turned to R. Itzeleh and complained; the Purim rabbi had not fulfilled the requirements of delivering a lecture that was not substantiable. R. Itzeleh laughed and said: "The legal reasoning on its own is true Torah, but the dictum and the ruling on which it was based do not exist."

Most of this material would have been largely unintelligible to anyone other than a small cadre of male students who had spent years in yeshiva study. Other material, though, was more intellectually accessible, like the parodies of disputations over matters of metaphysics and theology. While their actual counterparts were sources of deep anxiety to the Jewish community, as we saw earlier, their parodic counterparts are of far less import, except as entertainment value. Here are the Jewish holidays, for example, arguing over which is superior, in a Yiddish text from 1517:

> "I don't wish to put it off any longer," said Passover, stepping forward. "I want the prize. On my day they started to tell the story, God chose my night and He also parted the Red Sea."
>
> Hanukkah said, "I'm so delighted—I've got my revenge. No one can stomach your food, people cook a lot better on my day. Young and old are cheered by the sight of me. So keep quiet, you talk too much!"
>
> . . .
>
> "I, Purim, I'll catch you. On my day they cook the best and not the worst. Israel was saved, and Haman was hanged."
>
> Hanukkah replied wisely, "You are my inferior, for I last a whole eight days, and even that, I feel, is too brief."

And here are wine and water, in similar debate:

> "You should praise me," the wine cried haughtily. "I am poured on the sacrificial altar, two quarts of me each day. People pay high prices for me and they store me in a fine tent while they spill you on the ground."
>
> "Don't brag at my expense," the water yelled. "I'll tell about how you made Lot's daughters commit a horrible sin. Lot poured wine down his throat, and that's nothing to flaunt, for he made both his daughters pregnant!"

These parodies, despite their reliance on some information about custom or ritual which would have been basic knowledge in traditional Jewish society, are neither overly low or highbrow; not entirely unvulgar (there's that Lot reference), but not overly so; gently poking at the bounds of decorum, but going no further. There are other, similar creations, like Purim mock calendars/almanacs, which get the months mixed up and put the holidays consistently in the wrong place.

Mikhail Bakhtin, in his pathbreaking study *Rabelais and His World*, presents the early modern period as a world of constant struggle between official culture and marketplace culture, between the world of the ruling and the unruly, with carnival and carnivalesque humor as a legislated and licensed voice of rebellion—in other words, a safety valve that's really about reaffirming institutional control. Bakhtin didn't talk about the Jews, but in his and others' discussion of the Feast of Fools and the Boy-Bishop, the mock saints' lives, the liturgical parodies, the humorous centos where biblical verses are rearranged to make new texts, medieval and early modern parodies traverse the spectrum from high to low, elite to popular. The bottom was viewed as an essential part of the whole, even by the top.

In other words, whatever we might think of these works' ostensible blasphemy, or what pull their parody might exercise on the foundations of the culture and society, we should probably think twice. These works were produced, disseminated, and enjoyed by people who cherished traditional culture, and rabbinic culture. Many of those same Purim players were spending their months and years in yeshiva. These parodies were far more about love than distance.

Of course, as the centuries went on, not everyone felt exactly the same way.

MODERNIZING JEWS concerned about their acceptance into non-Jewish society were particularly anxious about much of this medieval comedy, feeling it wasn't ready for Enlightenment prime time. Haskalah activists were by no means the first to try to censor vulgar comic material: *The Alphabet of Ben Sira* had its share of outraged readers, including some suggesting it was an anti-rabbinic forgery, and there were opponents in the yeshiva world to the *purim-shpil*, feeling that it was inappropriate frivolity for the students. But the right-thinking members of the Haskalah might have taken it to a new level, making the reformation of the Purim play one of their first literary goals as part of their effort to present the kind of cultural face amenable to the salonnieres of Enlightenment Berlin. Plays like *Silliness and Sanctimony* were designed as refined Purim plays to be performed in the new educational institutions they were forming, to do nothing less than cultivate a new Jewish sense of humor.

This didn't last long: since it wasn't like the Haskalah reformists were immune to the blandishments of parody and vulgar, bodily comedy. This was especially so as the Haskalah movement encountered Hasidim in Eastern Europe, and increasingly switched to Yiddish, the so-called vulgar tongue. As we've mentioned earlier, Haskalah writers believed these Hasidim to be the living Jewish antithesis to the Age of Reason: foolish and superstitious, gullibly led around by their corrupt leaders. The Hasidim begged to differ: but their mystical notions of the necessity of elevating the physical world by engaging with it (thus the accounts of Hasidic rebbes dancing, singing, eating—they were attempting to invest those actions with sacredness) would make them easy targets for a series of accounts that present them as vulgar, gluttonous sex maniacs, inveterate gamblers, or vulgar ignoramuses.

We've already seen jokes to this effect. Many of these attacks were also achieved through parodies of the credulous accounts of followers, or of the typical hagiographic Hasidic tale, the kind you might find in a collection like *In Praise of the Ba'al Shem Tov*. And they're aided, not infrequently, by a healthy dose of obscenity and scatology. In Joseph Perl's *The Revealer of Secrets*, for example, the Hasidic rebbe expires ignominiously when he drunkenly falls out of a bathroom window; shades of the account of Eglon's death, two thousand years earlier. The resonances are entirely intentional. For the Haskalah, the Hasidim are just as dangerous to Israel as the Moabites were.

If *The Revealer of Secrets* parodies Hasidic speech in a Western literary form, the epistolary novel, Perl's fellow maskilic traveler Isaac Mayer Dik—who has *his* Hasidic rebbe meet a similar fate in the satire "The Gilgul"—takes on more traditional Jewish genres. Not just the supernatural testimonial of the reincarnated spirit of "The Gilgul": his pseudo-Talmudic tractate *Masekhet Aniyut* ("Tractate of Poverty"), credited pseudonymously to "The pauper, the head of the poor, Rabbi Great Pauper," which includes notes "from those sages of the paupers/idlers who have spent their days in the investigation of poverty." One pseudo-law reads:

> Anyone of Israel may be acceptable to perform the services of matchmaking, cantoring, and school-teaching, even those who have never read the Torah in all their days or who have never gone to school. Rabbi Pauper/Idler (*batlan*) says: even someone who is a stutterer and an ignoramus.

Dik's parody, like other Haskalah parodies, has polemical bite. Here, it critiques traditional educational and vocational practices. But if Dik could still hope his parodic efforts would subversively lead to social change, Mendele Moykher Seforim would use the form to dismiss such Enlightenment-oriented hopes as quixotic, in his parody of Cervantes's greatest work. We've already spoken about how 1878's *The Travels of Benjamin III* (translated into Polish as *The Jewish Don Quixote*) stands in as an attack on the possibilities of Jewish political power and action more generally; but what wasn't mentioned earlier was how brilliantly that point was couched along the lines of its illustrious comic predecessor. Mendele's Benjamin sets off on an epic quest for personal and national glory (and, it should be said, to get away from his harridan wife), but he isn't able to get much past his own backyard. Like Don Quixote, his quest is doomed to failure; but here—as his own cowardice, his Sancho Panza Sendrel's overly accommodating and quietistic nature, and the depredations of local Jews he encounters shows—the failure lacks the tragic nobility of Cervantes's hero. It's replaced by unease about

Jewish ignominity. (Especially since, to accentuate Benjamin's and Sendrel's low situation, Abramovitch occasionally covers them in sewage and ordure: scatological comedy continues to reign.)

Still, Yiddish parody—as it made its way toward the twentieth century—remained optimistic in a certain structural sense. With its dips into and nods toward Western literary currents and older Jewish strains, it could serve as a watchword for the possibilities of a self-consciously modern Jewish literature more generally. If you are parodying Western literature and culture, after all, it means you have internalized the thematic and stylistic turns and preoccupations of that culture—and are illustrating how they can thrive (albeit comedically, and in a slanted fashion) in your own cultural idiom. It didn't hurt that Yiddish was perceived by its speakers as a particularly flexible language open to the inclusion in its texts of various other languages, which meant parodic byplays were available in that context, too. It might be Yiddish songs whose melody and rhyme schemes were taken from Polish cabaret, songs which both embraced and questioned Jewish participation as a minority in that territorial culture. Or Itzik Manger's retelling of traditional Jewish Bible stories in ballad form, creating a natural tension between the elevated biblical figures and the earthy, melodramatic, pathos-driven characters who conventionally populated the form:

> Lot—it's disgusting—it's got to be said—
> You and your nightly carouse—
> Yesterday in the Golden Hart . . .
> What a terrible scandal that was.
> Manger the tailor can do such things,
> But it simply won't do for you.
> You've a couple of daughters to raise, you're rich—
> Knock wood—and besides, you're a Jew.

But Manger's treatment of the book of Esther sounded a more sobering note about the possibilities of cultural integration as symbolized by parody. There, he interpolates a love-struck tailor into the biblical book, one who attempts to assassinate Ahasuerus because of his love for the queen. But Haman, recast as the operator of a contemporary anti-Jewish newspaper who spreads *Protocols*-like messages of Jewish perfidy in the wake of his failed attempt, displays the failure of artistic wit in the face of encroaching, eliminationist anti-Semitism.

Other approaches to the "Jewish question" we've seen advanced in the face of emancipation's failures also were vulnerable to the possibilities of parody. Zionists arriving in prestate Palestine produced their own parodies on all sides of the ideological equation. A 1931 takeoff of the Passover haggadah, *From Egypt to Here*, for example, asks the reader to "pour out thy wrath" against the British, "the Gentiles who have deceived you and against the commissions whch did not invoke your name." At the same time, it cast, in the tale of the four sons, different representatives of modern Jewish politics in the three less complimentary roles (the wicked son is a revisionist; the simple son is a binationalist; the son who does not know how to ask, a communist). Other works from the pre-state period took on ultra-Orthodoxy, and one recondite Talmudic parody from 1913 satirized the debate over what language to teach in primary schools, Hebrew or Yiddish. Later generations of Israelis would be similarly sacrilegious: One example, from the Lebanon war, took a classic folk song about being buried in the first Jewish winery in pre-state Palestine and changed the lyrics. The original:

> When we'll die
> They will bury us
> In the winery of
> Rishon Le-Tsiyon.
> There are pretty gals there
> Who serve glasses
> Full of wine [which is]
> Reddish red

The parody:

> When we'll die
> They will scrape us
> With a scraping knife
> Off the tanks' walls.
> There are pieces there
> Of burnt flesh
> In the colors of
> Red and black.

As you can imagine, there was an outcry, and the army moved quickly to shut down the image of soldiers singing this on television.

But Zionism wasn't the only ideology employing—or rife for—parody. In the early Soviet Union, "red haggadot" used examples from the Passover service to discourage celebrating the holiday, or performing other religious rituals, for that matter. Socialists in England and in America used the book—and the story of the Exodus—to create works like the Socialist Haggadah (first appearing in the London *Worker's Friend* in 1887) and Morris Winchevsky's 1895 "A Socialist Parodies the Ten Commandments," which reads, in part:

> *I am the Lord thy God* and mammon is my name . . . *Thou shalt not take my name* . . . Never swear falsely unless by doing so you are adding to your bank account . . . *Thou shalt not murder* . . . No matter how vast your treasures, this is too heavy a sin for you, my son. On the other hand, do not upset yourself if someone brings you the news that one of your workers has had his head split open by a machine in your factory.

THE REAL RESONANCE of socialist movements among immigrant American Jews notwithstanding, the ideology embraced most quickly, and broadly, was Americanization itself. The traditional language of Jewish parody was often employed to address the questions acculturation brought. Gerson Rosenweig's Hebrew *Tractate America*, for example, included the Talmudically flavored passage: "The wise men have counted seven characteristics in greenhorns: they eat ravenously, walk in the middle of the street, curse the name of Columbus, corrupt their language [by mixing it with English words], ask advice but do not take it, and cheapen the labor market." But soon enough parody became a means to peek through the generational divide between immigrants and immigrants' children, and to provide a cymbal sting of ethnicity to the joke of Judaizing something that was deeply and firmly American—like the immigrants' children themselves had largely become, or, at least, could aspire to. Yiddish became, as it had with the *purim-shpils*, part of the parodic joke. But instead of bringing the epic past or transcendent present into the earthiness of the everyday, it became a reminder of something vaguely in the past, something at an increasing distance, which generated a complex mix of affection and alienation. Given the complicated twists and turns of Americanization, these parodic reminders took two forms. They suggested the distance between "American Jewish" and "American" identities, and, conversely, jabbed at how American cultural identity was actually becoming Jewish at its core, despite its Jewish creators' frequent efforts to elide the fact.

Let's take examples in song. Mickey Katz was a household name among Jewish communities in the mid-twentieth century, whose parodies mixed (or *shpritzed*) Yiddish liberally into songs from the American mainstream. Boys and girls everywhere knew "The Ballad of Davy Crockett," featuring the "king of the wild frontier" who was "born on a mountain top in Tennessee" and who "killed him a bear when he was only three." In a 1955 song, Katz reimagined the frontiersman as Duvid Crockett, born on Delancey Street, whose exploits as a three-year-old revolved around the flicking of chickens.

Both Crocketts go west: David to leave behind a glorious legend and legacy (in the song, at least); Duvid to go to Vegas, play craps, and lose his shirt. "He went home *"naket*," says the song—a final rhyme with "Crockett." Whether or not the listeners understood every one of the Yiddish words that speckled Katz's songs—and chances are a good number did, at least from childhood—the sense of comic minimization, the jarring mixing of worlds, that Yiddish provided came through. And it came through loud and clear: "Duvid Crockett, King of Delancey Street" sold two hundred thousand copies and hit number two on the charts. Katz's fifties antics—propping himself on a deli butcher's block surrounded by salamis on the cover of an album, wearing a cowboy outfit and claiming he came from the "Bar Mitzvah" ranch—led the way for other Jewish parodists in the decade to come.

And some of those parodists took slightly different approaches: like the far more popular Allen Sherman, who would grow famous by working in—and against—the quintessentially American idiom of the folk song. Sherman, who grew up in Chicago in the 1930s and attended the Yiddish theater there, first turned his comic attentions to Broadway, sensing—long before many others did—the Jewish heart and sensibility beating behind those all-American plays. He brought it out in parodies of Broadway musicals he performed for private audiences in the 1950s—*My Fair Lady* became "My Fair Sadie"; *South Pacific* "South Passaic." A Friars' Club roast for Jewish studio mogul Jack Warner featured a parody of *My Fair Lady* where the flower girl speaks too perfect English for anyone to understand in American Jewish circles, but a Yiddish-accented Jew "comes to Liza's rescue and promises to teach her how to speak English so perfect that in six months she will be elected president of Hadassah."

Sherman understood that his parody, as opposed to, say, Katz's, was about bringing out the hidden Jewishness behind American mass culture. Introducing those parodies to family and friends, he would say, "These songs are what would happen if Jewish people wrote all the songs—which, in fact, they do." But unable to produce his Broadway parodies due to copyright restrictions (i.e., the refusal of some of the writers to allow their works to be parodied), he turned to material in the public domain. *My Son, the Folk Singer* (1962), with songs like "Sir Greenbaum's Madrigal," "Sarah Jackman," ("How's your brother Bernie?/ He's a big attorney") and "Shake Hands With Your Uncle Max," sold over a million copies.

Sherman's songs were far more linguistically accessible to the general American than Katz's Yiddish-inflected parodies, and played on the key of an emerging set of American Jewish stereotypes that were widely recognized. But the increasing acceptance of American Jews in American society through the sixties was part of the story. One doctoral thesis of the time even went so far as to say that *My Son, the Folksinger*'s success stemmed from a secret American wish to be Jewish. (Sherman's response: "Won't that be news to the New York Athletic Club?")

Still, things were changing when a Jewish comedian could make a joke about the Chief Justice of the Supreme Court's putative Jewishness to his face and be lauded for it. For an event at the National Press Club in 1963, a celebration of its new president's installation, Sherman had been warned by an executive that his material might be too "ethnic," since the audience would only be about 10 percent Jewish. At the event, Sherman singled out Chief Justice Earl Warren in the front row and said: "I was warned before coming here that the audience would only be ten percent Jewish. Perhaps they thought I would be disappointed. On the contrary, I am delighted. Mr. Chief Justice, I am delighted to hear that you are even ten percent Jewish. I didn't know you were Jewish at all."

Sherman understood his audience had grown far beyond American Jewry; and comments he made on the subject were indicative of the turn in American Jewish comedy. "I realized I am at my worst in front of all-Jewish audiences," he said, "because they seem to want something from me that I can't give them. They want me to fit into a mold that I never made but they did. They want me to be a professional Jew, an inside Jew, and they want to sit there and laugh their version of the hipster's laugh—'I dig you, but the goys don't'— and I can't give them that—that's too much Jewish." Sherman was incalculably influential in inculcating the growing sensibility that you clearly didn't have to be Jewish to like Jewish-oriented comedy. Parody was, in many ways, the bridge that spanned Jewish and Jewish-oriented, yoking together disparate canons and forms of funny. For a broader culture, seeing something mocked from the majority culture, and seeing it mocked in a particularly Jewish way, were becoming increasingly common, and increasingly inextricable.

That combination was a central feature of *Mad* magazine, one of the most important institutions of American comedy of that, or indeed any, period. *Mad*—started as a comic book in 1952, transformed into a magazine three years later, and selling two and a half million issues a year by the early 1970s—was, in the words of Art Spiegelman, "more important than pot and LSD in shaping the generation that protested the Vietnam War." And its animating spirits, literally and metaphorically—Will Elder (Wolf William Eisenberg); Harvey Kurtzman (whose parents spoke Yiddish); Al Jaffee (raised traditionally observant and who lived in Lithuania from age six to twelve); and William Gaines (son of comics innovator Max Gaines, born Maxwell Ginzberg), created that seminal countercultural satire by framing it Jewishly, through Yiddishized parody.

Mad's spoofs of popular culture—epitomized, perhaps, in its groundbreaking "Superduperman" parody from the magazine's fourth issue in 1953—whittled down icons to size by presenting them as neurotic, overemotional, hyperverbal manics: in short, Jews. (*Mad* had a predecessor in this effort, albeit one slightly less explicitly Jewish. The products of the Fleischer animation studios, most notably Betty Boop, which were, in many ways, Jewish, parodic versions of Disney cartoons: urban, ethnic, racy, and raucous, in contrast to Walt's sweet rural creations.) *Mad*'s verbal and visual energy refused to stay within the limits of word balloons and panel frames, but escaped to dot the margins and interstices, where parody, metaphorically, always flourishes. Elder called the side doodles " 'chicken fat,' after that staple of Jewish cuisine: 'the part of the soup that is bad for you, yet gives [it] its delicious flavor.' " An early issue of an in-house knockoff, *Panic*, "was seized in Boston for ridiculing Santa

Claus"—*Santa Claus*, as Alvy Singer, or for that matter S. J. Perelman, might have said, meaningfully.

Jewish parents might have looked down their noses at their kids' copies of *Mad*, if they weren't confiscating them first. But they had their own equivalent, their own space for comedians to deliver English jokes with more risqué punch lines rendered in *mame-loshn*. In the Borscht Belt, the tables were turned: there, it was the newer generation who could tell something was going on, but what it was wasn't exactly clear.

THE BORSCHT BELT, for Jews, was born of physical needs. New York City was too hot, air conditioning not having been invented, and as early as 1893, the Rand McNally Guide to the Hudson River was calling Tannersville "a great resort of our Israelite brethren." Not everyone was so saturnine: several years earlier, *Puck* had published a dialect poem called "The Catskill Mountains Are Full of Jews" which depicted Jewish pawnbrokers wearing their customers' fancy duds to the mountains; a reminder that humor *about* Jews flourished in America, too, much of it not very nice. But if some mountain hotels restricted Jewish occupancy, a vast complex of Jewish-owned and -operated hotels, resorts, bungalow colonies sprung into the void with an appeal based, in no small part, on physical attractions.

There was the food available in copious, even gluttonous, portions; including, at Grossinger's, borscht in a glass, seven days a week, fifty-two weeks a year, which led the editor of *Variety*, Abel Green, to coin the region's unforgettable nickname. (Paul Grossinger, of the eponymous hotel: "Way down deep, we all thought it was an ethnic slur. Maybe it was. But there were some who took it as a red badge of courage.") But there were also the eligible men and women who went to look for mates, and the belly laughs provided by the entertainment, spotted and organized by indefatigable bookers who threw more and more people into the ever-increasing demand.

By the Second World War, there were about four hundred hotels in the mountains, and not nearly enough entertainers: especially comedians, who many thought were one of the most important draws of the mountains. The comedian Freddy Roman (née Fred Kirschenbaum) put the comedy-centered nature of the experience particularly well:

> This fellow checks into a hotel with his wife. He goes to breakfast, goes to Simon Sez, eats lunch, lays around in the pool, rows on the lake, plays softball, eats dinner, goes to the early show, then goes to the late show, then goes to the coffee shop. Finally, at four in the morning, the wife says, "Let's go to bed." "Why?" he asks. "Who's appearing there?"

It would be far easier to list the people who didn't play the mountains in those war and postwar years than those who did: Eddie Cantor, Milton Berle, Henny Youngman, Joey Adams, Danny Kaye, Jackie Mason, and Jerry Lewis appeared there among many, many others. (My favorite unexpected cameo in Borscht Belt history: Wilt Chamberlain, who worked as a bellhop at Kutsher's in the early 1950s while in high school.) So many entertainers worked the mountains then that a kind of natural comedic myopia resulted, a sense that the Catskills were the world. As dialect comedian Sam Levenson put it in a joke:

> RENTER: Is there a pleasant view from the bungalow?
> ANGENT: Well. . . . from the front porch there is an exquisite view of Grossinger's. . . . Otherwise there is nothing but blue lakes and snow-capped mountain peaks.

Those entertainers didn't have it easy, though. The constant necessity for new material—which required endless ferment of creativity, putting on a new near Broadway-caliber show every Saturday night, a schedule that would prove so similar to that of the early days of television—demanded instant rapport with the paying audiences, who were brutal: experienced, possessors of sky-high expectations, and willing to let their displeasure immediately be known. As the comedian Joey Adams, a veteran, bluntly put it: "The roughest thing in the whole world is to lay an egg at a show in the Catskills . . . when you bomb in the mountains, it's like a concentration camp with sour cream." One of the best ways to achieve that rapport was through parody, whether it be "bowdlerized versions of current Broadway shows" or Yiddished-up versions of current hits of the day. In that master-class training ground of the Borscht Belt (or, alternatively, the Sour Cream Sierras, or the Derma Road), at a time where Jewish experience in all its gustatory, sexual, and bodily versions came out, the comedy was—and I mean this in the best way—parodic.

To trace this path in its most profound incarnation, let's narrow our focus to one undistinguished Borscht Belt saxophone player whose comedic shows at the Avon Lodge attracted so much demand that people would leave the other hotels to see him, standing on the outside porch and peering through the windows of the casino to try to get a glimpse of his act. Sid Caesar's partnership with resort impresario Max Liebman—which had begun when the former's comedy bits in a wartime revue attracted the notice of the latter, who was directing—continued back in the Catskills, then in nightclubs around the country, and then back in Manhattan at the Roxy and the Broadhurst, and, finally and most famously, on television. *The Admiral Broadway Revue* and *Your Show of Shows* were packed with resort alums, most notably Lucille Kallen and Mel Tolkin from the Tamiment. Liebman would brag to the New York *World-Telegram*: "Whereas it takes months and months to put on a two-hour revue on Broadway, we do an original one-hour show, with singing, dancing, and comedy—in one week. Theatre die-hards speak of the thrill of opening night. Hell, we have one every night." This sounded a lot more like Borscht Belt than Broadway.

Befitting his Borscht Belt heritage, Caesar's most prodigious gift—what, in many ways, he remains most famous for—was his spirit of parody, of mock imitation. Caesar's comedy was like music—he'd picked up the sax when a tenant of some rooms his father rented out skipped out and left one behind—parodying language and speech; he caricatured action heroes and classical conductors. Caesar's parodic language, his famed double-talk, born of the ethnic mishmash of his surroundings (before the Great Depression wiped them out, his parents owned luncheonettes and he was exposed to a wide variety of nationalities and languages among the clientele), probably first flowered in a routine he did during the war depicting a conversation between Adolf Hitler and Donald Duck where he played both sides. The actual words were meaningless; the intonations and rhythms hilarious and uncanny.

Caesar's later parodies on *Your Show of Shows,* fraught with the decorum of tiptoeing into the new medium of television and the respect of a group of Jewish American writers concerned about mainstream cultural acceptance, are enormously entertaining but rather tame. Mixed with the fairly antiseptic surroundings, to say nothing of Caesar's nonspecific good looks and (unchanged, beyond all reason) gentile name, it was hard to imagine this breakthrough sitcom as being deeply Jewish. Still, many of its parodies, befitting the show's creators' backgrounds, rely, in small or large part, on the intrusion of an ethnic dimension into avowedly nonethnic material. (Said Larry Gelbart, one of Caesar's writers who would go on to craft *M*A*S*H*: "We were a bunch of very gifted neurotic young Jews punching our brains out.")

Caesar's double-talk featured a good deal of the Yiddish about it, like in the famous sketch "The German General"—and Yiddish snuck its way into some other linguistic parodies. A Japanese film parody, for example, rendered by the cast entirely in mock-Japanese, featured characters with names like *shmate, gantze mishpokhe,* and *gehakte leber.* When, in a parody of the Western *Shane* ("Strange"), Caesar plays on the typical cowboy's stereotypical thirst by explaining that he'd had herring for breakfast, audiences—and the early days of television, for reasons related to the demographic disposition and location of television set owners, yielded a more cosmopolitan and sophisticated audience than any audience until arguably the days of pay cable and "It's Not TV, It's HBO"—roared at the in-joke of a cowboy eating this most typically Jewish of food.

Caesar's parodic approach was enormously influential on the history of American comedy. His own writers' rooms boasted, among many other luminaries, Carl Reiner, Mel Brooks, and (later) Woody Allen. It's worth remembering that Reiner and Brooks's iconic "2000 Year Old Man" series of routines begins, explicitly, as a parody—a parody, according to Reiner, of a "news" show he saw that attempted to present a "you were there" approach to historical events. News parodies weren't, well, news. One of Brooks's earliest regular contributions to Caesar's show, "Nonentities in the News," featured a reporter interviewing strange characters played by Caesar and others. And Lenny Bruce, who was arguably as influential a parodist as he was a satirist, was doing show business interview parodies, too, including one in which the variety show host and bandleader Lawrence Welk attempts vainly to interview a fifties hipster. It was the Judaizing element—the presentation of Brooks, ad-libbing wildly and so brilliantly he was putting off sparks—that made Brooks and Reiner famously unwilling to present the 2000 Year Old Man to the world, simply preferring to play the bit at parties, until (in various iterations of the story) George Burns threatened to steal the material if they didn't put it to record. What's more, upon producing a limited, private set of records, thanks in part to the efforts and encouragement of Steve Allen, Cary Grant borrowed one to play for no less a gentile than the Queen Mother of England. If Archibald Leach and Queen Elizabeth the Queen Mother could enjoy it, Reiner and Brooks figured, who were they to stand in its way.

Brooks and Reiner's "2000 Year Old Man" skits are possibly the fullest demonstration of the thesis posed by *Mad*, Katz, Sherman, and others that parodying something was presenting its Jewish version (although contemporary reports, it should be noted, have Brooks's original 1960 recording not nearly as popular as Sherman's, or perhaps even Katz's), since they bend all of human time and space to their Jewish American middle-class tags and punch lines. The 2000 Year Old Man has 25,000 children . . . and not a single one of them writes; he mishears Paul Revere, the anti-Semite, insisting that the Yiddish are coming; he backed Shakespeare's failed play "Queen Alexandra and Murray." This approach would serve Brooks equally well in medieval times (his rabbi in *Robin Hood: Men in Tights*) and in outer space (too many characters in *Spaceballs* to count, and the Jews in space who are going to protect the Hebrew race in the trailer for *History of the World Part II*).

Considering Jews and space leads us back to Woody Allen, another Caesar alumnus, and his often-overlapping parodic sensibility. Allen's early stand-up piece "A Science Fiction Film," suggests, perhaps improbably, that the rampaging and hostile aliens bent on conquering the earth from the days of H. G. Wells are really interested in our skills as dry cleaners. The corollary—the triumph of the human race—comes in the punch line: "That they traveled twenty million light years to get here and they forgot their ticket." The point here, beyond an absurdist parody of a standard of popular culture, is the intervention of the Jewish ethnic element into it; of course the same man who joked that his parents' values were God and carpeting would turn the aliens into middle-class mid-twentieth-century Jews obsessed with getting the stains out. And there are plenty of other examples—the Jewish robot tailors in *Sleeper*, the Borscht Belt jester in the medieval scene in *Everything You Always Wanted to Know About Sex*, Virgil Starkweather's transformation into a rabbi in *Take the Money and Run*—that show how well Allen internalized that equation of Jewishness and parody.

But it was Brooks who truly wore the crown as Caesar's parodic heir. He'd come by it honestly: his own Borscht Belt debut was as a pool *tummler*—in Brooks's own definition, "resident offstage entertainers at Jewish mountain resorts, mostly after lunch"; Danny Kaye and Jerry Lewis both got their start as *tummlers*—is famously a parody in itself. Brooks dressed up in a suit, carried a briefcase, walked up to the diving board, and said, in a precise reflection of the businessmen who came up on Fridays, "Business is terrible! I can't go on!" and dropped off the diving board. The fact that he couldn't swim, and had to be pulled out on regular occasion, showed he took his craft seriously indeed.

Brooks and Caesar would have a famously close relationship, Caesar being responsible for bringing Brooks into the television business. (Perhaps more accurately, Caesar enjoyed having Brooks around, and Brooks scrambled and, in Caesar's words, "push[ed] his way into the writers' room through a combination of raw talent, inertia, and sheer chutzpah," despite Max Liebman's dismissal of him as a "meshuggener.") But it was more than just gratitude, or personal influence: Brooks understood the intimate connection between parody and live performance in a way that Allen, who wrote plays and playlets more frequently, never did, putting theater first and foremost, even in film. ("I never leave show business," he once said. "It's in everything I do.")

It's on display as early as the end of *Blazing Saddles,* which ends in a brawl that breaks through soundstages and onto other shows, but it hits its height, of course, in yet another parody (though it's not often considered as such): a parody of the "let's put on a show" movies that were such a staple of his childhood. Here, though, another conventional Judaizing *shpritz* occurs, by focusing less on the apple-eyed gentile ingénues at the front of house, but the nebbishy, schlocky backers behind. *The Producers* combines everything in this stream of Jewish humor: theater, parody, vulgarity, and "bad taste." That last, of course, is a charge that hangs over Mel Brooks's career; but of all the vulgarity and puerility that constitutes the charge—vulgarity and puerility that, as I think we've demonstrated, has a remarkably long history in Jewish comedy—the most powerful and profound version of it, the one that really hits a nerve, is the material that has to do with Jewish life, fate, and history. And of course by taking on the Holocaust, 1968's *The Producers* does that in its darkest moments.

Two important facts to know about *The Producers* right up

front. First, no matter how influential and popular it is now (and the success of its stage version, thirty-odd years after its film version saw theatrical release, is ample testament to that influence and popularity), it was a commercial failure at the time, nothing even close to what Brooks would accomplish just a few years later. But if it wasn't a commercial success, at least, as Brooks might have put it, it was also a critical failure. Renata Adler in the *New York Times* called it "shoddy and gross and cruel" (although also "funny in an entirely unexpected way") and opined that "I never thought black comedy of this dilute order could be made with the word or idea of Hitler in it anywhere. . . . I suppose we will have cancer, Hiroshima, and malformity musicals next." Pauline Kael opined, for her part: "*The Producers* isn't basically unconventional, it only seems so because it's so amateurishly crude, and because it revels in the kind of show-business Jewish humor that used to be considered too specialized for movies."

It wasn't rejected in *every* way. In fact, it won Brooks his second Oscar, for best original screenplay, at a time when the Academy was probably even more conservative than it is now. (To be fair, the other nominees—*2001*, *The Battle of Algiers*, *Faces*, and *Hot Millions*—were, with the exception of the last, a pretty radical bunch of possibilities, too. It's not impossible to suggest, given his history and industry connections, that Brooks was actually an insider candidate for this one.) But *The Producers*, as a film and a script, was always really about the question of how one might go about accepting *The Producers*, and the new, edgy comedy it represented.

Take, for example, the film's culminating scene, where the curtain goes up on the opening number, "Springtime for Hitler." Notably, this was Brooks's original title, his first conception of the idea; theater-iness and silliness all baked into one. Which leads to my favorite anecdote about *The Producers*. When Brooks started pitching it, it was turned down all over town; but Universal's uber-executive Lew Wasserman agreed to take it on—as long as Hitler was replaced by the less-controversial Mussolini. Brooks, wisely considering that "Springtime for Mussolini" wouldn't pack the same comic punch, declined.

The performance is funny enough—dancing girls with stereotypical pretzels and steins of beer—and it's certainly button-pushing (for me, the swastika kickline is probably the most suggestive). Brooks, wisely, trains the camera regularly on the very proper Broadway audience for the show—rich, white, middle-aged, elegantly dressed—who are, in a static shot, horrified into paralysis. One person stands up and applauds, and is roundly browbeaten—literally—by the other audience members. They begin to walk out in droves, one member saying, "Talk about bad taste!" And there it hangs, momentarily, and then the play's action begins, and we hear Hitler's ridiculous dialogue. "It's funny!" someone in the audience says, and then, licensed to laugh and mock rather than treat the show as a sober object of contemplation, the audience loves it—with the concomitant tragic results for Messrs. Bialystock and Bloom.

In the many, many interviews he's done, Brooks suggests fairly consistently that *The Producers* was part of a strong, aggressive strategy of getting revenge on Hitler and Nazism by reducing it to ridicule. And it's true that *Springtime*'s playwright's absurdist claims for Adolf Hitler's own magnificence, his frustrated drives to reveal the real Hitler—"Not many people know it, but the Fuhrer was a terrific dancer"; "Hitler . . . there was a painter! He could paint an entire apartment in an afternoon! Two coats!"—do their job at assaulting a little bit of the dictator's presence. But a large part of the (comparative) comfort the movie offers comes from its comfortable, affectionate frame of parody: its attraction to the conventions of theater movies even as the content is disturbingly unconventional.

Another sign of this radical movie's conservative comic frame— that push-pull between love and distance, incorporating majority attitudes while simultaneously kicking against them, is its attitude toward, well, the time's cultural radicalism. The things that date most in *The Producers* are the jabs at the drug culture, like the casting of the flower child Lorenzo St. Dubois, or LSD—jabs that not coincidentally position Brooks, if sides must be taken, as a member of the Establishment. Brooks is rarely, if ever, included in the established canon of seventies countercultural film rebels; some of this may be critical bias against his form of comedy, but it's probably in no small part born of the recognition that Brooks's reliance and affection for old conventions, necessary for parody, put him on the Establishment's side in certain fundamental respects.

IF A SWASTIKA kickline doesn't raise hackles or activate a bad taste meter, consider this joke, from a few decades later: "Had there been black people in Germany, the Holocaust would have never happened—at least, not to Jews."

That's the stand-up comic and actress Sarah Silverman, one of Brooks's most direct heirs: in her dedication to offend, in her wrapping that offensiveness in a kind of who-doesn't-love-me stereotypical Jewish persona (in Silverman's case, the sweet Jewish girl rather than the nice Jewish boy). Of course, that joke isn't *really* about the Holocaust; it's about the persistence of hatred, and the complex racial hierarchy of persecution, and about turning the phrasing of liberal pieties on its head—all specialties of Silverman, who spent most of one episode of her titular sitcom, a sitcom generally obsessed with bodily humor, going around in blackface. Similarly, Amy Schumer's sketch on "The Museum of Boyfriend Wardrobe Atrocities," on her show *Inside Amy Schumer*, is less about the Holocaust (though the set, dialogue and character reactions are brilliant caricatures of the current state of Holocaust memorialization, by institutions and their visitors alike), but about the state of American manhood (or lack of same), and the horror it invites in the women who observe it. Late in the first decade of the twenty-first century, the Holocaust, while by no means having lost its power to shock, has far less visceral effect on American viewers than comedy that puts Jews in an uncomfortable position vis a vis race, or gender. (Parodies like the 2003 Jewsploitation comedy *The Hebrew Hammer*, which recasts black power as black-hat ultra-orthodoxy, tread similar territory.)

Part of this is just a matter of the Holocaust receding into history: what was deeply controversial when Brooks released it in 1968 thrilled Broadway audiences in the twenty-first century. Holocaust humor is everywhere (along with Holocaust comparisons: see the 1990 invention of Godwin's Law, which states that "as an online discussion grows longer, the probability of a comparison involving Nazis or Hitler approaches one"), and, like anything that's everywhere, is increasingly diluted in its effect. This comes at a time where Jewish claims and concerns of anti-Semitism in America are at previously unimaginably low rates (although recent trends, and political events, may give troubling reason to reconsider this assessment). But what was vibrantly discomfiting when *The Producers* premiered a half century ago and still has the capacity to shock, may have begun—and this is said without any denial of the enormity, terror, and importance of the lessons of the Holocaust—to lose some of its comedic edge.

This isn't just the case in America. A skit by the 1990s Israeli group The Chamber Quintet features a tour guide pitching a trip to Poland: "There's a weekend in Poland that includes three concentration camps . . . there's a complete week in Poland that includes visiting seven concentration camps—and also a shopping day in Warsaw. And there's the extended Poland option. That includes visiting all the concentration camps, including Auschwitz, but without the day off for shopping in Warsaw." The guide recommends the last based on her niece's experience: "She really cried in Auschwitz."

But some of it doesn't have to do with Jewish history as much as the progress (if that's the word) of cultural institutions and their audience's tolerance for "offensive" comedy more generally. Film, radio, television, the recording industry, all had their own bans and censorship that would lead to different approaches. Brooks could get away with material on film that could never appear on television; the 1978 Supreme Court decision that upheld the FCC's right to ban "patently offensive" language during hours when children are in the audience, which led to the creation of TV's "family hour," certainly helped create a cultural lag when it came to envelope-pushing. At least until the development of pay cable, which then was able to televise material that had originally been concert films and develop stand-up specials of their own; and basic cable, most notably in the form of Comedy Central, which gave Sarah Silverman her venue. Now, as we move to other kinds of entertainment institutions—streaming video, internet channels, satellite radio, YouTube clips—gatekeeping is even more limited, and allows the development of the "bad taste"/"unpleasant Jew" perspective to new heights, for better and for worse.

There's Hulu's *Difficult People* (premiered 2015), where Julie Klausner and Billy Eichner can put on and discard masks of anti-Semitism in a way that would have launched a thousand ADL statements years before; and there's Rachel Bloom, whose 2013 song "Historically Accurate Disney Princess," which went viral on YouTube, not only cleverly intrudes Jewishness into one of the great American gentile narratives, but also features a healthy dose of ironic self-hatred along with a poke at Disney's own anti-Semitism, taking wide-eyed Sarah Silverman innocence to a new level. (There's also her 2012 song "You Can Touch My Boobies," where a boy fantasizing about his Hebrew school teacher is chastised by the spirit of Golda Meir.) Bloom's move to the CW in 2015, with her genre-bending *Crazy Ex-Girlfriend*, shows how blurred these lines and platforms are becoming now; as does Comedy Central's *Broad City*, which premiered the previous year, and whose physically fearless vulgarians, Abbi Jacobson and Ilana Glazer, produce line-crossing comedy of such breathtaking proportions that they can barely be mentioned in this book.

Suffice it to say that the fourth episode of *Broad City*'s second season, entitled "Knockoffs," is unquestionably the nimblest, and most discomforting, juxtaposition of Jewishness and matters corporeal since that campfire scene, and maybe since those Yiddish Purim plays. In the episode, Ilana (whose bucket list, we have learned in a previous episode, includes making her own Passover seder, and learning how to squirt) suffers the loss of her maternal grandmother: and her mother's own discomfort with her own emotional openness, displaced onto her love of counterfeit handbags, is matched by Abbi's own halting steps toward comfort with herself as a sexual being. This all sounds comparatively sedate, until I reveal much of this manifests—and here I will be coy—in the discovery of an apparently subpar sexual aid (a knockoff, that is) in Abbi's handbag at Grandma Esther's shiva, which she hopes will replace the one she has ruined after using it in a sexual act that she found surprising, somewhat off putting, but (perhaps) an opportunity for self-realization. Perhaps a bit taken aback by the reaction of Ilana's parents (who, befitting the nuanced take on sexual maturity and immaturity *Broad City* offers, are supportive rather than the opposite: "*Good* for you for trying something new," Ilana's mother says), she explains, citing the departed's zest for life: "Yeah, I pegged, but I kind of did it for Grandma Esther, you know?"

I'm not certain what Grandma Esther would have made of *Broad City*. I think I know what Mel Brooks would say; but the episode's delight in delving into New York's underbelly—Ilana and her mother literally go underground in search of their beloved counterfeit handbags—most powerfully evokes another iconic New York vulgarian. Howard Stern, for the early part of his career, was vilified as a "shock jock," with characters like Fartman who were, in the minds of his critics, simply walking personifications of obscene bad taste. But Stern—often by design—was interested in developing strategies for pushing the buttons of society and the sometimes arbitrary and punitive limits that ruled the airwaves; and his crudenesses opened conversations about sexuality that, in what now seems like either a simpler or more regressive time, were largely unequaled in public conversation. In addition, Stern—who, as he himself frequently joked, had a face and body made for radio—proved himself to be a revitalizing master of the form, using its capacities for discretion (that is, the way in which the lack of visuals necessarily leaves much to the imagination) like a concert violinist with a Stradivarius.

Stern's comedy was not always Jewish; in fact, it often wasn't—hard to simply hit that note when you're broadcasting so many hours a day—but he was the one most responsible for putting a Jewish face on the seamy side of eighties New York, the one who suggested, after Lenny Bruce and Lou Reed but before Seinfeld, that what made NYC dwellers Jewish was their ability to participate in the New York attitude. Dustin Hoffman did a good job of it in *Midnight Cowboy*, but he did it as Ratso Rizzo; for someone Jewish to be so . . . scuzzy . . . Howard Stern was your man.

This is another way of saying, of course, that vulgarity, bad taste, blasphemy, and the like can all be part of art: and the important thing is not to mistake simple gestures of the former (rude ones, with middle finger extended) for the other. Take, for example, one of the most evocative displays of public rudeness in recent memory by a Jewish comedian, a single moment that opened up a larger comic vista, and allows us, most pungently and in conclusion, to consider the role of the ethical in these comic works: not whether or not the jokes are funny, but whether they should, in fact, be told at all.

The stand-up comedian and actor Gilbert Gottfried, best known for that grating, unmistakable voice that has given life most famously to the Aflac duck and the parrot Iago in *Aladdin*, has, throughout his career, displayed a general habit of saying things that have gotten him into trouble. But one of them, a single moment three weeks after the greatest tragedy in the history of New York City, is one of the seminal moments in the history of offensive American comedy. Participating in a Friars Club Roast in honor of Hugh Hefner on September 29, 2001, Gottfried apologized for being late; he couldn't get a direct flight, he explained, because his plane had had to stop off at the Empire State Building on the way over.

Any fan of comedy is familiar with the phrase "too soon," and it's often uttered, dismissively, as a throwaway line. There's a warning in it, though, a suggestion that you're getting close to the transgressive edge. Many comics, would-be and professional, take that as a warning. Gottfried was not one of those comics, generally speaking, but the nature of the one-liner didn't give an opportunity—and even the Comedy Central crowd of roast attendees, who were hardly easily offended types, let their displeasure be mightily known. On the recording, one can see Gottfried visibly taken aback, losing his bearings: there are, it seems, moments in history sufficiently powerful to shake even the most hardened of comic sensibilities. And then he recovers, and tells "The Aristocrats," the dirtiest, most tasteless joke ever told.

Which I'm going to tell here.

Well, not in a particularly dirty or tasteless way, which, as you'll see, is very much to the point. Here's the joke, for those who haven't seen the documentary dedicated to it:

> A man walks into a booker's office at a vaudeville talent agency and tells the agent he has an act the agent might consider taking on. The agent, naturally, asks him to tell him what it is. The man complies, saying, "Well, it's a family act"—and cheerfully launches into a description of the vilest, most disgusting, offensive actions that members of a family, and their pets, and other passers-by, and various inanimate objects, and so on, can do with, on, near, and at each other. After what seems like an eternity of description, the man finally stops, and the agent (somewhat taken aback, to be sure) says, "Well, ah, well, that's quite an act. What do you call yourselves?" "Oh," the man says, "we're the Aristocrats."

Three things about this joke, which, as I've told it, is almost certain to be found unfunny.

1. The joke's comic effect clearly relies on the middle section, and the teller's inventiveness in creating the act's details.

2. Those details' composition are a Rorschach test of the comic sensibilities of the teller (what they find funny, or comedically provocative), their sense of the audience, and their willingness to engage the audience on those grounds. In that sense, "The Aristocrats" can be a Jewish joke, or not, depending on who and how it's told. The Upper West Side audience with whom I saw the documentary—catalyzed by Gottfried's delivery of the joke and consisting of many famous comedians delivering their versions—laughed smugly and confidently at versions of the joke with racism, incest, scatology, and necrophilia, but cringed in horror and offense when one of the comedians whispered those not-so-sweet nothings and concepts into the ears of his ten-month-old child, even though the odds of the latter understanding were nil. Insert your own psychological reading of a highly Jewish neighborhood's sensibilities here; I'll just note that offense differs from one community to the next.

3. And in that vein, Gottfried was, in September 2001, willing to tell a joke that would offend on many other grounds—just not dwell on the one that was truly offensive. And it worked. The show went on.

To be truly offensive and blasphemous, to be deeply vulgar, is easy and artless. To be meaningfully so, in a way that enlightens—that has a long tradition. And it's done with love.

5

The Divine Comedy

THE HOLIDAY OF PURIM ON WHICH THE BOOK OF ESTHER IS READ takes its name from the lots (*purim*) cast by Haman to determine the precise date of the Jews' destruction: a date which, in the topsy-turviness so common to comedy, would become a date of celebration, feasting, and merriment instead. Lots—lotteries—are in their essence and by their definition random. They are without meaning. And what transpires, through the book, are a great deal of events that lead to enormous consequences—both destructive and salvific—that happen as a result of sheer, random coincidence.

The timing of Ahasuerus's bout of insomnia; the overhearing by Mordechai of an assassin's plot; the fact that Esther's particular traits, of all the other women, are the ones that happen to strike the king's fancy, and that she happens to be Mordechai's cousin; the fact that Haman happens to trip and fall over Esther the moment that Ahasuerus returns from stewing in the garden . . . the book of Esther offers the possibility of the bleakest, blackest joke in Jewish history: the idea that the entire fate of a nation—of God's self-proclaimed, self-understood chosen people—depends on simple coincidence, nothing more. Especially since—uniquely among all the books of the Bible—God goes unmentioned in the text. That's the kind of joke that's no joke indeed.

The Bible, in general, is hardly reticent about showing or arguing for the divine hand behind the affairs of men. This omission—and its theological consequences and provocations—led to the most ironic strand of Jewish comedy: its attempt to juxtapose grand visions of chosenness and covenant with the strains and stresses of earthly conditions, to fuse metaphysics and humanity. From the Talmud to Tevye, from Hasidic masters to post-Holocaust novelists, Jewish artists weighed in on the meaning of Jewish history and fate in light of its grand beginnings and audacious claims, not least the promises made by their God. Many of them did so, despite—or because of—the stakes, in a comic key. And the sum of their responses, whether they be warm and joyful reaffirmations of faith, or blackly ironic rejections of what they had been taught, or an uneasy laughter from the effort of balancing between those two poles, is the story of this chapter.

THE BIBLE, taken as a whole, is not funny.

Given all the comic evidence of the last chapters, though, that might require some qualification. The Bible, taken as a whole, is actually Not Funny: from a God's-eye view, that is. Fittingly, He actually clarifies the matter during the Bible's first instance of laughter, Sarah's laughter during the episode of the birth of her son Isaac (whose name comes from the Hebrew word for laughing). The first time Sarah laughs, she's been told her aged husband Abraham has been promised, in violation of common sense and biology, that his wife will bear him a son as a reward for his hospitality. Her laugh is a laugh of irony: Sarah knows the way the world works, and she's mocking her foolish husband for his fantastic beliefs. But this is not the kind of laughter God chooses to embrace. In a universe centered on a divinity who regularly works miracles for his chosen people, belief isn't fantastic at all; it's wise, and irony fails. A child is born after all, God takes Sarah to task for her laughter, and Sarah laughs again, not the comic laughter of superiority but a humbled grin.

This story has the benefit of incorporating two of the three major approaches to comic theory that critics and philosophers have managed to come up with, resolving one into the other. (We've discussed the third, superiority theory, in the previous chapter.) *Incongruity theories* of comedy tend to suggest that the reason we laugh is that we see something that's incongruous: a monkey on a bicycle, or, in one of my favorite Jewish punch lines, a vampire faced with a cross saying, "Oy, bubbele, have you got the wrong idea." Sarah (and Abraham's) first laughter is of that type: it's a laughter which has to be predicated on knowledge of how the world is. My four-year-old, for example, is only beginning to understand why it would be funny for a monkey to be depicted riding a bike, and the currents at play in the intrusion of Jewish stereotypes into the vampire narrative are, it's safe to say, beyond him.

The second laughter, though, is predicated on what the philosophers of comedy call *relief theory*: the idea that laughter is connected with the joy of resolving tension, related to, but not precisely the same as, the Shakespearean sense that all's well that ends well and all's right with the world. Sarah's second laughter—and Isaac's naming—is of this sort. Isaac becomes a living example of this comfort of God's connection and covenant with Abraham's family, that an interventionist God will literally change the world to assist his chosen people. (Of course, that's tested when God asks Abraham to sacrifice Isaac, but you can't have everything.)

As the rebuke of Sarah illustrates, the Bible is tough on an ironic superiority that comes from earthly knowledge, the kind often on display in a Greek or Roman comedy. (The term *irony* comes from the Greek, and the final events chronicled in the biblical canon take place at virtually the same time Aristophanes was staging his plays.) But conversely, it engages deeply with a kind of structural irony based on knowledge from a kind of God's eye view of history—a readerly irony of a sort, related to a sense of metaphysical order.

Divine comedy, indeed; quite different from that practiced by lowly humanity. And whether and how the Jews could appreciate such comedy—and the inevitable and necessary gap between God, His laughter, and themselves and their own—is precisely our story.

Take two biblical figures who aren't normally thought of as laugh riots: Ecclesiastes and Job. Ecclesiastes is particularly down on laughter: "Laughter is madness," he says. It's like "the crackling of thorns under a pot," he says. "Better sorrow than laughter," he says. His opposition to a hearty chuckle seems to come from philosophical objections, and a surfeit of ironic knowledge. His awareness of the ironies of life—the same fate awaits all, wealth goes to fools who squander it, etc.—mean that for him, the only rational response is an abrupt dismissiveness of the world as (to use his favorite word) "vanity" (*hevel*). Or, to put it another way, life is Not Funny. One might ask, though, whether we're meant to admire his approach, or reject his lack of laughter for the same reasons we reject Sarah's inappropriate glee.

And then there's Job. Even readers familiar with his story's outlines—God champions Job as righteous man; Satan points out that the happy, wealthy Job doesn't have much to rebel about; Satan challenges God to a bet where Job loses children and possessions, and is afflicted with boils on top of it all; Job complains for many chapters, but does not curse God—may have forgotten its ending, which may make all the difference. After hearing God's voice from out of the whirlwind asking him who he thinks he is to fathom His power and plans, Job gets back everything he's lost, and more. It's a happy ending which makes it into a comedy, at least according to some technical definitions. Critics who identify the book of Job as a comedy in this sense also tend to focus on the satiric caricatures of Job's philosophizing, theologizing friends who come to comfort him, and who, in the process, forget about God's goodness and providence. Job castigates them, and down through the centuries we can practically hear *his* sarcastic tone: "No doubt you are perfect men and absolute wisdom is yours! . . . But I have sense as well as you." They are the ones who don't understand; Job does, and he is greeted, as a result, with joyous restoration.

On the other hand, it's easy enough *not* to read the book as a comedy. Job's history, what he's been through, matters, maybe just as much, maybe even more than, a payoff at the end. Job's children die early in the narrative; is the fact that he is granted others sufficient joyous recompense? We can argue about how the book's original readers might have answered that question; but the question of promised theological payoff balanced against the painful vicissitudes of history, and, indeed, life itself—if we apply it to the Jewish people writ large rather than Job—becomes the animating question of almost all of Jewish history, and of this strand of comedy.

The approach taken by Abraham and Job has everything to do with the joy that comes with understanding, or at least internalizing, the theological belief that the Jews, following their God, were on the right side of history. As the last chapter suggested, the Bible seems to be fine with the kind of smirking laughter that comes from being on the right side of the divinity in charge, and mocking all those people, from Egyptians to Moabites, who don't get with the program. Think of the song of Deborah's triumph in Judges, mocking Sisera's mother for standing by the window and listening to the blandishments of other women telling of his triumphant return: Don't they *know* that to go up against God will only lead in destruction? What *idiots*. And it's extra funny, because her son is dead!

But there's another kind of comedy the Bible seems fine with: metaphysical comic joy. This kind of joy replaces that evocation of the *incongruity theory* by something that's probably technically relief theory, but goes beyond it to what we might call *congruity theory*: when the world, to grievously misuse the philosophical terminology of another German thinker, matches the case. When everything fits, in a way that bespeaks divine harmony, and historical intent.

Demonstrations of this kind of fit can occur, in the Bible, on the most basic of levels: the word, and specifically the name. Names can be easily congruent, as in the case of Nabal ("fool"), who behaves as ill-advisedly as his name suggests, or ironically incongruent (Laban, whose name means "white," behaves—let's put the racism-tinged problems of such essentializing aside—darkly to Jacob throughout). Ahasuerus's name is probably analogous to something like "King Headache," but my favorite in this context has to be Cushan Rishathaim, which a listener—remember that the Bible, by and large, was designed to be orally delivered—"could have interpreted only as 'Superblack Doublevillain.'" But the comic relationship in the text between word and thing—or words and things, because the root-and-variation structure of Hebrew allows for a kind of comedy of familial resemblance harder to visualize in English—relied on, and indeed led to, a recognition of a metaphysically ordered universe: the smile of recognition that came with the humor was a smile of relief.

But this sense of order echoes on a historic scale in the Bible, too. The reader joyfully and pleasurably comes to recognize cycles, repetitions, and ironic reversals that constantly take place—and, they could say, could only take place—in a divinely ordered history. Most famously, and representatively, there's the story of Jacob, in which it is the younger who receives the birthright, not the older; and in which, later on, it is that deceiver who is deceived, his own deceptive actions in taking his brother's birthright carrying down the generations to the Joseph story. This dictate of "measure for measure" can extend to laughter, where the mocker can be mocked. A mocking Pharaoh who thinks he holds all the cards, for example, is in turn the defeated subject of mockery. (Later generations of interpreters, including whoever penned the song "One morning when Pharaoh woke in his bed/ there were frogs on his pillow, frogs on his bed," made this dynamic even more explicit.) God actively intervenes in history in order to protect his chosen, covenanted family who become a people (Jacob, that is, becoming Israel). Such ironies, properly recognized and appreciated—by protagonists as well as readers—can release a kind of laughter that can only be considered joy.

All this was fine when there was a clear congruence of Jewish history with Jewish theology, when the Jews were on top. It held through the humiliation of Egypt, the conquest of Israel, the growth of the kingdom of David, even through the division of that kingdom into Judah and Israel. But after the most profound event in Jewish history—the destruction of the Temple and the end of Jewish political independence for two thousand years—the old models of comedy don't hold up. How can you feel superior when your god's house is in ruins and your kingdom—the tangible sign of your god's strength on earth—now belongs to another empire? What does that say about your understanding of how the world works? Essentially, it boils down to one, great Jewish joke, the greatest Jewish joke of all time. You think, you Babylonians (or Romans, or Crusaders, or so on), you think that just because you came into our territory, burned our houses, slaughtered our families, destroyed our property, you think you *won*? What schmucks you are. We know we're God's Chosen People. We know we're getting the last laugh.

Of course, I'm paraphrasing.

I've just articulated the theologically orthodox approach to the massive challenge to Jewish self-understanding and identity posed by the Temple's destruction. There's an answer, of course, which is that the covenant between an all-powerful God and His chosen people still obtains; it's just that because the people have sinned, God's wrath has come upon them, leading to a temporary setback. But it'll all be fine. The return to Jerusalem several generations later by some representatives of the Babylonian leadership—empires had risen and fallen in the interim; new policies were adopted—didn't necessarily hurt this interpretation.

But it did lead to the possibility, sitting uneasily alongside the orthodox interpretation, that there was something more complicated going on. Maybe, that thinking went, all this was just whistling in the dark. Maybe this talk of covenant was just a joke. It's a joke that's Jewish in all the central ways: it's about resilience in the face of persecution, backed by faith, the humor that allows the persecuted to buck up and soldier on. But it's also extremely black comedy, as it's always, always told in the full knowledge that the joke might be on them. (The Jews of the Bible, after all, are as loath to be the butt of someone else's joke as anyone else, as the book of Lamentations suggests over and over again: "Jerusalem sinned grievously, so she has become a mockery," the mourning narrator intones.) There's that small, heckling voice in the back of the Jewish consciousness: *Who are we kidding, what with the superiority complex. Look at where **they** are and look at where **we** are: **we're** history's joke, not them.* Non-Jews made this point, too—as early as the fourth century, Julian the Apostate said, "Will anyone think that victory in war is less desirable than defeat? Who is so stupid?"—but the Jews listened to their own voices most of all. And so this aspect of Jewish humor—perhaps the grandest of them all—began.

THE BOOK of Esther's string of coincidences—along with its absent, unmentioned God—could well be Exhibit A in this new, theologically anxious, ironically saturated sensibility. Now, traditional authorities pointed out that this string of sheer coincidences are so deeply unlikely that there must—*must*—be an Author to them, and the rabbis expanded and retold the story, not just adding doses of scatology or buffoonery, but placing God back into the narrative. (Sometimes they accomplish both, sending the angel Gabriel to trip Haman and have him pratfall directly into Esther's lap and arranging a literal and metaphorical downfall as a result.) And Esther's name itself becomes a rabbinic theological statement in its own right; subjected to a bit of etymological wordplay, it is revealed to have thematic connections to the regnant term for the *deus absconditus*, for God's hiding his face from the world.

The rabbis' theology—which has a vested interest in matching God's emotional equilibrium to that of His chosen people's—accordingly takes on whether God, while hidden from those suffering and exiled people, has much to laugh about. Psalms provided an intriguing image to the rabbis for contemplation in this respect, a verse stating that "He who sits in Heaven shall laugh." But the frequently attributed cause of God's laughter—the heathen ("But as for You, God, You laugh at them; You mock all nations") and the wicked ("the Lord laughs at the wicked, for he knows their day is coming")—seemed to ring hollow, or perhaps even offensively, in a post-exile world where the wicked heathen seemed to have had their day at the chosen people's expense. Theologically speaking, the rabbis were congruity-making machines, trying to resolve stubborn and knottily contradictory elements of the Bible to their own satisfaction and match them to their ideas of God and history, and they're happy to use whatever approaches they can to do so.

Their first tack was to relocate divine laughter in time and space. That "their day is coming" in Psalms offered the glimpse of a later, final reckoning, either at the end of human life or national empire, which allowed the rabbis to assert that "since the day of the destruction of the Temple, there is no laughter for the Holy One except that day." At that point, though, at the time of national revival and return, to laugh would be to participate in the same messianic joy of the Jews described in Psalms, when God returns the exultants of Zion and their "mouth will be full of laughter and our tongue of song."

Some rabbinic authorities, in a move we've seen earlier, took this approach to mean that laughter *until* that messianic period was suspect. They interpreted the verse to mean that "filling one's mouth with laughter in this world" was to be discouraged, if not proscribed completely. They even recast a rare positive comment about laughter by Ecclesiastes—"I said of laughter, it is to be praised"—to refer to a metaphysical world to come and the laughter of the righteous there, which might have come as a bit of surprise to the author, who was grappling pretty clearly with the here and now. But there was still another approach, one which redefined divine laughter, rather than deferring it. It is illustrated in a widely cited example, valuable for a peek into the rabbinic mindset in regard to laughter rather than jurisprudence more generally, as it is usually employed.

The specific legal question before the rabbis in the case that has come to be known as "the oven of Akhnai" is less relevant to us than the outcome: the sages ruled against a single rabbi, despite his many arguments to the contrary. That rabbi, Rabbi Eliezer, miffed at what he felt was the contravention of the law as it was supposed to be, shouted, "If the law is as I said, then let the carob tree prove it!" Without further ado, the carob tree uprooted itself and moved about fifty yards. "You can't prove anything from a carob tree," responded the sages. "Fine," he said. "If the law is as I said, then let this stream prove it!" And immediately the stream flowed backward. "You can't prove anything from a stream," they responded. Rabbi Eliezer said the same thing about the walls of the house of study, which started to fall, until another rabbi, Rabbi Joshua, objected, "When the sages are arguing, what are you doing getting involved?" So they stopped falling—but didn't go back to their original place, in deference to Rabbi Eliezer; they stayed at a slant. Finally, Rabbi Eliezer said, "Heaven will set you straight." And no sooner did he say so than a voice from Heaven resounded, "Why are you arguing with Rabbi Eliezer? He always has the law right." To which Rabbi Joshua responded with a verse: "The Torah is not in heaven!" (Deut. 30:12) or, in other words, "Mind your own business." (The Talmud explains that he meant that the Torah had already been given, at Mount Sinai, and there it was written that it's required to follow the majority.) The upshot? The Talmud relates that Rabbi Natan met the prophet Elijah, and asked him what God's response was. Elijah (who, given that he'd never died and had been taken alive to Heaven on a chariot, was uniquely positioned to pass these sorts of messages back and forth) duly reported that God laughed, saying, "My children have defeated me, my children have defeated me."

In one sense, this seems terribly transgressive. It seems to fit into the strand of comedy whose celebration of reversals and inversions might be extended, after the destruction, to full-fledged religious revolt, a philosophical case that would threaten ultimately to overturn Jewish life and faith as a whole. (That revolt could well take its motto from a famous verse in our centrally indicative book of Esther:

venahafoch hu, "the world is turned upside down.") Indeed, many have used this Talmudic tale to advocate for quite radical change in Jewish law.

But I think that would be a misreading, at least comedically speaking. This actually seems to be a lived humor that comes out of an actual relationship with God. Such questioning—and yes, even and perhaps especially such laughter and joking—can be a sign of connection and closeness and love, and not antagonism, or not only antagonism. Heaven is both intimately involved in considerations of the law and considerately stays out of it when humans are settling their own legal affairs. God has even agreed to be bound by His own word—or, more precisely, the witty and apropos application of it. With enough wit and chutzpah, based on knowledge and cleverness, and an understanding of the straitened circumstances the God-Israel relationship reflects in its diasporic incarnation, you can get God to laugh, and thus to leave you alone. Lovingly.

LUDWIG WITTGENSTEIN once said that "a serious and good philosophical work could be written that would consist entirely of jokes." Is it true that a good work of Jewish theology—or philosophy, or thought—could be done the same way? Well, no, and also yes. This is not the only model for the relationship with God in Jewish theology; and maybe it's not surprising that some of the models and texts that accentuate distance and fear—the medieval Maimonideans, for example—are hardly what you'd call a great source of theological comedy. (I don't want to present that extraordinary jurist, scholar, philosopher, and medical professional as a total killjoy, though: in advice to other doctors, Maimonides—who attended the Sultan of Egypt as personal physician—noted that "One should strengthen the vital power . . . by telling patients joyful stories which widen his soul and dilate his heart, and by relating news that distracts his mind and makes him laugh as well as his friends.") On the other hand, as we move into the eighteenth and nineteenth centuries, the Hasidic movement, with its emphasis on divine proximity, its insistence that God is all around us and infinitely reachable, is full of humor of various sorts, joyous, wry, rapturous, and the like.

This sensibility was hardly limited to the Hasidic movement. One of the founders of what we'd now call modern Orthodoxy, Samson Raphael Hirsch, contemplating the verse in Exodus where the Jews complain "Are there no graves in Egypt that you have brought us to die in the wilderness?," wrote: "This sharp irony even in a moment of deepest anxiety and despair is a characteristic trait of the witty vein which is inherent in the Jewish race from their very beginnings." Indeed, it may be a hallmark of traditional societies for whom comfort with divinity in their lives is a given that joking is far less taboo than in societies where that faith is constantly in question. Here are two jokes that tell the tale:

> A man sits at the outskirts of the shtetl, paid two kopecks a week to watch out for the messiah. "Two kopecks?" he's asked. "Not very much." "No," comes the response. "But it's steady work."

Or:

> A man went to his tailor and asked him to make him a suit. The tailor told him to come back in six days. "Six days?" asked the buyer. "So long? Why, God was able to make the world in six days!" "True," replied the tailor, gesturing to his samples. "But just look at the world—and look at these pants!"

Both jokes would have passed without comment in traditional society. But this last, an oven of *akhnai* for the shtetl—humans can do things more perfectly than God—might epitomize the Hasidic comic sensibility in the extreme.

Some Hasidic humor, given the movement's evangelizing nature, features narratives of theological superiority, as we've seen in earlier chapters. Those narratives often feature Sarah-like happy endings, with the formerly skeptical individual now turned true believer. In the Hasidic milieu, though, it's rare to find God as the butt of the joke—that role goes to the apparent sophisticate unwilling to understand the wisdom in radical simplicity. There are tales about Hasidic rebbes switching places with their coachmen, for example, the coachmen displaying wisdom that could have come just as easily from the Hasidic rebbes.

This is not to say, though, that these believers don't have moments of struggle; and that struggle, comedically speaking, is most powerfully expressed through sardonic remarks about God, prayer, and the world. The Hasidic rebbe Levi Yitzchak of Berdichev, for example, fed up with the radical imbalance between rich and poor, decided to pray to change the situation. (This joke, it should be noted, relies on an understanding in the Hasidic milieu that their leaders can mystically—the technical term would be *theurgically*—change the fate of the world by persuading God to alter His destined plan for the universe.) As he prays, his disciples watch him eagerly. After a long time, he removes his hand from his eyes and says, "I prayed for the rich to give all of their money for the poor, so that everyone will be equal, and I can tell you that I am halfway there!" The disciples rejoice. "Really?" "Yes!" says the rabbi. "The poor have agreed to receive the money!"

On the one hand, this is a joke about the limits of human nature; but it's also a joke about the seeming incapacity or unwillingness of the divine to change people's lives in the ways that matter the most. This was no small issue for a movement which prided itself (at least in its literature and folklore) as a people's movement. With a sense of intimacy and a mystical-philosophical orientation that placed human activity at the center of the metaphysical action—humanity was capable of nothing less than repairing a broken Godhead—Hasidic rebbes were often unafraid to argue with God, to treat Him as a friend and companion who's sometimes taken the wrong path.

Take, again, Levi Yitzchak of Berdichev, known for his "God-arguing," and whose mien in mixing a light tone with the most serious of theological concerns can serve as the paradigm for a meaningful Jewish spiritual comedy. In a famous anecdote, a tailor tells the rebbe of a deal he's made with God one Yom Kippur. On the one hand, the tailor tells the Holy One, Blessed be He, he hasn't lived up to the commandments; minor sins, and the like. On the other hand, God hasn't been so good to the Jews either. So, he says, we'll call it a wash: you forgive us for our sins, we'll forgive you for Jewish history. It's a barbed joke if there ever was one, putting the grandest questions into a format generally applied to rag trade *hondling*—but it's the punch line that lingers. Levi Yitzchak, getting the last word, tells the tailor he let God off too easily: given the Jewish people's history, he should have pushed for the coming of the messiah! But such a gesture—to try, in the phraseology of Jewish mysticism in which it's sternly warned against, to "hasten the end," to try to short-circuit God's ultimately joyous plan for messianic redemption and to shape the course of Jewish and universal history—is ultimately the question of faith on which traditional theological comedy stops. Or, to put it in the words of the greatest God-arguer and comic theologian in Jewish literature: "It grieved me that I wasn't a more learned man, because surely there were answers to be found in the holy books."

Sholem Aleichem's Tevye, "author" of the above, only exists in speech. That is, in the original stories that Sholem Aleichem wrote—as opposed to his later incarnation in the universally successful musical *Fiddler on the Roof*—all we know about him are the monologues that he delivers to a character "Sholem Aleichem": one of the things he has in common with stand-up comics. But an essential part of Tevye's *shpiel*, his routine, are his arguments. Not just with his audience of one Yiddish author, trying to make him understand what he's gone through with his life and his fate and his daughters, but the faithful transcripts of his conversations with God, as he wanders with his horse on the roads.

One of the most marked features of those conversations is the way that he quotes snatches of the Bible, the Talmud, and the Jewish liturgy, and then offers his own Yiddish "translation." That last in quotes because—in contrast to the opinions of some American critics unfamiliar with the Jewish literary tradition—Tevye wasn't giving what he mistakenly thought was a faithful translation. He was no Mr. Malaprop; rather, he was a careful and wry commenter on the promises made by God and claims made by the Jewish people to God in return, as captured in those holy texts featured in liturgy he would have recited every day of his life. When Tevye, quoting from the holiday service, says "What does it say in the prayer book? *You have chosen us*—We're God's chosen people; it's no wonder the whole world envies us . . . , " he's both audaciously reflecting his author's modern orientation and also warmly locating himself within the bosom of traditional faith. Tevye exemplified a search to understand a traditional Jew's place in the modern world, but to treat the theological concerns that search raised with intimacy and warmth and connection.

Perhaps this was why Sholem Aleichem was the canonical author of modernizing Eastern European Jewry. We often tend to think of the Jews' entrance into secular culture as one of radical break; the image of throwing the *tefillin*, the phylacteries, off the boat as you reach the New World's shores. Or, to put it another way, take this joke:

Mrs. Cohen arrives on the boat from the old country and is met by her son. She barely recognizes him. "You've shaved your beard!" she says. "Oh, mama, in America everyone is clean-shaven," he says. "Do you keep kosher?" "It's so hard to do that here," he replies. "So expensive, and every penny counts." "And the Sabbath?" she asks, hopefully. "With competition so fierce, it simply has to be a seven day work week," he says. She leans forward. "Tell me something, son," she asks. "Are you still circumcised?"

But even as observance changed in both Eastern Europe and America—and the nature of that change was often subtle and complex—the equally subtle and complex conception of the relationship between Jews, God, and history also switched less quickly than we might have thought. New forms of nationalism allowed for people to think about their role in Jewish history in a transformative way. But the perpetuation of fundamental factors—like the continuing differences between Jew and non-Jew—meant that, even among those recognizing that times were changing, skepticism could plausibly reign. Sholem Aleichem's meditation on the Jewish people, their fate, their difference—as seen through Tevye's struggles to understand that question—balanced nicely between a Jewish group identity based on the higher ideas of God and covenant and one based on national, ethnic, and other factors. Which is what made the question of his third daughter, Chava, in love with a non-Jew, so hard for him. It's where the situation truly gets unfunny, since there's no way of—like in the best jokes—having it both ways. (This was particularly pointed in Tsarist Russia, where there was no such thing as interfaith marriage: to marry a Christian meant to convert to Christianity.) Chava's tale was composed in the turbulent years in the wake of the first Russian Revolution, when it seemed as if everything was changing. The question was how much Tevye, a man of faith and tradition, could change as well. The older man and his willingness or unwillingness to change is a staple of comedy—from Abraham to *All in the Family*—and Tevye, as Sholem Aleichem points out, was willing to go so far and no further.

But the world kept moving on nonetheless. Tevye aged, in the tales and as a text, and the delicate balance he exemplified seemed to be less and less viable, both in a Europe in which Yiddishland was totally destroyed and in an America in which the very grammar of Jewish existence was being rewritten. In Europe in 1939, Itzik Manger's *The Book of Paradise* takes on the grand narratives of Jewish metaphysics via a *Tristram Shandy*–like device. The narrator, because of a heavenly mix-up, is capable of recalling the circumstances before his birth and, as an infant, relates them to astonished onlookers. As a yet-to-be reincarnated soul, he was in Paradise: but it turns out the object of centuries of Jewish yearning is simply a homey recreation of the shtetl. Paradise is nothing more than its artistic recreation in the minds of comic authors—which doesn't say much for its prospects as a theological motivator of behavior.

The Warsaw-born Yiddish writer Isaac Bashevis Singer, for his part, marks out similar territory in his depiction of Jewish devils. In a tragicomic story like "The Last Demon," entities evinced by earlier pietists as the proof of God's omnipotence and providence are rendered as simple Jews, stunned into silence, the subversive comedy of their presence ripped away by the fact of the Holocaust. Here's the last demon, on himself, to himself, alone and orphaned in a murdered shtetl:

> I, a demon, bear witness that there are no more demons left. Why demons, when man himself is a demon? Why persuade to evil someone who is already convinced . . . I don't have to tell you that I am a Jew. What else, a Gentile?

The last demon ends his tale by looking for sustenance from within the letters of a Yiddish storybook. But Singer's specters suggest the frightening possibility that to him—and, perhaps, to others—the tension that came from measuring the possibility of God's providence against the earthly conditions the Jews faced would belong less to lived comedy than as a relic of a historical past, whose structures of belief and theology were shattered by the ghettoes and camps that killed so many millions of that storybook's potential readers.

IN THE vastly safer precincts of America, by contrast, the questions of theological attachment have the greater luxury to be worked out intellectually, and not in extremis. (Which is not to say that individuals breaking from their family's traditions and observances didn't have their share of personal emotional trauma in the process, of course.) Perhaps accordingly, the God-arguers become the subject *of* comedy rather than the tellers of a tale; most notably by a writer who deeply loved, and was raised with, Sholem Aleichem. Saul Bellow famously described the work of great Jewish literature as a mixture of laughter and trembling, not far from the common characterization of Sholem Aleichem's contribution to Jewish comedy as "laughter through tears." But while the latter characterization (not always correctly, in my opinion) views Jewish comedy as an emotional response to Jewish history, turning its melodramas into ironic recognition, Bellow's own formulation, in his introduction to a 1963 anthology of Jewish short stories, adds an intellectual, and perhaps even theological, component:

> I would call the attitudes of these stories characteristically Jewish. In them, laughter and trembling are so curiously mingled that it is not easy to determine the relations of the two. At times the laughter seems simply to restore the equilibrium of sanity; at times the figures of the story, or parable, appear to invite or encourage trembling with the secret aim of overcoming it by means of laughter. . . . Recently, one Jewish writer . . . has argued that laughter, the comic sense of life, may be offered as proof of the existence of God. Existence, he says, is too *funny* to be uncaused.

Bellow's theological metaphor, not far from name-checking Søren Kierkegaard, made sense in a postwar America increasingly attempting to think of Judaism as a confessional faith that could compete equally with Protestantism and Catholicism. It also made sense after a Holocaust that had horribly punctuated the challenges to theological thinking that had been growing since modernity began. Bellow's comedy often features individuals trying to find their way in a world of almost existential hostility or indifference, rendering them shrunken and, sometimes, laughable—although hand in hand with a certain moral, religiously inflected grandeur. There's Herzog, writing all those prayerful letters to the good and the great, without any hope of an answer. Or Mr. Sammler, the one-eyed Holocaust survivor making his way through the conservative Bellow's kingdom of the blind, New York City streets filled with the vapid, narcissistic, unintellectual youth culture of the late sixties. (America's youth, in Bellow's reading, are among much else unfunny: dead-serious *agelasts*, lacking in the intellectual's ironic sense, one of his more damning charges.)

This said, the storehouse of American Jewish literature has many rooms, and there were writers who took a more intimate, almost Hasidic approach to these questions. That same Kierkegaard, in his *Concluding Unscientific Postscript*, wrote that "an existing humorist is the closest approximation to one who is religious"; that a humorist recognizes suffering in life, but "makes the treacherous turn, revoking the suffering in the form of jest"—humor is the almost-faithful, the work of the one who wants to believe. Bernard Malamud, in stories like "The Magic Barrel," "The Jewbird," "Angel Levine," "The Last Mohican," and even his largely overlooked novel *God's Grace*, was able to create a set of alienated Jews, largely American, who accept the presence of something greater in their lives and worlds—a prospect Bellow's intellectuals are never afforded, at least not outside of their crania. And yet, the shrunken and diminished sensibility that Bellow diagnosed is there, too: sometimes in contrast to the grand settings of the American landscape, sometimes in the straitened circumstances of stereotypical American Jewish smallness, Malamud's protagonists comically ignore that possibility of transcendence, or actively spurn the possibility of that gift.

And then there are Stanley Elkin's kibitzers and criers—who are, in their own ways, the literary equivalent of Lenny Bruce's shpritzing: stuck in their own corners, all the protagonists of the stories in *Criers and Kibitzers, Kibitzers and Criers* (1966) and his novels *The Living End* (1979) and *The Rabbi of Lud* (1987) can do is offer up ethnically secular prayers. It would be funny if it weren't so pathetic—or, more accurately, it's funny because it's so pathetic. They're the theologically oriented equivalent of Bruce Jay Friedman's black comedy. But Elkin's Jewish comedy never reached a broad literary audience, and Malamud crossed over (literally) most when he turned his energy for writing religious allegories into a Christian idiom, like in *The Assistant*, *The Natural*, and even *The Fixer* (which takes a Jewish story and Christianizes it). Perhaps not coincidentally, none of these are comedies.

No, for the fullest and most popular Jewish American fiction that takes these issues by the throat—if not another part of the anatomy—we have to turn to Philip Roth.

"Doctor Spielvogel, this is my life, my only life, and I'm living it in the middle of a Jewish joke . . . *only it ain't no joke*!" screams Alexander Portnoy in *Portnoy's Complaint*, Philip Roth's most famous novel. Roth—ever since his debut collection *Goodbye, Columbus*, which combines pathos, caricature, slapstick, and a deep dive into American Jewish theology in a story cheekily titled "Conversion of the Jews"—is our great comic cosmic writer of the modern period, the one who understands that telling jokes is in no small part a way of trying to deal with staring into the void, of grappling with the crisis of meaning.

Roth, asked if *Portnoy* was influenced by the stand-up comics beginning to take on more serious fare in the sixties, famously replied he was actually influenced by a sit-down comic named Franz Kafka. Less well-remembered are the other influences he mentioned: some local candy-store cutups and living-room clowns, and Henny Youngman, "a Jewish nightclub and vaudeville comic, whose wisecracks, delivered in an offhand whine while he played atrociously on the violin from the stage of the Roxy, had impressed me beyond measure at the age of ten." The tradition in which Roth's indelible characters participate—the professor of desire who's turned one morning into a giant breast; the weeping, howling, pissing, masturbating puppeteer; the fast-talking Rothian double named after a Yiddish belly button— mixes high and low humor for the most transcendent of aims: to investigate nothing less than the Jewish place in a world permeated by a omnipresent and infinitely unreachable God.

Roth had blazed onto the scene in 1959, with a National Book Award–winning collection that was infamous, in the Jewish community at least, for its scabrous satire. *Goodbye, Columbus*'s title novella had sent up both the nouveau riche Jewish manufacturers and their spoiled princess daughters, along with the young man with a chip on his shoulder who encounters them. But it may have been even more controversial for three other stories: "Defender of the Faith"; "Eli, the Fanatic"; and "Conversion of the Jews." "Defender of the Faith" features a largely nonobservant Army sergeant wheedled by a coreligionist into cutting him some slack on the base; he finally stops doing so when he realizes the latter is essentially debasing religion, practically commodifying it as a unit of exchange between the two, to get what he wants. (Realist as Roth is, he's often fairly symbolic about his characters' names, and it doesn't seem coincidental that the sergeant's last name is Marx.) The story may have drawn blood then for presenting a non-model image of a group whose leaders desperately wanted it to be displayed as a model minority: thus the young Roth's bridling when Jewish leaders spoke about his work being "bad for the Jews," responding somewhat stiffly that portraying an individual Jew said nothing about the Jewish question. Even if it's hard to entirely disagree with this position, the broad, even allegorical nature of other stories later in the collection suggest he may have been being somewhat disingenuous.

"Never hit anybody over God" is a powerful, if simplistic, theological manifesto; it's the mantra everyone repeats at the close of "Conversion of the Jews," a powerful, if somewhat simplistic, tale. In it, with a lot of flapping and manic energy, sophisticated theology deforms into farce, if not exactly a joke. The story involves schoolchildren, and it has a kind of sniggering schoolboy energy to it that its occasional forays into genuine pathos don't entirely dissipate. But as its title suggests, the story's not-quite-comedy takes on broader questions, particularly with its dynamic of a dictum of American liberalism coming to hold sway in a Hebrew school classroom: What are the Jews converting to? And from?

A partial answer appears in the third story, one which takes a subtler, more ironic tone; and grapples with the theological challenges of the previous decade and of modernity and secularity more generally. "Eli, the Fanatic" follows on the theme of "Defender of the Faith" by suggesting that the real question is who gets to speak for the community, and who gets cast out. In suburban America, Eli's attempt to grapple with genuine questions of Jewish community and solidarity—catalyzed by the arrival of a group of Holocaust survivors, largely schoolchildren, into his white-picket-fence, everybody of every faith gets along as long as no one stands out too much suburban idyll—are dismissed as insanity and fanaticism by his neighbors. Roth here, in the late fifties, is handling a question of increasing import now: what place Jewish spirituality in a world that finds it, not threatening, but simply old-fashioned, old-world, ridiculous?

The nuclear impact of the collection—the number of seminal moments of American Jewish literature contained therein by a writer in his mid-twenties—is hard to overstate. It's the *Revolver* of American Jewish literature, and I don't use the comparison inadvisedly. Though Roth's writing is of a piece with other work of the late fifties—the draft-era experiences of "Defender of the Faith," the pathos of the man in the grey flannel suit meets Holocaust survivor vibe of "Eli the Fanatic"—that line between the Faded Fifties and the Swinging Sixties isn't as bright and firm as cultural historians would sometimes like to make it, and Roth wanders across it, firing countercultural shots in all directions. (Another reading of *Goodbye, Columbus,* for example, could focus on its harbingers of the Sexual Revolution; its complex pas de deux with organized religion and spiritual search that also characterized some of hippiedom; and its stark portrayal of the generation gap, particularly the older generation as, all too frequently, clueless know-nothings.)

There's an argument to be made, in fact, that Roth spends most of the sixties hiding from the sixties-esque rebellion he's posited in his first collection, in a fruitless attempt to be Henry James, until he bursts gloriously back into form in *Portnoy's Complaint*, a novel where he combines two of his main obsessions—his own autobiographical masks and the Jewish voice—to take on the largest questions of Jewish life, faith, and fate in fully mature comic style. There's sniggering in *Portnoy*, of course; and there's cheap irony; and there's satiric dismissals; and there's farce. But it's all now in the hands of a master artist who uses it expertly, like a magician who sets up an amateurish pass to disguise the real ledgerdemain going on behind it.

It's fun to read Alexander Portnoy's complaint; but I'm not sure how many of us would envy his psychological agonies, whatever their cause. (The book's final line—its bitter, black parting joke—suggests the unsettling thought that after all of this, Portnoy is just beginning his psychoanalytic journey.) Portnoy's attempt to blur life and fiction in his search to make himself understood to his own implied listener, to communicate, to tell his jokes and make them land, to work his way through wrongness and wrongness until finally reaching understanding—is tied to his own confusion about himself and his relation to a rapidly changing society.

Like with Tevye, we have no objective reality in *Portnoy*. It's all monologue, all opportunity to hear a reflection on *everything* (and *Portnoy* covers the gamut—religion, sex, Jewish life and fate, the temptations of and against liberal politics, American Jewish identity, Israel, sex, Jewish-gentile relations, sex . . .) filtered through an intensely individual and unreliable lens. Roth was dissociating himself from the opinions and perspectives of his characters well before *Portnoy*. But *Portnoy* and its reception led to a quantum leap forward in the process of (mis)identification of Roth with his characters—a process Roth has inveighed against while (fair is fair) being perfectly comfortable with baiting his readers and critics in a series of books that flaunt the tempting possibility of making those connections. But that's not *very* different from stand-up comedians, or anyone who works in texts that create distinctive voices and especially distinctive "I"-voices, who take what he or she sees as an excuse to wander around the world of their head and come back again, in what (when it's done right) seems like the ramblings of therapeutic confession on-stage but is really a very structured performance.

Roth's literature—the comic side of it, at least—is about the summoning of reality through voice and language, whether it's the way in which Moishe Pipik, the strange, Jewish double of Philip Roth, appears in *Operation Shylock*, or the bizarre baseball players and politicians who populate *The Great American Novel*. (Or, in his parody of *The Metamorphosis*, when a professor turns into a gigantic breast.) In all these cases, Roth is struggling with the metaphorical made real, the joke that is not a joke at all. If in Bellow, philosophical and theological questions receive no answer, just resound, and in Singer, Jewish mythic and religious culture are used to provide theological (tragi)comic relief, in Roth the questions find quasi-supernatural echo, and theology repeats itself not as tragedy but as farce.

Thus the arrival of a survived Anne Frank in *The Ghost Writer* produces something like a shocked laugh and an intake of breath, and where *Portnoy* is replayed, with greater sadness and greater maturity, in the face of what fate has assured can only occur in the ghostly imagination: "Virtuous reader, if you think that after intercourse all animals are sad, try masturbating on the daybed in E. I. Lonoff's study and see how you feel when it's over." Thus the return of another Philip Roth in the land of Israel in the bizarre geopolitical spy story of *Operation Shylock*, which is John le Carré if everybody involved had gone to Yeshiva or City College rather than Oxbridge. Thus the return of multiple Philip Roths in *The Counterlife*, with its ironic recognition that though multiple paths may be possible, those multiplicities are hardly infinite: they echo and redouble in a way that not only speaks to the expertise of literary structure but, largely speaking, the inescapability of fate and of identity. There is no escape—at least none beyond the body, and that only provides the illusion of such. Alexander Portnoy's comedy may seem to be of the body, but it's really of the mind: as the Monkey points out to him, the police he fears will arrest him, in all senses of that word, are " 'Only in your imagination' (a not unsubtle retort, if meant subtly)." Roth's characters are trapped, rehearsing the same questions as Singer's yeshiva students turned Schopenhauer readers, but unfettered by Roth's greater linguistic, stylistic, and erotic comic landscape.

Does it have something to do with American Jewish manhood that, in the waning decades of the twentieth century, connection with something greater than oneself is comically expressed through the release of bodily fluid? Roth's Mickey Sabbath pisses on his mistress's gravestone in *Sabbath's Theater*; and Walter Prior involuntarily tumesces, then ejaculates, whenever the Angel of America approaches. Admittedly, Walter Prior isn't Jewish, but Tony Kushner's "gay fantasia on national themes," *Angels in America* (premiered, in two parts, in 1991–1992) has more than its share of Jewish comic elements: the stereotypical Jewish male jokes, the use of Yiddish as punch line, and the transformation of the God-arguing tradition into something mixing the sublime and the ridiculous. Late in the play, Prior goes to Heaven, and he—and Kushner—confronts the magnificence of the transcendent with homey wit and chutzpah, following Manger's lead in turning Heaven itself into something prosaic, diminished, domesticated. Not all of this is put into the mouths, or the views, of Jewish characters in Kushner's play. For Kushner, the theological question of America is best expressed by its religious minorities: and his characters of multiple identity and affiliation—gay, Mormon, Reagan conservative—need their Jewish counterparts, and the "Jewish" city of New York, to become most fully realized as *comic* theologians.

Kushner's work—and other plays intertwining theology and

comedy, like Neil Simon's 1974 *God's Favorite*, which rewrites the book of Job, or even 1964's *Fiddler on the Roof*, with Tevye's soliloquizing—is about performance in a way that the work of Roth and Sholem Aleichem aren't. Alexander Portnoy and Tevye (in his original incarnation) are creatures consisting solely of language; Louis Ironside and Tevye (as embodied by Zero Mostel) are creatures of expression and gesture as well. Whither the stand-up theologians, the comedy of religious gesture?

MOST AMERICAN JEWISH comedians of the past few decades don't necessarily know—or care—enough about the big theological questions in order to take them on. Some of this is that comedy got small, focusing on Seinfeldian socks; some of it is that it became responsive to the American conditions around it, like Brooksian parodies; and some of it is simply that the big questions—race, gender, politics—are, in this secular age, largely not related to religious questions for most people, and for American Jews more than most. There are exceptions, particularly stand-up comics who work partially or entirely for religious Jewish audiences. Elon Gold has a very successful act with modern Orthodox audiences, often revolving around the minutiae of Jewish religious observance in a secular world; and there's Mordechai Schmutter, humor columnist for the ultra-Orthodox newspaper *Hamodia*, whose Erma Bombeck-in-a-sheitel approach portrays the foibles of a religious community in as quotidian a fashion as any other community's. But there are other comedians who very clearly take on religious issues in their work while aiming at a broader audience: the Bellows and Roths of the microphone scene.

David Steinberg grew up in Winnipeg, the son of an Orthodox rabbi; he came to Chicago in 1960 to attend yeshiva, then switched to study English literature at the University of Chicago. While there, he saw Lenny Bruce at the Gate of Horn—"it was like seeing the

Rolling Stones for the first time"—and noted, impressed, the way Bruce threw Yiddish into his monologues. Steinberg got involved with Second City, and quickly became known for his own jazzlike monologues: improvised mock Bible sermons fashioned around biblical names called out from the audience. (A generation later in Chicago, Robert Smigel, best known for creating Triumph the Insult Comic Dog and *Saturday Night Live*'s "TV Funhouse," would perform a slapstick version of similar mien; coming onstage as an Orthodox Jew complete with cotton-candy beard, he would lick his finger, turn a page of the Bible he was holding, tear off and eat a piece of his beard, and lick his finger once more.) Steinberg would eventually take his mock sermons to national television, where he would ruffle feathers. A Moses sermon on *The Smothers Brothers Comedy Hour* in October 1968 led to a deluge of letters; reappearing at Tommy Smothers's behest over the network's objections in April 1969, he gave a sermon on Jonah, in which he suggested that skeptical New Testament scholars "literally grab the Jews by the Old Testament"—complete with (in)appropriate hand gesture. That last led to a flap eventually resulting in the network cancelling the show.

Steinberg's controversial positions on religion, tame as they may seem now, had an almost incalculable effect in a culture whose entertainment was less stratified, whose discourse was far less coarsened (or more restricted: take your pick) and whose public culture was significantly more religious by many metrics. But it's still possible to raise hackles, perhaps most notably—though unsurprisingly—by writers who by dint of their own autobiographical circumstances are fighting battles most of the Jewish community took on many decades, if not centuries, ago.

In the stories collected in 2005's *Beware of God*, his 2007 memoir *Foreskin's Lament*, and his 2012 novel *Hope: A Tragedy*, Shalom Auslander takes his anger at the theologies drummed into him in his ultra-Orthodox upbringing and turns them into satirical explosions of absurdist fiction: hamsters arguing theology while musing about best-selling thriller author James Patterson, or a luckless protagonist discovering Anne Frank in his attic. (Though this Anne Frank is not the melancholy survivor of Roth's *Ghost Writer* but an irate force of wrath against metaphysical destiny: even Roth, in his wildest, might not have dared to place the words "Blow me" in Anne Frank's mouth.)

The novel's protagonist, like *Portnoy*, meets with a psychologist, who insists on telling him jokes with deflating punch lines.

> What did Jesus Christ say when they nailed him to the cross? . . . He said Ouch, said Professor Jove. I don't get it, said Kugel. There's nothing to get, said Professor Jove. It hurt. . . . There is hurt in this world . . . there is pain. Hoping there won't be only makes it worse.

Auslander, despite—or more precisely, because—of his upbringing, is still taking theology seriously, even if he doesn't want to. His jokes sting in a different way from that Sarah Silverman routine about Jesus being magic mentioned earlier. Yes, Silverman's joke is, in its own way, theological; but her dismissiveness of Christianity extends, really, to all matters metaphysical; as a joke-teller, she's embracing, as an increasing number of her compatriots do, the concept that life's a joke. Full stop, without consideration of the concomitant philosophical implications. In that, she's reflective of the increasing majority of Americans—and American Jews. What consequences this will have for this strain of Jewish comedy remains to be seen.

6

The Tale of the Folk

How popular is Jewish humor? Not very, so far.

I'm joking, of course; a not-so-witty play on words, resting on semantic sleight of hand over the twin definitions of "popular." As to whether Jewish comedy entertains and edifies large audiences—well, sometimes it did, and sometimes it didn't (as our chapters on satire and wit suggested). But whether it reflected the breadth and variety of Jewish society—well, that's something else again.

The overwhelming majority of the comedy we've discussed so far—certainly before the early twentieth century—was composed, disseminated, and often circulated among a small group of almost entirely male elites. The scholars in the Talmudic academies; the pamphleteers and propagandists of the Haskalah; even the salons of the Yiddish belletrists and mid-century American intellectuals—these were highbrow, or high-middle-brow, largely male precincts. And that, as much as anything else we've discussed, shaped the tone and contours of the comedy it produced. (The exception that proves the rule: the vulgar "low comedy" of the parodies—and even there, the "low" parodies were matched by their highbrow counterparts.) Which left a large portion of the Jewish world under-represented: notably, the less-well-educated part, and, even more notably, the female part.

Under-represented, but not undiscussed. When we look at ancient, medieval, and early modern comedy about women—and there almost all we have is work *about* women; vanishingly few works of Jewish literature written *by* women in those periods have survived—it's full of comedy at their expense, misogynistic and cruel, work that nonetheless tells us a great deal about women's role, their power, and the motives and personalities ascribed to them. Women aren't presented as rich, nuanced, complicated beings in their own right; they're reduced to caricature, to stereotype. They're not the jokers; and, all too often, they're the butt of the joke.

Take Esther, for example. Because make no mistake, Esther is a book, in no small part, about women's power and the fear men have of it. Esther's predecessor Vashti's refusal to come to the king's feast is, in the kind of exaggeration that is the province of comedy, blown up into an entire aria of anxiety that her action will lead to women disobeying their husbands throughout the empire: and so legislation is passed that explicitly forbids such an eventuality. As it turns out, of course—and here the comedy turns from satire to a deeper, more brilliant irony—Esther *does* use her sexuality to fatal effect, and she *is* disobeying her husband, to a certain extent. For the best of all causes, of course, to protect her people—domestic comedy, national stakes. And she does it with grace, and with charm, as endlessly noted and feted. But with wit? I've never seen a single suggestion that Esther herself has a sense of humor. Now, this isn't quite fair—from the moment we meet her, she's in extreme circumstances, and the stakes we see her in are constantly the very highest. But in the later expansions of the story, as we'll see, most of the other, male, characters get all the fun.

Esther's story through the ages, and the story of the domestic comedy she's part of—despite not being quite in on the joke—is the history of women in comedy, Jewish and otherwise, until far too recently. For most of that time, women were clearly identified with the domestic; with folk culture; with oral transmission. This doesn't make them joke tellers, necessarily, but it does make their story a good jumping-off point to discuss the domestic strand of Jewish comedy: the one that focuses on the everyday Jew, and which, along the way, takes in a great number of stereotypes, some loving and some deeply pernicious. These stereotypes—and as we'll see, played for comedy, they often gain in grandeur and essence to become something closer to archetypes—are not just evocations of the popular humor that was produced and circulated more generally. They give some sense—distorted and stretched through the comic lens as it is—of the imagination the Jewish people had of themselves: not history, but something closer to myth, to folktale.

Those stereotypes—of women, but also of rabbis and paupers and schlemiels and marriage-makers and many others—are most pithily expressed in jokes, so our focus will expand to the Jewish joke more generally: and include some history of those who told it, how they told it, and who got to tell it. But we'll keep circling back to the stories of, and about women, in and out of comedy; since that stereotype is the broadest and in many ways most resilient of all. And the story starts—once more—with the first laughing woman in Jewish literature.

LET'S LOOK at the story of Sarah's laughter again; this time a little less charitably. First, it's a story of a woman who doesn't get the joke, or, more precisely, thinks there's a joke when there isn't. Put another way, it's a story about how women don't get comedy. (The fact that Abraham actually laughs, too, but doesn't get faulted for it, may make this an early example of the comedic double standard often operative in such situations.) And the laughter Sarah *does* exercise is that mocking laughter we've seen so often in the Bible: but here the (presumed) inferior in her sights is the impotent, aged Abraham, rendering her, after perhaps Eve herself, the first of a long line of women viewed as potentially castrating figures in the Bible, and afterwards.

There's Miriam, talking down Moses's marital experiences (and punished with leprosy as a result, unlike her brother, who does the same thing); Delilah's constant attempts to emasculate Samson (although admittedly everyone comes off pretty poorly in that one), or Yael and that tent peg through the head, a story repurposed for the Apocryphal tale of Judith and Holofernes. In that story, Judith, who famously cuts off an Assyrian general's head, is portrayed as notably pious: so much so that she fasts for three and a half years without a break. In short, she's portrayed as a killjoy, an *agelast*—and she's not the only one. For speaking truth to power in a biting, sarcastic manner—telling David he looks like a fool for his joyous celebration of the return of the ark, dancing so happily that his genitals are on display—Michal, Saul's daughter, David's wife, is punished with childlessness, a monstrous fate in the ancient world, particularly for a woman. She's not the only one who makes David the butt of a joke: the prophet Nathan embarrasses him in front of his entire court. But it's Michal who's punished. Michal's role as the scolding harridan, the angry housewife, finds its echo in Proverbs. ("It is better to live in a desert than with a contentious and angry woman"; "It is better to live on a corner of the roof, than in a house of companionship with a quarrelsome wife.")

This is one side of the misogynistic coin when it comes to comedy: women's lack of humor. But don't worry; sexism can hold opposing negative stereotypes simultaneously, and the other might be best expressed by a slightly later writer, the Roman Jewish historian Josephus, who writes: "Let not the testimony of women be admitted, on account of the levity and boldness of their sex." Josephus presented an image of women as childlike, if not outright childish; proverbially curious and deeply untrustworthy, in no small part due to their inability to think rationally past their sexual desires. In the Joseph story, Potiphar's wife is portrayed as having what a less enlightened time used to call "hot pants": she chases after Joseph four times in six verses in Genesis. (Perhaps it's related to her marriage to a eunuch.) The midrashic explication of the story expands the image of female licentiousness into slapstick territory, having all of her friends who have come over to snack and ogle Joseph get so overwrought they actually stab their own hands with the knives they're using to peel their fruit.

And yet *another* linked misogynist stereotype (we've run out of sides of the coin; sorry) is the way that empowered women who act surprisingly out of conventional roles—Tamar and Rahab and Ruth, for example, exercising powers of initiative and intelligence—are often marginalized by reducing their efforts to the sexual sphere or limiting their ambit to sexualized actions. Of course, the limited sphere of women's action in ancient times meant they didn't have many other venues open to them—but not many isn't identical to none; and it reinforces those same castration fears. In one of the books of the Apocrypha, First Esdras, for example, three men play a riddle game in front of a king, asking what the strongest of all things is. The first suggests wine; the second, the king himself; and the third, women; since, as he puts it, a woman can even strike the king, and the *king* will beg forgiveness for whatever he has done wrong.

This paradigm—three men talking about women and no woman's voice to comment—pretty much sets the tone for most of Jewish (and general) literary history, where the women didn't get much of a chance to respond to these claims. (This, of course, despite a reputation for garrulousness: "Ten *kabs* of idle talk descended to the world," says the Talmud. "Nine were given to women.") This had to do with full-fledged misogyny within much of premodern culture, Jewish and otherwise, and in medieval and early modern Europe women were figures of Jewish fun in almost precisely the same way that they were in that of their territorial neighbors': either voluptuaries only willing to exercise their wits to get into adulterous trouble—the Talmud also says that women have nine kabs of sexual indulgence to one of continence—or vicious and sour harridans whose prime purpose was to make their husbands' lives living hells.

These last were expressed in comedic fables, folktales, or poetry, from the medieval period on. Whether it's Joseph Zabara's *Book of Delight* (ca. 1200) ("Take heed of a woman's counsel, for woman is evil and bitter in spirit and hard. Her heart is of flint, an accursed plague is she in the house. Wise and understanding men heed not their wives, for they are of light mind"); Yehuda al-Harizi's *Takhke-moni* (early thirteenth century), one of whose sections is entitled "Of Seven Maidens and Their Mendacity"; or Ibn Shabbetai's thirteenth-century "The Misogynist," a parodic work which, at the very least, shows a remarkable facility with the conventions and stereotypes of misogynistic literature, the portraits remain remarkably similar, written by men, or inhabited by male personas, who play their impatience with and hostility toward women for comedy. And the stereotype remained depressingly robust. Here's a brief quatrain from five centuries later, entitled "Epitaph for a Hen-Pecked Husband": "At last I can rest; I am free/ From the tongue of my termagant wife,/ But I fear very much what will be/ When we're both resurrected to life." A comic pamphlet from late eighteenth- or early nineteenth-century Amsterdam features a twenty-two–stanza quarrel between newlyweds (the number of letters in the Hebrew alphabet), each one starting with a liturgical, biblical, or rabbinic quotation and devolving into insult. The first, for example, subverts one of the warmest evocations of domestic bliss in the Bible, from Proverbs, still often recited by a husband to his wife on Sabbath eve:

> *Eshes chayil mi yimtso*
> "Where can a woman be found"
> Who doesn't hold her husband in regard
> When she is a shrew
> What does her beautiful face help me?

These images of women would set the table for their complicated position as subjects of and producers of comedy until the present day.

THESE STEREOTYPES didn't just circulate in the elite echelons, behind the screen of medieval erudite Hebrew poetry, of course. They didn't even limit themselves to the more populist and linguistically acces-sible Yiddish chapbook. The main way they spread—the way most stereotypes spread most easily—was orally; and the most efficient vector for oral transmission (so to speak) was the joke.

Jokes are old, of course, very old. A joke book from fifth-century Greece, the *Philogelos* (Laughter-Lover), still exists, and we know that centuries before that a favorite writer of the first-century Roman emperor Augustus apparently compiled one hundred and fifty joke anthologies. (Not one of which survives to this day, alas.) Explana-tions of the philosophy and the psychology of jokes, their structure, even their neurological basis, are manifold. Jokes, as a medium, exemplify the theories of humor we've mentioned particularly well: for the incongruity theory, there's the linguistic playfulness of puns and witticisms, or the surreally absurdist joke; and of course there are a wide variety of jokes dedicated to establishing the superiority of one group over another (and these days, in their telling, perhaps indicating the precise opposite).

And then there's the third theory, the relief theory. That's where that great Jewish joke analyzer, Sigmund Freud, comes in. Freud was a great lover of jokes, particularly Jewish jokes; and was fascinated by what they said about the people who told them and what they revealed of the way their minds worked. He looked close to home for his examples, and despite his complex and sometimes vexed relationship with his family's Judaism, wrote a book on humor in which Jewish jokes often stood in for the whole. Freud developed the idea that ethnicities and groups had all sorts of traits that reflected national character, and he noted that Jews, like everyone else, had a great deal of aggression. Aggression was part of the essential function of joking, in fact, a safety valve to push against our frustrations about the artificial forms of societal (and linguistic) restraint without actu-ally tipping over the apple cart. "Anti-rites," as the anthropologist Mary Douglas put it. They're social contracts, about how to push, and how not to push too far. Or, as dirty joke historian Gershon Legman put it, jokes contained "infinite aggressions," especially of men against women—but they *concealed* them. Though, for the joke to really work, not very well.

Freud also famously said, with regard to the Jews and *their* jokes, that "I do not know whether there are many other instances of a people making fun to such a degree of their own character." In the Jewish case, he noted, the aggression was turned *inward*. Freud's disciples in psychoanalytic thinking, like Theodor Reik and Martin Grotjahn, took this a lot further, and developed an entire theory of Jewish wit based on aggression, masochism, and the like. Jewish jokes were based on a specific understanding of Jewish nature; an argument not that dissimilar to the ones we've seen on display in earlier chapters. It was an argument that called for a specifically masochistic Jewish nature, and, as a result, could be understood to define Jewish humor as partaking of something of the (psycho)pathological. In fact, some of these claims would be taken on gleefully by pro-Nazi "scholars." In the years before the Final Solution, they attempted to "prove" that Aryan humor was the best, exemplifying shared Aryan values, and that Jewish humor was not only twisted and grotesque but simultaneously correctly diagnosed these hateful people's failings.

This was not Reik's and Grotjahn's approach. As Grotjahn put it:

> the Jewish joke, however, is only a masochistic mask; it is by no means a sign of masochistic perversion. The Jewish joke constitutes victory by defeat. The persecuted Jew who makes himself the butt of the joke deflects his dangerous hostility away from the persecutors onto himself. The result is not defeat or surrender, but victory and greatness.

Nonetheless, it's still a circumscribed approach—defining Jewish humor, or at least the Jewish joke, through this one lens entirely—and I hope that the variety and diversity of comedy discussed throughout this book has given us the comfort to suggest these Freudian statements, like some of the other critical approaches we've seen, are better taken as a part of the whole, not the whole thing. Freud, of course, was pretty well known for jumping to grand, universal conclusions on the basis of sporadic case evidence. But Freud's genius when it comes to jokes is like when it comes to everything else: flashes of lightning which illuminate the surroundings but don't necessarily give you the full picture.

Take, for example, the first entry in an early collection of modern Jewish jokes, Immanuel Olsvanger's *Red Pomegranates*. It's about the act of joke-telling itself:

> You tell a joke to a peasant and he laughs three times: when you tell it; when you explain it; and when he understands it. A landowner laughs only twice: when he hears the joke and when you explain it. For he can never understand it. An army officer laughs only once: when you tell the joke. He never lets you explain it—and that he is unable to understand it goes without saying. But when you start telling a joke to another Jew, he interrupts you: "Go on! That's an old one," and he shows you how much better he can tell it himself.

There's that aggression. Yes, like Freud said, it's aimed inward. But crucially, not only so: it's just that the last, and best, and perhaps bitterest laugh, is so aimed. Two-thirds of the joke is aimed outward. For a moment, we'll focus on the part we generally gloss over: the set up of peasant, landowner, army officer. It doesn't mean that much to us, and we can enjoy the joke—particularly that punch line—without dwelling on the details. But for someone in late nineteenth-century Eastern Europe, the distinctions, though stereotypical, were certainly to be savored as well.

When you get down to it, in other words, there are really three kinds of Jewish jokes: jokes that showcase particular Jewish conditions or circumstances, jokes that highlight particular Jewish sensibilities, and jokes that feature particular Jewish archetypes. Jokes of the first type—discussing how Jews live in the world and how they react to its changing circumstances—we've discussed in previous chapters as part of the general subject. Jokes of the second type, which discuss a kind of generalized Jewish nature or sensibility, are closest to Freud's approach. But even *that's* a moving target, both because of historical shifts and because, as we've seen, Jewish comedy has many natures and many sensibilities.

Which leaves the final category: archetype jokes. All jokes, of every type, are by definition related to the society they circulate in. This is true on the most basic level of language—a knock-knock joke makes no sense if you don't have the cultural ethos of signaling on a door before you enter, for example. It's a fine balance between reality and stereotype, though, and universal and particular. Jokes about, say, doctors, which have been around at least since that first Greek joke book, focus on a fairly static set of issues (quackery, overcharging) alongside others that are clearly culturally specific (a predilection for golf). Tracking the Jewish comic stereotypes—and whether and how they've changed—can be particularly illuminating. We've already begun to do this with the most powerful, enduring, and pronounced stereotype in Jewish comedy: the Jewish woman. We've traced that stereotype from the Bible to the edge of modernity, and we'll return to it in its more recent incarnation shortly, particularly—though not solely—in jokes. But there were other cards in the Jewish deck as well, and let's lay them out: first the specifically Jewish roles, that is, roles that have in one way or another very specific Jewish cultural circumstance, and then expand to more generalized character types with a Jewish spin.

Jokes have always stereotyped particular types of employment. So it's pretty clear that the Jewish job par excellence, the rabbi, would come in for its share of skepticism and scrutiny. Jews have always, since the days of Moses, treated their leaders with a modicum of disrespect. Rabbis are mocked for the length and boredom quotient of their sermons, their lack of qualification for their position, their personal hypocrisies given their role as moral example and instructor. These, naturally, differ from period to period in their instructive cultural details. Rabbi jokes become increasingly pronounced and defined as a subcategory with the increasing professionalization of the rabbinate in the modern period. A favorite American joke, which will have to stand in for many, tells of the rabbi who goes to play golf on Yom Kippur and scores eighteen holes in one, one after another. The angels protest to God for this seeming topsy-turviness in the matter of human affairs: such a sin, to play golf on the holiest of all days, and to be so rewarded? God, smiling, stroking his beard: "Yeah. But who's he gonna *tell*?" Rabbis—in their temptations, in their vanities—are no different than anyone else.

Overall, though, the rabbi jokes, in a process that dates as far back as the "Purim rabbi" we discussed earlier and maybe all the way back to the Talmud, are generally dedicated to perpetuating the system by poking fun at its bad apples. (With the exception of social satires in which a particular *branch* of rabbis—the Hasidic rabbinate, for example, or the Reform rabbinate—are lampooned harshly as a class, rather than as individuals.) There's this one, for example:

> A rabbi, having asked for advice on how to deliver a sermon, was given three tips. First, speak about the weekly Torah portion. Second, be honest with the congregation. Third, be brief. That Sabbath, the rabbi arose, walked to the pulpit, and said: "We are about to read this week's Torah portion. I'll be honest: I have no idea what it is. Thank you." And then he sat down.

In many jokes, though, the rabbi comes off with a witty sense of self-consciousness about his own situation, the lone possessor of common sense in a world of ignorance and superficiality. Some of my favorite jokes, enough that they might constitute a subcategory, are predicated on a very traditional rabbinical task: the need to write letters of approbation for a prospective but unworthy manuscript on rabbinical matters, or of recommendation for unworthy recipients. (One rabbi, writing a recommendation for an unqualified author, signed his name low on the page; when the author asked why, he replied with a biblical verse, "Keep your distance from an untruthful word.") And then there are the ones that deal with obstreperous congregants: Sholem Aleichem expanded one of these into a short story, "Tit for Tat," in which both rabbi and congregant tell stories poking fun at the other's expense, accusing each other of embezzlement.

This fondness toward the archetypal figure tends to spread to some of the other archetypes as well. Take, as the best example, the schnorrer, the beggar. The schnorrer figure must be seen against the incredible poverty in Jewish Eastern Europe, in which a tremendous number of people were trying to compete for the same kopecks and rubles and groschen in alms, and at times, it was wit, not to say chutzpah, that distinguished the recipient from the one turned away. (At least in the comedy version of the story; in real life the encounters between poor and rich were certainly far less enchanting.)

Take, for example, the story of the schnorrer who, every year, showed up at the same rich man's house for alms; one year he shows up with another man. Asked who the second man is, he says: "He's my son-in-law: I'm introducing him to the family business!" Or the one with a similar setup, in which the rich man says to the schnorrer: "I'm sorry, I can only give you half my usual amount. I had a bad year." To which the schnorrer, not batting an eye, responds. "So you had a bad year. Why should I suffer?" Or the one Freud references, where a schnorrer goes to a very expensive medical specialist, then pleads poverty when it comes time to pay. "Then why did you come to the most exclusive professional in the city?" the doctor demands. "For my health," the schnorrer says, "nothing is too expensive!" Or the one in which the schnorrer takes on the archetypal Jewish rich man of Eastern Europe, Baron Rothschild himself. After a donation has been wrangled out of him, the magnate comments: "If you hadn't made such a damned nuisance of yourself I would have given you twice as much." To which the schnorrer responds: "Do I give you financial advice? Well, I'm a professional schnorrer, so don't give me shnorring advice."

So maybe it *is* chutzpah, after all. (In fact, the London 1899

Jewish Year Book actually *defines* the schnorrer as "the technical name for a Jewish beggar, who is distinguished from all other beggars by his Chutzpah.") There was something about the schnorrer jokes that suggested an essential, if not dignity, at least attempt to show no shame in poverty. But it was a fine line between that and class aggression. One last joke, concerning a schnorrer with a literary legacy, the famed folk character Hershele Ostropolier. There were other famously witty schnorrers in Jewish Eastern Europe—Shmerl Snitkever and Lebenyu Gotsvunder of Podolia, Motke Chabad of Lithuania, Shayke Fefer of Poland—but only Hershele was famous enough to be immortalized by Isaac Babel. A classic Hershele story:

> Hershele visited an inn and asked for a meal, to which the innkeeper, no stranger to shnorrers, asked him whether he had the means to pay for it. Hershele admitted that he didn't, but said, meaningfully, that if they didn't provide him with a meal regardless, he'd have to do what his father did in such circumstances. Quite disturbed, the innkeeper and his wife served him a sumptuous repast, and then, once he had eaten his fill, timidly asked if they could find out what his father did. "Why," Hershele replied, "he went to bed without any supper."

Not the best of jokes, perhaps, but powerfully revealing the aggression, the energy aimed by the poor, the have-nots, at the haves. And it pays off: in these jokes, the schnorrer generally either gets the contribution he's begged for or at least the pleasure of one-upping his competition with a cutting remark or a witty line. (Although the schnorrer didn't *always* get the last word. The thirteenth-century medieval wit Gregory Bar Hebraeus told of a rich man who, in refusing to give to the poor, would say, "That which God hath not given him, how can I give him?")

Compare this to tales of the *luftmensh*, the air-man, who is incapable of any success whatsoever: nothing he does comes to fruition.

And he tries *everything*. One of Jewish literature's most famous *luft-menshen*, Sholem Aleichem's Menakhem-Mendl, tells of his constant failure in businesses ranging from stock trading to matchmaking in a series of letters to his wife that became comic touchstones for a generation of Eastern European Jews. The comic listing that perhaps best exemplifies the *luftmensh* as a jack-of-all-failures is composed by the major Yiddish comic talent, now virtually unknown, Joseph Tunkel (then better known as Der Tunkeler):

> As you see me, this Litvak, Bentze the son of Dvoira the Blintz Baker of your home town, has already been everything in the book: a Turk, a Tartar, a Gypsy, an echo-man, a waterfall spiller, a Moroccan, a Little Russian Cossack chieftain, a Chinese, an Apache.

The travails of this *luftmensch* have led him to contortions not just of trade, but of ethnicity itself: the only identity he can't eradicate is his humble Jewish luftmenschiness, though, and he's a failure in all of them. In that sense, he's not dissimilar to his two more famous brethren in the taxonomy of comic Jewish stereotype, the schlemiel and the schlimazel.

The distinction between the schlemiel and the schlimazel has lent itself to all sorts of characterization: I'm partial to the one that suggests the schlemiel is the one who spills the soup and the schlimazel is the one that's spilled on. There's not so much to say about the schlimazel, except to note that as the kind of avatar of Jewish misfortune, his troubles are always writ small—yes, for the schlimazel, the bagel always lands butter side down, but you won't tend to read about a schlimazel being caught in a pogrom; the stakes are just too disproportionate. The schlimazel's only option, his only power, is the right to complain.

The schlimazel's complaint was heard as early as medieval times, in a poem where the speaker bemoaned his bad fortune: "If I should undertake to sell candles, the sun would never set; if I should deal with shrouds, no one would ever die." A later joke, expanding the motif, encompasses a threat to go into the hat business—since with this man's luck, babies would all be born without heads—but the aggressiveness of this posture sits uneasily with the general resignation and, yes, masochistic tendency associated with the true schlimazel. We should take care not to confuse persona and person: the author of the preceding poetic complaint was Abraham ibn Ezra, one of the great scholars and intellects of medieval Spain. But the taint of schlimazeldom has affected its practitioners, especially its greatest ones, into the modern era.

Putting aside the matter of his last name, George Costanza is the schlimazel par excellence. Far be it from me to list the catalog of indignities wreaked upon him by a hostile universe (and the *Seinfeld* writers' room): not when he does it so much better himself. In an attempt to sway the co-op board of an apartment building from awarding a prized New York commodity—a sweet apartment—to a survivor of the capsized ship the *Andrea Doria*, this self-proclaimed "short, stocky, slow-witted bald man" launches into his own version of a greatest hits catalog. Handcuffed to the bed in his underwear? Check. In a compromising relationship with (unbeknownst to him) a Nazi? Check. Fiancée dies by licking the toxic envelopes he picked out for their wedding invitations? Check. Shrinkage? Yep.

Needless to say, of course, George does not get the apartment. Victory is not in the schlimazel's DNA. (In this, he is a close cousin to the particularly, peculiarly American schmuck: who, in an archetypal joke, is such a schmuck he comes in second place in a schmuck contest. Because he's a schmuck.) Any improvements in position are, at best, temporary. In an earlier episode, when George briefly attempts to better his self-confidence by wearing a toupee, Elaine wrestles the somewhat psychologically effective device from his head and throws it out the window: we take a deep breath at the sense of order restored.

The schlemiel, by contrast, is a soup-*spiller*; and often gets himself into trouble by his very nature. Heine provides a quasi-biblical providence for the archetype in his *Hebrew Melodies*: when the zealous Phineas (or Pinchas) attempts to slay the treacherous Zimri, a poor zhlub gets in the way of his spear, one Shelumiel ben Zurishaddai: "forebear," Heine says, "of the race and lineage of schlemiels." But, unlike in that mythic first case, the schlemiel usually bumbles himself *out* of trouble, too, and something in the way he does that, as in the picaresque novels that serve as the archetype's ancestors (Don Quixote has something of the schlemiel about him; so does Joseph Andrews), generates sympathy and maybe even some perverse admiration. If it's hard to imagine anyone feeling admiration for a schlimazel, and even sympathy, if we have it, is touched by alienation and perhaps even slight contempt, it's worth recalling that Ruth Wisse once referred to the schlemiel as a "modern hero." And he *does* seem particularly suited for an age in which we may have lost our metaphysical footing; being unbowed, in the modern age, with all the indignities that are visited upon us is something. Jewish humor is not *only* about psychic resilience, but some aspects of it *can* be about that, and the schlemiel's nobility in being—or, at times, playing—the fool, elevates accident and contempt to a kind of comic pathos.

One notable example, Isaac Bashevis Singer's "Gimpel the Fool," uses the figure of the schlemiel to make arguments about Jewish power, morality, and heroism. The title character is constantly fooled by other shtetl members, defrauded and mocked and cuckolded; but he makes clear that his own power of understanding—and of vengeance—are hobbled by blinders of his own making. His schlemielhood is a show; it is he, Heaven-bound, who will have the last laugh, and they who are the fools. What makes the story's great humor, though, of the blackest sort is the intimation—like in "Bontshe the Silent," which this story is explicitly modeled on—that Gimpel may have accepted this position, this contortion, for nothing at all, no reward. The joke, in the end, may be on him, and the moral system that encourages passivity and being wronged. Schlemielhood, as it turns out, can serve as the highest test of traditional society as it uneasily confronts modernity.

A LESS philosophical but more pervasive battleground between the forces of tradition and modernity was the institution of marriage, and the transition to its conception as a site for romantic love, rather than an economic arrangement. The figure of the matchmaker, or *shadkhn*, was central to that treatment.

It's an old business—one wry anecdote from the midrash has a rabbi telling a Roman matron who asks what God has been up to since the creation of the world that He's been making matches. (The matron then tries to show her superiority to the divine by trying to make matches herself, with comic results; it's another of the "stupid gentile" stories.) But matchmaker jokes really explode in the modern era: in which these representatives of the old guard, the literal arrangers of arranged marriage, were either presented as corrupt businessmen constantly out on the make, caring only about pocketing their fee rather than assuring the couple's compatibility, or total incompetents, the *luftmenschen*, schlemiels, and schlimazels trying their hands at their latest failed enterprise. A notable subgroup of matchmaker jokes and comic stories, for example, feature a pair of matchmakers collaborating to accidentally set up two boys or two girls—in an age long before gay marriage, a sign they haven't done their homework, to put it mildly.

Still, many of the jokes have an extra twist, an almost admiring quality for the *shadkhn*'s entrepreneurial and verbal audacity, for the way he *sells*, in violation of empirical truth, good sense, or even logic. One of the most famous examples of the type has a *shadkhn* calming down an anxious groom-to-be. He frets that she's blind; the *shadkhn* responds that she'll never see what he gets up to. When he points out that she's mute, the response is she'll never scold him. When it's brought to the *shadkhn*'s attention that she's deaf as well, he answers that the groom can yell at *her* all he wants. And finally, when the despairing young man says, "But she's a hunchback, too!," the reply comes, calmly: "So, you're going to throw the whole thing out over one small fault?"

But if you *could* get to the wedding—somehow—you'd get to witness the professional Jewish entertainer, the stand-up comic avant la lettre, in action. It's an old tradition. Not biblical; although there are prophets who employ satire and even throw out the occasional comic fable or riddle, their raison d'etre is hardly entertainment. The Talmud offers the first mention of merrymakers whose specific function it is to provide levity, but even there it's not a full-time job: rather, it's a task rabbis, students, and other individuals take upon themselves at particular moments, either on Purim or at festive events, particularly weddings. (Maybe because the only ancient equivalent, the comic actor, was associated with the pagan theater, so anathema to the rabbinic mindset.) It was those weddings that would eventually, in the late medieval and early modern period, provide the occasion for the development of the full-time Jewish comic entertainer. Yes, there were other types of clowns and entertainers in Eastern European Jewish culture—the *lets*, more of a slapstick performer, a music-making clown; the *marshalik*, the baton-wielding wedding master of ceremonies—but they've left less of a comic posterity, become less of a cultural touchstone, than the wedding jester, the *badkhn*.

Theodor Reik once wrote that "Jewish jokes in print are, properly speaking, incomplete. They should really be heard and seen. Their communication is not only verbal. The gestures and the facial expressions, the rise and fall of the voice of the storyteller, are essential parts of the telling." This is clearly true of Jewish entertainers writ broadly—the old line that a Martian watching a Borscht Belt comedian would have assumed his language was composed of hand gestures, with occasional mouth movements for emphasis, has its germ of truth. But the *badkhn*'s performance was perhaps the traditional apex of combining text and performance. The *badkhn*'s role in the nuptial festivities may seem somewhat unexpected, from our modern perspective: their rhymed speeches and jokey formulas were designed, at least in part, to make the bride cry, usually doing so by stressing the wedding as a time of lost girlhood and the often dull and occasionally dubious responsibilities of adulthood, particularly of womanhood, mixed with double entendres and vulgar in-jokes for the adult audience about the other entrance into womanhood associated with a bride's wedding night. In fact, when the Council of Four Lands, determining that a series of mid-seventeenth-century horrific pogroms were expressions of divine wrath at excessive levity, among other things, decided to outlaw such displays in 1661, they specifically exempted the *badkhn*. The reason: he was more abusive than funny.

The misogyny underlying some of the *badkhn*'s routines— and many of the matchmaker jokes—is so baked in it is almost impossible to imagine those subgenres without it. Unsurprisingly, a lot of that misogyny was about fear: fear of women's sexuality, fear of the power women had or could potentially have. There were ebbs and flows in women's social and economic power through Jewish history—the early modern period, for example, which offered new possibilities, also saw an upsurge in some of these comic opportunities and performances—but given the barriers to women's participation in writing and publishing before the modern period, much less performing, it was pretty difficult for them to get a chance to answer the *badkhn* back. Comedy can be about presentation of breaking down structures rawly, subverting them from the inside, or consolidating stereotypes, but women didn't get a chance to do any of those things, in any fundamental way, until the twentieth century provided the necessary upheavals.

ALLOWING WOMEN to explore and express their sexuality as performers, singers, actresses, and so forth was far more possible in the New and Newer Worlds. I use the latter term to refer not to America but to new settings for Jewish life in the rapidly reinventing cities of Jewish Europe, both in the West, like Berlin, with its swelling émigré population, and in the East, where cities like Warsaw provided the opportunities for anonymity and rawness in their cabaret and theater cultures. The birth of Yiddish theater in Romania in the second half of the nineteenth century allowed women to take their place on the professional stage for the first time; and as Yiddish theater—and its actors and actresses—traveled westward, starring in satires and farces along with the scenery-chewing melodramas and national pageants the Yiddish stage became famous for, comediennes began to strut their stuff, trodding the boards from Warsaw to Whitechapel to the Bowery.

Soon enough, acculturation being what it was, they weren't only doing it in Yiddish. Whether it was Sarah Bernhardt on the stage of the Comédie-Française, or Oscar Straus and Max Reinhardt reshaping German and Austrian cabaret culture, the Jewish voice became central to a kind of late nineteenth- and early twentieth-century European cosmopolitan entertainment. Venues like the Böse Buben ("Bad Boys") and Grössenwahn ("Megalomania") cabarets, created and founded by Jews, were essential in creating a witty, ironic interwar European style.

Much of this activity was less explicitly Jewish in content. But figures like Oscar Teller, among others, created particularly Jewish-oriented cabarets in the 1920s that addressed internal concerns, including Zionism. In Eastern Europe, Dzigan and Schumacher in Lodz and Warsaw offered Yiddish satirical takes on matters of the day in a less polemical, more entertainment-oriented context in cabarets like the Qui Pro Quo and the Morskie Oko and the Kleynkunst Teater, just one duo standing in for a flourishing Yiddish interwar culture. (Their head writer, Yosef Shimon Goldshteyn, wrote a highly influential humor column for the Warsaw Yiddish newspaper *Der Haynt*, which ran a brisk business in publishing readers' Jewish jokes along with professional satires.) Much of this material is difficult to translate or render in text, given its dependence on Yiddish, German, and Yiddish/German mashup, to say nothing of the intonations, gestures, and "business" in any successful act. But one fateful interwar routine resonates: an "upside-down world" skit—set in 1975 at the University of Vienna celebrating the twenty-fifth anniversary of Jewish world control, tweaked the Austrian and German right wing parties' insistence that Jews were out for world domination.

These entertainers—like their vaudeville counterparts in the United States—were happy to employ Jewish stereotypes in their acts as well. In the urban cauldrons where Jews from all different parts were engaging in levels of intra-ethnic interaction like never before, regional Jewish stereotypes abounded. German Jews, *yekkes*, came in for mockery for their overly formal nature; Lithuanian Jews, *litvaks*, for their rigorous commitment to an intellectually oriented approach to religion. One paradigmatic joke:

> A devout *litvak* is praying at the Western Wall when suddenly a terrorist grabs him from behind, putting a large knife to his throat. The Jew quickly recites the martyr's blessing, typically recited by someone about to die for his religion. Impressed with his intended victim's piety, the terrorist turns to walk away. The *litvak*, pointing to his throat, calls out impatiently to the terrorist: "Nu! Nu!"

So committed is the Lithuanian Jew to the structures of religion over real-world consequences that he insists that once he makes a blessing, in this case for martyrdom, the blessing's object be fulfilled. (There can also, according to Jewish law, be no speech between the blessing and its fulfillment, thus his use of the monosyllable.)

These stereotypes survived the Atlantic crossing. In 1914, for example, the comedian Lee Tully took on a classic subethnic rivalry—between Lithuanian and Galician Jews—as part of his standard act, focusing on the dialectal difference stereotypically present in each group's speech and expanding it into a patter song:

> From my wife, I get such aggravation,
> she's driving me out of my wits.

She's from a different denomination,
I'm a Litvak and she's a Galits.
We're happily married, I don't want to squawk,
We understand each other completely, except when we talk.
I say "mutter," she says "mitter,"
Er iz mir biter: ikh zog putter she says pitter.
What's the difference, mutter, mitter, pitter? Oy, how I shvitz
Cause I'm a litvak and she's a galitz.

But there were new stereotypes to explore—and new venues to explore them. Greenhorns, whose enthusiasm for America outmatched their competency to understand it, and *alrightniks*, whose confidence in their competency outmatched their actual expertise, were regular staples of comic fodder in the Yiddish press and theater. One of the best-known examples of the stereotype, surprisingly, appeared in the pages of *The New Yorker*, where Leonard Q. Ross first introduced that particularly vivacious greenhorn H*Y*M*A*N K*A*P*L*A*N to a wide American audience in the mid-thirties. Ross was better known as Leo Rosten, who would later be known as the figure most responsible for the popularization of Yiddish in America through the 1968 bestseller *The Joys of Yiddish* and its sequels. He was also, perhaps, as responsible as anyone else for the association of Yiddish with humor. *The Education of H*Y*M*A*N K*A*P*L*A*N* was one of the first paperback books of the Armed Services Editions, sent out to the army in September 1943, and the ethos of the book followed the ethos of the image of the army as great ethnic equalizer. The immigrant Kaplan's own innovative spelling and grammar in his English classes, to the bemusement of his instructor—he's the one who added the asterisks to his name, for example, to help him stand out—are the book's comedy. The stereotypical immigrant is also stereotypically eager to assimilate, and grateful to the classes for the opportunity to do so.

Kaplan's attempt to render the Jewish voice on the page may have attracted the highest, or at least most elite, profile, but Jewish dialect humor had made for popular reading for decades. There were collections like 1902's *Hebrew Jokes and Dialect Humor*, and the work of Milt Gross, who took the American Jewish dialect national with books like *Nize Baby* (1925). Gross's characters, with names like Mrs. Feitlebaum and Mow-riss and Mrs. Yifnif, live in a tenement and speak in language that has to be read aloud to be deciphered—if then. Characterizing it, Gross described the language as "a literal translation of the Anglicized American Jew. At least I try to make it so. It is the language of the people—conveyed at times in somewhat ludicrous character. But, so far as I know, it is never false, never out of register. . . . Its only departure from the actual might, as I've said, lie at times in its ludicrous element. That's necessary, of course, in the work itself."

Gross's mildly defensive tone may have come from the position, taken by some, that his dialect comedy was counterproductive to the prospects of American Jewish acculturation. Lillian Eichler, for example, commented in her column in the Yiddish press: "However we may chuckle with Milt Gross and his comic characters—and their still more comical pronunciation—we realize the importance of good speech." Gross had many defenders; the notable American rabbi Stephen S. Wise was among them, and Max Shulman, the creator of Dobie Gillis, said, "If this promotes anti-Semitism, so do lox and bagels." But you can understand how the easily offended might take Gross's description of Santa Claus in his 1926 parody of "The Night Before Christmas" (rendered, inimitably, as "De Night in de Front from Chreesmas") as pushing a few buttons: "De nose it was beeg like de beegest from peeckles/ I weesh I should hev sotch a nose fool from neeckles!"

Gross was a hugely popular comic strip artist. He popularized, in the strip of the same name, the phrase "banana oil," which is how you said something was bullshit in the 1920s, and his *He Done Her Wrong* (1930) is sometimes credited as the first graphic novel. His caricatured images of Jews could also be seen as playing on comic stereotypes, not all of them created by Jews, not all of them kind.

Other successors in Jewish comics—most notably Harry Hirshfield's Abie Kabbible, with "his striped trousers, saucer eyes, small bulb nose, familiar accent and peculiar syntax," and love of family, country, and pinochle—tried to navigate similar territory between Jewish aspirations to acculturation and productive employment of comic stereotype.

But the clearest image of the Jew in popular culture around the turn of the century came from the exploding entertainment form of the vaudeville stage, first in transmuted form as "German comics" and then, as *Deutsch* was misheard and transmuted, "Dutch comics," their Americanized Yiddish given a *Plattdeutsch* ring. (Some of this Yiddishization may have come also from the World War I-era unpopularity of explicit Germanness.) Probably the best known of the period was the duo of Joe Weber and Lew Fields, sons of Eastern European Jewish immigrants who trod the boards in the 1880s and 1890s and were successful enough to open up their own music hall on Broadway in 1896, and who inspired the Ziegfield Follies. They were known for their physical comedy, but, as a descendant of Fields noted, "when they needed a big laugh right away, they'd enter singing 'Here we are, an Irish pair,' with their hands covering their noses. The gesture never failed to delight the Bowery audience." An ethnic act of this sort would have been called, in vaudeville, a "double Hebe"; and this kind of peekaboo Judaism by a "Dutch comic" was picked up more famously—and far more subtly—by Groucho Marx.

These performances were often associated with an image of "Hebrew makeup." Here's a description from 1904: "A black and white vest, coat somewhat the worse for wear; large turned-down collar and red tie; light striped trousers, narrow at the bottom and short, showing the loud colored stockings; black wig and black whiskers; old derby hat in the back of the head and so large that it sets down over his ears." The Jewish look, though, was secondary to the Jewish voice, which would often introduce a wide range of Jewish stereotypes: "canny," clever, manipulative, cheap, cowardly, bullied.

Joe Welch was arguably the originator of the "Hebrew monologue," coming out in funereal garb and mien and asking the audiences, "with the saddest look ever on a human pap, 'Maybe you tink I'm heppy?'" As early as 1905, he would tell audiences:

> The other day my friend Rosenski took his boy in a restaurant to get a bowl of soup. Jakey commenced to eat, and he grabbed his father's arm an' says, "papa, there's a fly in the soup." Rosenski says "eat der soup an' vait till you come down to der fly, tell de vaiter and he'll give you another bowl for nothing."

Joe Hayman's "Cohen on the Telephone" monologues, first introduced in 1912, sold two million copies for Columbia Records. In "Cohen Telephones the Health Department," recorded in 1917, Cohen is in a lather because his office boy has just swallowed a half dollar.

> I want you should send down a doctor, yes, a doctor, not a lawyer, we don't want to sue him for the money. You know before we could get a judgment against him the boy might die of stomach trouble. . . . What do you say? If the boy swallowed a half a dollar, it won't do him no harm? Well, it ain't drawing any interest there, is it?

Sometimes even non-Jews got into the act, as vaudeville troupers would understand that towns with large Jewish audiences would react more positively if the performers would work Jewish words into their material. Frank Bush, the German-born Christian vaudeville comic, would sing:

> Oh, my name is Solomon Moses I'm a bully Sheeny man
> I always treat my customers the very best what I can
> I keep a clothing store 'way down on Baxter Street
> Where you can get your clothing I sell so awful cheap.

Performances like these were cited by institutions like the Chicago Anti-Stage Jew Ridicule Committee, along with the B'nai Brith and the Associated Rabbis of America, in an effort to push back against the ethnic stereotyping. But they went on and on, including many names largely lost to entertainment history, before the days of YouTube capture. There were Bickle and Watson; Andy Rice, who ditched the old Hebrew comic costume for snappier duds; Lou Holtz; Julian Rose (speaking about a Jewish wedding, where an Irish janitor started a fight: "Ah, he was no fighter, me and my two brothers and a cousin nearly licked him!"); the Howard Brothers; and on, and on. More prominently, there were Alexander Carr and Barney Bernard's Potash and Perlmutter, clothing sellers who were simultaneously sympathetic and stereotypically business-obsessed, and who featured in a book and a hugely successful 1913 Broadway run.

As the technologies of entertainment progressed, and the stars of vaudeville became mainstream radio stars and national celebrities, there was Al Jolson, who, before *The Jazz Singer*, did Hebrew acts like "The Hebrew and His Cadet" along with "coon songs" like "Where Did Robinson Crusoe Go with Friday on Saturday Night." And Eddie Cantor, the massive variety star who ad-libbed in Yiddish from the stage who, when he made the jump to movies and particularly to his weekly radio program, brought that nebbishy sensibility with him. These Jewish ethnic comics began to provide America with a soundtrack of what Jewish comedy looked and sounded like.

This doesn't even include the American *Yiddish* voice, which has persevered through all the periods of American mass entertainment. In vaudeville. (One program, at New York's Windsor Theater on April 17, 1895, featured a playlet called "Among the Indians" with scenes titled, among others, "Willie the peddler must be lynched!" and "Clothing! Clothing! Clothing!") In radio, like the parody commercials perfected by the Barton Brothers. And even in the age of streaming, as currently practiced by the Canadian duo known as YidLife Crisis. But, as the twentieth century went on, Yiddish comedy *in Yiddish* was firmly relegated to the margins of mass

American Jewish entertainment. What remained—what became the basis of the most enduring Jewish folk stereotype in America, the stereotype of "Jew" itself—was an Americanized version of the folk voice, something indebted to, but quite different from, its Eastern European counterpart. Yiddish-y, but not Yiddish; embattled, but not quite persecuted; baroquely articulate, but not Talmudic.

Its clearest manifestation may be in free-floating jokes:

> An old Jewish man in a theater taps a person sitting beside him on the shoulder and asks, "Do you speak Yiddish?" "No," says the person. He then taps a person sitting on the other side of him and asks, "Do you speak Yiddish?" "No," says the person. He then taps a person sitting in front of him on the shoulder and asks, "Do you speak Yiddish?" "Yes," says the person. "Vell, vot time is it?"

A 1950 survey indicated that over a third of contemporary Jewish jokes relied on dialect humor. But its willful blurring between Yiddish and "Yiddish"—which is not just the incursion of a Yiddish word, but an accent, a syntax, a sensibility which often combined aggrievedness and pugnaciousness in varying proportions—would serve as the template for the dozens of Borscht Belt comics who took their acts out of the Catskills and across America.

There were still traditional "dialect comics" in mid-century, perhaps most notably Sam Levenson (who had a bit about *chazzerai* that, twisted, could easily be the basis for an Alex Portnoy routine, perhaps the one where Levenson is name-checked). But Levenson himself would argue that, in the title of a piece he wrote in 1952, "The Dialect Comedian Should Vanish," and the institution was soon supplanted by comedians who often seemed like near descendants. The most famous might be the fast-talking Jacob Maza, better known as Jackie Mason, who made a career on ringing the changes on Lenny Bruce's Jewish/goyish routine ("There's no bigger schmuck than a Jew with a boat. . . . The only things Jews know about boats is how many people a boat sleeps. My boat sleeps 6, this boat sleeps 12"; "I love Italians. They're the greatest people. My best friend is half Italian and half Jewish. If he can't buy it wholesale, he steals it") or that voice of the 2000 year old man, based on Mel Brooks's Uncle Sol. "I never forgot his voice," Brooks has said. "That sound meant a great deal to me—safety, protection, strength, that loud, vigorous voice with the Jewish accent."

But there was also the exasperated Alan King, who said, in what could be an epigraph for this group, "If you're dying, talk louder and faster"; Freddy Roman, Shecky Greene, Buddy Hackett, Don Rickles, and the many others who founded a second temple across the country from the Catskills. This one—befitting a community of Jews—was in the desert. Comedians who entertained the upwardly mobile types who flew into "Lost Wages" solidified the idea that the stand-up comic voice was Jewishy show biz. And comedy being, like other subcultures, constantly fascinated by its own history—paying homage and studying older work Talmudically when not trying to burn it down or lift it wholesale, which may end up being the same thing—this voice was channeled, ventriloquized, echoed, in a particular strain of comedians to come. Billy Crystal, in *Mr. Saturday Night* and *700 Sundays*, has spent much of his career exploring this Jewish vocal vein; fellow travelers in this historical ventriloquism include Harry Shearer, Hank Azaria, and members of the contemporary Friars' Club, probably most notably Jeffrey Ross. It remains instantly recognizable, even if the conditions and circumstances that generated it—and the audience whose speech patterns it echoed—have changed almost beyond recognition, and many of the grand Borscht Belt hotels have fallen into picturesque ruin.

IF THE MALE COMICS were happy to turn out stereotypical portraits for the masses, there were women who—given the far more groundbreaking nature of their performance at all—were willing to smash far more barriers than simply showing up on stage. The history of the "unkosher comediennes," as they've been termed, includes the incomparable Fania Borach, better known as Fanny Brice, considered "one of the great, great clowns of all time" by no less an authority on the subject than George Cukor. Brice is probably closest in tone and topic to the ethnic comedians of vaudeville than the Borscht Belters, with the broad physical humor and magnificent parody skills that served her well in the nine Ziegfeld revues she performed in between 1910 and 1936. But she is also remembered for her range of Jewish characters—the American Indian Jewish girl Rosie Rosenstein; the Yiddish-accented evangelist and neophyte nudist; Sascha, a Jewish girl that became a sultan's wife; and Mrs. Cohen at "Mrs. Cohen at the Beach," a consummate yenta who puts her marker down amongst all those male Cohens who spent their time talking on telephones. Brice put it as well as anyone in explaining what this group of Jewish comedians were doing, and how they were appealing: "My best audiences . . . are composed of 'American Jews'—who combine, in a certain sense, the Jew and the gentile. They have seen the awkward gesticulation; they have heard the comic speech at close range, but they have passed beyond that stage, and so it is they who see the ludicrousness of Fanny Brice, it is they who appreciate her imitations, it is they who laugh at her exaggerations."

But if the carefully composed statement betrays an anxiety over acceptance and authenticity in both camps—an authenticity snidely questioned by Dorothy Parker's famous line about Brice's "cutting off her nose to spite her race" after she had a rhinoplasty—that's hardly an apt description of her act. Take, for example, her Yiddish-accented delivery of the tale of Sadie Salome, who left home to become an actress; but when her sweetheart Mose saw her on stage, he realized what kind of act she actually did: "That's not a business for a lady!" he yells, asking: "Oy oy oy—where's your clothes?"

"Sadie Salome" (music and lyrics by Irving Berlin, incidentally) is of a piece—maybe a slightly tamer piece—in its daring, its willingness to trade on depictions of unbridled Jewish, feminine sexuality, with the work of Sophie Tucker, the "last of the red-hot mamas." Tucker (born Sonia Kalish) helped her parents run a kosher-style restaurant as a teenager in Hartford, which may be where she received the inspiration to belt out lines like "I've put a little more meat on. So what, there's more schmaltz to sizzle when I turn the heat on." Combined with songs like "Mistah Siegel, You Better Make It Legal," Tucker would strike a tone in her stage performances in the twenties and thirties: the knowing grin that hovered between a wink and a leer, the strategic use of Yiddish to not-quite-cover the *shmutz*, what people rarely said in polite society and liked to pretend women didn't know—until their laughter at these comediennes' jokes showed otherwise. That laughter would grow substantially when the long-playing record allowed for stand-up and nightclub routines banned from airplay and sold only under the counter to be replicated in the privacy of one's own home.

A trio of Jewish bawdy working-class comics, less well known today, had seven-figure sales of these "party records" in the late fifties and early sixties. Belle Barth sold over two million copies of albums like *If I Embarrass You, Tell Your Friends* (1960); *I Don't Mean to Be Vulgar, But It's Profitable* (1961); and *My Next Story Is a Little Risque* (1961). Barth's cheerful scatology—she referred to herself as an MD, or Maven of Dreck, as well as the "Doyenne of the Dirty Ditty"—is best expressed, I think, by the one she tells about the man who can sing out of his rectum who, asked to do so, defecates liquidly all over the floor. Challenged, he replies, "Well, I had to clear my throat, didn't I?" Pearl Williams' seven albums included the million-plus seller *Pearl Williams Goes All the Way* and the immortally, if obscenely, titled *A Trip Around the World Is Not a Cruise* (1961). Besides the plethora of Jewish accents, the humming of "Hava Nagila" during the comic interludes, the generous sprinkling of Yiddish—remind me to tell you about the one with the cord attached to the *beardzl*—Williams also continues to develop the role of a cheerfully horny American Jewish housewife, adding that to the other stereotypical attributes. You don't even need to know the setup to the exchange—"Madame, would you like a screw for this hinge? No, but I'd blow you for that toaster up there"—to see where it's coming from.

If Williams played, at least at times, a kind of *balaboosta* of Bath, Patsy Abbott took on the other side of the stereotypical spectrum: the kvetch, the nagger, with her classic joke about the man who keeps asking God that chestnut of theodicy, why he suffers while others thrive: "Why should he have when I ain't got? Why? Tell me why?" And God answers, with a bolt of lightning: "Cause you're *nudging* me. That means you bug me, man." And then there were those who turned that hostility on themselves, not just as Jew, but as woman. The four-foot-ten, one-hundred-and-ninety-pound Totie Fields (born Sophie Feldman), started her career in 1944, and once remarked, mock-wistfully: "I'm so tired of being everybody's buddy. Just once to read in a newspaper, Totie Fields raped in an alley." She'd later lose a leg to phlebitis; and, concurrently having lost weight, duly switched from making self-deprecating fat jokes to self-deprecating handicapped jokes.

The unkosher comediennes took on every flavor and every role Jewish comedy had to offer—the vulgarian, the ironic, even hipster theologian, the self-deprecating schlimazel, and so on. But this remained a hidden, if not exactly minor (remember: millions of albums sold) counterpoint to a far more socially acceptable role for Jewish women in comedy: as stereotypical Jewish mothers.

Strange as it may seem, it's a lot harder to find Jewish mother jokes before the twentieth century than you'd think. As we saw, when the Jewish women of the medieval and early modern period come in for comic roles, they aren't seen as mothers, but as wives and sexual beings (not nicely, of course, but that's how they're seen). They're seen as mothers, too, of course, but that sacred task of maternity (literally: perhaps in some response to Marian culture, the *shalosh imahot*—the three matriarchs—are elevated almost as intercessory saints in a pantheon) isn't mocked, primarily.

Modernity started changing things. Heine, in his 1844's *A Winter's Tale,* has a somewhat familiar portrait:

And when I came to my mother at home, you could knock
her down with a feather. She shouted "My boy, my boy!" and
clapped her old hands together. "My boy! It's all of thirteen
years! Let me look, are you fatter or thinner? Thirteen years:
You must be hungry for sure. Now what would you like for
dinner?"

But the stereotype really took off in America, when the maternal
values of protection and proximity, keeping someone close to home,
became increasingly seen as rife for mockery, rather than simply
an evocation of traditional values—that is, they become the source
of a satire against parochialism, particularly when the mothers in
question are immigrants. In addition, the comparative affluence
and emphasis on domesticity in the (especially postwar suburban)
American household allowed for the creation of a space which was
both powerful and powerless. Add to that the spread of Freudian
ideas which psychosexualize the relationship between, particularly,
mother and son, that allow for the relationship to be expressed at
times as something "unhealthy"; and, complementarily, the melodramatic elevation of the American and American Jewish cult of
motherhood which turned the mother into a romantic, and even
quasi-erotic, object. Think, most powerfully, of Al Jolson down on
his knees singing "Mammy."

This wasn't just in comedy. In his National Book Award-winning
World of Our Fathers, Irving Howe depicted the Jewish mother as
a "brassy scourge, with her grating bark or soul-destroying whine,
silver-blue hair, and unfocused aggression . . . Daughters paled,
sons fled" at her "groaning, cajoling, intimidating." Alfred Kazin
remembered his mother as shouting "Eat! Eat! May you be destroyed
if you don't eat! What sin have I committed that God should punish
me with you! Eat! What will become of you if you don't eat! Imp
of darkness, may you sink ten fathoms into the earth if you don't
eat! Eat!" But these descriptions, and others of their ilk, constituted
a kind of epic portrait that would inevitably repeat itself as farce.

The jokes that resulted were fairly straightforward: of the Jewish mother as someone constantly yearning to tie their children more tightly to their apron strings (a metaphor which, of course, suggests they're in the home, cooking). The title of the best book on the history of the Jewish mother, Joyce Antler's *You Never Call! You Never Write!*, shows how easily this sentiment was easily put into a catchphrase, a punch line. The jokes are clear enough that they can often be offered without their setups—"He can walk, all right, but thank God he doesn't have to" may be my favorite, combining as it does the infantilizing maternity with the braggadocio of the American Jewish noveau-riche, with "Help! My son the doctor is drowning!" a close second.

Perhaps the most powerfully developed treatment of the stereotype is the Mike Nichols and Elaine May routine "Mother and Son," from their 1960 Broadway show, which was immortalized on record. There, over the course of six or seven minutes, Elaine May's mother reduces Nichols's rocket scientist son (no more elite, respected, or for that matter gentile job in those Mercury days), to a quivering, baby-talking mess, literally goo-gooing and gah-gahing as the skit ends, via the judicious application of guilt and passive-aggressiveness. May's character prays, for example, that her son will have children of his own one day—that way they'll make *him* suffer, the way she's suffering now. "That's a mother's prayer," she concludes. The routine, though, was only a drop in the maternal Jewish bucket. Dan Greenburg's *How to Be a Jewish Mother*, published in 1964, sold over three million copies in fifteen editions, and went to Broadway in an adaptation featuring Molly Picon. That same year saw the publication of Bruce Jay Friedman's novel *A Mother's Kisses*, whose protagonist's mother insists on escorting him off to college—and staying there with him. Comic greats like Woody Allen and Albert Brooks took the theme late into the twentieth century; in Allen's contribution to the 1989 anthology film *New York Stories*, "Oedipus Wrecks," his dead mother literally *nudzhes* him from the sky above; Brooks's 1996 movie *Mother*, as one critic put it, "descends, in spirit, from an entire generation of Jewish-mother jokes," the fact that the mother in question is played by Debbie Reynolds notwithstanding.

As Sophie Portnoy, perhaps the literary apotheosis of the type, teaches so well, guilt is the animating sentiment of the comic Jewish mother, and in many of the jokes that circulated and circulate about her, the guilt is a double-edged weapon: aimed *at* the children, but *through* herself. (The difference between Jewish and Italian mothers, the joke goes, is that the former will kill you if you don't eat and the latter will kill herself.) If the old joke about how many Jewish mothers it takes to change a lightbulb is any guide—none, of course; she'd rather sit in the dark—it's a guilt based on demanding and deserving recompense for the work of maternity.

And that hostility is harnessed to the rigorous verbal and intellectual dexterity of the stereotypical comic Jew more broadly, allowing it to flow in every way, through every channel. One of the most famous Jewish mother jokes, told, in its manifold variations, in almost all the literature on the subject, is a case in point:

> A Jewish mother buys her son two ties for his birthday. When he comes down wearing one, his mother says, "What's the matter? You don't like the other one?"

This kind of hostility—maternity means they know their children, their sons, more deeply than anyone else, and so they can see into their weak, neurotic, self-doubting hearts—wasn't just a stereotype. When Mel Brooks bragged about his success and high pay on *Your Show of Shows*, his mother, Kitty Kaminsky, would simply ask: "Have they found out yet?" It may be that nothing her infinitely more famous son ever wrote was more biting. He wasn't the only one. Larry David's mother, after *Seinfeld* was number one in the ratings, would ask him: "Do they like you? Do you think they're going to keep you?" Norman Lear's mother, hearing he was one of the inaugural honorees for the Television Hall of Fame, responded, "Well, if that's what they want to do, who am I to say?"

This of course hit particularly home when (as it did in Mrs. Kaminsky and Mrs. Lear's cases) it directly took on the narrative of American Jewish success—defined often, though not always, as acculturation. Mothers in these sort of jokes are truth-tellers, being cruel to be kind, although, perhaps, crueler than absolutely necessary. Take, for example, the joke about the nouveau riche man who buys a yacht and insists on wearing a captain's hat everywhere. The mother's response—"Solly, by you you're a captain, and by me you're a captain, but by a captain you're no captain"—expresses the point rather nicely.

If the most famous targets of the Jewish mother stereotype are her neutered, infantilized, Jewish sons, an equal victim of the culture's misogyny are those mothers' daughters and granddaughters, who grow up just in time to become the Jewish American princesses of the eighties. The litany of jokes about the stereotype generally ring the changes on charges of sexual frigidity. "How do you get a Jewish girl to stop having sex? Marry her." "Definition of a Jewish porn film? Five minutes of sex, followed by an hour and a half of guilt." "What is Jewish foreplay? Twenty minutes of begging." There's also the intertwined commodity fetishism ("Why do JAPs like circumcised men? They like anything with 20 percent off"; or the one about the American Jewish matriarch who asks for her ashes to be scattered over Bloomingdale's so that her daughters will visit her twice a week.) Gilda Radner, who always referred to herself as "this Jewish girl from Detroit" and whose combination of unbridled physicality, musical energy, and femininity made her the most plausible heir to Brice and Tucker in the age of American television, was known for her character Rhonda Weiss, the Jewish American princess, and her 1980 "Jewess Jeans" parody ad on *Saturday Night Live*, alongside her famous characters Emily Litella and Rosanne Rosannadanna.

Was the rise of the Jewish American Princess joke, as at least one critic has suggested, a movement of female empowerment related to the rise of feminism? Barbra Streisand channeled Fanny Brice in a movie that was as much about her life story and comedic talents as her character's; the titular *Funny Girl* reminded audiences in 1968, four years after *How to Be a Jewish Mother* hit the best-seller list, that Jewish women were not just Jewish mothers, or the butt of jokes. There were responses to *Portnoy* on the page, as Erica Jong and Grace Paley wrote works (*Fear of Flying* and "Mom") that presented the image of the Jewish woman and mother as sexualized, liberated, neurosis-free. And two seminal Jewish comic performances on nineties television may provide some very limited support for this approach: Debra Messing's portrayal of Grace Adler on *Will and Grace* and, particularly, Fran Drescher's character on *The Nanny*. Drescher's own transformation, as an actress who literally played an embodied JAP as one of the titular *Princesses* on the sitcom of the same name to the creator/star/producer/occasional director of *The Nanny*, where she presented the character as a romantically desirable, erotically fixated, well, JAP, overturned decades of conventional thinking in a sitcom whose sit was as unbelievable as com could come up with: A Jewish nanny to a gentile British Broadway producer? Who somehow manages to come up with designer gowns and outfits for every and any occasion? But Drescher made it work.

Drescher responded to an article charging *The Nanny* with providing a "demeaning depiction of Jewish womanhood" by suggesting that if the author "was offended by someone like Fran Fine, simply because her mother has plastic slipcovers and speaks with a strong New York accent, [that] suggests that she is a victim of post–World War II culture, which says that the only good Jew is an assimilated Jew." Drescher's powerful argument notwithstanding—and of course, she's making in support of her own show—expanding the argument to the whole field seems somewhat unlikely; the gleeful trading and circulation of JAP jokes, both orally and in books, seem generally speaking to be told at women, rather than with them.

BUT MUCH of the battle against misogyny in the Jewish comic tradition—and in the institutions of American comedy, full stop—wasn't televised, but took place in the stand-up trenches. Many of those institutions were created and operated by Jews for a broad audience, unlike the Borscht Belt before them. There was Paul Sills, the genius behind the explosion of improv comedy, whose Second City flourished in a converted Chinese laundry in Chicago; Budd Friedman, the creator of the Improv in the mid-sixties in a former Vietnamese restaurant in midtown Manhattan, and Rick Newman, who founded Catch a Rising Star on the Upper East Side a few years later; Sammy and Mitzi Shore, who co-founded The Comedy Store in LA; and Jamie Masada, an Iranian Jew who opened the Laugh Factory on Sunset Boulevard after two years working as a dishwasher at The Comedy Store. And then there were the agents and managers, including Jack Rollins (née Rabinowitz), the impresario who broke Nichols and May and helped Woody Allen with his stage fright, and Bernie Brillstein, who did more to make comedy a business in Hollywood than almost anyone.

Not all of these institutions—and the ones who followed them, like Johnny Carson's *Tonight Show* and the HBO comedy specials—were committed to egalitarianism, to put it mildly. Of the forty-three specials aired on HBO between New Year's 1975 and the end of 1980, only one was headlined by a woman (Phyllis Diller). Elayne Boosler, the pathbreaker, asked the difference between a comedian and comedienne, famously replied, "Ten thousand a week." Boosler was one of a number of female Jewish comics who attacked the problem from a variety of angles: Rita Rudner, who'd moved away from the early days where she played Jewish venues (and delivered jokes like "I used to go to a very fancy temple—they read the Torah in French") to take on the gender wars in her own inimitable, mock–space cadet, delivery; Merrill Markoe, the hidden genius partially responsible for David Letterman's offbeat, acerbic sensibility; Sandra Bernhard, who put her sexually pugnacious, combative Jewish self front and center in her stage routines; Carol Kane, with her batty faux-ethnic personae; Bette Midler, who accepted her fans' adoration and imitation as her due; and most of all Roseanne Barr, whose spat-out delivery of the phrase "I'm a domestic goddess" put a generation of men on anxious notice long before her religion-neutral television show stood in for a heartland ignored by both *The Cosby Show* and *Family Ties*.

In more recent years, the comfort—and encouragement—of a wider range of ethnic specificity in American comedy has allowed for even more pointed Jewish comedy to emerge. Corey Kahaney created a tribute to Barth, Pearl Williams and others whose title, *JAP: Jewish Princesses of Comedy,* is explicitly about reclaiming that stereotype. Jessica Kirson talks about "fat, ugly" girls like herself and says: "I'm an angry Jew . . . but I feel like an angry black man." Susie Essman's rages on *Curb Your Enthusiasm* are legendary ("You fat *fuck*"); as are the solo shows of Judy Gold, which include "25 Questions for a Jewish Mother" and "Mommy Queerest," and of Obie Award–winner Jackie Hoffman ("The Kvetching Continues"; "Jackie's Kosher Khristmas"). And as specifically Jewish, and as groundbreakingly nondefensive, as Fran Fine was in the nineties, it may be that broadcast television has never seen as powerful a rejoinder/love letter to this problematic tradition of American Jewish comedy as Rachel Bloom's "JAP Rap Battle" on the CW's *Crazy Ex-Girlfriend*.

The battle in question, occurring between "two hard-as-nails Shebrews from Scarsdale," encompasses Yiddish and Hebrew words ("*shondeh*" and "*sheket bevaka*-shut the hell up"); staples of millennial American Jewish life (it name-checks Birthright Israel and the Matzo Ball); and throws enough vulgar shade to make Belle Barth and her fellow unkosher comediennes proud, if not blush. That same Matzo Ball, for example, is where our protagonist boasts of banging her rival's hedge fund manager fiancé. In a bathroom stall. Bloom, as she's done in her other musical-comedy works, takes cultural traditions with long legacies, often hostile to female (and Jewish) participation, and makes them gloriously her own.

But if there's one summary figure who speaks for all these voices, for all these figures—who contains multitudes—it would have to be Joan Rivers.

If the great metaphysical comedians' efforts to bridge the

unbridgeable gulfs between human and divine were sifted, sublimed, and reduced to three words, I'm not sure that any of them could do better than "Can we talk?" That phrase—invitation to empathic communication and an aggressive put-up-your-dukes warning, cozy and polemical, warm and spiky all at once—that was Joan Rivers in a nutshell. (The same combination of distancing and encouragement is equally visible in her other catchphrase, "Oh, please!"—or, more accurately, "Oh, puh-LEEZ,"—since, as any accomplished comedian will tell you, the delivery matters as much as the words.) Rivers's subject has always been herself, or, maybe more properly, "herself," the persona every stand-up comic and artist creates: but her routines encompassed everyone.

Rivers, born Joan Molinsky in 1933, a doctor's daughter and Barnard grad from Larchmont, New York, was no stranger to how rough women had it in comedy: working strip clubs under the name Pepper January, grinding it out in the early sixties as part of Jim, Jake, and Joan, a sketch comedy trio born out of her years in the Second City circle, before turning back to stand-up. Rivers wrote briefly for Phyllis Diller, one of the other women on the frontlines in those years, and Diller's "woman as alien" shtick, ostensibly as far from Rivers's ethnographically grounded approach as you could imagine, shared a proclaimed discomfort with women's bodies, with images of femininity projected by others and internalized within themselves.

Over her career, Rivers moved from mocking the neuroses of a young Jewish American princess who can't get married to savagely excoriating sexism in marriage and the workplace to chronicling the travails and indignities of old age on the body—the woman's body in particular. Nothing and no one is excused before her withering gaze, as carefully wrought and evolved, over time, as the stereotypes and jokes and images of the Jewish world she discusses. She was the Jewish mother ("I want a Jewish delivery—to be knocked out in the delivery room and wake up at the hairdresser.") The Jewish American princess. ("Jews get orgasms in department stores.") The *kurveh*, the sexual voluptuary (through her adopted persona, Heidi Abromowitz, in a book chronicling the life and times of the same). The ironist locating American and American Jewish womanhood at the corner of eros, commerce, and domesticity. ("My mother is desperate for me to get married. Outside our house she put a sign: 'Last Girl Before Freeway'"; "Why should I cook for my husband? So he can tell a hooker I make a delicious cake?") The self-deprecating body comic. ("Dress by Oscar de la Renta, body by Oscar Meyer"—and, of course, the plastic surgery.) But when Rivers did it—more and more, as the decades continued—it seemed like an act of self-liberation.

Rivers claimed she learned from Lenny Bruce that "personal truth can be the foundation of comedy, that outrageousness can be cleaning and healthy. I was becoming a nice Jewish girl in stockings and pumps saying on stage what people thought but never said aloud in polite society." The fact that Rivers cited Bruce is unsurprising— *everyone* of that period cited Bruce as an influence—and it's a way of reminding us that reducing any of these comics to their gender is doing a disservice. But, in cataloging a long and wide set of Jewish stereotypes in comedy, the stereotyping of women is the central one, the one we can't ignore. And Rivers's personal truths, variously and hilariously expressed, paved the way for others, both male and female, to follow in her footsteps.

Rivers was hardly populist in her lifestyle (she lived in an Upper East Side triplex that she once described as the way Marie Antoinette would have lived if she had the money) or ordinary in her genius. But she, along with the many others in this chapter, trafficked in an enduring Jewish comedy that is, in its own way, as transcendent as the ironic metaphysics of the comic philosophers. Its power comes from its focus—in its treatment of women, of comic archetypes based on character, on the Jewish voice—on aspects of Jewish life that range widely, and, in ranging widely, range deeply as well. It might be possible to have a Jewish comedy without these kinds of voices represented. But one couldn't have the history of Jewish comedy without them.

7

Jewish Comedy—Hold the Jewishness

POSSIBLY *THE* CENTRAL PHENOMENON OF THE JEWISH EXPERIENCE in diaspora has been Jewish difference, and the feelings and sensibilities that come along with it. And all too often that difference has been associated with hostility and persecution: which in turn generates a comedy of counteraggression and of soul-searching. (That's not *all* of Jewish comedy, as we've seen, but it's definitely an important part.) But what about when hostility and persecution are replaced with indifference, or even outright support and welcome? And where, as a result, a creative person's Jewishness ceases to matter, socially, culturally; where the writer or performer, by all rights and accounts, should slip easily and smoothly into the comedic currents of the majority culture . . . and yet they *don't* ease in, because it *does* still matter? Which raises two related questions in turn. First: *How* does it matter? That is, how does that Jewishness manifest itself comedically, if it's not through our classic markers of Jewish comedy, a deep engagement with Jewish text, community, history, or even anti-Semitism? And second: Why might it still do so? Telling that story not only offers a crucial insight into the most difficult cases for our study—the ones that *seem* Jewish, that clearly *are*, and yet don't fall into our other drawn circles nearly so neatly—but also, it should be stressed, illuminates a central part of the lived Jewish experience.

And not just the modern Jewish experience, even though we might think of this kind of state of affairs as a peculiarly modern concern. It seems to go back to the earliest days of Jewish comedy. As legions of scholars have noted, Esther's situation was an honest reflection of the complicated world that Esther (whose name is taken from the pagan goddess Ishtar) and Mordechai (from the pagan god Marduk) lived in. It's a world in which the protagonists aren't necessarily thinking of themselves as taking part in a Jewish story, until circumstances, Haman's decree, thrust them into that role. This isn't totally accurate—the fact that Esther is told by Mordechai to hide her heritage even before Haman's rise to power suggests a sense of threat. But even that heritage is, in the text, little more than a name, to be disguised and revealed. Nonetheless, Esther's proclamation—a simple matter of stating her identification with a people—is a triumphant embrace of an aspect of her own identity that has previously gone largely unnoticed. As opposed to, say, being someone's cousin, someone's wife, someone's queen, someone's object of erotic fixation.

Esther spends much of the book that bears her name in disguise. (Perhaps all of it, depending on your reading: Esther also has a Hebrew/Semitic name, Hadassah, and so perhaps the final joke is that she is known throughout history by a name that, *pace* the previous paragraph's argument, she might indeed have preferred.) Comedy loves disguise, of course. Think of *Twelfth Night,* or *Some Like It Hot*, or *Nuns on the Run*—and those are only the ones involving cross-dressing. Variations rung on the change of ethnic disguise rather than gender disguise, or class disguise (ah, *Trading Places*), and so on, are practically infinite. But the book of Esther is one of the earliest examples of Jews disguising themselves as gentiles to make their way easier in a gentile world. But disguises of any sort are, in the end—at least at comedy's end—temporary. Either they're ripped off to reveal the essential, unchanged self; or, if change has indeed occurred, to show that change is only partial, to allow the former self to peek back through, to insist on itself. And that insistence on Jewishness—even if the insistence itself is the sum and substance of the Jewishness involved—*means* something. Something important, and perhaps even something profound.

This strand of Jewish comedy tells the story of these attempts at disguise—attempts out of necessity, attempts out of desire, attempts out of inertia and inclination—and how they fail, and succeed, and the comedy that comes about in the process. Because in no small part, those attempts, in their varying forms, are metaphors for the attempts to define and isolate the nature of Jewish identity itself under conditions where that identity is most in question.

Often, as it turns out, those comedic attempts revolve around Jewish manhood. Since the history of Jewish literature before the modern period is, like every other literature and history in the world, largely by and about Jewish men, questions about identity are often strongly linked to questions about *male* identity, and disguising as a non-Jew means "passing" as a non-Jewish man, with whatever images and stereotypes that entails. Which then, in turn, provides comic inspiration whenever the disguise seems somehow incongruous.

A case in point: Consider the throwaway joke in the Zucker-Abrahams-Zucker disaster parody *Airplane!*, when a flight attendant, asked by a passenger for light reading, proffers a short leaflet entitled *Famous Jewish Sports Legends*. "Since when are Jews sports heroes?" the viewer asks, chuckling in familiarity, since the ridiculous mismatch is clear. A sustained comic piece in this vein, though—rather than a throwaway joke—necessarily has to present the process, the *struggle* to look like and act like the general culture's depiction of a hero, sports or otherwise. (And for most of Western culture, of course, "hero" and "male" were largely interchangeable.)

But the "since when are Jews" question—which bears within it the disruptive, failure-drenched answer, "Never!"—has a wide range of consequences. Failure, disruption of expectation, mismatch: that's funny. But what happens when Jews *do* become heroes, of the screen, erotic, and yes, even sporting variety. How does the comedy maintain itself, in a world where the phrase "Jewish leading man" is less likely to raise an eyebrow? What happens to the comedy of disguise, when disguise is no longer necessary, or, maybe, even possible?

To figure it out, let's go back a bit, and meet a Jew in shining armor.

THE BOOK of Esther, as we've said, is a diasporic book, and these questions of disguise belong, most powerfully, to the diaspora. (The inhabitants of pre-diaspora Judah and Israel were considered different by denizens of other kingdoms, but, it seems, largely as simply another people with their own odd customs, like monotheism and the Sabbath). By the medieval period, though, Christianity had defined the Jew as an emasculated, feminized, impotent male (even, in a common anti-Semitic trope, insisting that he menstruated), and the Jews had had the time to internalize some of this critique. So the idea seeped into Jewish comedy. Two contrasting examples from the early modern period, both written in Italy in the late fifteenth–early sixteenth century, illustrate how and whether the idea resonated.

Judah b. Leone Somo's 1515 *An Eloquent Marriage Farce* is Jewish in some of the most important ways we've discussed—it's written in a Jewish language (it may be the first Hebrew play), and it's constantly discussing Jewish law and society (the farce revolves around the efforts of the two ingenues to marry, and the Jewish legal tactic to which they resort creates complications). Somo, a theorist of aesthetics as well as a dramatist, attempted to address the tension he lived and breathed—is it possible to create a Jewish work of art using Western, Christian, foreign aesthetic principles? On one level, he succeeds: the characters could be Renaissance courtiers thrown into Hebrew, and the structure, plot, and approach are smoothly integrated into the contours of Renaissance comedy. But, despite the fact that these Jews aren't actually disguised, the disguise they're wearing, comedically speaking, is an awfully good one: so good that it dilutes the play's energy, making it almost a mechanical transposition of contemporary themes into a Judaic context. It seems like nothing more than a pale variation of its surroundings, and falls flat, feeling neither Jewish nor Italian.

Before we jump to conclusions about the work translation and adaptation can do for comedy, though, take the second case, written under a decade earlier. Elijah Levita, sometimes known as Elye Bokher, took a chivalric tale of Bevis of Hampton by way of an Italian adaptation and rendered it into Yiddish, Judaizing it along the way. Joseph Heller, anticipating our questions in this chapter, once asked, "Since when do Jews ride horses?"; much of the adaptation, known as the *Bovo bukh*, is in its own way an answer to the question. Which is to say: "not as well as their gentile counterparts." Bovo, the main character, is rarely mentioned or identified as a Jew—it's not impossible to suspect the main reason he *is* so identified is to make the book permissible to audiences who'd have been uncomfortable with Christian chivalric motifs in their households. But even the limited Jewishness that is displayed opens up comic vistas.

Bovo is not, certainly through the first part of the book, a very good knight. He's so bad, in fact, that it's called attention to by the book's narrator, who is something of a wise-ass. He's also not much of a man. He doesn't know how to please a woman or react to her sexual advances ("I wouldn't have that problem!" the narrator boasts); he offers to play bride of the regiment to a few sailors into whose clutches he falls, and so forth. Now, some of this was conventional—the young fledgling stumbles before becoming a full-fledged knight—but some of it unquestionably plays into readers' expectations: What kind of figure does a Jewish knight cut? What kind of man can a Jew be in a gentile world? Not much of one, to be honest. And that failure is funny.

As modernity came to Eastern Europe, and the equivalent of knightly prowess—participation in the armed forces of the newly constituted nation-state—became a hallmark of the emancipation conversation, Jewish unwillingness or failures in this regard, perceived or otherwise, tapped into a wide variety of analogous issues. We began this book with a joke about a Jewish marksman in the Tsar's army, one which illustrated a certain kind of overmastering ingenuity. But there are other, less positively oriented jokes. Like the one about the Jewish recruit who, despite his expertise in marksmanship, fires into the air at the time of battle. When challenged by his superior officer, he explains, calmly: "Don't you see? There are people there! Someone might get hurt!" The military—that possible venue for Jewish emancipation and equality by virtue of participating in the man-making institution of European state society—simply becomes a venue for Jewishness to reassert itself in all its stereotyped, unmanly ingloriousness.

The military here was not only about masculinity, but about modernity: and "modern" was a disguise all of its own. New technologies, and the changes in lifestyle they enabled, allowed for all sorts of disguising possibilities. If you could get on a train and travel hundreds of miles away from the shtetl where everyone knew you, you could reinvent yourself—as a success, as an unmarried man, even, perhaps, as a gentile.

Or could you? Otto Kahn, the American banker who converted to Christianity, was walking by a synagogue with a hunchbacked friend, the humorist Marshall P. Wilder. Kahn: "You know, I used to be a Jew." "And I used to be a hunchback," his companion replied. Freud, in his book on jokes, tells the one about the traditional Jew in a train compartment who'd gotten comfortable—put his feet up on the seat—when a man dressed in the latest fashion enters. After a moment, the man asks when Yom Kippur is. "Oho!" said the first Jew, then puts his feet back up before answering. This famous— and famously subtle—joke has two dimensions to it. The first is illustrating a technique omnipresent in the comedy of disguise and revelation, how moments of encounter and stress force a revelation of one's Jewishness. There's a direct line from Esther's banquet through the fashionable man on the train confronting, and being confronted by, the appearance of his coreligionist to Mrs. Green shouting "Oy vey!" when that soup spills on her.

But the second dimension is how the first Jew takes this act of disguise—or, really, the removal of the other's "modern," which is to say gentile-seeming, mask—as an excuse to return to what the joke portrays as a willing indulgence of comfort over decorum. *We're all Jews*, it says. *No need to stand on civility*. But what does this say about Jewishness and civility more generally? Does the joke think that non-Jews behave similarly when there are no Jews around to watch them? What does it say, in other words, about Jews themselves, the disguises that they don in modernity, and the way that they live up—or don't—to the promises and potentials of the non-Jewish world?

The prospect of Jewish failure to flourish in modern disguise, due to internal, cultural, or other immanent aspects probably received its most profound airing in the greatest Jewish short story ever written, Sholem Aleichem's "On Account of a Hat" (1913). Naturally, it's a comic narrative—but with a tremendous twist.

By the time Sholem Aleichem was writing, the phenomenon of Jewish disguise had taken on an entirely different complexion. In the modern world, flush with emancipatory spirit and ideology that allowed for action and behavior to replace old notions of identity and ethnicity, disguise—or perhaps its successor, actual cultural transformation—should have been possible. But "On Account of a Hat" takes the disruptive, potentially disqualifying lack of self-consciousness expressed in Freud's joke to a new level. Or, more precisely, regresses it to a preconscious one.

The tale, itself based on an old Jewish joke, recounts the attempts of one Sholem Shachnah to return home by train for Passover. An accidental hat switch with a Ukrainian official while asleep on a station bench, which should have allowed him to travel home in time and in style, fails catastrophically: looking in the mirror, Sholem Shachnah fails to see himself, only the hat, and believes he's been left sleeping on the platform. He misses the train to wake himself up. We're left, bemused and disturbed, by the thought that there's something in the character—the Jewish character—that prevents successful ends, something that peeks through the disguise and disallows the fulfillment of grand goals. It was so impossible, Sholem Shachnah believed, for a Jew to become a potent, manly official, part of the gentile power structure, that he refused to recognize his own identity in the mirror, preferring to accept the absurdist explanation that in his contortions of identity was the only "reasonable" one. Such, Sholem Aleichem suggests, are the wages of Jewish identity in the modern world. The prospect of change is itself simply an illusion, a very good disguise, and the schism that at its widest can be played for farcical comedy can, looked at through a narrower lens, yield a valley of the uncanny.

This kind of revelation—man sees double in mirror; double gets the better of it; nervousness over identity results—is practically a type scene in modern Jewish comedy. The "father" of the modern Yiddish theater, Avrom Goldfaden, created an indelible comedy in just this vein. In the culminating scene of his 1880 comic operetta *The Two Kuni-Lemls*, the titular character, a malformed, stuttering, idiotic representative of the old world, comes face to face with his modernized cousin, who has dressed up just like him. Kuni-Leml, a stunted man if there ever was one, has been betrothed to our ingénue, and her beloved, Max, is trying to extricate her while having a little fun at everyone's expense in the process. Max "proves" to Kuni-Leml that *he* is actually the real Kuni-Leml, imitating his stutter and his hobbled walk, and, turning the tables, insists that it's Kuni-Leml who's faking. Kuni-Leml wilts, and, as Max leaves, asks a simple question: What should he do if someone addresses him as Kuni-Leml? Max tells him, mock-angrily, that he should remain silent. Kumi-Leml slinks off.

It's unfortunate that this single example has to stand in for all the comic moments in the history of the vagabond stars of the Yiddish theater who made their way across stages from Buenos Aires to Whitechapel to Second Avenue, but at least it's the very finest. (Maurice Schwartz, arguably the Yiddish theater's greatest actor, referred to Kuni-Leml as "our Hamlet" and this scene as "our 'to be or not to be,'" which also says something about the roles of comedy and drama in the Jewish imagination.) Critics have begun to realize that if superficially Max is another in the line of satirical Enlightenment types making fun of Old World recalcitrance, his ability to take on Kuni Leml's attributes, to don his disguise, is a little bit . . . well, too easy. They *are* cousins, after all. And the mirror looks through disguise: it reveals similarities, and family resemblances.

WE'LL RETURN to a third mirror scene in a bit. But before we get there, a brief pause to examine one of the best-known fans of the Yiddish theater and one of the masters of twentieth-century Jewish comedy.

Of course, I'm talking about Franz Kafka. Kafka possesses a sustained, if mordant, comic vision. Not in all of his works, of course: I would hardly call *In the Penal Colony* a laugh riot, and certainly his "Letter to His Father" isn't a great source of comedy (though it certainly does explain a lot). But there's an argument to be made that in enough of his works—"Blumfeld, an Elderly Bachelor"; "A Report to an Academy"; "The Village Schoolmaster"; and yes, *The Metamorphosis*, to name just four—Kafka, building on the Yiddish theatrical comedy that was a surprisingly important factor in his Jewish identity, created a template for twentieth-century comedy, Jewish no less than otherwise. And Kafka's Jewish comedy, in the frequently non-Jewish forms it takes, relies for its Jewish effect, as well as its comic effect, on literary disguise: or, to put it another way, the sustained presence of allegory.

It's easy to simply throw around terms like "post-Enlightenment" and "the failure of reason" and nod to how the Great War changed everything by using the miracles of industrialization to dispense death in mass qualities. It's harder to make them funny. But all this does seem to have been grist for Kafka's comedic mill. With his particular gift for portraying the eruption of the mysterious, the irrational, the uncanny, into the present world situation—whether it's about two floating balls tormenting an elderly bachelor, the discussions of scholarship around an enormous and possibly mythical vole, an intelligent ape making a report to a society of scholars, or Gregor Samsa just waking up to discover that he's been transformed into a monstrous vermin—you can say that Kafka is taking on and incorporating advances in technology, science, governance, bureaucracy. Think about the balls, for a moment, as floating particles of light; of the vole as the scientific search for the historical Jesus; of advances in physics, evolutionary biology, and the replacement of a type of dogmatic certainty with another type of studied blurriness and genuine unknowingness. In this sense, Kafka's work is a satire of science and intellectualism.

This nods back to Freud, obviously, whose idea that we're mostly the sum and substance of irrational drives that we paper over with talk about reason (I'm simplifying outrageously, of course) and that humor comes in no small part of our dawning, if partial, awareness that the knowledge and certainty we have about our lives is highly illusory. All of these mirror situations—which reveal the monstrously misunderstood distortions peeking out, in a way so horrible that you just have to laugh—undergird so much of the argument that has been made for the Jewishness hidden in Kafka's work. (Hidden in his fiction, that is; it's there, manifest, in the letters and diaries.)

That is, these stories seem so clearly to be allegories that it's easy to spot questions of Jewishness in them. "A Report to an Academy" (1917), which appeared in the Max Brod–edited Zionist journal *Der Jude*, is about the dubious welcome of the Jew to the European family; *The Metamorphosis* is the same, but in reverse; and so on. If we're suggesting that disguise, and the question of whether change is really just a disguise, is a central theme of the non-Jewish Jewish comedy, who better to explore that than the author of *The Metamorphosis*?

Not Proust, I think, Kafka's almost precise contemporary; despite the brilliant sense of the *comédie humaine* and the nervous comic energy that bristles around disguised Jewishness, and gayness, in Proust's work—especially the joke, one, as we've seen, of long standing, that the disguise isn't particularly good. On one occasion, for example, Albert Bloch, a Jewish friend of the narrator's, is embroiled in a socially charged conversation concerning the Dreyfus Affair. When his Jewishness is snidely alluded to, Bloch's reaction—how could they have known?—is presented as not-so-simple self-deception: "given his name, which had not exactly a Christian sound, and his face, his surprise argued a certain naivete," the narrator notes.

But to simply cast Kafka in Proust's model of acculturative anxiety is, I think, selling him short. The weirdness in his fiction suggests, in its blunt *thereness*, that life isn't just stranger than we can imagine but that, *pace* Freud, *we* are stranger than we *do* imagine. A lot of it *is* sexual, of course—those two balls haunting an elderly bachelor aren't really Einsteinian (or Rutherfordian) particles, are they? They're really *balls*, genitalia, taunting him with his own impotence. And, given the connection between anxiety over Jewish disguise and Jewish masculinity in this strand, it's hardly insignificant that many of the protagonists are, in their varying ways, unmanned (as ape and as vermin, to name just two).

But it's not so much the fact of the uncanny itself that places Kafka in the ranks of the comic; it's the way that his protagonists react to that uncanniness. The natural first response of readers of *The Metamorphosis* is to focus on the horror of Gregor Samsa's situation: How did he get that way? What's going to happen to him? Can he change back? What's the explanation? The fact that there is no explanation, and no hope of escape or transformation, naturally tends to lead to a focus on the horror of the story. This has led to a portrait of Gregor Samsa (or Blumfeld, or Joseph K.) as the victim of a terrifying and terrible world, a world that's either metaphysically unfair or politically totalitarian. It's not coincidental that Kafka's reputation really gains traction in the West during the Cold War:

the fact that he was writing under a monarchy notwithstanding, it's pretty easy to see how anti-Communists saw Kafka as expressing their precise concerns with the terrors of their hated regimes.

What all that overlooks is that mostly Kafka focuses on the protagonists' *reactions* to the uncanny event. He doesn't seem to care very much about the whys and wherefores. He cares about reactions and situations. In effect, what Kafka has created is a pool of stone-faced straight men negotiating the absurd world they suddenly find themselves in. Gregor Samsa is the classic example: When he discovers that he has been turned into a monstrous vermin, his reaction is not, as I suspect many of ours would be, "Oh my god oh my god oh my god what is happening to me?" Rather, it is simply a long aria about being late for work. And then, as time goes on, and everyone who he knows, including someone from his office, shows up outside his door, we realize we're in the province of something resembling an anxiety dream, but one which is actually happening (the truth status, so to speak, of Samsa's experiences are never in doubt). The elderly bachelor Blumfeld acts similarly; his response to the floating balls is not to question the overturning of everything science and society knows about gravity, but simply to display asperity and annoyance.

If Kafka's jokes are Jewish, which I think in many ways that they are, then their Jewishness *had* to be quite strictly and scrupulously stripped from the work in order for it to achieve the aesthetic effects that it did. Because those aesthetic effects—those comic effects—are about studied attempts at normality in the face of weirdness: the precise situation, I think Kafka felt, that Jews have in acculturated modernity, where they don't have the luxury of acting weird or acting out or acting big, whatever the provocation. Even if it's floating balls.

It may be that the closest moments in literature to Gregor Samsa's excruciating, emasculating embarrassment and discomfort are (and you'll forgive the blasphemy, but I think it fits) the opening moments of the 1998 movie *There's Something About Mary*, where a young Ben Stiller has accidentally had a horrible accident involving his genitalia and everyone in the world is parked outside the bathroom door. Samsa—and "Stiller"—are fairly normal (if neurotic) individuals caught in extraordinary circumstances. Which is another way of saying that Kafka's comedy has strong resemblances to film comedy, especially slapstick.

The great theorist of comedy in Kafka's day, the French Jew Henri Bergson, suggested, in the shadow of industrialization, that the essence of comedy was the reduction of the human being to a machine. The iconic image is Chaplin caught inside the gears of the machine in *Modern Times*. But the robotic reactions of Buster Keaton and the frantic smile of Harold Lloyd were all part of the same piece. None of these three masters of American physical comedy were Jews. The gold medal for "most influential Jewish slapstick comedian or comedians" probably belongs to the Three Stooges, with the silver to Jerry Lewis and the bronze to Soupy Sales. But the Stooges—despite titling a powder puff Schlemiel No. 8 in their 1949 movie *Hokus Pokus*, an occasional foray into Yiddish in their shorts, and even producing an anti-Nazi film—had little interest or evocation of the themes related to identity in the world around them, and Sales even less.

Compare this to the Marx Brothers, two of whom find each other, in 1933's *Duck Soup*, in the third of our triptych of mirror scenes. Moving in unison, siblings in sensibility as well as of course in real life, the brothers would, as Philip Roth suggested, work wondrously in a film version of Kafka's *The Castle* (Groucho as K., and Harpo and Chico as his two assistants). But their comedy—which, in a manner not dissimilar to Kafka's, at times traded on how to portray ethnic difference, and Jewishness in particular, in a medium studiously opposed to that presentation—set the course for a century of a kind of Jewish mass entertainment.

Sons of Jewish immigrants to America, the Marx Brothers made their bones in vaudeville; in part on the success of their lightning-quick wits, in part on the power of their knockabout physical comedy, and in part on their ability and willingness to trade on the then-pervasive humor of ethnic stereotypes. Chico was the comic Italian, Harpo the comic Irishman, and Groucho the comic "German," which, as we've seen, was often vaudeville for "Jew": in an early notice, he was described as "Master Marx, a juvenile soprano singer and impersonator of the Yiddischer."

What made the Marx Brothers so successful was their ability to serve as the blast of anarchy into the stuffed-shirt world that, after the First World War and during the Depression, needed shaking up. ("Whatever it is," Groucho sings in 1932's *Horse Feathers*, long before Brando and James Dean, "I'm against it.") Whether it was the university, the mansions of the rich, the opera, or even the halls of government, the Marx Brothers came in and upended everything. But they did so as the mustachioed, hatted, bewigged and trench-coated assistants of classical comedy. Understanding a Marx Brothers movie is really in part about understanding how the traditional conventions are maintained: the young lovers still end up together; the hypocrites are unmasked and banished; and the spectators (in the movie, not just watching it) get a good show into the bargain. Groucho, when asked to replace his greasepaint mustache for a more realistic one so that the audience would believe in it more, replied, "The audience doesn't believe in us anyhow." But this isn't quite true: they believe *implicitly* in the Brothers' good hearts and good graces and good aims. Groucho may have advocated anarchy and disbelief, but in the service of higher causes.

This is ultimately why Philip Roth was wrong: none of the Marx Brothers would really have been right to play K. (though admittedly Groucho would have been closest). Kafka's characters are the straight men to the world that the Marx Brothers seem to create, and then uncreate by the movie's end. Kafka's characters or worlds are, largely speaking, changed forever or destroyed by the events which take place around them; the Marx Brothers simply move on to the next movie. Looked at this way, Kafka's the one that champions a comedy unmoored from all verities, that strives for the universal; whereas the Marx Brothers—as we'll see—are, in their particular anxieties, willing to embrace ethnic details, including the circumstances of their Jewishness.

Take one scene from 1930's *Animal Crackers*, a classic set piece of comedy: the unmasking of the hypocrite. In this scene, Roscoe W. Chandler, a villain of the film, is recognized by Chico, who tries to place him, though Chandler huffily claims never to have seen him before. Chico and Harpo finally hit on it: he's Abie the fish peddler from the old country: that is, a Jew. (The name Abie, for Abraham, and the peddler job are dead giveaways; more subtly, they discover a birthmark that identifies him as "Abie"—shades of circumcision, another bodily change that marks off Jews.) Abie confesses, using a turn of Jewish voice: "I *vas*! I *vas* Abie the Fish Peddler!" he says, using that v instead of a w, the bête noire of all Eastern European Jewish immigrants. Chico then asks him how he got to be Roscoe W. Chandler: to which Chandler, without missing a beat, asks him how *he* got to be Italian.

Chico replies that it's none of his business, but it's our business very much indeed. There's a lot of ethnic masking and changing and unmasking going on here; in the same way that in the same movie, during the song "Hurray for Captain Spaulding," Groucho nervously asks: "Did someone call me schnorrer"? Of course, Spaulding *is* a schnorrer, as are Otis Driftwood, Rufus Firefly, Hugo Hackenbush, and so many other characters in Groucho's oeuvre. What are those names if not the efforts of someone trying to pass, fearful he won't, and knowing he doesn't? But if he's pretending not to be a Jew, the movie is making it clear that they're also interested in us finding them out. (Although maybe not *all* that interested. When one critic "anointed him the 'symbolic embodiment of all persecuted Jews for 2000 years,' Groucho carped, 'What sort of goddamned review is that?'") That anxiety—about being in and out—is at the root of this kind of Jewish comedy.

Actors were hardly the only ones anxious about their Jewish identity in the film industry, and committed to disguise as a result.

The studio executives were, famously, a lot less playful about it. Though they probably weren't regular readers of Henry Ford's *Dearborn Independent*, they certainly heard its 1921 shot across the bow: "As soon as the Jews gained control of the 'movies' . . . we had a movie problem, the consequences of which are not yet visible. It is the genius of that race to create problems of a moral character in whatever business they achieve a majority." And those problems were expressed precisely phrased in terms of the possibility, or rather impossibility, of Jews being like other Americans: "It is not that producers of Semitic origin have deliberately set out to be bad according to their own standards, but they know that their whole taste and temper are different from the prevailing standards of the American people. . . . Many of these producers don't know how filthy their stuff is—it is so natural to them." And they were aware of the flourishing of certain negative Jewish stereotypes in vaudeville-to-film comedies like the Cohen shorts, such as the Edison Company's *Cohen's Fire Sale* (1907), which trades on the popular impression, often disseminated in joke form, of Jews burning down stores to recoup insurance money. My favorite of these jokes:

> A man approaches Cohen. "I'm so sorry, Cohen, I heard about your store burning down yesterday."
> "Sh! Tomorrow!"

Or take the earlier Edison 1904 film *Cohen's Advertising Scheme*, where the enterprising, not to say unscrupulous, Cohen turns a client's coat into a billboard advertising his wares.

The results were a doubling down on disguise: not everyone had the autonomy, or anarchic take-it-or-leave-it sense, of the Marx Brothers. Take the case of the well-known actor Max Davidson, a "maestro of reaction shots," who played an "unmistakably Jewish" character in a number of two-reel shorts he did for the Hal Roach Studios in the 1920s (including *Jewish Prudence*, *Should Second Husbands Come First*, and *Why Girls Say No*). His contract ended in 1928; the reason might have been that Nicholas Schenck and Louis B. Mayer, who ran MGM (which distributed Hal Roach), were embarrassed by the ethnic stereotyping. George Jessel, known on the vaudeville stage for his telephone comedy (telephoning his Jewish mother on stage, he learns she's cooked a bird he bought her that spoke five languages), had the title of a projected 1927 movie *Schlemiel* changed to *Mamma's Boy*. After his first screen test for MGM, Danny Kaye was pressured by Sam Goldwyn to get his nose fixed (they settled on bleaching his hair); Carl Reiner's show about his experiences writing television comedy was "de-Judaized" with his replacement by Dick Van Dyke (who, to be fair, added his own inestimable comic gifts to the mix—they were just different comic gifts); among many other examples.

But the Marx Brothers' exploration of the cracks and fissures in the American Jewish disguise—and playing that exploration for nervous laughs—was picked up over the next decades nonetheless. There's Jerry Lewis and his 1963 movie *The Nutty Professor*: in the transformation of Julius Kelp (and is it a coincidence, that we hear the word "Jew" in that not atypically for the time Jewish first name?) to Buddy Love, the crooner and sex object of everyone's desire, we see Lewis's suggestion that giving up one's identity for conventional success isn't what it's cracked up to be—and the resulting dissonance when most of the audience didn't feel they necessarily agreed with the movie's moral. Or Woody Allen's *Zelig* (1983), in which Allen invites no less eminent a personage than Irving Howe to pontificate on the case study of the eponymous human chameleon, with the explanation that Zelig was a living metaphor for the American Jewish experience—"he just wanted to assimilate like crazy." Zelig, who is all disguise, all protective coloration, in the movie's climax finds questionable solace in the arms of a group where everyone is exactly like everyone else—the Nazi party. The Jew so turned around by his unmooring from firm identity that he becomes its diametrical opposite: now that's dark comedy, and sound allegory. But all too often the disguise was of the Jessel type, from *Schlemiel* to *Mamma's*

Boy; that is to say, not a very good one. The explicit representation was gone, but it was simply replaced by a slightly more complex stereotyping.

Alternatively, Jews donned other disguises to play similar games of peekaboo Judaism, dressing up as other ethnicities, other genders, other *others*. Jews were performing in blackface on the vaudeville stages from its inception, for example. And Eddie Cantor, in his 1930 movie *Whoopee*, pretends to be a Native American. When a Native American insists to Cantor he's white—"I've gone to your schools," he says, Cantor replies: "An Indian in a Hebrew school?" This particular disguise had a long tradition even before Cantor. There was Fanny Brice's "Yiddishe Squaw" Rosie Rosenstein; or, more esoterically, the 1908 song "I'm a Yiddish Cowboy (Tough Guy Levi)," along with 1909 and 1911 silent movies of similar title; and Milt Gross had turned his dialectal attentions to the situation by producing a Longfellow parody, 1926's *Hiawatta witt no odder poems*. And of course Cantor would have his successors, most famously Mel Brooks's casting Native Americans as Yiddish speakers; and several years later, on the other side, 1981's *The Frisco Kid* would present Brooks's favorite actor, Gene Wilder, as the unlikeliest cowboy in the world. After all, as Leslie Fiedler once wrote about the Bernard Malamud novel, *A New Life*, which he called the author's "travesty Western": "The very notion of the Western Jew is, like that of the Irish Jew, a joke in itself." Replace "Western" or "Cowboy" with "knight" and we have the *Bovo-bukh* all over again.

Notions of sexual orientation and manhood, Jewish and otherwise, have had a long history in comedy, and it's not surprising that an aspect of identity long revolving around disguise and revelation, closeting and coming out, had a role in American Jewish comedy as well. Milton Berle's drag peformances as Carmen Miranda were a central part of the early history of television; and, on one 1949 show, when his wig slipped, he said, "my *sheytl* is falling," connecting the traditional Jewish married woman's wig to his own gender-bending theatrics. In the late eighties and early nineties, Paul Rudnick took up the masquerade via his occasional female Jewish alter ego, assistant buyer of juniors activewear and film columnist Libby Gelman-Waxner; and a more sustained effort, one that focused on comic character rather than comic caricature, came in 1992 from William Finn. *Falsettos* was one of the few Broadway shows to include a treatment of a bar mitzvah—and one of the fewer to include the bar mitvah boy's gay father and his lesbian kosher caterer. The musical, which encompasses AIDS and adolescent anxiety along with its more comic stings, took remarkable strides in presenting a different kind of Jewish family to American audiences; that progress has been built upon by the Amazon show *Transparent*, which premiered in 2014. *Transparent* (which, in Jimmy Kimmel's words at the 2016 Emmy Awards, "was born a drama, but . . . identifies as a comedy") has been called, by *New Yorker* television critic Emily Nussbaum, "the most Jewish show I've seen on TV"; and it's a show which sometimes neatly, sometimes with the messiness the best art uses to capture life, weaves together the revelations Jeffrey Tambor's Maura (formerly Mort) Pfefferman comes to and shares with others about his own personal identity with those Jill Soloway, the show's creator, articulates about Jewishness. Not only Jewishness in the lives of modern American Jews, but the ones presented—now more boldly than ever before—on American laptops and television screens by entertainment media.

All these displays, in their own individual ways, reminded audiences of Mel Brooks's comment, speaking about himself but, I think, more widely applicable, that "comedy comes from the feeling that, as a Jew, and as a person, you don't fit into the mainstream of American society. It comes from the realization that even though you're better and smarter, you'll never belong." And you didn't need greasepaint, or war paint, to make that point. Sometimes—and increasingly, over the course of the twentieth century—the joke was more about hiding in plain sight.

TAKE BENNY KUBELSKY. Under the name Jack Benny, he was one of the most popular comedians in American history; certainly in the history of American radio. He started on NBC radio in 1932; became its most popular star by 1937; and by the 1940s was considered to be the medium's most recognizable voice (in second place: FDR). So widespread was the ritual of tuning in to listen on Sunday night at 7 that in 1943 NBC announced that no matter what sponsor bought the slot, the time belonged to Benny. Probably part of the reason was because of "the brainstorm that revolutionized radio: situation comedy based on the lives of the performers, complete with sophisticated sound effects. Instead of revue skits and strings of jokes, each show would be a variation on a constant theme: life with Jack Benny." But the fact that he was hilarious didn't hurt either.

Was it Jewish comedy? Did his legions of fans think about it that way? Well, no, and yes. On the one hand, he never identified himself as a Jew; he didn't speak in dialect. On the other hand: He had sidekicks named Schlepperman and Kitzle, who often Judaized cultural names and icons (referring to Ed Sullivan as "Ed Solomon," for example, or the singer Nat "King" Cohen). He was proverbially known for his stinginess. (Robber: "Your money or your life." Benny, after a long pause: "I'm *thinking*." And he played a one-hundred-dollar Stradivarius—"one of the few *ever* made in Japan.") And—perhaps most interestingly for our purposes—he was constantly portrayed as unmanly: cowardly, sensitive about his age, effeminate. A schnook, in short, a word perhaps first shared with the general American public on Benny's radio broadcast in 1951, used to describe Benny's character by his (real and on-the-show) wife. Benny said that he made his character the target of the jokes so that "the minute I come on, even the most hen-pecked guy in the audience feels good." Of course, this was a persona. Gracie Allen, who famously played a not-very-bright character to George Burns's straight man, was once asked if Benny was really cheap. Her response was: "Am I stupid?" But it was a persona that traded on certain archetypes. At least, that was what Benny thought. In 1945, his show, characteristically enough, offered a prize for the best explanation of "Why I Hate Jack Benny" in twenty-five words or less. While Benny okayed the idea, he insisted that any anti-Semitic responses be pulled. Of 270,000 entries, only three were offensive.

Which once more raises the question of how good the disguise was, or, put another way, who saw through it. Jews weren't the only stereotypical cheapskates, in vaudeville and other popular cultural media. Scrooge McDuck, that archetypal tightwad, is a reminder of a generally forgotten anti-Scottish slur of the same ilk. Some people thought George Burns was Irish; Groucho believed people thought the Marx Brothers were Italian, given the sound of their stage names; the Kitzle character's dialectal intonations were at least partially based on an African-American hot dog salesman one of Benny's writers had heard in Houston. Sometimes the game of peekaboo Judaism seemed to be by the few, for the few. Nobody else knew, and, in not knowing—moguls' anxieties notwithstanding—didn't care.

For those *in* the know, though, disguised Jewishness, and the questions about masculinity that went with it, continued to flourish. Benny's reign would extend into the television era as well, as *The Jack Benny Show* ran from 1950 to 1965; and at a time when New York accounted for 42 percent of television sets, and, in 1952, when 63 of the 108 operating stations were in metropolitan regions, Mr. Television himself, Milton Berle, killed with his brand of cross-dressing comedy. Berle was no stranger to the "did someone call me schnorrer" sidebar—recall that tossed-off line about the *sheytel*—but the most interesting thing about the episode is that it's the *audience* that cracks up, clear on the Yiddish word. Of course they did: television was New York, then.

Disguised Jews were everywhere in a small, centered popular culture then. *Your Show of Shows* was joined by Phil Silvers's *Sergeant Bilko*, with its brilliantly byzantine central character (along with Privates Fender and Zimmerman) and the Jewish Bronx of *Car 54, Where Are You?*, featuring the iconic Molly Picon as Mrs. Bronson, thanks in no small part to the presiding comic genius behind these shows (and involved early on in Berle's career), Nat Hiken, a Sholem Aleichem fan whose most famous character also had an ongoing dialogue with God. Lenny Bruce would provide his own echo of the pop culture act, where iconic characters are revealed, after a closer look, to be Jews: when one slows down the Lone Ranger's iconic call, "Hi-Ho Silver" is revealed to be "Hi, Yosl-Ber," and Mr. and Mrs. Dracula are shown to be nagging Jewish parents.

But as television became less New York and more American, things changed: or, at least, the view of things from the top office changed. This kind of Yiddish gameplaying, of peekaboo Judaism, smoothed over some of the ethnic and other idiosyncracies of television with more of a glass-teat homogeneity. As two of the writers from *Your Show of Shows*, that iconic example of the first period, put it: "We were a big hit in all the urban areas, but the minute TV began to spread out into the suburban and rural areas, they didn't get our kind of comedy. We couldn't be as sophisticated as we once were, and the ratings eventually started to drop." Or, more pungently: "As the price of sets came down, so did the IQ of the audience." Those two writers? Neil Simon and Larry Gelbart, respectively.

A perfect case study is the tale of perhaps the most important explicit Jewish presence in early American radio and television. Gertrude Berg, the daughter of a Catskills resort owner who did skits there to entertain guests, approached CBS during the Depression with an idea for a radio show inspired by Milt Gross dialect stories. (She herself, it should be noted, was American-born and spoke accentless English.) CBS took it on, and cast Berg in the lead as a result of her ingenuity—she delivered the script in unintelligible handwriting so they would ask her to read—and aired from 1929 to 1945, a run second only to *Amos 'n' Andy*. Berg was writer, producer, and star, making her one of the most important people in radio.

When *The Goldbergs* switched to television, it shot to number seven in the ratings in 1949 and Berg won an Emmy for best actress in 1950, as well as being named "TV mother of the year." But then Philip Loeb, the male lead, was blacklisted. Berg kept him on salary for as long as she could, but after intense pressure from the show's sponsor, General Foods, he was forced off the show in 1952 and would later commit suicide. Given that, and the changing nature of the television audience, Goldberg was doubling down on Americanization, backpedaling the show's early Yiddishisms, its New-Americanesque malapropisms ("Sit down. Take your feet off"; "David, throw an eye in the soup until I get back"), and its vanishingly rare ethnic distinctiveness. In a 1956 *Commentary* interview, Berg said:

> You see, darling, I don't bring up anything that would bother people. That's very important. Unions, politics, fundraising, Zionism, socialism, inter-group relations, I don't stress them. And after all, aren't such things secondary to daily family living? The Goldbergs are not defensive about their Jewishness, or especially aware of it . . . I keep things average. I don't want to lose friends.

In its final 1955–1956 season, at NBC's behest, the characters moved from the Bronx to the suburbs, and dropped their last name, at least in the TV listings: the show was retitled, simply, *Molly*.

Four years before, Henry Popkin had charged that "what may be called 'de-Semitization' is by now a commonplace in the popular arts . . . this law originates not in hate, but in a misguided benevolence—or fear; its name is 'sha-sha'. . . . If we pretend that the Jew does not exist, the reasoning goes, then he will not be noticed; the anti-Semite, unable to find his victim, will simply forget about him." Popkin noted particularly the loss of the dialect comedian. One of those comedians, Sam Levenson, addressed the issue head-on, writing of his concern that explicit displays of Jewishness lost you friends—personally and as a people. Watching a dialect comic in a predominantly gentile audience, he wrote, in a 1952 article:

the audience howled. The laughter frightened me. The entire scene recalled the Nazi beer hall where comedians with derby hats and beards told the same type of story to those who were later to become the executioners of our people. This may sound extreme, but it is my belief that any Jew who, in humor or otherwise, strengthens the misconceptions and the prejudices against his own people is neither a good Jew nor a responsible human being. There are such things as "inside jokes" . . .

And yes, inside jokes there were. There were, of course, the wild men who insisted on bringing those jokes out unapologetically—Allen Ginsberg sending William Carlos Williams a poem he described as "a mad song (to be sung by Groucho Marx to a Bop background)"; Lenny Bruce stalking strip club stages and shpritzing; the comedienne Jean Carroll, addressing a United Jewish Appeal benefit at Madison Square Garden in 1948, saying, "I've always been proud of the Jews, but never so proud as tonight . . . Because tonight I wish I had my old nose back."

But there were less-wild men, too; a lot of them, in their latest, postwar iteration. You don't have to agree with everything in the critic Albert Goldman's late sixties thesis statement to find resonance in it:

> The Jewish comic is the adolescent urban funny boy— hysterically intense. The key to his comedy—and the ironic clue to his tragedy—is that he is intellectually and verbally overdeveloped at the same time that he is emotionally and sexually underdeveloped.

Goldman, who wrote the book on Lenny Bruce and was a perceptive pop culture critic at a time when most critics were dismissive, seems to have captured an important connection that would suit a broad range of postwar Jewish comedy particularly well. It covered Neil

Simon's evocations of nostalgic ethnicity on the Broadway stage. Starting with 1961's *Come Blow Your Horn*, about his and his brother's experiences moving away from their Jewish home, Simon would go on to chronicle different aspects of American Jewish identity whose comic sensibility stemmed largely from conformity to easily recognizable stereotype. Often, for Simon, that was tied to different stages in the life cycle of the American Jewish man: Goldman's intellectually overdeveloped, sexually underdeveloped adolescent (1983's *Brighton Beach Memoirs* and its successors); the idiosyncratic, self-pitying, self-martyring, neurotic adult (Felix Unger in 1968's *The Odd Couple*; the description is Simon's, of how he wrote the character Jewish); and the wise-cracking, crotchety senior citizen (1975's *The Sunshine Boys*). The new disguise of American Jewish identity—a kind of not-quite-man—was in full bloom.

But it also covered the alienated allegorists, the comedians whose struggles against the restrictions on comedy emerged as war on "comedy," in its contemporary institutionalized practice. Albert Brooks's assault, in his various talk show appearances, on the conventions of ENTERTAINMENT! (the world's worst ventriloquist, the animal trainer whose elephant has gotten sick and he has to replace it with a frog at the last minute), and his iconic appearance on *The Tonight Show* where he tells the audience that he's run out of "bits" and that he could do cheap jokes but "that isn't me," were an essential act of alienation, of being not-quite-able-to-handle "the normalcy" of comedian life, if there ever was one. And Brooks was absolutely mainstream next to Andy Kaufman's brand of conceptual art, whose most famous roles—the terrible comic from a Caspian island who, at the end of his disastrous routine, would pivot to a remarkable Elvis impersonation; his obnoxious Tony Clifton, the alter ego to end all alter egos; the sexist "Andy Kaufman" who baited talk-show hosts with horrific comments about women culminating in a staged bout with a female wrestler—took disguise to a level so dazzling/wearying/frightening that it's the closest real-life equivalent to Sholem Shachnah and his fractured identity crisis. "Kaufman"'s antics, of course, reflected—or, more precisely, satirized—the fear of male impotence at the heart of so much misogyny; and Goldman's point resonates again.

But late-night appearances aside, you wouldn't find these figures on television—at least not in anything resembling their truly dangerous form. (Think of Kaufman's hilarious but neutered Latka on *Taxi*, for example.) The balancing act that Berg and Levenson suggested—and the television executives mandated—resulted in an increasingly homeopathic strain on America's television sets, and, to a lesser extent, film screens. But, almost paradoxically, that same presentation resulted in the reinforcing and amplifying of certain conventionally understood "Jewish" stereotypes, part and parcel of an increasing identification of the idea of Jewishness—in its own way and by itself—with being funny.

This could be symbolized by a rim shot of Yiddish, or Yiddish-like linguistic behavior, which had already been "comedified" by the Borscht Belt comedians, among others. (One scholar, interviewing Jewish television writers and producers about how they "wrote Jewish" in their shows, found that they were only able to come up with a single specific method: "putting the object of the sentence at the start rather than at the end." This immediately recognizable sentence type—"*This* you give me?"—is adopting a kind of Yiddish syntax.) Or references to American Jewish lower-middle-class behaviors that were a little different but not too different. Like Hanukkah, which America turned into a secular Jewish Christmas, complete with greeting cards that provided a convenient occasion and punch line. Greeting cards that read "Deck the halls with loaves of challah" or "Oh, you wanted Hanukkah GELT. I thought you said GUILT" were about demonstrating how Jewish humor was mainstream.

Not all of this mainstreaming, or the comedy that went with it, was about masculinity or male sexuality. There was Wendy Wasserstein's exploration of the neuroses and desires of a certain American Jewish female demographic (especially in 1992's *The Sisters Rosensweig*); Grace Paley's hilarious, wistful, pugnacious, and unique portraits of American Jewish women; and Erica Jong's *Fear of*

Flying, which chronicled the flights of fancy and freedom of a newly liberated—or were they?—American Jewish womanhood. But all too often, when women were involved in explorations of Jewish Americanism, they were non-Jewish women, who provided the ultimate test case for becoming part of the body general: marrying into it.

Intermarriage, by whatever name, has been part of this story from its beginnings: Esther, after all, marries a non-Jew, which perplexed rabbis so much that they devoted much effort to explaining it away. (My favorite apparently unintentionally comic solution: it was actually a "ghost body" of Esther's that cohabited with Ahasuerus.) The prospect of intermarriage, until the twentieth century, was necessarily intertwined with conversion: in Tsarist Russia, for example, Tevye's daughter Chava had to become a Christian to marry her Chvedka. Which upped the stakes considerably, and made the prospect of intermarriage, if not impossible to serve as a subject for comedy, more naturally fall into the realm of melodrama or tragedy. (In the case of Tevye's Chava, Sholem Aleichem manages to dance among all three genres, brilliantly.) But in an American context, the historical circumstances of separation of church and state along with the comparatively rapid transformation of Jewish identity from religion to ethnicity offered more room to breathe, and to laugh.

The questions at the heart of many of these intermarriage or interfaith comedies—which far more frequently featured a Jewish man and a gentile woman than the reverse—played on the possibility of the Jewish male escaping the bonds of the comic stereotypes that rendered him a possibly unfit lover. The granddaddy of all of these treatments, the play *Abie's Irish Rose* (which ran for 2,327 performances from May 1922 to October 1927, setting a Broadway record broken by another chronicle of an interfaith relationship, *Fiddler on the Roof*), presented what had not long before been anathema as a set of situations and stereotypical misunderstandings to be worked out—a situation comedy in search of an American resolution. *Abie's Irish Rose* spawned a herd of on-screen imitators: films like *Private Izzy Murphy* (1926), *Sailor Izzy Murphy* (1927), and *Clancy's*

Kosher Wedding (1927). There was also *Kosher Kitty Kelly* (1926), one of the long-running Cohens and Kellys series, which starred Jewish comedian George Sidney as a paterfamilias trying, like an American Tevye, to understand this new thing that was happening. Unlike the Tevye of Sholem Aleichem's stories, he came to embrace a new pairing for a new world with a smile.

Perhaps these films were less troubling to the producers of mass entertainment when what they depicted was a vanishing rarity off-screen, a metaphor for American acceptance rather than an actual sociological phenomenon. In the twenties, intermarriage rates were well below 5 percent; but that changed radically over the succeeding half century. By 1975, the number of Jews marrying non-Jews had reached 25 percent—triple what it had been just ten years earlier. Perhaps this explained the fate of a groundbreaking sitcom dedicated solely to the topic of interfaith romance.

Or, more precisely, inter*ethnic* romance. *Bridget Loves Bernie*, which first aired on CBS in 1972, was never really about matters theological, but rather the question of how an uptown WASP and an outer-borough Jew could ever possibly overcome their differences, codified in whatever classic stereotypes a sitcom writing staff could come up with. (Spoiler alert: love, it turns out.) In the pilot episode, lines like "Now, Bernie, do you take one lump or two in your Jew?" (Bridget's parents) and "I don't believe this. I've lived with you people all my life. Now why is everyone all of a sudden being so Jewish?" (Bernie, to *his* parents) told the tale. There's a little anti-Semitism, a little ethnocentrism, but nothing a good romance can't get over. This was a message that most Americans seemed to be fine with. *Bridget Loves Bernie* placed fifth in the ratings in its first, and only, season. It was cancelled nonetheless, the victim of protests, and presumably a victim of studio concern that its Jewishness was *too* assertive.

There aren't many opportunities for comparison: from 1954 to 1972 not one leading character on prime time clearly identified as Jewish (*Bridget Loves Bernie*'s Bernie Steinberg broke the streak), then again a drought from 1978 to 1987. Seventeen years after

Bridget, Jackie Mason's short-lived *Chicken Soup* (1989) suffered a similar fate: despite high ratings and critical approbation, Jewish opposition to the show (the *Jewish Journal* of Los Angeles called it "as inappropriate and offensive to Jews as *Amos and Andy* [sic] would be to blacks today") helped cancel it after a month. It was the second-highest-rated series in history to be canceled, ranking thirteenth in the ratings. The highest? *Bridget Loves Bernie*.

There were occasional exceptions that proved the rule—most notably Richard Lewis's show *Anything But Love* (1989–1992). As a stand-up comedian, Lewis was "known for being neurotic, obsessive, wired, an essential unhappy man with trust issues; he was famous for pacing restlessly onstage, stooping as he walked, running his hands through his long hair—what one critic called a 'kvetch ballet.'" It was a shtick so character-based that it transferred well to the sitcom format. But the persona he created was such a full embodiment of a certain Jewish stereotype it needed no explanation. ("We went to see *Les Miserables*. I thought it was going to be like a play about one of my family's seders.") But the title itself indicated how complicated the romance in this romantic comedy was going to be, as opposed to the easy attraction displayed by the comic partners in *Bridget Loves Bernie* or *Chicken Soup*.

Despite their popular (if short-lived) success with fans at the time, these three sitcoms hardly thrive in syndication and streaming. Paradoxically, it was de-Semitization taken to its extreme that opened the door for a wider variety of explicit Jewish experience in mass culture than ever before. By 1999, there were twelve "Jewish" sitcoms from the 1990s in first-run and syndication available on TV, and thirty-three with Jewish protagonists between 1989 and 2001. And almost all of this could be laid at the feet of one show that specialized in the comedy of Jewish disguise, rather than its opposite: *Seinfeld*.

JERRY SEINFELD's first role in sitcomland was as a joke writer for the governor on the 1980–1981 season of *Benson*; the gag was he wrote jokes no one liked or wanted to hear. One joke he tried out: "Did you hear about the rabbi who bought himself a ranch? Called it the Bar Mitzvah." After the joke fails, he asks: "Too Jewish? Too Western?" Seinfeld wasn't the only one to worry about being too Jewish on television; but he obviously didn't suffer from the problem. By 1981, he appeared on *The Tonight Show*, that anointed path to bigger and better things if you hit—and boy, did he. He became a fixture there, on Letterman, on Merv Griffin, and toward the end of the 1980s was getting up to twenty-five thousand dollars a weekend to do stand-up and doing 300 performances a year.

It was easy to see why Carson, paradigmatic Midwestern gentile, liked Seinfeld. Sure, Seinfeld had been a kibbutz volunteer; but his observational humor—the discussions of socks, of baseball uniforms—was exactly the kind that removed ethnic specificity. *Everybody* knew what Seinfeld was talking about; that was the point. And no one would ever be left behind, be alienated, or take offense. If anything, they'd admire the cut-glass precision of the jokes, the rigorous attention to the loops and whirls of language in its specific absurdities. Sure, there was weirdness there, and hostility, and occasional flashes of misanthropy; but it was buried beneath a general impression of professionalism and bonhomie.

Maybe that's why Brandon Tartikoff, NBC's president at the time, despite (or because of) being Jewish himself, was so interested in Seinfeld—and so nonplussed by the show that Seinfeld and Larry David, someone who was far more focused on the unlikable, the lack of connection, produced. Tartikoff had said in 1983 that *The Goldbergs* "would not work today. It worked when television was new, television sets expensive, and the owners were disproportionately Jewish." It's not surprising to see how his distaste for exploring explicit Jewish storylines on the network would be connected to his horror at a show whose famed "no hugging, no learning" credo was almost diametrically opposed to the network's monster Thursday night hits like *The Cosby Show* and *Family Ties*.

After seeing the pilot, Tartikoff dismissed it as "too New York Jewish" and gave it the smallest order in television history, four episodes. The way Tartikoff told it, the only reason he was convinced to put it on the air at all was that Rob Reiner told him he was making the biggest mistake of his life. And this was the *self-justifying* version of the story: success has a thousand fathers, and Tartikoff wanted to at least take *some* credit for getting the show on the air. More credit for airing *Seinfeld* goes to NBC's head of late-night programming, Rick Ludwin, who paid for the order out of his own budget, cancelling a Bob Hope special to come up with the money. Ludwin, a non-Jew, didn't have Tartikoff's concerns about the show's Jewishness. But any explicit mention of Jewishness that could be avoided—unlike, for example, Jerry's Jewishness, which had been established via his stand-up routines—was changed and coded.

Thus Elaine, a classic example of the Jewish American princess, now possesses a famed "shiksappeal" and crosses herself before entering an apartment to retrieve a misplaced manuscript; and the Costanzas, the avatars of a certain kind of Jewish ethnic zhlubiness, were—as the noted Jewish comic Jerry Stiller, who played Frank Costanza, put it—"a Jewish family living under the witness protection program under the name Costanza."

Only Kramer seems different, somehow. Kramer began life as "Kessler," but at Tartikoff's insistence that only Jerry, whose persona had been established, remain Jewish, his name was changed to Kramer. But something different happened in the nomenclatural transfer than did with Costanza and Benes: Kramer, rather than being a disguised Jew, actually transmutes into a non-Jew, seen through Jewish eyes. As Michael Richards said, not only was he a "hipster doofus," but, more importantly, "I liked the idea of him being like a fourth element, just coming in from nowhere." In the increasingly cocooned and internal atmosphere created by the three others, Kramer was something different, something other, something goyish. In this respect, he epitomizes the nature of Jewish-gentile relations—and the humor that this engenders—in America: harmless, largely, but incomprehensible, and, as it turns out, incomprehensibly successful. (George: "Kramer goes to a fantasy camp. His whole *life* is a fantasy camp. People should plunk down two thousand dollars to live like him for a week. Do nothing, fall ass-backwards into money, mooch food off your neighbors and have sex without dating. *That's* a fantasy camp.")

Maybe the disguise worked, to some extent, for some people; thus, at least, a partial explication of the Anti-Defamation League's Abe Foxman's comment that "there were no bizarre or eccentric Jews on *Seinfeld*, which is a development for Jews in America"— technically true, arguably, if you take Elaine and George at face value. And the rare occasions that *Seinfeld does* deal with Jewishness explicitly are fairly telling. In one episode, Seinfeld's dentist (played—to perfection—by Bryan Cranston in his pre–*Breaking Bad* days, when he was still known in the business almost entirely as a comic actor, to the extent he was known at all) converts to Judaism and immediately begins telling Jewish jokes. Seinfeld, immediately seized by the suspicion that he has converted solely to be able to tell such jokes with impunity, begins complaining about this, but finds few if any takers. Kramer, in an inspired verbal run by the show's writers (in this episode's case, Peter Mehlman and Jill Franklyn), takes on Seinfeld for his discriminatory tendencies, culminating in calling him an "anti-dentite."

The way *Seinfeld* walked the fine line between anti-Semitism and accusations of self-hatred isn't limited to this episode. (Most famously, I'd suspect, there's the episode where Jerry is caught making out during *Schindler's List*; and a number of episodes float the prospect that Jerry's obsessive cleanliness and orderly behavior are Nazi-like.) Ultimately, though, this blurring of lines is designed to suggest a higher allegiance, as the episode's end reveals. Jerry, frustrated in his attempts to find any sympathy for his position, goes to confession to tell a priest his story. It's actually one of the few times on the show he explicitly identifies himself as Jewish, although it's not particularly a secret. When the priest asks him if the notion of his dentist's conversion for the jokes offends him as a Jew, he replies that it doesn't—it offends him as a comedian. In some sense, this is a capper, a throwaway line, designed to end a scene which has served as the basis for any number of Jewish jokes. But in another sense, it's key to understanding Seinfeld, and *Seinfeld*'s, perspective on these matters—Jerry's other identities come first.

The outsize success of *Seinfeld*—and the undenied, if not undeniable, Jewishness of its lead protagonist, along with its other characters' often Jewish or quasi-Jewish sensibilities—led to an increasing comfort with other depictions of Jewishness on television in the 1990s. In terms of explicit Jewishness, these range along the spectrum from *Mad About You* (where Paul Reiser's Jamie Buchman displayed almost no sign of ethnic stereotype, outsourcing the Jewish hijinks to Mel Brooks's Uncle Phil) to *The Nanny* (arguably, one long riff on Jewish-gentile relations, brilliantly anchored in Fran Drescher's conscious overperformance) with shows like *Dr. Katz: Professional Therapist* and *Will and Grace* somewhere in between.

For the cognoscenti, the harder-core comedy fans, there was the delicate pas de deux of Garry Shandling and Jeffrey Tambor on *The Larry Sanders Show* on HBO, which treaded in ethnic parody of that (at the time) gentilest of television settings, the late-night talk show. Shandling's arias of neurosis and the incorporation of backstage and business manipulations into the show brought the behind-the-scenes dynamic into public view in a groundbreaking way that we now all take for granted. Included in that was putting the industry's "too Jewish" concerns on display: Judd Apatow, who wrote for *Sanders*, once said that "the Larry Sanders writers had debated behind the scenes about whether Larry was Jewish and had concluded that he was a self-hating Jew"; though Sanders "fastidiously" avoids the subject of his possible Jewishness, his sidekick Hank Kingsley (Tambor) is another story, and his flirtation with explicit Jewishness in the episode "My Name is Asher Kingley" encapsulated the series' overarching theme: "If you want to survive in the entertainment business, much less in public life, don't let your kippah—i.e., your Jewishness—show."

For those without HBO, though, or whose parents wouldn't let them watch it, or who simply weren't clued-in enough, the most important moment in the post-*Seinfeld* revolution also came on NBC, just a little later at night, when an impossibly young dorky-looking man-child took his guitar and, in a warbly voice, created a new Jewish anthem.

From his days as a cameo performer who did bit parts on the bizarrely delightful MTV game show *Remote Control*, Adam Sandler graduated to creating an indelible set of characters on *Saturday Night Live* in the early nineties. Sandler's characters, particularly the ones who appeared on "Weekend Update" (looking at you, Operaman) were mostly—as the audience knew—essentially Sandler mugging and speaking in silly voices. But Sandler's limited range as a sketch actor made his "Weekend Update" appearances even more important.

Sandler's introduction to what became an anthem for a certain generation of Jews in the early 1990s—it was performed on December 3, 1994—is, in its own stuttering way, a manifesto against Tartikoff's, and much of the mainstream cultural media's, presentation of Jews. "When I was a kid," he begins, "this time of year always made me feel a little left out because in school there were so many Christmas songs and all us Jewish kids had was the song 'Dreidel dreidel dreidel.' So I wrote a brand new Hanukkah song for all you Jewish kids to sing, and I hope you like it!"

The song's first public appearance was, of course, live; and so Sandler's reactions to the audience's rapturous response are unfeigned. He and Norm MacDonald look genuinely surprised at just how well it went over. Sandler might well have considered it just another trifle—after all, it's got some mildly clever wordplay (particularly focused around the difficulties of finding things to rhyme with "Hanukkah"), but it boiled down to, in the words of the song, "a list of people who are Jewish just like you and me."

It's a bit different from its 1990 predecessor, Tom Lehrer's "Hanukkah in Santa Monica." That song, while similarly outing its author/performer as a Jew who lights his menorah amid the California flora, doesn't portray itself as a manifesto, or give a sense of earnestness; it's touched with the same witty, ironic alienation that pervades so much of Lehrer's work. Sandler, on the other hand, is explicitly trading on the current Jewish condition: comfortable individually, alienated collectively. In addressing that, the song plays into our dynamic of disguise, "outing" some people who seem unlikely to be Jewish (Arthur Fonzarelli, half of Paul Newman); but doing so in a way that's equally heir to two generations of desaturated Jewish content on TV. It propounds the equation, "this is Jewish because I say it's Jewish, and therefore it's funny." There's almost no content whatsoever to "The Hanukkah Song," except for the assertion of Jewishness and, of course, the celebration of that most American of Jewish holidays, Hanukkah. But that was enough.

If Sandler became the poster boy for a new generation of American Jews, and for a new construction of American Jewish identity, a second, more continuous aspect of that identity was embodied in his one significant character on *SNL* not on "Weekend Update": Canteen Boy, the man-child sexual plaything of Alec Baldwin. If a good part of this strand of American Jewish comedy is about a crisis of manhood, about the possibility for a Jewish man to be potent, erotic, and the comic consequences of that potential failure, Sandler puts all that front and center.

He wasn't the first, of course. Groucho Marx, aided and abetted by his quartet of brothers, constantly resists the temptation to settle down with any Margaret Dumont–type: not when comic anarchy is a possibility. Marx's descendants include Dustin Hoffman's character in Mike Nichols's *The Graduate*; Eugene in Neil Simon's *Brighton Beach Memoirs*; Elliott Gould; Richard Benjamin's portrayals of various Philip Roth characters on film; Benny, Shandling, Allen, Seinfeld. ("We are not men," Jerry bemoans to George, sitting across from him at the diner. "No, no, we are not men," George replies, introducing a bizarre scheme where they both work together to be a single boyfriend to a girl, on the assumption that neither of them could really be satisfactory.) But Sandler goes the other way, both because his manic comedy is given to extroversion rather than introversion, and because the dictates of his sort of film comedy suggest that he must also be the romantic lead—and thus a new kind of Jewish humor is born; one of the current age of success.

There would be others at the same time; perhaps most notably Ben Stiller, whose identifiably Jewish characters in movies like *Keeping the Faith* and the *Meet the Parents* movies, would pick up on the theme. (Stiller's rabbi character's Yom Kippur sermon in the 2000 romantic comedy *Keeping the Faith*—"We live in a really complex world in which boundaries and definitions are blurring and bleeding into each other in ways that I think challenge us not just as Jews but as human beings"—could almost be an epigraph for this chapter.) But Sandler opened the floodgates, and, perhaps, provided an absurdist apotheosis in his totally bonkers (I don't think there's another technical term for it) 2008 film *You Don't Mess with the Zohan*, in which Sandler's Mossad agent becomes a New York hairdresser, John Turturro plays a member of the PLO, piranha are stuffed down bikini briefs, and hummus is used as a toothpaste and a flame retardant. A Hebraic *Shampoo*, Sandler comes off as the least and most possible man at the same time. It's not coincidental, I think, that this film of Sandler's was co-written by his old friend Judd Apatow, the man who in the first two decades of the twenty-first century became probably the most important impresario in comedy and who has done more to put forth these images than anyone else.

Apatow himself—the noted writer, director, and producer, responsible, in one way or another, for a spate of highly successful features and shows ranging from *The Ben Stiller Show* to *Freaks and Geeks* to *The 40-Year-Old Virgin* to *Knocked Up* to *Bridesmaids* to *Girls*—doesn't at first glance seem to have much Jewish content in his works, or even much of a Jewish sensibility. Almost all the authors he advises would-be comedy writers to read, for example—

Chandler, Carver, Agee, Dubus, Exley, Fitzgerald—aren't Jewish. But a closer look—starting with comedians he idolized like Seinfeld, Paul Reiser, Robert Klein, and Mel Brooks, and especially the stable of actors he's surrounded himself with, a regular troupe composed largely if not almost entirely of a Jewish comic generation of actors including Seth Rogen, Paul Rudd, Jason Segel, Jonah Hill, and Jason Schwartzman, sometimes referred to as "the Jew-tang Clan"—may suggest otherwise.

In a 2009 interview with the *Jewish Journal* of Los Angeles, Apatow explained this casting choice by saying: "It's just a sensibility that's almost an unspoken, unconscious thing. You can't quite put your finger on why. . . . I'm not a religious person, but I couldn't be more Jewish." Put perhaps slightly less abstractly, it is clear that one of his major comic themes is the question of what it means for an outsider—an ethnic, Jewish outsider—to get the girl, and to become a man in so doing; that is, to be integrated into regular social norms. To fit into the mainstream, whether it be American society or the model of the Hollywood leading man, remaking it in the process. When Seth Rogen, in *Knocked Up*, tells Katherine Heigl that he has a special hairstyle called *Jew*—and she laughs, and sleeps with him, and (spoiler alert) bears his child, and makes him into a better man—this is quite different from Woody Allen's curmudgeonly neurotics. Alvy Singer knew he had a problem, and he knew everyone else knew, too; only he knew his problem better. Here, there's no problem at all—nothing that can't be solved, anyway. Or in the Apatow/Sandler/Rogen project *Funny People* (2009), where Rogen's character's line that "my face is circumcised" is indicative of how Judaism has also become the scrawny, the geeky, the funny-looking, the objective correlative for the "sense of humor is the way to get girls."

This isn't a question that Apatow has tackled alone in recent years, but he's probably the loudest expositor of the theme. Others include Seth Cohen et al. on the teen soap *The O.C.*, whose 2003 popularization of "Chrismukkah" was, in its own way, a "Chanukkah song" for a new generation even more comfortable with interfaith romance, coming as they were more and more frequently from blended families; the Bluths on Mitchell Hurwitz's *Arrested Development*, for whom Jewishness, especially for Jeffrey Tambor's crooked paterfamilias, is a convenient disguise to be donned and doffed; and Andy Samberg and Akiva Schaffer, who along with Jorma Taccone, created the enormously influential Lonely Island digital videos for *Saturday Night Live*.

In songs and videos like 2009's "I'm On a Boat" and 2011's "I Just Had Sex" and "Jack Sparrow," Samberg, Schaffer, and Taccone are boys posturing as men, letting us know that the joke is that they're totally unworthy of getting the girl. On the other hand, get the girl they do, otherwise they couldn't boast about it. But the videos are dedicated to the idea that the whole thing is ridiculous. But *that* said, they're filmed with love and affection for the video conventions of their young adulthood, which is why they work so well. . . . and we're back to some of the earliest kinds of disguise in American Jewish comedy, since the hip-hop wannabeism of "I'm On a Boat" is a kind of Jewish blackface, too. And they're not the only ones doing it: there was the blackface episode of Sarah Silverman's show we mentioned earlier, along with a skit she did on Jimmy Kimmel where she purported to be preparing to take over Dave Chappelle's show after his sudden departure.

True, not all of these neo-schlemiels get the girl. In Sam Lipsyte's novel *The Ask*, Jewishness comes not with success, but failure; the protagonist finds his ethnicity as he slips down the ladder of fortune. And Jonathan Ames has dedicated his recent work, like the essays in *I Love You More Than You Know*, to the prospect of erotic and creative failure in Brooklyn. But more and more do: even if the getting is in ironic quotes, the evidence is there, on screen, in front of us, as the music swells.

Apatow has also, it should be said, become dedicated in recent years to the proposition that the unassimilable man can become a woman, as *Bridesmaids* and *Girls* eloquently (and profanely and hilariously) testify. If *Girls* as a whole is occasionally unfocused and messy, Dunham's performance is a cringe-inducing wonder as well carried off as David's on *Curb Your Enthusiasm*. Will Horvath ever grow up and become the kind of person that Sandler and Rogen and Segel and Stiller become in the last reel? Will she become a mature, unconflicted American? The show's final season, coming to a close just as this book goes to press, suggests significant steps in that direction, with maternity taking the role marriage so often plays in the male-focused movies.

And if many of these last examples rarely, if ever, explicitly mention Jewishness at all—well, is that a sign of the end of an era of Jewish comedy? Or just a new iteration of the cycle of Jewish disguise? Ask Queen Esther; maybe she'd have something to say on the matter.

EPILOGUE

Bringing this history to an end—which is, must be, only a stop rather than an end, since Jewish comedy has continued to be produced as this sentence was typed, proofed, printed, and bound between covers—nonetheless requires some concluding thoughts about the future of Jewish comedy. And, in its own way, the Jewish story: because each of the book's chapters illustrate, in varying manners, how Jewish history and the comedy made in and of it can be seen not as a progression, but a series of constantly repeating conditions. Which makes sense, since any comic observer of human nature comes away with one unavoidable conclusion: that the essential aspects of our condition are inescapable, eternal, and unchanging. And it's that impossibility of change that results in our greatest disappointments, but also, luckily, the wisdom that allows us to laugh at our frailty.

Mrs. Grenville can never escape being Mrs. Greenstein; even Sholem Aleichem's train rider, with his new hat, and Alexander Portnoy, with his fancy career and beautiful gentile girlfriends, can't escape the Jewish joke. And why would they want to? The appeal of Jewish humor is that there's always someone around to get the joke. Interacting with the outside world—pushing back and out—that's hard and dangerous work. Better to endure and joke among ourselves.

But is that true in America today? In America, where the best jokes aren't about Jewish failure, but about Jewish success? That Fred Allen statistic about the over-representation of Jewish comedians in America—there are lots of reasons for that. There's the low social barriers to entry of the institutions of entertainment that would carry comedy to the masses, and there's the particular Jewish institutions and family networks that acted as training and recruiting grounds for upcoming comics. But all of these, in their own way, are based—especially when we compare it to other periods of the Jewish diaspora—on the ease of getting it right, even as comedy depends on somehow, in some way, getting it wrong. Whatever happened inside the church of that classic joke suggests, as much as anything else, another side of the Jewish experience—not the difficulties of communicating with the outside world, but the ease; not the inassimilability of the Jew, but the utter ease in which it takes place, given the right soil.

What that success bears within it, of course, is loss as well as gain: Esther marries Ahasuerus, but what about Mordechai? Speaking to everyone means, in certain ways, not speaking to just someone: not the loss of communication with a fellow Jew, but the loss of that ironic, loose, comic ease that can be an essential content of that communication. Whither Jewish humor in a land of success, where communication with others is far more frictionless? In the 2013 Pew Research Center study "A Portrait of Jewish Americans: Overview," 42 percent of respondents felt that "having a good sense of humor" was part of "being Jewish in America today," 14 percent more than "being part of a Jewish community" and 23 percent more than "observing Jewish law." Many generations of Jews would have thought that this was swapping the cart for the horse; many might have thought of it as, well, as a joke.

What the punch line of that joke is still remains to be determined.

ACKNOWLEDGMENTS

THIS BOOK HAS BEEN A LONG TIME IN THE MAKING: ARGUABLY, since the days when my parents stood me in front of their dinner-table guests and allowed an eight-year-old me to recite the joke about a Dalai Lama named Sheldon. (I'm not saying I understood it; just that I recited it.) Accordingly, it has generated many debts, which I can only briefly—and all too poorly—repay here.

This book has come out of almost two decades of teaching and research at Columbia University, and I am incredibly grateful to my colleagues in the Department of Germanic Languages and at the Institute for Israel and Jewish Studies, as well as those institutions' staffs. Their support, advice, and assistance has been invaluable. My thanks also to the staff of the Columbia University Library, especially the Interlibrary Loan Division. And I could not have done the research for this book without the assistance of Adam Shapiro and, particularly, Joshua Price.

There is a rabbinic dictum to the effect that you learn much from your teachers, and more from your students: this one, unlike some that I cite in the book, is no joke. To the latter, I am indebted to their questions, comments, and responses in lectures, seminars, and assignments. (There have been numerous times, over the years, when I've said, in response to a particular comment, "I'm going to use that in my book!" It always got a laugh. Now they know I wasn't kidding. Thank you.) To the former—particularly Ruth Wisse, whose comic genius, and genius for comedy, knows no bounds—I know that I stand on giants' shoulders. And I can't thank Jason Zinoman and Adam Kirsch enough for reviewing a draft of the manuscript and giving invaluable advice.

My agent, Dan Conaway, is a perfect example of one of the book's themes: despite his comic protestations of ignorance or folly— "Explain it to me again. Like I'm an idiot," I would hear—he is the brightest, most imaginative person in the business. This book would look very different, and not for the better, without his advice and guidance. His only contender for that title is my editor at Norton, Matt Weiland, whose perspicacity and laser-like brilliance when it comes to the printed word has radically improved every page of this book. My deepest thanks to both of them, as well as to Remy Cawley and William Hudson for their editorial assistance, and to Taylor Templeton, for going above and beyond.

It was a particular honor, and a sweet joy, to work with my dad's copy of Nathan Ausubel's *A Treasury of Jewish Folklore*, one of the great Jewish joke collections, in writing this book. My mom and dad created a house full of joy, and laughter, and Jewishness, for me and my brothers growing up: and seeing them laugh and joke with my children, now, is one of my greatest happinesses. Thanks, so much, Mom, and Dad, for everything you've done, for the example you set every day: you are, quite simply, the models I strive to follow in my own life as a parent, and a person. My brothers Noah and Andrew, and my sister-in-law Sara, and Boaz, Jordana, Moses, and Delilah, my in-laws Bob and Sherry Pomerantz, and my other sister-in-law, Rachel: thanks for your support, your love, your hospitality, your senses of humor, your advice, and your incredibly cute requests for me to read to you (not all of these may apply to everyone).

And to my own family. My older son, Eli, who tells me stories of Batman and airports, is a wonder and a delight; my younger, Ezra, who is coloring on everything we let him get his little hands on, is the same, but in reverse. The love I have for them is boundless; my wishes for them, even more so. And for my love, my Miri, I am so thankful for you, for your love, your support, your wisdom, and for the home we have made together. I am—there should be no evil eye, as many of the figures in this book would say along with me—an extraordinarily lucky man.

NOTES

Introduction: A Joke, Two Definitions, Seven Themes,
Four Warnings, and Another Joke

ix **"You want to hear a joke?":** One version of this joke appears in William
Novak and Moshe Waldoks, *The Big Book of Jewish Humor* (New York:
Harper and Row, 1981), 24.

x **a tale of the Preacher of Dubno:** As recounted in Nathan Ausubel, *A
Treasury of Jewish Folklore* (New York: Crown, 1948), 4.

x **approaching 80 percent:** Steve Allen, *Funny People* (New York: Stein
and Day, 1981), 11, 30.

xi **any attempt to define:** See Hershey H. Friedman and Linda Weiser
Friedman, *God Laughed: Sources of Jewish Humor* (New Brunswick,
NJ: Transaction Publishers, 2014), 5.

xii **Johnson's . . . Swift's:** Johnson quote from J. W. Whedbee, *The Bible
and the Comic Vision* (Cambridge, UK: Cambridge University Press,
1998), 5; Swift quote from *The Works of Jonathan Swift* (London: Henry
Washbourne, 1841), I:615.

xii **defines their Jewishness:** See, for example, Shaye Cohen, *The Beginnings
of Jewishness: Boundaries, Varieties, Uncertainties* (Berkeley: University
of California Press, 1999).

xii **Charlie Chaplin:** On Chaplin's "Jewishness," see J. Hoberman and Jeffrey Shandler, *Entertaining America: Jews, Movies, and Broadcasting*
(Princeton, NJ: Princeton University Press, 2003), 34–39, and Groucho
Marx's testimony in his letter of Sep. 5, 1940, reporting a conversation
with the comedian: "He told me, among other things, that he's not Jewish

but wishes he were." Groucho Marx, *The Groucho Letters* (New York: Simon and Schuster, 1967), 24.

xii **second trickier condition:** Elliott Oring has a similar, if slightly more capacious, definition in "The People of the Joke," *Western Folklore* 42 (1983): 261–271, 262, although, like many others, characterizes "Jewish humor" as a particularly modern phenomenon.

xiii **@crazyjewishmom's Instagram account:** https://instagram.com/crazy jewishmom/; on the account's ambiguously comic nature, see R. Einstein, *Stop Lol-ing at My Crazy Jewish Mom*, http://forward.com/opinion/214827/stop-lol-ing-at-my-crazy-jewish-mom/.

xvi **are absolutely certain:** On these uncertainties, see, for example, David Marcus, *From Balaam to Jonah: Anti-Prophetic Satire in the Hebrew Bible* (Atlanta, GA: Scholars Press, 1995), 4–5.

1. What's So Funny About Anti-Semitism?

1 **Whitehead . . . Eliot:** Whitehead quote: Lucien Price, *Dialogues of Alfred North Whitehead* (Boston: Little, Brown, 1954), 59. Eliot quote: from Yehuda T. Radday, "On Missing the Humour in the Bible: An Introduction," in Radday and Athalya Brenner, *On Humour and the Comic in the Hebrew Bible* (Sheffield, UK: Sheffield Academic Press, 1990), 21–38, 21. Carlyle's opinion can be found in James Anthony Froude, *Thomas Carlyle: A History of His Life in London*, 1834–1881 (New York: Scribner's, 1904), II:384.

2 **Prichard:** James Cowles Prichard, *Researches Into The Physical History of Man* (London: John and Arthur Arch, 1813), 186.

2 **"the lachrymose approach":** Salo Baron, "Ghetto and Emancipation: Shall We Revise the Traditional View?" *The Menorah Journal* 14 (1928): 515–526, 526.

2 **"The facetious element":** Hermann Adler, "Jewish Wit and Humour," *The Nineteenth Century* 33 (1893): 457–469, 457–458.

3 **"a people":** Price, 59.

4 **story of Esther takes place:** Its dating is famously nebulous; see, for discussion, Erich Gruen, *Diaspora: Jews Amidst Greeks and Romans* (Cambridge, MA: Harvard University Press, 2002), 145n34, who suggests a date of composition no earlier than the late fifth century, and accepts the possibility of a late Persian or Hellenistic date.

5 **suspiciously nearby:** It almost makes you wonder whether Haman himself was behind that assassination attempt, though there's no evidence of this in the text.

6 **The prophet Isaiah:** See Isaiah 10:15 and discussion in Ze'ev Weisman, *Political Satire in the Bible* (Atlanta, GA: Scholars Press, 1998), 84–93.

6 **Similar portraits:** Compare Michael J. Chan, "Ira Regis: Comedic Inflections of Royal Rage in Jewish Court Tales," *JQR* 103:1 (Winter 2013), 1–25, 4, 13.

6 **"Some say the Emperor":** BT Sanhedrin 39a; for other stories, such as the one featuring R. Joshua b. Hanania and Caesar's daughter, see BT Nedarim 50b and BT Taanit 7a. See Meyer Heller, "Humor in the Talmud" (Rabbinical thesis, 1950), 14–15.

7 **But the impunity:** For a comparative speculative example in the early Islamic world—one scholar's imagined spectacle of Jews heckling Muhammad through publicly satirizing his teaching—see Reuven Firestone, "The Failure of a Jewish Program of Public Satire in the Squares of Medina," *Judaism* 46:4 (1997), 439–452.

8 **hardly an accurate reflection:** See, for example, Jonathan Elukin, *Living Together, Living Apart: Rethinking Jewish-Christian Relations in the Middle Ages* (Princeton, NJ: Princeton University Press, 2013).

8 **one of the minor judges:** Judges 9:7–20; see discussion in Weisman, 26–36.

9 **particular popularity:** As they'd been in earlier times: the Talmud notes that Rabbi Meir had no less than three hundred fox parables, of which three remain. See Heller, 105–106.

9 **"A sick lion":** Adapted from the midrash; this version from Ausubel, *Folklore*, 626.

10 **Versions of this comedy:** See, for example, Robert Gnuse, "From Prison to Prestige," *Catholic Biblical Quarterly* 72 (2010): 31–45.

10 **another animal joke:** Adapted from version in Rufus Learsi, *Filled With Laughter* (New York: Thomas Yosseloff, 1961), 254.

11 **neither clothed nor naked:** See Ausubel, *Folklore*, 95–103.

11 **"If they're laughing":** Quoted in James Robert Parish, *It's Good to Be the King: The Seriously Funny Life of Mel Brooks* (Hoboken, NJ: John Wiley & Sons, 2007), 25.

12 **being urinated on:** And, in some versions, ejaculated on. See Michael Meerson and Peter Schäfer, *Toledot Yeshu: The Life Story of Jesus* (Tübingen: Mohr Siebeck, 2014), I:195, and Sarit Kattan Gribetz, "Hanged and Crucified: The Book of Esther and Toledot Yeshu," in Peter Schäfer, Michael Meerson, Yaacov Deutsch, eds., *Toledot Yeshu Reconsidered* (Tübingen: Mohr Siebeck, 2011), 159–180, 178.

12 **might have been read communally:** The communal reading, similar to the reading of the book of Esther, may have been part of a medieval

tendency to thematically conflate Haman and Jesus; see Kattan and Elliot Horowitz, *Reckless Rites: Purim and the Legacy of Jewish Violence* (Princeton, NJ: Princeton University Press, 2008).

12 **Profiat (or Profayt) Duran:** Maud Kozodoy, "The Hebrew Bible as Weapon of Faith in Late Medieval Iberia: Irony, Satire, and Scriptural Allusion in Profiat Duran's Al Tehi Keavotekha," *JSQ* 18 (2011): 185–201, 185–186, 193; Elazar Gutwirth, "From Jewish to 'Converso' Humor in Fifteenth-Century Spain," *Bulletin of Hispanic Studies* 67:3 (1990), 223–233, 228–229.

13 **"Do not be":** Cited in Kozodoy, 187.

13 **"I worship thee":** Quoted in Gutwirth, 230. Notably, in both cases, the satirical jabs were from fellow converts. A much later joke expresses that apparently paradoxical dynamic well. Three Jewish converts to Christianity are sitting around explaining their rationales for doing so. The first said he did it to get a better position in society. The second converted for romantic reasons: he was in love with a Catholic, and she insisted. The third said, "I converted for theological reasons; I believe that Jesus Christ was sent to this earth, a god made flesh, to save all mankind from original sin." The other two looked at him. "What do you take us for, a bunch of goyim?" Adapted from Joseph Telushkin, *Jewish Humor: What the Best Jewish Jokes Say About the Jews* (New York: William Morrow, 1992), 137.

13 **Jewish pope:** On this subject, see Joseph Sherman, *The Jewish Pope: Myth, Diaspora, and Yiddish Literature* (Oxford, UK: Legenda, 2003).

14 **"Once there was a wicked bishop":** A shorter version of this joke is recorded in Ed Cray, "The Rabbi Trickster," *The Journal of American Folklore* 77 (1964): 331–345, 342–343; a slightly different, lengthy one, in Simon R. Pollack, *Jewish Wit For All Occasions* (New York: A&W Visual Library, 1979), 176–179.

16 **In the *Decameron*:** Giovanni Boccaccio, *The Decameron* (New York: Penguin Books, 1972), 37–41, quote 40.

17 **"It is extremely difficult":** Quoted in Chaim Bermant, *What's the Joke?: A Study of Jewish Humour Through the Ages* (London: Weidenfeld and Nicolson, 1986), 47. Heine would also say toward the end of his life that he had not returned to Judaism, because he had "never left it." See Heinrich Heine, *Jewish Stories and Hebrew Melodies* (New York: Markus Wiener Publishing, 1987), 12.

18 **"a mystery that only":** Heine, *Hebrew Melodies*, 134.

18 "no longer": Heine, *Hebrew Melodies*, 93. See also S. S. Prawer, *Heine's Jewish Comedy* (Oxford, UK: Clarendon Press, 1983), 28.

18 in marked contrast: On this dynamic, see Ruth Wisse, *No Joke: Making Jewish Humor* (Princeton, NJ: Princeton University Press, 2013), 14, 16, 29ff.

18 "when people talk": Lore and Maurice Cowan, *The Wit of the Jews* (Nashville, TN: Aurora Publishers, 1970), 41.

19 "That all men are beggars": Israel Zangwill, *The King of Schnorrers: Grotesques and Fantasies* (New York: Macmillan and Co., 1909), 6. Not that Zangwill was leaving the Jews out of his comic sights: he twitted the Anglo-Jewish notables for their mistaken belief that there was much difference between their royal airs and those of the king of the schnorrers. Compare Edna Nahshon, *From the Ghetto to the Melting Pot: Israel Zangwill's Jewish Plays* (Detroit, MI: Wayne State University Press, 2006), 393 and Wisse, *No Joke*, 107.

19 "if there were no Jews": Cowan, 74.

19 a post–Great War joke: Henry D. Spalding, ed., *Encyclopedia of Jewish Humor: From Biblical Times to the Modern Age* (New York: Jonathan David, 1969), 183.

21 "He creeps and crawls": Aaron Halle Wolfssohn, *Silliness and Sanctimony*, in Joel Berkowitz and Jeremy Dauber, *Landmark Yiddish Plays* (Albany, NY: SUNY Press, 2006), 81–111, 87.

22 "Once a bear escaped": Adapted from a version in Howe, "Nature," 21–22.

23 *The Travels of Benjamin III*: The roman numeral alludes to two previous real-life Jewish explorers named Benjamin, the medieval Benjamin of Tudela and a more recent mid-nineteenth-century figure, Israel Joseph Benjamin. Dating the novel is tricky: the textual history and chronology of most of Abramovitch's novels is complex, because they often went through several revisions, revisions which reflected a rapidly changing political perspective. But the point, generally speaking, holds.

24 "We hereby declare": S. Y. Abramovitch, *Tales of Mendele the Book Peddler* (New York: Schocken, 1996), 389.

24 "Let [the mare] become more presentable": S. Y. Abramovitch, "The Mare," in Joachim Neugroschel, *Great Tales of Jewish Fantasy and the Occult* (Woodstock, NY: Overlook Press, 1987), 545–663, 610–611.

25 " 'It's all very clear' ": I. L. Peretz, "The Shabbes Goy," (ca. 1894), in Ruth Wisse, ed., *The I. L. Peretz Reader* (New York: Schocken, 1990), 131–138.

25   "You're laughing?": "Shabbes Goy," 138.

25   An iconic joke: On this joke and its moral consequences, see Paul Lewis, "Joke and Anti-Joke: Three Jews and a Blindfold," *Journal of Popular Culture* 21:1 (1987), 63ff.

25   the Jewish men: The historicity of these episodes has been debated by critics; see the special issue dedicated to Kishinev in *Prooftexts* 25 (2005): 1–2.

26   "Haim is walking": Cited in Wisse, *No Joke*, 163. See also David Harris and Izrail Rabinovich, *The Jokes of Oppression: The Humor of Soviet Jews* (Northvale, NJ: Jason Aronson, 1988).

27   "A Jew was stopped": Steve Lipman, *Laughter in Hell: The Use of Humor During the Holocaust* (Northvale, NJ: Jason Aronson, 1991), 206.

27   "Two Jews are sitting": A slightly different version in *Laughter in Hell*, 197.

28   "The writer L. F.": Feuchtwanger, "Balance Sheet of My Life," in Nathan Ausubel, ed., *A Treasury of Jewish Humor* (Garden City, NY: Doubleday, 1956), 51–54, quotes 52–53.

28   in a 1935 sketch: John Efron, "From Lodz to Tel Aviv: The Yiddish Political Humor of Shimen Dzigan and Yisroel Schumacher," *JQR* 102:1 (2012), 50–79, 61.

29   "My great crime": Franz Werfel, *Jacobowsky and the Colonel* (New York: Viking Press, 1944), 15. The play was turned into a Danny Kaye movie, *Me and the Colonel* (1958), which has a less bleak tone than its theatrical antecedent.

29   "It was a good *khokhme*": Romain Gary, *The Dance of Genghis Cohn* (New York: World Publishing Company, 1968), 59, 142 (italics author's).

29   humor *did* flourish: For an extensive discussion of this position, see Chaya Ostrower, *It Kept Us Alive: Humor in the Holocaust* (Jerusalem: Yad Vashem, 2014), *passim*, esp. 57–61; 146–148; 235–236; songs quoted from 184, 186, 305–306. See also Roy Kift, "Comedy in the Holocaust: The Theresienstadt Cabaret," *New Theatre Quarterly* 48 (1996): 299–308, for this and other songs.

31   "songs, poems, jokes": Viktor Frankl, *Man's Search for Meaning* (New York: Washington Square Press, 1984), 65.

31   "God grant": See Ruth Wisse, *No Joke*, 154, where this is cited as ghetto folklore in the Ringelblum archives.

31   Frankl, for example: *Laughter in Hell*, 14–15, 137.

31   A children's play: *Laughter in Hell*, 148.

31   "A man is saved": Joke in Spalding, 197–198.

32   "A Nazi sees a Jew": Arthur Asa Berger, *The Genius of the Jewish Joke* (New Brunswick, NJ: Transaction Publishers, 2006), 78.

32 "joke courts": Jim Holt, *Stop Me If You've Heard This* (New York: Norton, 2008), 102; Nat Schmulowitz, *The Nazi Joke Courts* (San Francisco: Nat Schmulowitz, 1943), 7; Lynn Rapaport, "Laughter and Heartache: The Functions of Humor in Holocaust Tragedy," in Jonathan Petropolous and John K. Roth, eds., *Gray Zones: Ambiguity and Compromise in the Holocaust and Its Aftermath* (New York: Berghahn Books, 2005), 252–269, 254.

32 Dzigan was called: Efron, 63.

32 An inmate: *Laughter in Hell*, 18, 144, 146, 208.

32 Radu Mihaileanu: See David A. Brenner, "Laughter Amid Catastrophe: *Train of Life* and Tragicomic Holocaust Cinema," in David Bathrick, Brad Prager, and Michael D. Richardson, eds., *Visualizing the Holocaust* (Rochester, NY: Camden House, 2008), 261–276, 267.

32 "Cheer up": *Laughter in Hell*, 151. Though even to that, there was, apparently, a response: "Yes, but while they make toilet soap from my fat, you'll be a bar of cheap laundry soap!" Ostrower, 91.

32 "Jewish humor died": Irving Kristol, "Is Jewish Humor Dead?: The Rise and Fall of the Jewish Joke," *Commentary* 12 (1951): 431–436, 431, 433.

33 "A Jew survived": Telushkin, *Jewish Humor*, 108. A more contemporary telling has a slightly different punch line: "Haven't you got another globe?" Theodor Reik, *Jewish Wit* (New York: Gamut Press, 1962), 48; on this joke and its history (as well as its adoption to refer to Jewish rootlessness more generally and less stingingly), see Richard Raskin, "Far From Where?: On the History and Meanings of a Classic Jewish Refugee Joke," *American Jewish History* 85:2 (1997), 143–150.

34 "all our family": Sholem Aleichem, "Otherwise, There's Nothing New," in *Some Laughter, Some Tears* (New York: Putnam, 1968), 237–242; this quote from translation in Maurice Schwartz, *The World of Sholom Aleichem* (New York: Schocken, 1943), 189. See also Kristol, 432–433.

34 "During the Great Depression": A version of this joke told in Avner Ziv, "Psycho-Social Aspects of Jewish Humor in Israel and the Diaspora," in Ziv, ed., *Jewish Humor* (Tel Aviv: Papyrus, 1986), 47–71, 63.

36 An infamous mid-century postcard: See Bernard Saper, "Since When is Jewish Humor Not Anti-Semitic?" in Avner Ziv and Anat Zajdman, eds., *Semites and Stereotypes* (Westport, CT: Greenwood Press, 1993, 71–86, 72.

36 "that you should never be mean": Quoted in Rachel Gordan, "When 'Gentleman's Agreement' Made Jewish Oscars History," *Forward*, Feb. 21, 2013, http://forward.com/culture/171133/when-gentlemans-agreement-made-jewish-oscars-histo/.

36   **rise and fall:** We don't have much time to talk about the rise and fall of different kinds of Jewish jokes, except by implication, but similarly historicized processes take place: jokes about keeping kosher, for example, receded in popularity as the taboo against eating *treyf* grew less and less powerful among the majority of American Jews. Christie Davies, *Ethnic Humor Around the World: A Comparative Analysis* (Bloomington: Indiana University Press, 1990), 282.

37   **the use of Yiddish:** See Stanley Brandes, "Jewish-American Dialect Jokes and Jewish-American Identity," *Jewish Social Studies* 45:3–4 (1983), 233–240, 236, on considering these as dialect jokes.

37   **even in people:** With respect to Yiddish, this is now technically known in the field of Jewish studies as "postvernacularity." See Jeffrey Shandler, *Adventures in Yiddishland* (Berkeley: University of California Press, 2006).

37   **Belle Barth tells a joke:** Cited in Giovanna P. Del Negro, "The Bad Girls of Jewish Comedy: Gender, Class, Assimilation, and Whiteness in Postwar America," in Leonard J. Greenspoon, ed., *Jews and Humor* (West Lafayette, IN: Purdue University Press, 2011), 140.

38   **"Now I neologize":** John Cohen, ed. *The Essential Lenny Bruce* (New York: Ballantine Books, 1967), 41–42.

38   **"Now, a Jew":** *Essential Lenny Bruce,* 40–41.

38   **shock value:** Wisse makes a similar point about *Portnoy's Complaint,* published a decade later; see *No Joke,* 137. For her comments on Bruce (primarily concerning the Jewish/goyish routine), see 138–139.

39   **Bruce's flaying:** *Essential Lenny Bruce,* 125–131.

39   **"Palestine has the size":** Cowan, 51.

39   **Ephraim Kishon:** Born in Hungary, Kishon arrived in Israel in 1949 in his mid-twenties. He is also well known for having created the character of Sallah Shabati, a Moroccan immigrant who felt victimized by the Ashkenazic majority. See Bermant, 156–159.

39   **in newspaper columns:** See, for example, "Caterwauling in A Major" and "I Placed Ushers on Your Walls, Jerusalem" (in which Kishon can't get into his own lecture—on "Is There a Genuine Israeli Humor," no less), in *Noah's Ark: Tourist Class* (New York: Athenaeum, 1962), 7–14, 86–90.

40   **"on the shores":** Kishon, *Noah's Ark,* 143–149, quotes, 145, 149.

40   **during the first Gulf War:** See Ofra Nevo-Eshkol and Jacob Levine, "Jewish Humor Strikes Again: The Outburst of Humor in Israel During the Gulf War," *Western Folklore* 53:2 (1994), 125–145. One joke that illustrates these continuities (132): "What's the difference between

Saddam and the wicked Haman? First, Haman was hanged and then we wore masks. With Saddam, first we wear masks."

40 **"We'll meet on the memorial plaque"**: See Yael Zerubavel, *Recovered Roots: Collective Memory and the Making of Israeli National Tradition* (Chicago: University of Chicago, 1995), 173–174.

40 **"Sara in Jerusalem"**: Cited in Wisse, *No Joke*, 218.

41 *The Finkler Question*: Howard Jacobson, *The Finkler Question* (New York: Bloomsbury USA, 2010).

42 **far more explicit Jewish content**: Of course, David has his own opinions on some of these subjects. Asked about " '*Curb*''s obvious Jewishness," he replied, grinning, "Jews think that all the time . . . They think no one else will get it, that it's a secret show just for them." Alexandra Schwartz, "Festival Dispatch: Life Lessons From Larry David," *The New Yorker*, Oct. 13, 2014.

42 **differences between a Jew and a Christian**: This apparently wasn't planned from the start: all accounts agree that David and his crew were originally casting for a Jewish or Jewish-looking actress to play David's wife, analogous to his Jewish (then-) wife, but that the comedic chemistry between David and the self-evidently gentile Cheryl Hines was too good to pass up. In fact, Hines's hair was dyed dark in the HBO mockumentary that retroactively serves as a quasi-pilot for the show so she would look more Jewish; it lightened every season. Hines has said, "We were in the middle of shooting our first episode when Larry said, 'I don't think anybody's going to believe you're Jewish.' And I said 'I don't think so either.' And he said, 'Well, I guess you don't have to be.' " Josh Levine, *Pretty, Pretty, Pretty Good: Larry David and the Making of Seinfeld and Curb Your Enthusiasm* (Toronto: ECW, 2010), 52–61; Deirdre Dolan, *Curb Your Enthusiasm: The Book* (New York: Gotham Books, 2006), 31; quote Dolan, 82.

42 **expelled from Hebrew school**: Dolan, 11–12.

43 **Larry eats some of the cookies**: Season 3, Episode 9: "Mary, Joseph, and Larry."

43 **urinates on a picture**: Season 7, Episode 7: "The Bare Midriff."

43 **chased down the hall**: This is also the episode, it should be noted, where David hangs a mezuzah with a nail from the 2004 Mel Gibson movie *The Passion of the Christ*, notoriously controversial for its anti-Semitic tropes. "The Christ Nail," Season 5, Episode 3. See Levine, 101.

43 **attacked by gentiles**: Season 2, Episode 3, "Trick or Treat." They're not explicitly identified as such, but the context presumes it.

43 **Larry Charles:** Charles, often considered David's right-hand man on *Seinfeld*, was the writer responsible for some of its darker episodes, like "The Baby Shower," "The Library," and "The Fix-Up." See Levine, 141. For more on this, compare Roberta Rosenberg Farmer, "Larry David's 'Dark Talmud': Or, Kafka in Prime Time," *Studies in American Jewish Literature* 32:2 (2013), 167–185, 170–171. Charles would go on to become a frequent collaborator with Sacha Baron Cohen.

44 **series finale:** The episode was not well-received—the *Houston Chronicle* called it "one of the least loved conclusions in the history of television." See Levine, 7–9, quote 9.

44 **end up in jail:** For more on the finale, see Farber, "Talmud," 172–177.

45 **from Woody Allen:** David had played small parts in two Woody Allen movies, *Radio Days* and *Another Woman*, before *Seinfeld* premiered; after *Curb* had made him exponentially more famous, he took the lead Allenesque role in another, *Whatever Works*.

45 ***Annie Hall*:** Co-written with Marshall Brickman, who would go on to co-write Jersey Boys and (less well known, but far more importantly) suggest the Swedish Chef to Jim Henson during some work he did on a 1975 pilot called *The Muppet Show: Sex and Violence*. (He also helped create Statler and Waldorf.) Mike Sacks, *And Here's the Kicker: Conversations with 21 Top Humor Writers on Their Craft* (Cincinnati, OH: Writer's Digest, 2009), 149, 160.

45 **neurotic obsessiveness:** Think, for a moment, of the Jew viciously angry about failing to get a job as a radio announcer. "A-a-a-a-nti-s-s-s-emites!" he complains bitterly to his friend. Brandes, 237.

45 **Granny Hall:** This was based on an incident from Allen's life, when he met Diane Keaton's family for the first time: "It was the quintessential kind of Gentile family. I was very conscious of my Jewishness when I met them originally, over Christmas dinner. . . . And there is a Granny Hall—that was Keaton's grandmother. She always had a dim view of Jews, as moneylenders and people who usurp all the good jobs and start wars and things." Cited in Myles Palmer, *Woody Allen: An Illustrated Biography* (New York: Proteus, 1980), 92.

45 **"The Schmeed Memoirs":** Woody Allen, "The Schmeed Memoirs," in *The Insanity Defense: The Complete Prose* (New York: Random House, 2007), 17–23.

45 **David invited two survivors:** Season 4, Episode 9.

46 **deprived of snacks:** Other cringe/laugh inducing Holocaust references on *Curb* start with the very first episode, where Larry refers to his wife as "Hitler" in a conversation with his agent, not knowing others were

listening in on the speakerphone, and include Larry's inability to fire a chef at his restaurant because he is a survivor. (What David believes to be an indicative "tattoo" is revealed at episode's end to be a phone number penned on to the chef's skin.) David's interest in the subject had long predated *Curb*, or even *Seinfeld*'s episodes about Jerry making out during *Schindler's List* or getting caught up accidentally in a neo-Nazi rally. In his early stand-up days, David told one joke that he'd have been friends with a Nazi if the latter had complimented his hair, and another about admiring Hitler for not "taking any shit from magicians." Levine, 17.

46 **For David:** In *Curb*, perhaps the most intriguingly relevant example of this was David's instantly notorious treatment of the most vexed locus of contemporary anti-Semitism—the Arab world—framed through the most complex and sensitive topic of the modern Jewish era—the Israel-Palestine question. In the *Curb* episode "Palestinian Chicken," Larry and his agent begin to dine regularly at a restaurant rife with anti-Israel (and anti-Semitic) sentiment, and Larry begins seeing a beautiful Palestinian woman whose erotic attraction to him is based on her ability to call him anti-Semitic names and his willingness to accept them and even participate (after all, on the show at least, Larry's prime sexual appeal is to those expressing either their own self-hatred or allowing him to express his own). What we get, despite some critics' arguments about David's "statement" on the geopolitical question, is David returning to behaving like George Costanza: for food, and for sex, he's willing to accept the most degrading circumstances to this aspect of his identity. Or, as David put it in an interview with *The New Yorker*'s David Remnick, "It occurred to me one day, Would I have sex with a Palestinian? . . . I thought, Sure. And what if, when we were having sex, she shouted all these anti-Semitic things? It wouldn't bother me in the least!" (According to Remnick, the law professor Alan Dershowitz sent the episode to Benjamin Netanyahu with the hope he'd watch it with Mahmoud Abbas.) Schwartz, "Festival Dispatch."

47 **"It was cute":** Sarah Silverman, *Sarah Silverman: Jesus Is Magic* (2005, dir. Liam Lynch).

49 **in 2006:** Cited in Sander L. Gilman, "Jewish Humour and the Terms by Which Jews and Muslims Join Western Civilization," *Leo Baeck Institute Year Book* 57 (2012): 53–65, 65.

2. Not-So-Nice Jewish Doctors

51 **plenty of Yiddish fiction:** See Dan Miron, "The Literary Image of the Shtetl," *Jewish Social Studies* 1:3 (1995), 1–43; Jeffrey Shandler, *Shtetl: A*

Vernacular Intellectual History (New Brunswick, NJ: Rutgers University Press, 2014).

51 **satire:** For a more conventional definition of satire—topical (related to the here and now), realistic (if exaggerated or distorted), shocking, informal (linguistically speaking, colloquial), funny, hoping to evoke in its readers a combination of amusement and contempt—see Gilbert Highet, *The Anatomy of Satire* (Princeton, NJ: Princeton University Press, 1962), esp. 5, 16–18, 21, 158, 190.

52 **George S. Kaufman:** On Kaufman, see Louis Harap, *Dramatic Encounters: The Jewish Presence in Twentieth-Century American Drama, Poetry, Humor and the Black-Jewish Literary Relationship* (New York: Greenwood Press, 1987), 89.

52 **"lampoons and satires":** Joseph Addison, *Maxims, Observations, and Reflections: Moral, Political, and Divine* (London: E. Curil, 1719), 74.

52 **"The true end of satire":** John Dryden, "Preface: To the Reader," *Absalom and Achitophel* (London: J.T., 1681).

53 **"They lie":** Amos 5:4–6.

53 **the prophet Hosea:** Hosea 13:4. See Michael B. Dick, "Prophetic Parodies of Making the Cult Image," in Dick, ed., *Born in Heaven, Made on Earth: The Making of the Cult Image in the Ancient Near East* (Winona Lake, IN: Eisenbrauns, 1999), 1–53, esp. 11, 30–34.

53 **Northrop Frye:** See Northrop Frye, *The Anatomy of Criticism* (Princeton NJ: Princeton University Press, 1957), 223–242; as well as discussion in Thomas Jemielity, *Satire and the Hebrew Prophets* (Louisville, KY: Westminster/John Knox Press, 1992), 21–22, 87.

53 **"What has the carved":** Hab. 3:18–19.

54 **"For the objects":** Jer. 10:3–5, with accepted critical emendation. For discussion, see Dick, 17–20. Compare a similar account in Hosea 13:2.

54 **"consults its stick":** Hosea 4:12; see Jemielity, 88. Compare also Isa. 40:18–20 and 41:6–7; Isa. 44:9–22.

54 **comic set piece:** 1 Kgs 18:27. Note the scatological element as well.

54 **"all joking is prohibited":** BT Meg. 25b; cited in Chan, 20.

54 **reinterpreted by the rabbis:** See Genesis Rabbah 74:4. And there's yet another attempt to add a scatological element to the mockery: Rachel menstruates on top of them.

55 **similar expansions:** Daniel's mockery of those who believe Bel to be a living god in Bel 6–7, and the Letter of Jeremiah, for example. See discussion in Toni Craven, "Is that Fearfully Funny?: Some Instances from the Apocryphal/Deuterocanonical Books," in Athalya Brenner, ed.,

Are We Amused?: Humor About Women in the Biblical Worlds (London: T&T Clark International, 2003), 65–78, 74 and Chan, 20.

55 **satiric sketch:** Genesis Rabbah 38:19.

55 **Elisha:** See 2 Kings 2:23–24.

55 **Isaiah went naked:** See Isaiah 20:2–4; Jeremiah 27:2–28: 17; Ezekiel 3:22–5: 17; as well as discussion in Jemiely, 137.

56 **"I have become":** Jeremiah 20:7–8.

56 **a king so uninterested:** On Ahasuerus' competence or lack of same, compare Barry Dov Walfish, *Esther in Medieval Garb* (Albany, NY: SUNY Press, 1993), 183–184.

56 **Jewish life, and fate in the diaspora:** Compare Kathleen M. O'Connor, "Humour, Turnabouts, and Survival in the Book of Esther," in *Are We Amused?*, 52–64, 56–62. On Esther as a diasporic work, see Gruen, *passim*; W. Lee Humphreys, "Life-style for Diaspora: A Study of the Tales of Esther and Daniel," *JBL* 92:2 (1973), 211–223; Alexander Green, "Power, Deception, and Comedy: The Politics of Exile in the Book of Esther," *Jewish Political Studies Review* 23:1–2 (2011), 61–78; and especially Elsie Stern, "Esther and the Politics of Diaspora" *JQR* 100:1 (2010) 25–53.

57 **nothing much changes anyway:** This isn't the only satire of gentile bureaucracy in the Bible: the book of Daniel also, in its enumerations of officials and instruments of the pagan governments in the third chapter, satirizes "the mechanistic and thoughtless behavior of the pagan worshippers, of the pagan bureaucracy in particular." See H. Avalos, "The Comedic Function of the Enumerations of Officials and Instruments in Daniel 3," *Catholic Biblical Quarterly* 53: 4 (1991), 580–588, 582 and David Valeta, "The Satirical Nature of the Book of Daniel," in Christopher Rowland and John Barton, eds., *Apocalyptic in History and Tradition* (Sheffield, UK: Sheffield Academic Press, 2002), 81–93, 87–91.

58 **too abstruse to go into:** See, however, Christine E. Hayes, "Displaced Self-Perceptions: The Deployment of Minim and Romans in B. Sanhedrin 90b–91a," in Hayim Lapin, ed. *Religious and Ethnic Communities in Later Roman Palestine* (College Park: University Press of Maryland, 1998), 249–289, on this last point.

59 **"Though he seems pious":** Translation from J. Chotzner, *Hebrew Humour* (London: Luzac and Co, 1905), 109. On Kalonymus and his most important satirical work, *Even Bochan*, written between 1318 and 1323, "as a reprimanding moralistic message of 'repentance of the past, morals for the present and warning for the future'," see Moshe

Feinsod, "A Distant Reflection: The Physician in the Eye of the Jewish Medieval Satirist Kalonymus Ben Kalonymus (1287–1337?)," *Korot* 22 (2013–2014): 239–253, quote 243.

59 **Meshullam da Piera:** James H. Lehmann, "Polemic and Satire in the Poetry of the Maimonidean Controversy," *Prooftexts* 1:2 (1981), 133–151.

60 **Yiddish-language broadsides:** Marion Aptroot, *Storm in the Community: Yiddish Polemical Pamphlets of Amsterdam Jewry, 1797–1798* (Cincinnati, OH: Hebrew Union College Press, 2002).

60 **"semi-neutral" spaces:** On semi-neutral society, see Jacob Katz, *Out of the Ghetto: The Social Background of Jewish Emancipation* (Cambridge, MA: Harvard University Press, 1973), 43–56. For more on this, especially as it applies to wit, see Moses Mendelssohn's comments on humor and "a higher form of wit" in his comments in the 1761 "On the Sublime and Naïve," and the discussion in Gilman "Muslim," 58.

60 **a less delineated sphere:** I'm not speaking about the special case of conversion: for our current purposes we'll consider those Jews as if they've fully left the Jewish community behind.

61 **"the way of education":** Menachem Mendel Lapin, *Sefer Cheshbon Hanefesh* (Lemberg: 1808), 50; cited in Yahil Saban, " 'Folded White Napkins': The Etiquette Discourse in Haskalah Literature," unpublished paper, 2015, p. 23.

62 **"if from my words":** On Wolfssohn, see Jeremy Dauber, *Antonio's Devils: Writers of the Jewish Enlightenment and the Birth of Modern Hebrew and Yiddish Literature* (Stanford CA: Stanford University Press, 2004), and Dauber, "The City, Sacred and Profane: Between Hebrew and Yiddish in the Fiction of the Early Jewish Enlightenment," *JSQ* 12:1 (2005), 43–60, quote from 47; on Euchel, see Marion Aptroot and Roland Gruschka, "The Manuscript Versions of Isaac Euchel's 'Reb Henokh oder vos tut me damit,'" *Zutot* 1 (2001): 165–179.

63 **Swift's contention:** See discussion in Simon Critchley, *On Humour* (London: Routledge, 2002), 14–15.

63 **" 'Perish the thought!' ":** Joseph Perl, *Joseph Perl's Revealer of Secrets: The First Hebrew Novel*, trans. Dov Taylor (Boulder CO: Westview, 1997), 44.

65 **"What's the difference":** Telushkin, *Jewish Humor*, 100.

65 **ideological discomfort:** Often due to issues related to Enlightenment linguistic theory, which don't need to be discussed here; for more discussion, see *Antonio's Devils*.

66 **"A rabbi is trying to get home":** Adapted from Ausubel, *Folklore*, 221.

66 "Two groups of disciples": Adapted from Ausubel, *Folklore*, 376.

68 "Our holy Talmud says": Introduction to *Di genarte velt*, reprinted from M. Viner, ed., *Di Genarte velt* (Moscow: Melukhe-farlag, 1940), 51–52. Translation from Jeremy Dauber, "Between Two Worlds: Antitheatricality and the Beginnings of Modern Yiddish Theatre," in Joel Berkowitz and Barbara Henry, eds., *Inventing the Modern Yiddish Stage* (Detroit, MI: Wayne State University Press, 2012), 27–39, 35.

68 Others followed: Chotzner, *Satire*, 29–56; *Humour*, 126–139. Erter's satirical work was published seven years after his death in 1858; both "Gilgul Nefesh" and "Tashlikh" appear there, in *Watchman of the House of Israel*.

68 scriptorial irregularities: On the role of Jewish law in this satirical material, see Yehuda Friedlander, "Halachic Issues as Satirical Elements in Nineteenth Century Hebrew Literature," in *Jewish Humor*, 135–147.

69 "Put a skull": I. M. Dik, "The Gilgul," in Joachim Neugroschel, *The Dybbuk and the Yiddish Imagination* (Syracuse, NY: Syracuse University Press, 2000), 154–183. Quotes 178, 157–158, 166.

70 When he began to entertain: See Jeremy Dauber, "Linetski, Yitskhok-Yoyel," *YIVO Encyclopedia of Jews in Eastern Europe* http://www.yivo encyclopedia.org/article.aspx/Linetski_Yitskhok_Yoyel.

70 Anger: Jemielity, 40.

70 "When it comes to worldly things": Israel Aksenfeld, "The Headband," in Joachim Neugroschel, ed. and trans., *The Shtetl* (New York: Richard Marek, 1979), 169.

71 "Maybe you want to say": S. Y. Abramovitch, *The Little Man*, in Marvin Zuckerman, Gerald Stillman, and Marion Herbst, *Selected Works of Mendele Moykher-Sforim* (Malibu, CA: Pangloss Press, 1991), 53–167, 113.

72 Sholem Aleichem: On Sholem Aleichem more generally, see Jeremy Dauber, *The Worlds of Sholem Aleichem* (New York: Schocken, 2013).

72 "I want your idea": Quoted in Dauber, *Worlds*, 84.

73 "But what shall I do": Quoted in Dauber, *Worlds*, 83.

73 stories like "Dreyfus in Kasrilevke": "Dreyfus in Kasrilevke," in Irving Howe and Ruth Wisse, eds., *The Best of Sholom Aleichem* (Washington, DC: New Republic Books, 1979), 111–114; "Lunatics" and "The Red Little Jews" in Sholom Aleichem, *Why Do the Jews Need a Land of Their Own?* (Tel Aviv: Beth Sholom Aleichem, 1981), 90–124.

74 "Poor Reb Yosifel!": Sholem Aleichem, "A Yom Kippur Scandal" and "On Account of a Hat," in *Best of Sholom Aleichem*, 37–42, 103–110, quotes 42, 109–110.

76 **"Bontshe the Silent":** In *The I. L. Peretz Reader*, 146–152.

76 **"Neila in Gehenna":** In *The I. L. Peretz Reader*, 258–262.

76 **around 25 percent:** The figure doesn't include joke booklets and chapbooks; these last were mostly in the nineteenth century, and most of the satirical materials come out after 1905. See Eddy Portnoy, "Exploiting Tradition: Religious Iconography in Cartoons of the Polish Yiddish Press," *Polin* 16 (2003): 243–267, 245–250, and "Follow My Nose: Self-Caricature in Cartoons of the Yiddish Press," *International Journal of Comic Art* 6:1 (2004), 285–303, 297 (Broom quote).

77 **"the only bluffer":** Marian Fuks, "Mirthful Pessimism: The Humoristic/Satiric Press in Poland Between the Two World Wars," Kesher, 21 (1997): 80–90; translation from English abstract. *Der Bluffer* ran from 1926 to 1930.

77 **"Tales of a Thousand and One Nights":** Very partial translation as "The Krushniker Delegation" in *Best of Sholom Aleichem*, 232–244.

78 ***Zelmenyaner*:** For a detailed discussion of the novel, see Sasha Senderovitch, "Introduction," in Moyshe Kulbak, *The Zelmenyaners: A Family Saga* (New Haven CT: Yale University Press, 2013), vii–xxxiv. Compare discussion in Wisse, *No Joke*, 167–172.

78 **"A left-wing intellectual":** A slightly different version of this appears in Harris, 135.

79 **" 'The sun cannot enter' ":** Isaac Babel, "Gedali," in Nathalie Babel, ed., *The Complete Works of Isaac Babel*, (New York: Norton, 2001), 227–229, quotes 228–229.

80 **Babel was disappeared:** The reasons for Babel's disappearance and execution are complex and manifold, and almost certainly had as much, if not more, to do with his affair with the wife of the head of the NKVD as it did his own criticisms of the Soviet Union. That said, the writing was hardly an insignificant factor.

80 **a strong contender:** However, he left Warner Brothers while the movie was still being planned. Lubitsch was also, by some accounts, an uncredited director of scenes in Wegener's *Der Golem*. See Gerald Mast, "Woody Allen: The Neurotic Jew as American Clown," in Sarah Blacher Cohen, ed., *Jewish Wry* (Detroit, MI: Wayne State University Press, 1987), 125–140, 127–128; and Joel Rosenberg, "Jewish Experience on Film— An American Overview," *The American Jewish Year Book* 96 (1996): 3–50, 18.

81 **Satire, it seems, fails:** For a slightly different perspective that takes Lubitsch's comedy seriously as well, particularly as an example of "exile cinema," see Joel Rosenberg, "Shylock's Revenge: The Doubly Vanished

Jew in Ernst Lubitsch's *To Be or Not to Be*," *Prooftexts* 16 (1996): 209–244; see also Gerd Gemünden, "Space Out of Joint: Ernst Lubitsch's 'To Be Or Not To Be'," *New German Critique* 89 (2003): 59–80, especially on the "implicit Jews" played by Felix Bressart before he becomes *To Be or Not to Be*'s Greenberg (70–71). The movie was later remade by Mel Brooks; not surprisingly, given his interest in theater and Nazis. Sander Gilman's comment that "the strained nature of the remake was to no little degree the result of that oppressive if unspoken presence of the Shoah in the audience's awareness," absent in the original, seems largely apt. "Is Life Beautiful? Can the Shoah Be Funny? Some Thoughts on Recent and Older Film," *Critical Inquiry* 26:2 (2000), 279–308, 288.

82 **Whether it was discussing politics:** Tashrak, "Chaim Does His Duty as a Citizen," in Henry Goodman, ed., *The New Country* (Syracuse, NY: Syracuse University Press, 2001), 135–139; Tashrak, "Chaim Becomes a Real-Estatenik," in *New Country*, 61–65.

82 **Zalmon Libin:** Zalmon Libin, "Why the Taracans Are My Enemies," *New Country*, 131–134.

83 **Yiddish satirical journals:** See Portnoy, "Follow," 294 and "Exploiting," 247.

83 **The first story:** Sholem Aleichem, "Mister Green Has a Job," in *Some Laughter, Some Tears*, 233–236.

83 **the tale of a man:** Moishe Nadir, "I-As Echo," *New Country*, 144–146. Nadir also penned a story—whose pointedness would mark it for comic failure were the portraiture of the immigrant entrepreneurs in it not so tender—of a couple whose efforts at opening a delicatessen are stymied by the horseshoe of flowers reading SUCCESS they attempt to put up as advertising: the American promise and its lack of fulfillment in a nutshell. Nadir, "Ruined By Success," in Ausubel, *Treasury*, 36–39.

84 **a wised-up former greenhorn:** Sholem Aleichem, "A Story About a Greenhorn," in *Some Laughter, Some Tears*, 243–248.

84 **"laughing with lizards":** On this phrase, see Michael Wex, *Born to Kvetch* (New York: Harper Perennial, 2005), 171–172.

84 **"Hard, it's hard":** Abraham Raisin, "His Trip to America," in *New Country*, 39–42, 42.

84 **hungry i:** There is some debate whether the "I" stood for "id," or "intellectual," as often thought; see Gerald Nachman, *Seriously Funny: The Rebel Comedians of the 1950s and 1960s* (New York: Pantheon Books, 2003), 9–13.

84 **Will Rogers:** Rogers, perhaps the least likely person to be involved in this narrative, took part in an episode indicating how deeply enmeshed

Jewishness was in all parts of the industry: he emceed a testimonial dinner for Eddie Cantor in 1925—in Yiddish. (As soon as he was asked to participate, he hired a tutor.) Eddie Cantor, *Take My Life* (New York: Doubleday, 1957), 111.

85 **"There's quite a bit of difference"**: See "The Third Campaign," *Time*, Aug. 15, 1960, and John Matthew Taylor, "Outside Looking In: Stand-Up Comedy, Rebellion, and Jewish Identity in Early Post–World War II America" (M.A. thesis: Indiana University, 2010), 6–7, 24.

85 **"a symptom"**: "Nightclubs: The Sickniks," *Time*, July 13, 1959.

86 **"a cadre"**: Taylor, 102–103; quote Nachman, 57.

86 **"I don't have any kinship"**: Quoted in Nachman, 69.

87 **"vertical negro plan"**: Harry Golden, *Only In America* (Cleveland, OH: World Publishing Company, 1958), 121–122.

87 **"I am a satirist basically"**: *Essential Lenny*, 117; Arthur Asa Berger, *Jewish Jesters: A Study in American Popular Comedy* (Cresskill, NJ: Hampton Press, 2001), 90.

87 **play to the band**: His first fans were, as Steve Allen put it, "adult jazz musicians, nightclub employees, comedy writers, wives and girlfriends of men in the business, and 'hip' people generally in the mid-thirties age bracket." *Funny People*, 79.

88 **"the jargon of the hipster"**: Lenny Bruce, *How to Talk Dirty and Influence People* (New York: Fireside, 1992), 5. See, similarly, Sanford Pinsker, "Lenny Bruce: Shpritzing the Goyim/Shocking the Jews," in *Jewish Wry*, 89–104, 90; and Frank Kofsky, *Lenny Bruce: The Comedian as Social Critic and Secular Moralist* (New York: Monad Press, 1974), 72–74.

88 **"Give it to me"**: "Litvak Lolita": *Essential Lenny*, 250. On his Yiddish and "Yiddish" humor, see Maria Damon, "The Jewish Entertainer as Cultural Lightning Rod: The Case of Lenny Bruce," *Postmodern Culture* 7:2 (1997); Damon, "Talking Yiddish at the Boundaries," *Cultural Studies* 5:1 (1991), 14–29; "Gertrude Stein's Doggerel 'Yiddish': Women, Dogs and Jews," in *The Dark End of the Street: Margins in American Vanguard Poetry* (Minneapolis: University of Minnesota Press, 1993), 202–235; and Ioan Davies, "Lenny Bruce: Hyperrealism and the Death of Jewish Tragic Humor," *Social Text* 22 (1989): 92–114, esp. 98.

88 **"All you guys"**: Quoted in Nachman, 397.

88 **jazz labels**: Verve and Fantasy, respectively; Sahl used to tour college campuses with the Dave Brubeck Quartet. See Taylor, 28–30.

88 **Tom Lehrer**: See Nachman, 124–150, in which it is also bruited that Lehrer may have invented the Jello shot (130).

89 psychoanalysis: "What's the difference between a tailor and a psychoanalyst? One generation." Cited in David Meghnaghi, "Jewish Humour on Psychoanalysis," *International Review of Psycho-Analysis* 18:2 (1991), 223–228, 224.

89 rarely explicitly so: For a more explicitly Jewish-based satire of Feiffer's, see his "The Deluge," reprinted in Novak and Waldoks, 221–223, in which government (mis)intervention disrupts Noah's plans for human salvation from the eponymous deluge; for general discussion of Feiffer's Jewish comedic sensibilities, see Stephen J. Whitfield, "Jules Feiffer and the Comedy of Disenchantment," in Sarah Blacher Cohen, *From Hester Street to Hollywood* (Bloomington: Indiana University Press, 1983), 167–182, esp. 178–179.

89 Heller suggested otherwise: Harap, 41–42.

90 black humor: Bruce Jay Friedman, *Black Humor* (New York: Bantam, 1965).

90 "tense comedy": See Mike Sacks, *Poking A Dead Frog: Conversations With Today's Top Comedy Writers* (New York: Penguin, 2014), 151.

90 "a nervousness": Friedman, *Black Humor*, viii–x.

91 "No playing": Bruce Jay Friedman, *Stern* (New York: Grove Press, 1962), 10.

91 "When You're Excused": Bruce Jay Friedman, "When You're Excused, You're Excused," in Jules Chametzky et al., *Jewish American Literature: A Norton Anthology* (New York: Norton, 2001), 1006–1014.

91 Epstein: "Epstein" and "Goodbye Columbus" in Philip Roth, *Goodbye, Columbus* (Boston: Houghton Mifflin, 1959).

91 Bellow's early shvitzers: Saul Bellow, *The Victim* (New York: Vanguard Press, 1947); *Seize the Day* (New York: Viking Press, 1956).

92 the "right copies": Though Friedman noted, "I remember wondering what it would have been like if it sold a hundred thousand wrong copies." Sacks, *Poking*, 152.

92 In books like *Only in America . . . For 2¢ Plain*: "from sha sha to cha cha": *Only in America*, 155. "From shul to pool": *Long Live Columbus* (New York: G. P. Putnam, 1975), 61. Jessel: "Life in the American Middle Class," *For 2¢ Plain* (Cleveland, OH: World Publishing Company, 1959), 58–67.

92 buying a child a suit: *Only in America*, 54–59. See also his *Long Live Columbus*.

92 gleeful puerility: See David Greenberg, "Little Rascal," http://tabletmag.com/jewish-arts-and-culture/books/784/little-rascal.

92 Klein, whose dad: Richard Zoglin, *Comedy at the Edge: How Stand-Up in the 1970s Changed America* (New York: Bloomsbury USA, 2008), 73, 76ff.

93   **"didn't have a hook":** Zoglin, 81.

93   **incorporate Jewishness:** This wasn't only a Jewish turn to the autobiographical. There are just as many—if not more—non-Jewish stand-ups central to the history of American comedy of this generation who can be so characterized, since everybody, it should go without saying, has a background and a cultural milieu they can render in a comic vein. Klein's similarly inclined compatriots include, among others, Jay Leno, David Letterman, Robin Williams, Steve Martin, and, perhaps most importantly, George Carlin and Richard Pryor. See Zoglin, 4.

93   *Soft Pretzels with Mustard*: New York: Arbor House, 1983.

93   *Wet Hot American Summer*: On *Wet Hot American Summer*'s Jewishness, especially in contrast to the hidden Jewishness of its predecessor, the 1979 Ivan Reitman (Candian Jew) movie *Meatballs*, see Josh Lambert, "Wet Hot American Jewish Summer Camp," July 30, 2015, http://www.tabletmag.com/jewish-arts-and-culture/192063/wet-hot-american-jewish-summer-camp?Src=longreads.

94   **Lear insisted:** Norman Lear, *Even This I Get to Experience* (New York: Penguin Press, 2014). Archie Bunker, hardly the expositor of the liberal Lear's favored positions, would become a hero to many; in part, it should be said, due to the nuance of the writing and Caroll O'Connor's layered performance.

95   **isn't particularly Jewish:** Its other foundational influence—the more recently mainstreamed countercultural currents like the *National Lampoon*, whose orbit, which gave the SNLers Michael O'Donoghue, John Belushi, and Chevy Chase, among others, wasn't particularly Jewish, either. (A notable exception: Ed Bluestone, who came up with the infamously iconic "If You Don't Buy This Magazine, We'll Kill This Dog" cover.)

95   **less and less intertwined:** An exception from the period that, perhaps, proved the rule was the comic cowboy county singer Kinky Friedman, who wove pictures satirizing the image of the hyperliberal Jew into his mock-redneck performances of songs like "Ride em Jewboy," "They Aint Making Jews Like Jesus Anymore," and "We Reserve the Right to Refuse Service to You." On Friedman, see Theodore Albrecht, " 'They Ain't Making Jews Like Jesus Anymore': The Musical Humor of Kinky Friedman and the Texas Jewboys in Historical and Geographical Perspective," in *Jews and Humor*, 211–224; and Jarrod Tanny, "Between the Borscht Belt and the Bible Belt: Crafting Southern Jewishness Through Chutzpah and Humor," *Southern Jewish History* 15 (2012): 119–167, 153–156.

95 **There's Tova Reich's take:** Tova Reich, *My Holocaust* (New York: HarperCollins, 2007); Tova Mirvis, *The Ladies' Auxiliary* (New York: Ballantine, 2000); Shalom Auslander, *Beware of God: Stories* (New York: Simon and Schuster, 2005).

95 *The Russian Debutante's Handbook*: *The Russian Debutante's Handbook* (New York: Riverhead, 2002). His subsequent novels—*Absurdistan* (New York: Random House, 2006) and *Super Sad True Love Story* (New York: Random House, 2010), are even funnier, but, though featuring similar protagonists, operate in a more farcical, imagined space than the territory explored in *Handbook* and are slightly less relevant to the discussion here.

96 **when President Eisenhower met:** Telushkin, *Jewish Humor*, 82–83.

96 **Levi Eshkol:** See Ofra Nevo, "Jewish Humor in the Service of an Israeli Political Leader: The Case of Levi Eshkol," in *Semites and Stereotypes*, 165–176.

96 **Two illustrative jokes:** See Spalding, 80, 171.

97 **a new Jewish culture:** This movement was also associated with a new, or, more precisely, revived, Jewish language; and that linguistic debate over the language of Zionism and the Yishuv—Hebrew, rather than Yiddish—was played out in satirical cartoons, among other venues. See Joshua A. Fishman, "Cartoons About Language: Hebrew, Yiddish, and the Visual Representation of Sociolinguistic Values," in Lewis Glinert, ed., *Hebrew in Ashkenaz* (New York: Oxford University Press, 1993), 151–166.

97 **"They came":** On the "chizbat," a word roughly meaning "lie" taken from the Arabic, see Elliot Oring, *Israeli Humor: The Content and Structure of the Chizbat of the Palmah* (Albany, NY: SUNY Press, 1981), 23–38, 53–54, 57–66. Joke quoted in Oring, 101.

98 **A skit:** See Liat Steir-Livny, "Holocaust Humor, Satire, and Parody on Israeli Television," *Jewish Film and New Media* 3:2 (Fall 2015), 193–219, 198. Compare Wisse, *No Joke*, 195.

98 ***bourekas* films":** Elise Burton, "Ethnic Humor, Stereotypes, and Cultural Power in Israeli Cinema," in Gayatri Devi and Najat Rahman, eds., *Humor in Middle Eastern Cinema* (Detroit, MI: Wayne State University Press, 2014), 104–125, 106.

98 *Hagashash Hahiver*: Wisse, *No Joke*, 200–201.

98 **popular series of jokes:** See Hagar Salamon, "The Ambivalence over the Levantizination of Israel: 'David Levi' Jokes," *Humor* 20:4 (2007), 415–442.

98 **a newer immigrant community:** See Narspy Zilberg, "In-Group Humor of Immigrants From the Former Soviet Union to Israel," *Israel Social Sci-*

ence Research 10:1 (1995), 1–22, joke 17; and also Maria Yenelevskaya, "Humor in the Russian-Language Media in Israel: Cultural Antecedents, Genres, and Themes," *Israel Studies in Language and Society* 1:2 (2008), 36-58; and Anna Ronell, "Russian Israeli Literature Through the Lens of Immigrant Humor," *Journal of Jewish Identities* 4:1 (2011), 147–169.

100 **at the Emmy Awards:** "Jon Stewart and The Daily Show at the 2003 Emmy Awards," https://www.youtube.com/watch?v=0achuXf3fg8.

3: The Wit of the Jews

101 **For most of biblical literature:** Exodus 32:19; Jeremiah 36:23; 2 Kings 22.

101 **the riddle game:** On the larger view of the Samson story as comic, compare J. Cheryl Exum and J. William Whedbee, "Isaac, Samson, and Saul: Reflections on the Comic and Tragic Visions," in Radday and Brenner, 117–159, 136.

102 **As biblical commentators:** See Dan Pagis, "Toward a Theory of the Literary Riddle," in Galit Hasan-Rokem and David Shulman, eds., *Untying the Knot: On Riddles and Other Enigmatic Modes* (New York: Oxford University Press, 1996), 81–108, 95.

102 **hardly a shining example:** Another, more positive riddle game appears in the Apocryphal/Deuterocanonical books; the contest in 1 Esdras 3.5–4.41, to which we'll return in a later chapter.

102 **In the most famous biblical story:** 1 Kings 3:16–28.

103 *God Knows*: Joseph Heller, *God Knows* (New York: Knopf, 1984), 249; the biblical allusion is never mentioned explicitly on Seinfeld (in the episode "The Seven," from 1996), but it's obvious.

103 **cruelty empathy:** A similar Solomonic riddle with a unifying effect, this one in the romantic vein (riddles, incidentally, often featured as part of wedding rituals), concerns Solomon's encounter with the Queen of Sheba. See Dina Stein, "A King, A Queen, and the Riddle in Between: Riddles and Interpretation in a Late Midrashic Text," in Hasan-Rokem 125–147, esp. 129.

104 **even reshape the riddle:** See Pagis, 103.

105 **smart-assery:** Compare Novak and Waldoks, 51–57.

105 **some reasons to wonder:** For some discussion of this question, see Holger Zellentin, *Rabbinic Parodies of Jewish and Christian Literature* (Tübingen: Mohr Siebeck, 2011), 43, 216.

105 **"A baby pigeon":** BT Bava Batra 23b.

106 **a knife flying:** Knife: BT Chullin 31a; wagon: BT Bava Kama 55a. See Hershey H. Friedman, "Talmudic Humor and the Establishment of

Legal Principles: Strange Questions, Impossible Scenarios, and Legalistic Brainteasers," *Thalia: Studies in Literary Humor* 21:1 (2004), from which some of these cases are taken. See also David Brodsky, "Why Did the Widow Have A Goat in Her Bed? Jewish Humor and Its Roots in the Talmud and Midrash," in *Jews and Humor*, 13–32, 40–42.

106 **"If one has two heads":** BT Menachot 37a.

106 **Witty mockery:** This is different than the kind of insults or putdowns delivered in the course of normal Talmudic discourse, which themselves can possess (or lack) a certain degree of wit. See Arthur E. Helft, *Talmudic Insults and Curses* (Arthur Helft, 2012).

106 **"A certain heretic":** BT Sukkah 48b.

107 **the case of Hillel:** BT Sabbath 31a.

108 **another kind of display:** See Brodsky, 13–14.

108 **the pun:** For a different analysis of puns and their wit with relation to religion, in which their dualism can lead to complex relationships with faith (or, alternatively, though he doesn't say this, an almost mystical sense of the capacities of the divine Word), see Sten H. Stenson, *Sense and Nonsense in Religion: An Essay on the Language and Phenomelogy of Religion* (Nashville, TN: Abingdon Press, 1969), 136–137.

108 **walking the ruins:** BT Makkot 24b.

109 **laughs, for example, at the suffering:** BT Sanhedrin 101a.

109 **laughter and frivolity:** Avot 3:13; see Chaim W. Reines, "Laughter in Biblical and Rabbinic Literature," *Judaism* 21:2 (1972), 176–184, 182, and Samuel E. Karff, "Laughter and Merriment in Rabbinic Literature," in Abraham J. Karp, *Threescore and Ten* (Hoboken, NJ: KTAV, 1991), 75–86.

109 **"since the day":** See BT Avoda Zara 3b and Avot 6:5.

109 **"Whoever has guffawed":** Cited in Ingvid Saelid Gilhus, *Laughing Gods, Weeping Virgins: Laughter in the History of Religion* (New York: Routledge, 1997), 68.

109 **"Just as if a full container":** Song of Songs Rabbah 1:2; see also BT Avodah Zarah 18b–19a.

110 **"If your inclination comes":** BT Shabbat 30b.

110 **the prophet Elijah:** See BT Berakhot 31a and BT Taanit 22a; compare Reines 183.

110 **Kopl told his friend:** Adapted from version in Learsi, 248.

111 **"You ruthless flea":** Quoted in Gustav Karpeles, *Jewish Literature and Other Essays* (Philadelphia: Jewish Publication Society, 1895), 212.

112 **that transcends theological fidelity:** A slightly less subversive example of the process appeared in the work of the thirteenth-century *payyetan*

Rabbi Yehosef Ha-Ezovi: B. Bar-Tikva, "Humor in the Piyyutim of Rabbi Yehosef Ha-Ezovi," Ulf Haxen et al., eds., *Jewish Studies in a New Europe* (Copenhagen: European Association for Jewish Studies, 1994), 54–63.

112 **long riddles in verse:** See Pagis, 82.

112 **provides its own source:** And it would continue into the Eastern European milieu, where Yiddish folksongs would freely and playfully mix Hebrew, Yiddish, and Slavic to reflect, ironize, and parody the lived circumstances of Jewish life in that rapidly changing landscape. See David Roskies, "Ideologies of the Yiddish Folksong in the Old Country and the New," *Jewish Book Annual* 50 (1992): 143–166, esp. 150–151.

112 **A medieval wedding song:** Kirsten Fudeman, " 'They Have Ears, But Do Not Hear': Gendered Access to Hebrew and the Medieval French Wedding Song," *JQR* 96:4 (Fall 2006), 542–567.

113 **The Dante-modeled comedy:** See Chotzner, *Humour*, 82–102.

113 **"If anyone among you":** 1 Corinthians 3:18.

113 **In First Samuel:** 1 Samuel 21:11–16; Proverbs 26:9. See also Proverbs 26:3.

113 **knowledge can itself:** See discussion in Andrew Stott, *Comedy* (New York: Routledge, 2005), 47–48.

114 **best known as Chelm:** I'm simplifying here, because in Jewish folklore, this fools' town, and the stories associated with it, was not identified as Chelm until the late nineteenth century; at this point in the historical narrative, the stories were generally set in the German town of Schild-burg. But it is with their association with Chelm that they've achieved immortality in Jewish folklore, and so I'm presenting it that way here. For the full story, see now the excellent scholarly treatment in Ruth Von Bernuth, *How the Wise Men Got to Chelm: The Life and Times of a Yiddish Folk Tradition* (New York: NYU Press, 2016).

114 **Singer would go on:** See R. Barbara Gitenstein, "Fools and Sages: Humor in Isaac Bashevis Singer's 'The Fools of Chelm and Their History,' " *Studies in American Jewish Literature* 1 (1981): 107–111.

114 **In another story:** See Learsi, 138.

114 **"The Tumblers":** Nathan Englander, "The Tumblers," in *For the Relief of Unbearable Urges* (New York: Knopf, 1999).

115 **whose culture they admired:** See Ismar Schorsch, "The Myth of Sephardic Supremacy," *Leo Baeck Institute Year Book* 34:1 (1989), 47–66.

115 **to an identification of "Jewish humor":** For a nice overview of the history of this approach, see Efron, 51–52.

116 **"The Tale of the Wise Man":** "The Hakham and the Tam (The Clever

Man and the Ordinary Man)," in *Nachman of Bratslav: The Tales* (New York: Paulist Press, 1978), 139–161.

117 **"If your friend"**: BT Bava Kama 92b; Heller, 109.

117 **Judeo-Spanish *refrán***: See Matilda Cohen Sarano, "Jewish Themes and Thoughts in the Judeo-Spanish Refrán," in *The Sephardic Journey, 1492–1992* (New York: Yeshiva University Museum, 1992), 156–171.

117 **the Yiddish curse**: Yosef Guri, *Let's Hear Only Good News* (Jerusalem: Hebrew University, 2004), 12, 102, 94, 108, 70, 65. See also Wex 118–139, and James A. Matisoff, *Blessings, Curses, Hopes, and Fears: Psycho-Ostensive Expressions in Yiddish* (Philadelphia: Institute for the Study of Human Issues, 1979).

117 **There was a saying**: Cited in Telushkin, *Jewish Humor*, 17.

117 **"You should have a lot of money"**: Telushkin, *Jewish Humor*, 105.

117 **"Yiddish curses for Republican Jews"**: Michael Schulman, "Yiddish Curses for Republican Jews," *The New Yorker*, Aug. 30, 2012, http://www.newyorker.com/humor/daily-shouts/yiddish-curses-for-republican-jews

118 **"A rabbi who is trying"**: Ausubel, *Folklore*, 22.

118 **William Hazlitt**: William Hazlitt, *Lectures on the English Comic Writers* (London: John Templeman, 1844), 24.

118 **"Two Jews traveling"**: Cited in Wisse, *No Joke*, 231–232.

119 **Shteynbarg's fables**: See Eliezer Shteynbarg, *Mesholim* (Tel Aviv: Y. L. Peretz, 1969); one of his works, "A Tale Without an End," is translated in Ausubel, *Humor*, 415.

119 **Agnon's novels**: For two examples, see 1931's *The Bridal Canopy* (New York: Schocken, 1967) and 1935's *A Simple Story* (New York: Schocken, 1985).

119 **in Odessa**: See Jarrod Tanny, *City of Rogues and Schnorrers: Russia's Jews and the Myth of Old Odessa* (Bloomington: Indiana University Press, 2011), 2–3, 99–100.

119 **"A newly Enlightened young man"**: See alternative version in Spalding, 60–61.

120 **According to Bellow**: See Saul Bellow, *Great Jewish Short Stories* (New York: Dell, 1963), "Introduction," 9–16, 14–15.

120 **Bellow's literary reputation**: See Mark Schechner, "Saul Bellow and Ghetto Cosmopolitanism," *Studies in American Jewish Literature* 4:2 (1979), 33–44, 33–34; and the special issue of *Saul Bellow Journal* 18:2 (2002) dedicated to Saul Bellow as a comic writer, especially the articles by Siegel and Kremer cited below.

121 **Bellow was frustrated**: See Ben Siegel, "Confusion Under Pressure: Saul Bellow's Look at Comic Society and the Individual," *SBJ* 18:2 (2002),

3–22, 6–7, 18, and S. Lillian Kremer, "High Art/Low Life: The Human Comedy in Saul Bellow's Fiction," *SBJ* 18:2 (2002), 78–94, 78–81.

122 **"A parasite":** S. J. Perelman, *The Most of S. J. Perelman* (New York: Simon and Schuster, 1958), 3.

122 **Perelman described his style:** Douglas Fowler, *S. J. Perelman* (Boston: Twayne, 1983), 4–6, 93–108, quote 97; Harap 46.

122 **an inseparable twosome:** See Nachman, 325ff.

122 **a simulacrum of wit:** This is slightly different from other kinds of mock-authority individuals, who were also specialized in by Jews like Sid Caesar and Irwin Corey.

123 **"I object to the whole thing":** Nachman, 336, 343–345, quote 348.

123 **In the same period:** Nachman, 298, 307, 321.

123 **painting word pictures:** See Eric Lax, *On Being Funny: Woody Allen and Comedy* (New York: Charterhouse, 1975), 6, and Foster Hirsch, *Love, Sex, Death, and the Meaning of Life: The Films of Woody Allen* (New York: Da Capo, 2001), 24–25, 48–51.

124 **Allen had idolized Perelman:** See Eric Lax, *Conversations with Woody Allen* (New York: Knopf, 2009, expanded edition), 91; Fowler, 106.

124 **Allen's reputation:** For just a few examples of that reputation, see Gerald McKnight, *Woody Allen: Joking Aside* (London: Star, 1983), 59–62; Diane Jacobs, . . . *But We Need the Eggs: The Magic of Woody Allen* (New York: St. Martin's Press, 1982), 5.

124 **Allen's own intellectualism:** McCann, 27; McKnight, 109.

124 **"I submit to you":** *On Being Funny*, 17. See also McCann, 3–4.

124 **often confused:** Compare Stephen J. Whitfield, "The Distinctiveness of American Jewish Humor," *Modern Judaism* 6:3 (1986), 245–260, esp. 256–257.

124 **Hebrew in school:** McKnight, 47.

124 **"The Scrolls":** *Insanity Defense*, 140, 45.

125 **" 'I cannot get my mind' ":** *Insanity Defense*, 255.

125 **"Teachers were amazed":** Lax, *Conversations*, 121.

126 **"This list":** Cited in Palmer, 120.

126 **New Yorker:** On Allen as New Yorker, see Graham McCann, *Woody Allen: New Yorker* (New York: Polity Press, 1990), esp. 20–21. Part of the New York complex: "The View of the World," *The New Yorker*, Mar. 29, 1976.

127 *Science—For Her!*: Megan Amram, *Science—For Her!* (New York: Scribner, 2014).

127 **Twitter:** Another strong voice on Twitter, this one practically divinely

so: David Javerbaum, whose tweeting as the Supreme Being (@TheTweet OfGod) was later turned into a Broadway show.

127 **"No one knows"**: @meganamram; May 19, 2016; Apr. 23, 2016; Apr. 4, 2016.

127 *Witz*: Joshua Cohen, *Witz* (New York: Dalkey, 2010).

128 *The Book of Numbers*: Joshua Cohen, *The Book of Numbers* (New York: Random House, 2015).

128 *Everything Is Illuminated*: Jonathan Safran Foer, *Everything Is Illuminated* (New York: Houghton Mifflin, 2002).

4. A View from the Bottom

129 **Soon after its release**: Parish, 13.

130 **"In every cowboy picture"**: Quoted in Parish, 11. For the technically minded reader: none of the sounds were actual flatulence; all were produced by wet soap, air pockets, and an occasional vocal assist from Brooks.

130 **"we're trying to use"**: Quoted in Parish, 7. He partnered on the script work with Andrew Bergman, Norman Steinberg, Alan Uger, and perhaps most notably, Richard Pryor.

130 **it rises below vulgarity**: See Parish, 12.

130 **To be a parodist**: A briefly annoying technical footnote to the effect that parody, in the most formal sense of the word, doesn't have to be funny in the sense we usually use the term. Although it's often used to satirize, or to ridicule, or to subvert, or to produce a comic effect (though those themselves aren't identical), it isn't always. Most critics consider parody a subcategory of satire, in fact: see Highet, 68ff, for example. See also Simon Dentith, *Parody* (London: Routledge, 2000), esp. 9–21, 32, 36–37. For a good overview, see also W. Kynes, "Beat Your Parodies into Swords, and Your Parodied Books into Spears: A New Paradigm for Parody in the Hebrew Bible," *Biblical Interpretation* 19 (2011): 276–301, 280–289.

131 **"Jewish jokes almost never"**: Reik, 111–112.

131 **Ehud**: See Judges 3:12–30; Athalya Brenner, "On the Semantic Field of Humour, Laughter, and the Comic in the Old Testament," in Radday and Brenner, 39–58, 45; and James K. Aitken, "Fat Eglon," in Geoffrey Kahn and Diana Lipton, eds., *Studies on the Text and Versions of the Hebrew Bible in Honour of Robert Gordon* (Leiden: Brill, 2012), 141–154, though he's less salient about the episode being humorous than many other critics.

132 **The sniggering intimation:** Compare Marcus, 24.

132 **Sisera:** Judges 4:18–21; See Lowell K. Handy, "Uneasy Laughter: Ehud and Eglon as Ethnic Humor," *Scandinavian Journal of the Old Testament* 6:2 (1992), 233–246.

132 **the prophet Balaam:** Numbers 22–24; BT Sanhedrin 105a–b; Marcus 34–36.

132 **the great and mighty:** Dan. 5.6; see Brenner, "Semantic," 43. Valeta (87) suggests he shits himself. Another non-Jewish royal who may come in for a similar comic treatment is Abimelech, king of Gerar; compare Tzvi Novick, " 'Almost, At Times, The Fool': Abimelekh and Genesis 20," *Prooftexts* 24 (2004): 277–290.

133 **"The passion of laughter":** Thomas Hobbes, *The Moral and Political Works* (London: 1750), 20.

133 **at people who are less knowledgeable:** Technically, they're ridiculous by not understanding themselves, having improper self-knowledge. Aristotle even took it further, suggesting the "laughable to be a species of the ugly"; see Holt, 67.

133 **that condition:** Yes, I know he's talking about in the state of nature, as opposed to under government. Still, the worldview shines through.

133 **so common in the Bible:** John Morreall, "Sarcasm, Irony, Wordplay and Humor in the Bible: A Response to Hershey Friedman," *Humor* 14:3 (2001), 293–301, 300–301. Or, as Miles puts it ("Laughing at the Bible," 180), "ancient humor was typically a laughing at rather than a laughing with."

133 **this "ethnic humor" is manifested:** Athalya Brenner, "Who's Afraid of Feminist Criticism? Who's Afraid of Biblical Humour? The Case of the Obtuse Foreign Ruler in the Hebrew Bible," *Journal for the study of the Old Testament* 63 (1994): 38–55, esp. 42–43.

133 **coming from the confidence:** Perhaps the exception that proves the rule here—viewing Balaam as a parodic prophet—reinforces the sensibility: he's parodied because he doesn't get with the Jewish God's mission for him.

134 **book of Jonah:** The first mention of the Twelve Prophets (which contains the book of Jonah) as a canonical book is in Ben Sira (around 180 BCE); and the first mention of the custom to read it dates from centuries later, in the Talmud (BT Megila 31a).

134 **something of an overreaction:** See, for example, E. M. Good, *Irony in the Old Testament* (Philadelphia: The Westminster Press, 1955), 49.

134 **not rendered unto Jews:** See Elias Bickerman, *Four Strange Books of the Bible* (New York: Schocken, 1967), 17.

135 **generally dour mien:** On the odd character that is Jonah, see Yvonne

Sherwood, "Cross-Currents in the Book of Jonah: Some Jewish and Cultural Midrashim on a Traditional Text," *Biblical Interpretation* 9:1 (1998), 49–79, 53. Luther, among others, took this as proof of Jewish hatred of gentiles; see Bickerman, 18.

135 **that has puzzled readers:** For one possible explanation, see Rob C. Barrett, "Meaning What They Say: The Conflict Between YHWH and Jonah," *Journal for the Study of the Old Testament* 37:2 (2012), 237–257.

135 **Most of the book's puzzles:** Including some linguistic matters a little too technical for our purview here, like an extended run of puns on the word "vomit" (including the gourd tree, the *kikayon*, whose name could literally be translated as something like a "vomit tree"). On punning as a source of humor in the book, see Willie Van Heerden, "Humour and the Interpretation of the Book of Jonah," *Old Testament Essays* 5 (1992): 375 388.

135 **"A fit story for ridicule":** Thomas Paine, *The Age of Reason* (London: B. D. Cousins), 132. Paine believed, it should be said, that the book was more a satire of a bad prophet than a parody of the prophetic mission more generally. For other attempts to determine the parody's point precisely—was it ridiculing prophecy? Satirizing those who take Hebrew scripture too seriously? Criticizing those who fail to live up to proper prophetic behavior, whether prophets or unrepentant and disobedient people?—see John A. Miles, Jr. "Jonah as Parody," *JQR* 65:3 (1975), 168–181; Marcus, 145–146; and Kynes, 300–303.

135 **parody of the psalmic cry:** On this last, see particularly Judson Mather, "The Comic Art of the Book of Jonah," *Soundings* 65 (1982): 280–91, 284–285.

135 **The name Jonah:** 2 Kings 14:25. Other stories about Jonah might have circulated at the time, of course; the earlier prophet lived at least a century before the book of Jonah could have been composed. On name aspects, see Yehuda T. Radday, "Humour in Names," in Radday and Brenner, 59–97, 75–76.

135 **The comedy there:** See R. P. Carroll, "Is Humour Also Among the Prophets?," in Radday and Brenner, 169–189, 180–181.

136 **The Greek origins:** Compare Harry Levin, *Playboys and Killjoys: An Essay on the Theory and Practice of Comedy* (New York: Oxford University Press, 1987), 156–157.

136 **"Two rabbis":** BT Megila 7b.

137 **Rabbis' bodies:** See BT BM 84a; Daniel Boyarin, *Socrates and the Fat Rabbi* (Chicago: University of Chicago, 2009), *passim*, esp. 177–186.

137 **Apocryphal book of Tobit:** See discussion in Gruen, 148–158. For a

dissenting opinion as to Tobit's comedic value, see J. R. C. Cousland, "Tobit: A Comedy in Error?" *Catholic Biblical Quarterly* 65: 4 (2003), 535–553, esp. 546–547.

138   **a mocking, scatological scenario:** BT Megila 16a.

139   **"the pompous fool":** Quote from Good, *Irony*, 14; compare discussion in Arkadi Kovelman, "Farce in the Talmud," *Review of Rabbinic Judaism* 5:1 (2002), 86–92, 87–89.

140   **"King, my dear":** Quote from Jean Baumgarten, *Introduction to Old Yiddish Literature* (New York: Oxford University Press, 2005), 377. It comes from the 1697 *Eyn sheyn purim-shpil.*

140   *Halt mir der shtekn:* Quoted in Ahuva Belkin, "The 'Low' Culture of the Purimshpil," in Joel Berkowitz, ed., *Yiddish Theatre: New Approaches* (London: Littman, 2003), 29–43, 37.

140   **old news:** There are other examples, too, like the Apocryphal book Joseph and Aseneth, which—although much about it is unclear, like its author and its dating (it was probably written in the first or second century CE)—has a title character who's much less resolute and virtuous than he is in the original, in a narrative that seems to borrow from Greek traditions of comedy and mime. See Angela Standhartinger, "Humour in Joseph and Aseneth," *Journal for the Study of the Pseudepigrapha* 24 (2015): 239–259.

141   **"FOR I go gladly":** Translation from Baumgarten, 279.

142   **Witty parodies of rabbinic interpretation:** See Zellentin, *passim.*

143   **" 'The son of Sira' ":** On this text, see David Stern, "The 'Alphabet of Ben Sira' and the Early History of Parody in Jewish Literature," in Hindy Najman and Judith H. Newman, eds., *The Idea of Biblical Interpretation: Essays in Honor of James L. Kugel* (Boston: Brill, 2004), 423–448, quote 430–431.

143   **specific biblical and midrashic:** See Stern, 433ff; texts include Job 1:10, as well as lots of Jeremiah-related midrashim.

143   **"Purim rabbis":** Peter J. Haas, "Masekhet Purim," *Jews and Humor*, 55–65, 57–58; Ariella Krasny, "Rav shel purim—teatron shel yom echad," *Bikoret ufarshanut* 41 (2009): 93–110; Dentith 50; Gilhus 85–104.

144   **tradition goes back centuries:** See Israel Davidson, *Parody in Jewish Literature* (New York: Columbia University Press, 1907), 19.

144   *Hymn of the Night of Purim:* See Chotzner, *Humour*, 110–112. The parodic hymn appears in the *Mahzor Vitry.* See Davidson, 4–5.

144   **"Said R. Keg":** Translation taken from Haas, 61.

145   **"It is no exaggeration":** Davidson, xix.

145   **"During R. Itzeleh's tenure":** Cited in Daniel Z. Feldman, "The Lomdus of Laughter: Toward a Jewish Ethic of Humor," in Yehuda Sarna, ed.,

Developing a Jewish Perspective on Culture (New York: Yeshiva University Press, 2014), 408–429, 417–418, slightly glossed.

146   " 'I don't wish' ": Zalman Khazak, "The War of the Holy Days" (1517, Oldendorf, Germany), in Joachim Neugroschel, *No Star Too Beautiful: Yiddish Stories From 1382 to the Present* (New York: Norton, 2002), 11.

146   " 'You should praise me' ": Zalman Sofer, "Debate Between Wine and Water" (1517), Neugroschel, *No Star*, 9.

147   Bakhtin: See Mikhail Bakhtin, *Rabelais and His World* (Bloomington: Indiana University Press, 1984); and Stott, 32–38, for discussion.

148   opponents in the yeshiva world: See Shulchan Aruch, *Or hachayim* 307:16, based on a reading of Psalms 1:1 ("Happy are those who do not . . . sit in the seat of scoffers.")

149   "Anyone of Israel": *Masekhet Aniyut* (Vilna: 1878), 26. On this text, see also Derek Penslar, "The Continuity of Subversion: Hebrew Satire in Mandatory Palestine," *Jewish History* 20:1 (2006), 19–40, 23–25.

150   It might be Yiddish songs: See David Roskies, "Major Trends in Yiddish Parody," *Jewish Quarterly Review* 94:1 (2004), 109–122.

150   "Lot—it's disgusting": "Abraham Scolds Lot," in Itzik Manger, *The World According to Itzik* (New Haven CT: Yale University Press), 8.

151   Zionists: Penslar, 27–32.

151   "When we'll die": Taken from Zerubavel, 175.

152   "red haggadot": Penslar, 22.

152   Socialist Haggadah: Eddy Portnoy, "Paschal Lampoon," http://www.tabletmag.com/jewish-life-and-religion/65090/paschal-lampoon.

152   "I am the Lord thy God": In Gary Phillip Zola and Marc Dollinger, eds., *American Jewish History: A Primary Source Reader* (Waltham, MA: Brandeis University Press, 2014), 144–145, 144.

153   "The wise men": Cited in Davidson, 103.

154   mixing of worlds: The mixed worlds, as Jarod Tanny, points out, are also those of the "Jewish" north and south. See "Borscht Belt," 126–129.

154   sold two hundred thousand copies: See Donald Weber, "Taking Jewish American Popular Culture Seriously: The Yinglish Worlds of Gertrude Berg, Milton Berle, and Mickey Katz," *Jewish Social Studies* 5 (1998–1999): 124–153, 140.

154   Katz's fifties antics: Josh Kun, "The Yiddish Are Coming: Mickey Katz, Antic-Semitism, and the Sound of Jewish Difference," *American Jewish History* 87 (1999): 343–374, esp. 349, 371–373.

154   "comes to Liza's rescue": See Mark Cohen, "My Fair Sadie: Allan Sherman and a Paradox of American Jewish Culture," *American Jewish History* 93:1 (2007), 51–71, quote 68.

154 "These songs": Mark Cohen, "Sadie," 56.

155 Sherman's response: Nachman, 18.

155 "I was warned before coming here": Quoted in Steve Allen, *More Funny People* (New York: Stein and Day, 1982), 243.

155 "I realized I am at my worst": Quoted in Allen, *More Funny People*, 243.

156 "more important than pot": Cited in Harry Brod, *Superman is Jewish?* (New York: Free Press, 2012), 59–60.

156 a predecessor in this effort: Brod, 72; Hoberman and Shandler, 164.

156 " 'chicken fat' ": Cited in Brod, 63.

156 An early issue: Paul Buhle, *Jews and American Comics: An Illustrated History of an American Art Form* (New York: New Press, 2008), 63.

157 "a great resort": Esther Romeyn and Jack Kugelmass, *Let There Be Laughter: Jewish Humor in America* (Chicago: Spertus Press, 1997), 56.

157 *Puck* had published: In *Puck* 17 (1884/1885): 356, cited in Rudolf Glanz, *The Jew in Early American Wit and Graphic Humor* (New York: KTAV, 1973), 35–37.

157 "Way down deep": Myrna Katz Frommer and Harvey Frommer, *It Happened in the Catskills* (New York: Harcourt Brace Jovanovich, 1991), 223.

158 who many thought: Frommer, 68, 82–83.

158 "This fellow": Frommer, 182.

158 My favorite unexpected cameo: Frommer, 124.

158 "RENTER": Sammy Levenson, *Meet the Folks: A Session of American-Jewish Humor* (New York: Citadel Press, 1948), 91.

159 "The roughest thing": Joey Adams, *The Borscht Belt* (New York: Bobbs-Merrill, 1966), 57.

159 "bowdlerized versions": Parish 37.

159 Sour Cream Sierras: Lawrence J. Epstein, *The Haunted Smile: The Story of Jewish Comedians in America* (New York: PublicAffairs, 2001), 111.

159 peering through the windows: As reported in Frommer, 65.

159 packed with resort alums: Parish, 61. Note that the Tamiment was actually located in the Poconos, rather than the Catskills (Nachman, 113).

159 "Whereas it takes months": Cited in Parish, 64.

160 famed double-talk: See Sid Caesar, *Where Have I Been?: An Autobiography* (New York: Crown, 1982), 13, 18.

160 Hitler and Donald Duck: Caesar, 51.

160 Caesar's later parodies: In that sense, they also bear the DNA of numerous other Jewish talents who turn their hands to parodying the American media; perhaps most notably Jerry and David Zucker and Jim Abrahams, who directed *Airplane!* (1980) and *Top Secret!* (1984), as well as the

breakthrough *Kentucky Fried Movie* (1977), based on their sketch and comedy work.

160 **"We were a bunch":** Cited in Nachman, 108.

160 **"The German General":** "The German General," *Caesar's Hour* (New York: NBC, Sept. 26, 1954), https://www.youtube.com/watch?v=5m6Czgl1acU.

160 **A Japanese film parody:** See Romeyn and Kugelmass, 60.

160 **herring for breakfast:** Caesar, 114.

161 **"Nonentities in the News":** Parish, 65.

161 **in various iterations:** See, among other accounts, Allen, *Funny People*, 54–55 and Lear, 162.

161 **contemporary reports:** See Mark Cohen, "Sadie," 55n21.

162 **"That they traveled":** Woody Allen, *Standup Comic* (1979, recorded 1964–1968).

162 **equation of Jewishness and parody:** It's not the only arrow in his parodic quiver—the bravura routine "Kidnapped," for example, which ends as an extended aria taking off on the final hostage scenes from a dozen mob movies, where the interchange between police and hostage-takers turns into verbal absurdity worthy of the Marx Brothers—but he returns to that well, over and over.

162 *tummler*: See Romeyn and Kugelmass, 58. Brooks quoted in Sanford Pinsker, "The Instruments of American-Jewish Humor," *The Massachusetts Review* 22:4 (1981), 739–750, 743.

162 **dressed up in a suit:** See Maurice Yacowar, *Method in Madness: The Comic Art of Mel Brooks* (New York: St. Martin's Press, 1981), 14.

163 **"push[ed] his way":** Caesar quoted in Parish, 70. The Caesar/Brooks relationship has been endlessly discussed and presented and represented; see Parish, 62–63; 76–77 gives a full account of the iconic scene where Caesar, exasperated by Brooks to his wit's end, dangled him by his legs out of an eighteenth story window of Chicago's Drake Hotel. (Caesar, in his autobiography, relates his behavior to his alcoholism; see Caesar, 118.)

163 **"I never leave show business":** Cited in Parish, 141.

163 **the "let's put on a show":** Sanford Pinsker strikes a similar note in "Mel Brooks and the Cinema of Exhaustion," in *From Hester Street*, 245–256, 246.

164 **Renata Adler:** "Screen: The Producers at Fine Arts," *New York Times*, Mar. 19, 1968; "Anyone for a Good Cry?" *New York Times*, Mar. 31, 1968.

164 **Pauline Kael:** Cited in Parish, 181–182; See James D. Bloom, *Gravity Fails: The Comic Jewish Shaping of Modern America* (Westport, CT: Praeger, 2003), 121.

164   **the new, edgy comedy:** Holocaust and Holocaust comedy being the apotheosis of this; see Gilman, "Is Life Beautiful?," *passim*.

164   **When Brooks started pitching it:** Parish, 173.

165   **licensed to laugh:** Wisse makes a similar point in *No Joke*, 181.

166   **"Had there been black people":** Quoted in David Gillota, *Ethnic Humor in Multiethnic America* (New Brunswick, NJ: Rutgers University Press, 2013), 57.

166   **going around in blackface:** Gillota, 57.

167   **Godwin's Law:** Mike Godwin, "Meme, Counter-Meme," *Wired*, Oct. 1, 1994.

167   **"There's a weekend in Poland":** Quoted from Eyal Zandberg, "Critical Laughter: Humor, Popular Culture, and Israeli Holocaust Commemoration," *Media, Culture, and Society* 28:4 (2006), 561–579, 572.

168   *Difficult People*: http://www.slate.com/blogs/browbeat/2015/08/27/ difficult_people_reviewed_the_show_may_not_be_great_but_its_ jewish_jokes.html.

168   **"Historically Accurate Disney Princess":** https://www.youtube.com/ watch?v=g5wFS6Gnkk4.

168   **shows how blurred:** http://www.tabletmag.com/jewish-arts-and-culture/ 178143/rachel-bloom.

170   **Howard Stern was your man:** Compare Hoberman and Shandler, 201–202. In 1998 Stern, who'd previously called himself a half-Jew, announced he was all Jewish.

170   **the role of the ethical:** See Berys Gaut, "Just Joking: The Ethics and Aesthetics of Humor," *Philosophy and Literature* 22:1 (1998), 51–68, 67; J. P. Steed, "'Can Death Be Funny?': Humor, the Holocaust, and Bellow's The Bellarosa Connection," *Saul Bellow Journal* 19:1 (2003), 30–44, 34.

171   **the documentary:** *The Aristocrats* (2005), dirs. Penn Jillette and Paul Provenza.

5. The Divine Comedy

173   **The holiday of Purim:** The exact interrelationship between the holiday and the book which provides its backstory is not our purview here; for more, see Kovelman, 90–91, and Sandra Beth Berg, *The Book of Esther* (Ann Arbor MI: Scholars Press, 1979), 3–4.

174   **God goes unmentioned:** On this, see, as one of many, Michael V. Fox, "The Religion of the Book of Esther," *Judaism* 39:2 (1990), 135–147.

174   **a laugh of irony:** See Exum and Whedbee, 123–124.

175   *Incongruity theories*: See Arthur Schopenhauer, *The World as Will and Idea*, trans. R. B. Haldane (London: Kegan Paul, 1907), Book 1, section 13, p. 76, who writes that "the cause of laughter in every case is simply the sudden perception of the incongruity between a concept and the real objects which have been thought through it in some relation and laughter itself is just the expression of this incongruity." Earlier philosophical efforts in this vein come from Kant ("Laughter is an affectation arising from the sudden transformation of a strained expectation into nothing"), and Francis Hutcheson (that "which seems generally the cause of laughter is the bringing together of images which have contrary additional ideas"; *Reflections on Laughter*, 1750). On this progression, see John Morreall, *Taking Laughter Seriously* (Albany, NY: SUNY Press, 1983), esp. 15–19.

175   **Isaac becomes a living example**: Isaac also, to some critics, becomes an exemplum of humor himself: see Joel S. Kaminsky, "Humor and the Theology of Hope: Isaac as A Humorous Figure," *Interpretation* 54:4 (2000), 363–375.

175   **a kind of structural irony**: For comments on how this sensibility plays out throughout the entire book of Genesis, see Good, *Irony*, 81–114.

176   **"Laughter is madness"**: Ecclesiastes 2:2, 7:6, 7:3.

176   **life is Not Funny**: Compare Friedman, "Humor in the Hebrew Bible," 266; Edward L. Greenstein, "Sages with a Sense of Humor: The Babylonian Dialogue between a Master and His Servant and the Book of Qohelet," in Richard J. Clifford, ed., *Wisdom Literature in Mesopotamia and Israel* (Atlanta, GA: Society of Biblical Literature, 2007), 55–65, 62, 64; and Etan Levine, "Qohelet's Fool: A Composite Portrait," in Radday and Brenner, 278–294.

176   **"No doubt you are perfect men"**: Job 12:2–3. Compare James William Whedbee, "The Comedy of Job," *Semeia* 7 (1977): 1–39, *passim*; Brenner, "Semantic," 41n9; Good, *Irony*, 214–215.

177   **Sisera's mother**: See Judges 5:28–30. On irony in the book of Judges more generally, see Lillian Klein, "Irony in the Book of Judges," in Athalya Brenner and Frank H. Polak, *Words, Ideas, Worlds: Biblical Essays in Honor of Yaira Amit* (Sheffield, UK: Sheffield Phoenix Press: 2012), 133–144.

178   **"could have interpreted only"**: See Radday, "Names," 61–63, quote 61, and Radday, "Esther with Humour," in Radday and Brenner, 295–313, 296. This wasn't only a biblical approach: as far back the fourth century, the Roman aesthetician Donatus suggested that "names should fit." See Levin, 73.

178 the root-and-variation structure: See Ernst Simon, "Notes on Jewish Wit," *Jewish Frontier* 15 (1948), 42–48.

178 "measure for measure": See Marcus, 16.

178 even more explicit: For more traditional interpretations in this vein, see Reines, "Laughter," 179.

178 All this was fine: Compare John Morreall, "Sarcasm, Irony, Wordplay and Humor in the Bible: A Response to Hershey Friedman," *Humor* 14:3 (2001), 293–301, 300–301.

180 "Jerusalem sinned": Lamentations 1:8. On how terrible a fate the idea of being a laughingstock and a byword is in the Bible, see Psalms 44:14–15, and compare Jemielity, 26.

180 "Will anyone think": Cited in Wisse, *No Joke*, 105.

180 placing God back into the narrative: For a contemporary examination of this approach, see Gordon H. Johnston, "A Funny Thing Happened on the Way to the Gallows!: Irony, Humor, and Other Literary Features of the Book of Esther," in David M. Howard Jr and Michael A. Grisanti, eds., *Giving the Sense: Understanding and Using Old Testament Historical Texts* (Grand Rapids, MI: Kregel, 2003), 380–406, 392–395; compare Walfish, 74–94.

180 sending the angel Gabriel: See BT Megila 16a and Bickerman, 183.

180 "He who sits": Psalms 2:4.

181 "But as for You": Psalms 59:9.

181 "the Lord laughs": Psalms 37:13.

181 "since the day": BT Avoda Zara 3b; see also Kovelman, 87.

181 "mouth will be full": Psalms 126:2; compare Reines, *passim.*

181 was to be discouraged: See BT Berakhot 31a for one example; for various positions, including the question of "excessive laughter," see for discussion Feldman, "Lomdus," 414–415.

181 recast a rare positive comment: BT Shabbat 30b; see also Craven, 71.

182 "the oven of Akhnai": BT Bava Metzia 59b.

182 follow the majority: Exodus 23:2.

183 *venahafoch hu*: Esther 9:1. On the structures of reversal in the book of Esther, see Johnston, "Gallows," esp. 389–390; and Berg, 104–113.

183 "a serious and good": Norman Malcolm, *Ludwig Wittgenstein: A Memoir* (London: Oxford University Press, 1966), 29.

183 "One should strengthen": Cited in Feldman, "Lomdus," 410.

184 "This sharp irony": Cited in Feldman, "Lomdus," 409. The verse is Exodus 14:11.

184 A man went to his tailor: A version of this joke can be found in Spalding, 14–15. Or the complaining man who, when told by his rabbi that God

would provide, responds: "Oh, I know, I know; I just wish He would provide until He provides." From Pollack, 33.

185 **The Hasidic rebbe:** A version of this appears in Spalding, 90.

186 **a tailor tells the rebbe:** One version appears in Ausubel, *Folklore*, 160–161.

186 **"It grieved me":** Sholem Aleichem, *Tevye the Dairyman and the Railroad Stories* (New York: Schocken, 1987), 81.

187 **"What does it say":** Tevye, 5.

187 **"Mrs. Cohen arrives":** See version in Spalding, 160–161. Or, in the song of the great Yiddish singer and performer Aaron Lebedev in the show *Der litvisher yankee*, "I spared no effort to get to America/ Thinking I'd become a rabbi and grow a beard./ I had a beautiful pair of peyes, like every observant Jew,/ Now, instead of the beard, I've lost the peyes, too!/ Now, you may ask me, what's it all about and how can it be?/ The answer, my friends, is this;/ What can you do? It's America!/ That's how people look here./ What can you do? It's America!/ Here the Jews look just like goyim!" Cited in Roskies, "Ideologies," 164.

189 **"I, a demon":** Isaac Bashevis Singer, "The Last Demon," in *Collected Stories* (New York: Farrar, Straus and Giroux, 1983), 179–187, 179. Compare discussion in Robert Alter, "Jewish Humor and the Domestication of Myth," in *Jewish Wry*, 25–36, 26–27, 30–31.

190 **"I would call the attitudes":** Bellow, "Introduction," 12.

191 **Herzog:** Saul Bellow, *Herzog* (New York: Viking Press, 1964); *Mr. Sammler's Planet* (New York: Viking Press, 1970)

191 **"an existing humorist":** Søren Kierkegaard, *Concluding Unscientific Postscript to the Philosophical Crumbs* (Cambridge, UK: Cambridge University Press, 2009), 375.

191 **Bernard Malamud:** See S. Lillian Kremer, "Mentoring American Jews in Fiction by Bernard Malamud and Philip Roth," *Philip Roth Studies* 4:1 (2008), 5–18, esp. 5–8.

191 **largely overlooked novel:** *On God's Grace*, not set in America, see now Estelle Gershgoren Novak and Maximillian E. Novak, "Bernard Malamud's God's Grace as Ironic Robinsonade, Ironic Akedah," *Prooftexts* 34:2 (2014), 147–169.

191 **Malamud's protagonists:** On the ironic, dark, and twisted endings of Malamud's tales in this respect, see Sanford E. Marovitz, "Malamud's Early Stories: In and Out of Time, 1940–1960, with Humor, History, and Hawthorne," *Studies in American Jewish Literature* 29 (2010): 114–122, 114–115.

191 **Stanley Elkin's kibitzers:** *Criers and Kibitzers, Kibitzers and Criers*

(New York: Random House, 1966); *The Living End* (New York: Dutton, 1979); *The Rabbi of Lud* (New York: Scribner, 1987). See, on Elkin, Maurice Charney, "Stanley Elkin and Jewish Black Humor," in *Jewish Wry*, 178–195; and Daniel Green, "The Rabbi as Vaudevillian: Stanley Elkin's Comic Rhetoric," *Contemporary Literature* 34:1 (1993), 88–102.

192 **"Doctor Spielvogel":** Philip Roth, *Portnoy's Complaint* (New York: Random House, 1969), 36–37.

192 **great comic cosmic writer:** On Roth's comic vision more broadly, see Lawrence E. Mintz, "Devil and Angel: Philip Roth's Humor," *Studies in American Jewish Literature* 8:2 (1989), 154–167.

192 **"a Jewish nightclub and vaudeville comic":** Philip Roth, *Reading Myself and Others* (New York: Penguin, 1985), 80.

193 ***Goodbye, Columbus*'s title novella:** Philip Roth, *Goodbye, Columbus* (New York: Houghton Mifflin, 1959).

193 **young Roth's bridling:** See Roth, "Writing About Jews," *Commentary* 36:3 (December 1963), 446–452.

195 **wrongness and wrongness:** Evoking Roth's famous line in *American Pastoral* that "the fact remains that getting people right is not what living is all about anyway. It's getting them wrong that is living, getting them wrong and wrong and wrong and then, on careful reconsideration, getting them wrong again." Philip Roth, *American Pastoral* (New York: Houghton Mifflin, 1997), 35.

196 **the comic side:** Although not only on the comic side: there's something akin to this when we look at the arrival of the unearthed but long-buried African American identity of Coleman Silk in *The Human Stain*, or even the anti-Semitism of a Lindbergh-influenced alternate world America in *The Plot Against America*.

196 ***Operation Shylock*:** Philip Roth, *Operation Shylock* (New York: Simon & Schuster, 1993); *The Great American Novel* (New York: Holt, Rinehart & Winston, 1973); *The Breast* (New York: Houghton Mifflin, 1972).

196 **"Virtuous reader":** Philip Roth, *The Ghost Writer* (New York: Farrar, Straus and Giroux, 1979), 112.

197 **" 'Only in your imagination' ":** *Portnoy's Complaint*, 212.

197 ***Sabbath's Theater*:** Philip Roth, *Sabbath's Theater* (New York: Houghton Mifflin, 1995); Tony Kushner, *Angels in America: A Gay Fantasia on National Themes* (New York: Theatre Communcations Group, 1993).

197 **domesticated:** The last term is Alter's; see Alter, "Jewish Humor," *passim*.

198 **Mordechai Schmutter:** Mordechai Schmutter, *A Clever Title Goes Here* (Lakewood, NJ: Israel Bookshop Publications, 2009).

199 **Robert Smigel:** Sacks, *Kicker*, 249.

199 **reappearing:** Zoglin, 70–71. In that same routine: "And the Gentiles, as is their wont from time to time, threw the Jew overboard." Quoted in *Haunted Smile*, 226.

199 **Shalom Auslander:** *Foreskin's Lament: A Memoir* (New York: Riverhead, 2007); *Hope: A Tragedy* (New York: Riverhead, 2012). This could be compared to the kind of quotidian comic metaphysics of the Israeli writer Etgar Keret (see, for example, *The Bus Driver Who Wanted to Be God* [New York: Thomas Dunne/St. Martin's Press, 2001]), in a manner which might suggest some hints about how Jewish theology manifests in a thoroughly Jewish and secular society.

200 **"What did Jesus Christ say":** *Hope: A Tragedy*, 40–41.

6. The Tale of the Folk

202 **the comedy turns from satire:** On irony more generally in Esther, see Stan Goldman, "Narrative and Ethical Ironies in Esther," *JSOT* 47 (1990): 15–31.

203 **Abraham actually laughs:** A technical note: some of the story's complexity in this regard seems to stem from its composition as a combination of two different texts from two different biblical authors.

203 **There's Miriam:** Numbers 12; Judges 16; the Book of Judith. On Judith, see Craven, 74–75.

204 **Michal:** 2 Sam 6.20–22; See Brenner, "Semantic," 43.

204 **"It is better":** Proverbs 21:19; 25:23.

204 **"Let not the testimony":** Antiquities 4.219; cited in Athalya Brenner, "Are We Amused?: Small and Big Differences in Josephus' Re-Presentations of Biblical Female Figures in the Jewish Antiquities 1–8," in *Are We Amused?*, 90–106, 91.

204 **presented an image:** See Brenner, "Are We Amused?," 98–99. Brenner intriguingly suggests this position is related to Josephus's family life (104), but acknowledges this is unprovable.

204 **chases after Joseph:** Genesis 39:12, 14, 15, 18. Eunuch: Saris, 39:1; Compare Yehuda T. Radday, "Sex and Women in Biblical Narrative Humor," *Humor* 8:4 (1995), 363–384, 374–375. See also BT Megila 11b.

205 **empowered women:** For a slightly alternative view, see F. Scott Spencer, "Those Riotous—Yet Righteous—Foremothers of Jesus: Exploring Matthew's Comic Genealogy," in *Are We Amused?*, 7–30. On Tamar's activity, see Mary E. Shields, " 'More Righteous Than I': The Comeuppance of the Trickster in Genesis 38," *Are We Amused?*, 31–51.

205 First Esdras: See 1 Esdras 3.5–4.41 and Craven 69–70.

205 "Ten *kabs*": Cited in Heller, 111.

205 "Take heed": Joseph Ben Meir Zabara, *The Book of Delight* (New York: Columbia University Press, 1960), 57.

206 "Of Seven Maidens": Judah Alharizi, *The Book of Takhkemoni* (Oxford, UK: Littman, 2001), 195–200.

206 a remarkable facility: This last phrase is Raymond Scheindlin's; see his introduction to his translation in David Stern, ed., *Rabbinic Fantasies: Imaginative Narratives From Classical Hebrew Literature* (New Haven, CT: Yale University Press, 1990), 269–294, 271.

206 portraits remain remarkably similar: And there are many examples in Ashkenazic and Sephardic folktales: see, for example, Reginetta Haboucha, "Brides and Grooms: A Judeo-Spanish Version of Well-Known Literary Parallels," *Shofar* 11:4 (1993), 1–17.

206 "Epitaph": See J. Chotzner, *Hebrew Satire* (London: Kegan Paul, 1911), 23–26. Quatrain from Yeiteles (1763–1813), 161.

206 "*Eshes chayil*": Marion Aptroot, "Western Yiddish 'Yontev-Bletlekh': Facing Modernity With Humor," *Jewish Studies Quarterly* 15:1 (2008), 47–67, 56, 58–59.

207 A joke book: See Holt, 8–11.

207 Freud was a great lover of jokes: See Sigmund Freud, *Jokes and Their Relation to the Unconscious* (London: Hogarth Press, 1905); and Elliott Oring, *The Jokes of Sigmund Freud: A Study in Humor and Jewish Identity* (Philadelphia: University of Pennsylvania Press, 1984), 2–3.

207 "Anti-rites": See Mary Douglas, "The Social Control of Cognition: Some Factors in Joke Perception," *Man* 3:3 (1968), 361–370; Critchley, 4–5; Berger, *Genius*, 26–27.

207 "infinite aggressions": See Holt, 35.

208 "I do not know": Freud, *Jokes*, 112.

208 developed an entire theory: See Reik, *passim*, esp. 41, 218–220, 226, and Martin Grotjahn, "Jewish Jokes and Their Relation to Masochism," in Werner M. Mendel, *A Celebration of Laughter* (Los Angeles: Mara Books, 1970), 135–137.

208 Jewish jokes were based: Compare Wisse, *No Joke*, esp. 10, 33.

208 some of these claims: This was seen in works like Siegfried Kadner's *Race and Humor* (1930, reprinted 1936, 1939) and J. Keller and Hanns Andersen's *The Jew As Criminal* (1937), which suggested that Jewish murderers were protected and camouflaged by their ability to provoke laughter! See Mel Gordon, "Nazi 'Proof' That Jews Possessed the Worst

Humor in the World," *Israeli Journal of Humor Research* 1:2 (2012), 97–100.

208 "the Jewish joke, however": Grotjahn, 139. Also, not all of the jokes these individuals analyze live up to their masochistic billing. On this, see Christie Davies, *The Mirth of Nations* (New Brunswick, NJ: Transaction Publishers, 2002), 53–67.

208 better taken as part of the whole: For a fuller assault on this hypothesis, see Dan Ben-Amos, "The 'Myth' of Jewish Humor," *Western Folklore* 32:2 (1973), 112–131.

209 "You tell a joke": Immanuel Olsvanger, *Royte Pomerantsn: Jewish Folk Humor* (New York: Schocken Books, 1947), 3. This translation from Irving Howe, "The Nature of Jewish Laughter," in *Jewish Wry* 16–24, 16–17.

211 the rabbi who goes to play golf: Adapted from Pollack, 124–125.

211 "A rabbi, having asked for advice": Adapted from Ausubel, 72.

211 witty sense of self-consciousness: Compare Cray, esp. 338.

212 "Keep your distance": Exodus 23:7. The story is ascribed to the Vilna Gaon in Ausubel, *Folklore*, 358.

212 "Tit for Tat": Alfred Kazin, ed., *Selected Stories of Sholem Aleichem* (New York: Modern Library, 1956), 212–228.

212 the story of the schnorrer: Cited (slightly differently) in *God Laughed*, 26.

212 the one Freud references: See Freud, *Jokes*, 55–56 (although it's told differently there, with a bathing-spa, the thrust is the same).

212 Or the one in which the shnorrer": Spalding, 30–31.

213 "the technical name": Quoted in Nahshon, *Zangwill*, 389.

213 if not dignity: Compare Howe, "Nature," 23.

213 other famously witty schnorrers: See Wisse, *No Joke*, 77–79. There's a similar trickster figure in Sephardic literature, Djuha; see Tamar Alexander, "'The Wealthy Senor Miguel': A Study of a Sephardic Novella," in William Cutter and David C. Jacobson, eds., *History and Literature: New Readings of Jewish Texts in Honor of Arnold J. Band* (Providence RI: Brown University Press, 2002), 189, 192.

213 to be immortalized by Isaac Babel: In the 1918 story "Shabbes nakhamu," itself based on another joke, one a little too complicated to be rendered here.

213 "Hershele visited an inn": A slightly different version appears in Learsi, 165.

213 "That which God hath not given him": Cowan, 12.

214 One of Jewish literature's most famous *luftmenshen*: On an earlier figure,

Osip Rabinovich, and his 1860 "Story of How Reb Khaim-Shulim Feige Traveled From Kishinev to Odessa and What Happened to Him," see Tanny, *City*, 39–45; Rabinovich puts this material into Russian really for the first time.

214 **"As you see me"**: Der Tunkeler, "From What a Litvak Makes a Living," in Ausubel, *Treasury*, 20–24, 24.

215 **Abraham ibn Ezra**: See discussion in Chotzner, *Humour*, 61; one translation of the plaint appears in Ausubel, *Humor*, 448.

215 **"short, stocky"**: http://www.seinfeldscripts.com/TheAndreaDoria.htm, aired Dec. 19, 1996.

215 **In an earlier episode**: "The Beard," aired Feb. 9, 1995.

216 **"forebear . . . of the race"**: See Heine, *Jewish Melodies*, 127–128.

216 **unlike in that mythic first case**: There is also a textured portrait of Jewish foolishness in Heine's "The Rabbi of Bacherach"; see Heine, *Jewish Melodies*, 50–57, especially Jäkel's comment that "a man is often celebrated far and wide for being a bigger fool than he has any idea of" (57).

216 **Ruth Wisse**: Ruth Wisse, *The Schlemiel as Modern Hero* (Chicago: University of Chicago Press, 1971). For more on the schlemiel's etymology, see 13–14.

216 **"Gimpel the Fool"**: "Gimpel the Fool," in Singer, *Collected Stories*, 3–14.

217 **one wry anecdote**: Genesis Rabbah 68:4.

217 **A notable subgroup**: For a joke version of this, see S. Felix Mendelsohn, *Let Laughter Ring* (Philadelphia: Jewish Publication Society, 1941), 20–21.

217 **One of the most famous examples**: Adapted from Freud, *Jokes*, 61.

218 **other types of clowns**: See E. Lifschutz, "Merrymakers and Jesters Among Jews," *YIVO Annual* 7 (1952): 43–83; Efron "Dzigan" 58; and Ziva Ben-Porat, "Ideology, Genre, and Serious Parody," in *Proceedings of the Ninth International Congress of the ICLA* (New York, 1982), 380–387.

218 **the *badkhn***: Ariela Krasney, "The Badkhn: From Wedding Stage to Writing Desk," *Polin* 16 (2003): 7–28.

218 **"Jewish jokes in print"**: Reik, 33–34.

219 **entrance into womanhood**: Although legally girls assumed legal adulthood at the age of twelve, the bat mitzvah as a ceremony of rite of passage is a product of the American twentieth century.

219 **Council of Four Lands**: *God Laughed*, 23.

220 **In Eastern Europe**: See Efron, "Dzigan," *passim*, esp. 65n45.

220 **one fateful interwar routine**: See Hans-Peter Bayerdörfer, "Jewish Cabaret Artists Before 1933," in Jeanette R. Malkin and Freddie Rokem, eds.,

Jews and the Making of Modern German Theatre (Iowa City: University of Iowa Press, 2010), 132–150, 132–133, 140–141.

221 **"A devout *litvak*"**: Cited in *God Laughed*, 22.

221 **"From my wife"**: Quoted in Romeyn and Kugelmass, 23–24.

222 **one of the first paperback books**: Kenneth C. Davis, *Two-Bit Culture: The Paperbacking of America* (Boston: Houghton Mifflin, 1984), 73. Rosten based the stories on his experience teaching a night class in English to immigrants in Chicago in 1931. He wrote them while finishing a Ph.D. in political science at the University of Chicago, using the Ross pseudonym because he didn't want people to know about his non-academic work. The stories were first published in *The New Yorker* in 1935 and published in book form in 1937. See Dan Shiffman, "The Comedy of Assimilation in Leo Rosten's Hyman Kaplan Stories," *Studies in American Humor* 3:7 (2), 49–58, 56; Dan Shiffman, "The Ingratiating Humor of Leo Rosten's Hyman Kaplan Stories," *Studies in American Jewish Literature* 18 (1999): 93–101, 96; Simon J. Bronner, "Structural and Stylistic Relations of Oral and Literary Humor: An Analysis of Leo Rosten's H*Y*M*A*N K*A*P*L*A*N Stories," *Journal of the Folklore Institute* 19:1 (1982), 31–45.

223 *Hebrew Jokes and Dialect Humor*: Philadelphia: Royal, 1902.

223 **"a literal translation"**: Quoted in Craig Yoe, ed., *The Complete Milt Gross Comic Books and Life Story* (San Diego, CA: IDW, 2009), 11.

223 **"However we may chuckle"**: In her Der Tog column of July 11, 1926: Cited in Ari Y. Kelman, "Introduction: GEEVE A LISTEN!" in Kelman, ed., *Is Diss A System?: A Milt Gross Comic Reader* (New York: NYU Press, 2010), 1–56, 24. The whole essay is crucial.

223 **"If this promotes anti-Semitism"**: Yoe, 14.

223 **"De Night"**: Originally published in the *New York World*, Dec. 19, 1926; reprinted in *System*, 165–186. Quote from 171.

224 **"his striped trousers"**: See Joseph Boskin and Joseph Dorinson, "Ethnic Humor: Subversion and Survival," *American Quarterly* 37:1 (1985), 81–97, 88.

224 **The vaudeville stage**: On the "Hebrew comic" which became popular in the 1870s and lasted through English and American vaudeville, see Nahshon, 49–50.

224 **Some of this Yiddishization**: Henry Popkin, "The Vanishing Jew of Our Popular Culture," *Commentary* 14 (July 1952): 46–55, 48.

224 **"when they needed a big laugh"**: Cited in Romeyn and Kugelmass, 30. See also Michael W. Rubinoff, "Nuances and Subtleties in Jewish Film Humor," in *Jews and Humor*, 121–136, 122.

224 "double Hebe": Mintz, 22.

224 "A black and white vest": Cited in Harap, 29.

224 wide range of Jewish stereotypes: Lawrence E. Mintz, "Humor and Ethnic Stereotypes in Vaudeville and Burlesque," *MELUS* 21:4 (1996), 19–28, 21.

225 "with the saddest look": Joe Laurie, Jr., *Vaudeville: From the Honky-Tonks to the Palace* (New York: Henry Holt, 1953), 176. His brother, Ben, would take the opposite tack, presenting "a lively, cheerful, wise-cracking Jew, in contrast to his brother Joe's sad Jew" (179).

225 "The other day my friend Rosenski": From monologue "Troubles" in *New Hebrew Jokes and Monologues, by the Best Jokers* (Baltimore, MD: L & M Ottenheimer, 1905), 7–11, 11.

225 "I want you should send down": Quoted in Michael G. Corenthal, *Cohen on the Telephone: A History of Jewish Recorded Humor and Popular Music, 1892–1942* (Milwaukee, WI: Yesterday's Memories, 1984), 54–55; Columbia Records A2192.

225 Sometimes even non-Jews: John E. DiMeglio, *Vaudeville USA* (Bowling Green, KY: Bowling Green University Popular Press, 1973), 41.

225 "Oh, my name is Solomon Moses": Cited in Gary Giddins, "This Guy Wouldn't Give You the Parsley Off His Fish," *Grand Street* 5:2 (1986), 202–217, 211; see also Hoberman and Shandler, 40.

226 Performances like these: DiMeglio, 42.

226 including many names: See Jay, "Nathanael," 10; Laurie, Jr., 178, 180; and *Haunted Smile*, 33.

226 Potash and Perlmutter: See Harap, 30, and Romeyn and Kugelmass, 35.

226 Al Jolson: Romeyn and Kugelmass, 40.

226 Eddie Cantor: Hoberman and Shandler, 156–157.

226 One program: See Mark Sloban and H. I. Minikes, "From Vilna to Vaudeville: Minikes and 'Among the Indians' (1895)," *The Drama Review* 24:3 (1980), 17–26. Minikes is the author of the playlet.

226 Barton Brothers: See Irv Saposnik, " 'Joe and Paul' and Other Yiddish-American Varieties," *Judaism* 49:4 (2000), 437–448, who mentions others like Eli Basse, Benny Bell, Lee Tully, and Billy Hodes, who "created comic sketches of Yiddish–American life: the oxymoron of a glaitzyner rhumba" (439–440).

226 YidLife Crisis: www.yidlifecrisis.com.

227 "An old Jewish man": Versions in Brandes, 235, and Berger, 88.

227 A 1950 survey: See Brandes, 234.

227 a bit about *chazzerai*: Levenson, 17. Portnoy (*Portnoy*, 111–112)

name-checks a number of "old-school" Jewish comedians of this type (Levenson, Myron Cohen, Henny Youngman, Milton Berle), suggesting that the classic Jewish stereotypes they employ in their rapid-fire routines—particularly, as far as Portnoy's concerned, the nice Jewish boy—pay no attention to the genuine pain that lay behind the stereotype.

227 "The Dialect Comedian": *Commentary* 13 (1952): 168–170.

227 "There's no bigger schmuck": Cited in Berger, *Jewish Jesters*, 119, 124. See also Jackie Mason, *How To Talk Jewish* (New York: St. Martin's Press, 1990), 1–8.

228 "I never forgot": Qtd Parish, 115.

228 "If you're dying": Compare *Haunted Smile*, 165; quote Nachman, 27.

228 Freddy Roman: Nee Kirschenbaum, whose uncle and grandfather owned the Borscht Belt hotel the Crystal Spring. Wisse, *No Joke*, 122.

228 the stand-up comic voice: And on some occasions, like in Danny Thomas's case, the Jewish dialect comedians weren't even Jewish. (Norman Lear's breakthrough in show business was writing him a Yiddish joke.) See Allen, *Funny People*, 53, and Lear, 118.

229 "one of the great, great clowns": See Joyce Antler, "One Clove Away from a Pomander Ball: The Subversive Tradition of Jewish Female Comedians," in *Jews and Humor*, 155–174, 159–160, quote 159.

229 her range of Jewish characters: Eddie Cantor, who should know, wrote: "All the persecution of a race was in her heart and in her throat; when she poured out a ballad you cried." Cantor, 43.

229 "My best audiences": Cited in Romeyn and Kugelmass, 42–43.

230 "I've put a little more meat on": Cited in Sarah Blacher Cohen, "The Unkosher Comediennes: From Sophie Tucker to Joan Rivers," in *Jewish Wry*, 105–124, 107.

230 seven-figure sales: "Empty album jackets [because people stole them] forced customers to ask clerks for the actual record, sotto voce, as if purchasing condoms." Nachman, 213.

230 Barth's cheerful scatology: On this, see Cohen, "Unkosher," 111.

230 "Madame": Del Negro, 141–143. Another honorary member of this group, Rusty Warren (nee Eileen Goldman), was breast-obsessed (she closed her act with "Mammaries" to the tune of "Memories," for example), but didn't do anything Jewish in her act. Barth called her a "Jewish shiksa." See also Nachman, 213–214.

231 her classic joke: Del Negro, 144–145.

231 "I'm so tired": Cited in Cohen, "Unkosher," 113.

232 "And when I came": Quoted in Reik, 83.

232 **Irving Howe:** Irving Howe, *World of Our Fathers* (New York: Simon & Schuster, 1976), 177; Alfred Kazin, *A Walker in the City* (New York: Harcourt, 1951), 32.

232 **constituted a kind of epic portrait:** Compare discussion in Joyce Antler, *You Never Call! You Never Write!: A History of the Jewish Mother* (New York: Oxford University Press, 2007), *passim*, esp. 8, 15–17, 102, 107. There's something interesting to be said about the prevalence of strong personality mothers among American Jewish comedians; see *Haunted Smile*, 18.

233 **"He can walk":** Adapted from version in Alan Dundes, "JAP and JAM in American Folklore," *Journal of American Folklore* 98:390 (1985) 456–475, 457–458.

233 **"Mother and Son":** Nichols remarked that he and May had the same, extremely difficult Jewish mother, and finding them funny was the beginning of a kind of self-liberation. See Nachman, 326.

233 **a drop in the maternal Jewish bucket:** Romeyn and Kugelmass, 74–75.

233 *A Mother's Kisses*: Bruce Jay Friedman, *A Mother's Kisses* (New York: Simon & Schuster, 1964); compare Antler, 135–138.

234 **as one critic put it:** Owen Gleiberman, "Mother," *Entertainment Weekly*, Jan. 17, 1997. Note that Brooks himself actually has a non-Jewish mother.

234 **The difference between Jewish and Italian mothers:** Dundes, *JAP*, 458.

234 **"A Jewish mother buys":** Cited in Berger, 75.

234 **Larry David's mother:** Benjamin Wallace, "Why Larry David the Schmuck Was the Best Thing to Happen to Larry David the Mensch," *New York*, Jan. 26, 2015; Philip Galanes, "Norman Lear and Seth MacFarlane and Their TV Families," *New York Times*, June 26, 2015; Lear, 3.

235 **"Solly, by you you're a captain":** Joke can be found in Novak and Waldoks, 274.

235 **"What is Jewish foreplay?":** Telushkin, *Jewish Humor*, 93.

235 **"Why do JAPs like:** Dundes, *JAP*, 464, 462.

235 **American Jewish matriarch:** Telushkin, *Jewish Humor*, 72.

235 **"this Jewish girl":** Antler, 165.

235 **known for her character:** See, on this and more generally, Riv-Ellen Prell, "Why Jewish Princesses Don't Sweat: Desire and Consumption in Postwar American Culture," in Howard Eilberg-Schwartz, ed., *People of the Body* (New York: SUNY Press, 1992), 329–359, esp. 336–337.

235 **as at least one critic:** Dundes, *JAP*, 469–470.

235 **the titular *Funny Girl*:** See Henry Bial, *Acting Jewish: Negotiating Ethnicity on the American Stage & Screen* (Ann Arbor MI: University of Michigan, 2005), 87–88.

236 **Erica Jong:** Erica Jong, *Fear of Flying* (New York: Holt, Rinehart, and Winston, 1973); Martha A. Ravits, "The Jewish Mother: Comedy and Controversy in American Popular Culture," *MELUS* 25:1 (2000), 3–31, esp. 17; *Gravity Fails*, 84–85.

236 **where she presented the character:** The Sheffield family was based on Twiggy's family in London; see Fran Drescher, *Enter Whining* (New York: Regan Books, 1996), 123–124.

236 **"was offended by someone":** Cited in Romeyn and Kugelmass, 82.

236 **to be told at women:** For a survey of some of this humor that reaches similar conclusions, see Gary Spencer, "An Analysis of Some JAP-baiting Humor on the College Campus," *Humor* 2:4 (1989), 329–348.

237 **whose Second City flourished:** Zoglin, 65. Its predecessor, the Compass Players, had featured Barbara Harris, Alan Arkin, Shelley Berman, Mike Nichols, and Elaine May.

237 **Budd Friedman:** Zoglin, 78–88, 145, 202–205; Nachman, 15–16.

237 **Of the forty-three specials:** Zoglin, 182, 190, 192.

237 **Rita Rudner:** http://www.thejc.com/lifestyle/the-simon-round-interview/48785/interview-rita-rudner.

237 **Merrill Markoe:** See Sacks, *Kicker*, 73.

238 **Corey Kahaney:** Antler, 168–171.

238 **"JAP Rap Battle":** *Crazy Ex-Girlfriend*, "Josh and I Go to Los Angeles!," aired Feb. 29, 2016.

239 **no stranger:** Zoglin, 184–185.

239 **Heidi Abromowitz:** On Heidi, see *Gravity Fails*, 88.

240 **"personal truth":** Cited in Antler, 163–164.

7. Jewish Comedy—Hold the Jewishness

242 **a sense of threat:** See Green, "Power," 64.

244 ***An Eloquent Marriage Farce:*** *A Comedy of Betrothal*, translated by Alfred S. Golding (Ottawa, ON: Dovehouse Editions, 1988).

245 ***Bovo bukh:*** It's actually where the phrase *bubbe-mayse* comes from. But that's another story. Levita wrote the book in 1507–1508; first printing (of many) was in 1541.

246 **the Jewish recruit:** Ausubel, *Folklore*, 11.

246 **Otto Kahn:** Telushkin, *Jewish Humor*, 125; Reik, 90, identifies the hunchback as Wilder. Kahn is always identified as the subject of the joke, though he may not have actually converted.

246 **Freud:** Freud, *Jokes*, 80.

247 **as an excuse:** In Freud's telling of the joke, the first Jew is an *Ostjude*,

a Galician, which also makes this a complex example of the self-hatred we discussed in an earlier chapter. The fact that Freud was himself of Galician ancestry, though, makes this assignation increasingly complex. For a good discussion, see Oring, *Jokes*, 43–44, 48–49.

248 **In the culminating scene:** Avrom Goldfaden, "The Two Kuni-Lemls," in Berkowitz and Dauber, 201–245.

248 **vagabond stars:** For numerous other examples of Yiddish theatrical comedy, see Nahma Sandrow, *Vagabond Stars: A World History of Yiddish Theater* (New York: Harper and Row, 1977).

249 **"Blumfeld":** All stories can be found in Franz Kafka, *The Complete Stories* (New York: Schocken, 1984).

250 **Zionist journal:** Compare Wisse, *No Joke*, 53–54.

251 **"given his name":** Marcel Proust, *In Search of Lost Time: Vol. 3, The Guermantes Way* (London: Chatto & Windus, 1992), 282. See discussion in, most importantly, Sam W. Bloom, "Marcel Proust and the Comedy of Assimilation," in Bloom et al., *Forging Modern Jewish Identities: Public Faces and Private Struggles* (London: Vallentine Mitchell, 2003), 140–155, and Hollie Markland Harder, "Proust's Human Comedy," in Richard Bales, ed., *The Cambridge Companion to Proust* (Cambridge, UK: Cambridge University Press, 2001), 135–150.

253 **Henri Bergson:** Henri Bergson, *Laughter: An Essay on the Meaning of the Comic* (Rockville MD: Wildside Press, 2008), 18, 70–71.

253 **anti-Nazi film:** *You Nazty Spy* (1939); see *Haunted Smile*, 96 and Wex, 38. And Sales, perhaps, even less, with the possible exception of naming one of his characters, a mock detective, Philo Kvetch. See Soupy Sales, *Soupy Sez!: My Zany Life and Times* (New York: M. Evans and Co., 2001), 153–154.

253 **as Philip Roth suggested:** See Novak and Waldoks, 172.

254 **"Master Marx":** See Simon Louvish, *Monkey Business: The Lives and Legends of the Marx Brothers* (London: Faber and Faber, 1999), 48. See also 30, 87, 99, 161.

254 **"The audience":** Groucho Marx, *Groucho and Me* (New York: Random House, 1959), 225.

255 **that is, a Jew:** In the stage version, he'd been the even more ethnically clear "Rabbi Cantor." Louvish, 196.

255 **What are those names:** Compare *Jewish Jesters*, 33–34.

255 **they're also interested:** In a less famous example from 1937's *A Day at the Races*, Groucho, singing "My old Kentucky Home," says it's brought to you "by the house of David." See Rubinoff, 126.

255 "anointed him": Cited in Lester D. Friedman, *Hollywood's Image of the Jew* (New York: Frederick Ungar, 1982), 65.

256 "As soon as the Jews": Quoted in Neal Gabler, *An Empire of Their Own: How the Jews Invented Hollywood* (New York: Doubleday, 1988), 277.

256 trades on the popular impression: Discussed in Stephen J. Whitfield, "Towards an Appreciation of American Jewish Humor," *Journal of Modern Jewish Studies* 4:1 (2005), 33–48, 35–36.

256 "A man approaches Cohen": A version of this can be found in Corenthal, 3. On arson jokes and their relation to anti-Semitism, see Davies, *Ethnic Humor*, 118–121.

256 Cohen turns a client's coat: See *Entertaining America*, 32–33; Friedman, *Hollywood*, 21–22. For more on the Levi and Cohen films, from Edison and Biograph, see Patricia Erens, *The Jew in American Cinema* (Bloomington: Indiana University Press, 1984), 30–31.

256 Max Davidson: Discussion of Davidson taken from Kenneth Turan, *Not To Be Missed* (New York: PublicAffairs, 2014), 10–13, and Erens, 92–94. He'd also done shorts for Mutual in the previous decade, where he played a character named "Izzy" with "a propensity for trouble and ill-fated love affairs" (Erens, 33). Titles from this period include: *Foxy Izzy* (1911); *Such a Business* (1914); *Levitzky's Insurance Policy: Or, When Thief Meets Thief* (1908); *The Firebugs* (1913); *Levi's Luck* (1914), and my favorite title for a romantic comedy, *Cupid Puts One Over on the Shadchen* (1915: Vitagraph). Erens, 34–40.

257 George Jessel: Erens, 95; Romeyn and Kugelmass, 40, 49.

257 Carl Reiner's show: Vincent Brook, *Something Ain't Kosher Here: The Rise of the "Jewish" Sitcom* (New Brunswick, NJ: Rutgers University Press, 2003), 45; David Zurawik, *The Jews of Prime Time* (Hanover, NH: Brandeis University Press, 2003), 51–54; Friedman, *Hollywood*, 64–67. There was a remaining Jewish presence on the show: Buddy Sorrel, played by Morey Amsterdam. But the Jewish presence had moved from the center to the margin. Zurawik, 226, rehearses the oft-cited maxim: "Write Yiddish, cast British."

257 Jerry Lewis: Compare analysis in Epstein, 121–122, and Murray Pomerance, "Who Was Buddy Love? Screen Performance and Jewish Experience," in David Bernardi, Murray Pomerance, and Hava Tirosh-Samuelson, eds., *Hollywood's Chosen People: The Jewish Experience in American Cinema* (Detroit, MI: Wayne State University Press, 2013), 193–210, 207–210.

258 blackface: See Hoberman and Shandler, 93–99.

258 *Whoopee*: Mast, "Woody Allen," 129.

258 **even before Cantor**: Who started out with business cards printed "Eddie Cantor, Dialectician"; he did, among other acts, Italian, Dutch, and "a Hebrew comedian." Cantor, 63–65.

258 **along with 1909 and 1911 silent movies**: Friedman, *Hollywood*, 20.

258 **"The very notion"**: Leslie Fiedler, "Malamud's Travesty Western," *Novel* 10:3 (1977), 212–219, 217.

258 **on one 1949 show**: Weber, 135; Parish, 57.

259 **Libby Gelman-Waxner**: Libby Gelman-Waxner, *If You Ask Me* (New York: Ballantine Books, 1995).

259 **in Jimmy Kimmel's words**: http://www.hollywoodreporter.com/news/jimmy-kimmel-s-best-monologue-emmys-2016-host-jokes-930197.

259 **"the most Jewish show"**: Emily Nussbaum, "Open Secret," *The New Yorker*, Sept. 29, 2014, http://www.newyorker.com/magazine/2014/09/29/open-secret.

259 **articulates about Jewishness**: Compare Josh Lambert, "Pfefferman Family Matters," *Tablet*, Dec. 7, 2015, http://www.tabletmag.com/scroll/195620/pfefferman-family-matters.

259 **"comedy comes from the feeling"**: Parish, 3.

260 **by the 1940s**: See Berger, *Jewish Jesters*, 39.

260 **in 1943 NBC announced**: Giddins, 204.

260 **"the brainstorm"**: Giddins, 208.

260 **he never identified**: Although he once inserted a joke on his show in order to let his audience know he hadn't recorded the broadcast on Yom Kippur. See Milt Josefberg, *The Jack Benny Show* (New Rochelle, NY: Arlington House, 1977), 282.

260 **He had sidekicks**: See Irving A. Fein, *Jack Benny: An Intimate Biography* (New York: G. P. Putnam, 1976), 69–70, 101 on the "Jewish dialectician Sam Hearn" who played Shlepperman, among other characters, and Artie Auerback, who played Kitzle; see also Josefberg, 107–109, on the duo.

260 **schnook**: See Josefberg, 316–317. He was also referred to as a schlemiel on the show (by Ronald Colman, no less).

260 **"the minute I come on"**: Cited in Nicholas Mirzoeff, *Seinfeld* (London: BFI, 2007), 76. See also Romeyn and Kugelmass, 55.

260 **Gracie Allen**: Giddins, 205.

260 **In 1945**: Fein, 100.

261 **Some people thought**: Compare *Haunted Smile*, 47, 61, 64–65, and Josefberg, 107.

261 *Sergeant Bilko*: Technically, *Sergeant Bilko* was titled *You'll Never Get*

Rich or *The Phil Silvers Show*. On Hiken, see David Everitt, *King of the Half Hour: Nat Hiken and the Golden Age of TV Comedy* (Syracuse, NY: Syracuse University Press, 2001), 44–45, 98–123, 150–151, 169–171. See also Romeyn and Kugelmass, 20, and Gravity Fails, 29–30.

262 provide his own echo: Bruce, *Essential*, 72, 174–175.

262 "We were a big hit": Quoted in Nachman, 110.

262 American-born: Hoberman and Shandler, 114. On Goldberg, see also Antler, 47ff.

262 her ingenuity: Stephen J. Whitfield, "Gertrude Berg," Jack Fischel and Sanford Pinsker, cds., *Jewish-American History and Culture: An Encyclopedia* (New York: Garland Publishing, 1992), 59–60, 60.

263 blacklisted: For full account, see Zurawik, 38–45.

263 doubling down: See Bial, 41–43; Zurawik, 24.

263 "You see, darling": Morris Freedman, "From the American Scene: The Real Molly Goldberg," *Commentary* 21 (1956): 359–364, 360. See also Romeyn and Kugelmass, 53–54.

263 the characters moved: Brook, *Kosher*, 14, 22; Zurawik, 28–30; Hoberman and Shandler, 124–126.

263 "what may be called": Popkin, 46.

264 "the audience howled": Levenson, "Vanish," 168.

264 "a mad song": Probably "Bop Lyrics." See Craig Svonkin, "Manishevitz and Sake, the Kaddish and Sutras: Allen Ginsberg's Spiritual Self-Othering," in *College Literature* 37:4 (2010), 166–193, citation 174, discussion 174–175.

264 Jean Carroll: Margalit Fox, "Jean Carroll, 98, Is Dead; Blended Wit and Beauty"; *New York Times*, Jan. 2, 2010. Carroll was a regular on *Ed Sullivan* who did adult and sophisticated jokes about marriage. Zoglin, 184.

264 "The Jewish comic": Albert Goldman, *Freakshow* (New York: Atheneum, 1971), 176–177.

265 description is Simon's: Brook, *Kosher*, 64. Compare Edythe M. McGovern in an early critical work who characterizes Simon's characters as "sometimes Jewish, but only nominally so." *Neil Simon: A Critical Study* (New York: Frederick Ungar Publishing, 1979), 10; and compare Daniel Walden, "Neil Simon's Jewish-Style Comedies," in *From Hester Street*, 152–166.

265 Albert Brooks's assault: Brooks came by his comic genius honestly: born (really) Albert Einstein, his father, Harry Einstein, was the well-known Greek dialect comedian Parkyakarkus.

266 to a lesser extent: Film was ahead of television here by about fifteen

to twenty years, in part because the studio system broke up, and more
independent sensibilities were allowed to shine through than in TV. See
Zurawik, 80.

266 **reinforcing and amplifying:** This is the argument made by Sig Altman,
*The Comic Image of the Jew: Explorations of a Pop Culture Phenome-
non* (Teaneck NJ: Fairleigh Dickinson UP, 1971).

266 **One scholar:** Zurawik, 133–134. A version of this—where the punch
line is delivered in Jewish American dialect—is also a central part of
the American Jewish joke. See Philip Nusbaum, "Some Notes on the
Construction of the Jewish-American Dialect Story," *Keystone Folklore*
23:1–2, 28–52.

266 **Greeting cards:** See Nancy-Jo Silberman-Federman, "Jewish Humor,
Self-Hatred, or Anti-Semitism: The Sociology of Hanukkah Cards in
America," *Journal of Popular Culture* 28:4 (1995), 211–229, 212.

267 **"ghost body":** This was added to the problem that many rabbinical
authorities also believed her to be married to Mordechai, thus putting
both members of the couple in the position of committing bigamy. See
Walfish, 122ff, and Barry Walfish, "Kosher Adultery?: The Mordechai-
Esther-Ahasuerus Triangle," *Prooftexts* 22:3 (2002), 305–333.

267 *Abie's Irish Rose*: The play was written by a non-Jew, though many Jews,
perhaps for understandable reasons, thought otherwise. In December
1923, *The American Hebrew* wrote, inaccurately: "the most unique
playwright in the galaxy of our dramatic firmament is none other than
Anne Nichols, who happens to be a Jewish woman despite her stage name
and who has written the most successful play of Jewish life within recent
memory." Cited in Ted Merwin, "The Performance of Ethnicity in Anne
Nichols' 'Abie's Irish Rose,'" *Journal of American Ethnic History* 20:2
(2001), 3–37, 26.

268 *Bridget Loves Bernie*: Zurawik, 83–103.

268 **from 1954 to 1972:** Zurawik, 7–9.

269 **"as inappropriate":** Brook, *Kosher*, 69; Zurawik, 144.

269 **"known for being neurotic":** Levine, 71.

269 **"We went to see":** Quoted in *Haunted Smile*, 229.

269 **By 1999:** More generally, see Zurawik, 140–200; Brook, *Kosher*, *passim*,
statistic from 3.

270 **One joke:** See Josh Levine, *Jerry Seinfeld: Much Ado About Nothing: A
Biography* (Toronto, ON: ECW Press, 1993), 22.

270 **kibbutz volunteer:** He'd spent a summer in Israel between his junior and
senior years of high school. Zoglin, 216.

270 **"would not work":** Quoted Mirzoeff, 74. And of course, Tartikoff wasn't

alone; a 1983 survey found 59 percent of TV's "elite producers" were Jewish. Brook, *Kosher*, 59.

271 **"too New York Jewish":** On Tartikoff's (and, among others, Lorne Michaels' concern) about being "too Jewish" in American television comedy, see Zurawik, 2–6. Until the mid-1980s, all three networks were Jewish-owned.

271 **Rick Ludwin:** See Zurawik, 204, and Stephen Battaglio, "The Research Memo That Almost Killed Seinfeld," *TV Guide*, June 27, 2014.

271 **changed and coded:** A caveat: Various writers contributed to these characters, and the characters deepened and blossomed over the 180 episodes of television, the equivalent (it should be noted) of 45 feature-length films, over the course of almost a decade. It's not worth holding Seinfeld to an overly universal and foolish consistency—though the rabbis attempt to make every Talmudic text and commentary accord with every other, things are messier than that on network television.

271 **"a Jewish family":** There are numerous opinions on this vexed question. Gregg Kavet, for example, said that George was; Carol Leifer said he wasn't, but she had worked some of her own experiences as a Jew into the character; Jason Alexander, who ought to know, modeled the character on a cross between Woody Allen and Larry David. In a recent interview, David has said that "when we were naming characters for the pilot, we don't think too far in advance. Jerry had a friend named Costanza. O.K., we'll call him that. That's how much thought we put into it. Then of course, he had to be half-Italian, half-Jewish. So Frank Costanza, his dad, was Italian, only because of that whim. That's the reason he's not Jewish." Jason Zinoman, "Larry David on Broadway Theater, 'Seinfeld,' and Death Etiquette," *New York Times*, Feb. 18, 2015. See also Brook, *Kosher*, 129–147.

271 **"Kessler":** Or, according to Levine, *Seinfeld*, 69, "Hoffman."

272 **"Kramer goes to a fantasy camp":** "The Visa," aired Jan. 27, 1993.

272 **"there were no bizarre":** Cited in Brook, *Kosher*, 106.

272 **the episode's end:** The episode's "The Yada Yada," by the way (aired 4/24/97), famous for another kind of Jewish comedy, the talking kind.

273 **any number of Jewish jokes:** Like the one about the old man who's spent the night with the two young Swedish stewardesses. You don't know it? Look it up.

273 **in another sense:** Mirzoeff, 85–86, brings up the parallel but treats it differently. There's another, conversion episode, almost a mirror of this one ("The Conversion," aired Dec. 16, 1993), where George almost converts to Latvian Orthodox Christianity for a girl. George's willingness to

submerge his own identity to have sex shows what, in the end, matters the most.

273 *Mad About You*: On *Mad About You*'s Jewish sensibility, or lack of same, see Brook, *Kosher*, 120–123. Though highly successful at the time, it's hardly become the cultural touchstone that Seinfeld has.

273 "If you want to survive": See Vincent Brook, " 'Y'all Killed Him, We Didn't!': Jewish Self-Hatred and *The Larry Sanders Show*," in Vincent Brook, ed., *You Should See Yourself: Jewish Identity in Postmodern American Culture* (New Brunswick, NJ: Rutgers University Press, 2006), 298–317, 309.

274 "When I was a kid": https://www.youtube.com/watch?v=WNisJddhIkA; compare a similar discussion by Jonathan Miller, "How Adam Sandler's 'Chanukah Song' Helped Save the Jews," in Zola and Dollinger, 428-430; it originally appeared as a *Huffington Post* blog piece in 2011.

275 that most American: On Hanukkah's increasing centrality to the American Jewish experience, see Dianne Ashton, *Hanukkah in America: A History* (New York: NYU Press, 2013).

276 a bizarre scheme: Mirzoeff also notes this episode, and has a later discussion about the episodes in which George is concerned that he's gay (Mirzoeff, 100), including the iconic phrase, "not that there's anything wrong with that."

276 Yom Kippur sermon: See Vincent Brook, "Boy-Man Schlemiels and Super-Nebishes: Adam Sandler and Ben Stiller," in *Hollywood's Chosen People*, 173–191, 177, and Vincent Brook, "Chameleon Man and Unruly Woman: Dustin Hoffman and Barbra Streisand," *Shofar* 33:1 (Fall 2014), 30–56. Other relevant Stiller movies: *Flirting With Disaster* (1996), where he seeks out his Jewish birth parents; *Permanent Midnight* (1998), where he played the writer Jerry Stahl; 2004's *Along Came Polly*, where he played Reuben Feffer, and his portrayal of the eponymous *Greenberg* in 2010.

276 Almost all the authors: Sacks, *Kicker*, 33.

277 idolized: Judd Apatow, *Sick in the Head: Conversations About Life and Comedy* (New York: Random House, 2015), x–xi, 331.

277 In a 2009 interview: http://www.jewishjournal.com/hollywoodjew/item/judd_apatow_i_couldnt_be_more_jewish_20090730.

277 to become a man: Apatow has said that he doesn't think he's ever met a man who's not a man-child: see *Sick*, 21.

277 nothing that can't be solved: Although there's a sub-subgenre of unmasculine Jewish men who can't be civilized: Judah Friedlander comes to mind, as does infamous joke thief "The Fat Jew."

277 the objective correlative: Compare Brook, "Boy-Man," 181–183.

277 *The O.C.*: "The Best Chrismukkah Ever," aired Dec. 3, 2003.

277 interfaith romance: Whose spiritual ancestor was, in some ways, David Schwimmer's Ross on *Friends*—the lines are a bit muddied here because Rachel Green was, technically, also Jewish, but after a bit of playing with the JAP stereotype early on, the show did its best to make the audience forget that.

278 boys posturing as men: And borrowing the tropes of rap culture to do so; remember that Jew-Tang Clan.

278 blackface episode: "Face Wars," aired Oct. 17, 2007; see Gillota, 48–75.

278 *The Ask*: Sam Lipsyte, *The Ask* (New York: Farrar, Straus and Giroux, 2010); Jonathan Ames, *I Love You More Than You Know* (New York: Grove Press, 2005); http://www.tabletmag.com/jewish-arts-and-culture/books/28057/look-out.

INDEX

Page numbers followed by *n* refer to endnotes.